Statistical Analysis with Excel® for

dummies®
A Wiley Brand

Statistical Analysis with Excel®

for dummies®
A Wiley Brand

4th edition

by Joseph Schmuller, PhD

for dummies®
A Wiley Brand

Statistical Analysis with Excel® For Dummies®, 4th Edition

Published by: **John Wiley & Sons, Inc.**, 111 River Street, Hoboken, NJ 07030-5774, www.wiley.com

Copyright © 2016 by John Wiley & Sons, Inc., Hoboken, New Jersey

Published simultaneously in Canada

For general information on our other products and services, please contact our Customer Care Department within the U.S. at 877-762-2974, outside the U.S. at 317-572-3993, or fax 317-572-4002. For technical support, please visit https://hub.wiley.com/community/support/dummies.

Wiley publishes in a variety of print and electronic formats and by print-on-demand. Some material included with standard print versions of this book may not be included in e-books or in print-on-demand. If this book refers to media such as a CD or DVD that is not included in the version you purchased, you may download this material at http://booksupport.wiley.com. For more information about Wiley products, visit www.wiley.com.

Library of Congress Control Number: 2016943716

ISBN: 978-1-119-27115-4; 978-1-119-27116-1 (ebk); 978-1-119-27117-8 (ebk)

Manufactured in the United States of America

10 9 8 7 6 5 4 3 2 1

Contents at a Glance

Table of Contents

Introduction

What? Yet another statistics book? Well . . . this is a statistics book, all right, but in my humble (and thoroughly biased) opinion, it's not *just* another statistics book.

What? Yet another Excel book? Same thoroughly biased opinion — it's not just another Excel book. What? Yet another edition of a book that's not just another statistics book and not just another Excel book? Well . . . yes. You got me there.

So here's the story — for the previous three editions and for this one. Many statistics books teach you the concepts but don't give you a way to apply them. That often leads to a lack of understanding. With Excel, you have a ready-made package for applying statistics concepts.

Looking at it from the opposite direction, many Excel books show you Excel's capabilities but don't tell you about the concepts behind them. Before I tell you about an Excel statistical tool, I give you the statistical foundation it's based on. That way, you understand the tool when you use it — and you use it more effectively.

I didn't want to write a book that's just "select this menu" and "click this button." Some of that is necessary, of course, in any book that shows you how to use a software package. My goal was to go way beyond that.

I also didn't want to write a statistics "cookbook" — when-faced-with-problem-#310-use-statistical-procedure-#214. My goal was to go way beyond that, too.

Bottom line: This book isn't just about statistics or just about Excel — it sits firmly at the intersection of the two. In the course of telling you about statistics, I cover every Excel statistical feature. (Well . . . *almost.* I left one out. I left it out of the first three editions, too. It's called "Fourier Analysis." All the necessary math to understand it would take a whole book, and you might never use this tool, anyway.)

About This Book

Although statistics involves a logical progression of concepts, I organized this book so you can open it up in any chapter and start reading. The idea is for you to find what you're looking for in a hurry and use it immediately — whether it's a statistical concept or an Excel tool.

On the other hand, cover to cover is okay if you're so inclined. If you're a statistics newbie and you have to use Excel for statistical analysis, I recommend you begin at the beginning — even if you know Excel pretty well.

What You Can Safely Skip

Any reference book throws a lot of information at you, and this one is no exception. I intend it all to be useful, but I don't aim it all at the same level. So if you're not deeply into the subject matter, you can avoid paragraphs marked with the Technical Stuff icon.

Every so often, you'll run into sidebars. They provide information that elaborates on a topic, but they're not part of the main path. If you're in a hurry, you can breeze past them.

Because I wrote this book so you can open it up anywhere and start using it, step-by-step instructions appear throughout. Many of the procedures I describe have steps in common. After you go through some of the procedures, you can probably skip the first few steps when you come to a procedure you haven't been through before.

Foolish Assumptions

This is not an introductory book on Excel or on Windows, so I'm assuming:

>> You know how to work with Windows. I don't spell out the details of pointing, clicking, selecting, and so forth.

>> You have Excel 2016 installed on your Windows computer or on your Mac and you can work along with the examples. I don't walk you through the steps of Excel installation.

>> You've worked with Excel, and you understand the essentials of worksheets and formulas.

If you don't know much about Excel, consider looking into Greg Harvey's excellent Excel books in the *For Dummies* series.

How This Book Is Organized

I've organized this book into five parts and four appendixes (including two that you can find on this book's companion website at www.statisticalanalysis wexcel4e).

Part 1: Getting Started with Statistical Analysis with Excel: A Marriage Made In Heaven

In Part 1, I provide a general introduction to statistics and to Excel's statistical capabilities. I discuss important statistical concepts and describe useful Excel techniques. If it 's a long time since your last course in statistics or if you've never had a statistics course at all, start here. If you haven't worked with Excel's built-in functions (of any kind), definitely start here.

Part 2: Describing Data

Part of statistics is to take sets of numbers and summarize them in meaningful ways. Here's where you find out how to do that. We all know about averages and how to compute them. But that's not the whole story. In this part, I tell you about additional statistics that fill in the gaps, and I show you how to use Excel to work with those statistics. I also introduce Excel graphics in this part.

Part 3: Drawing Conclusions from Data

Part 3 addresses the fundamental aim of statistical analysis: to go beyond the data and help decision-makers make decisions. Usually, the data are measurements of a sample taken from a large population. The goal is to use these data to figure out what's going on in the population.

This opens a wide range of questions: What does an average mean? What does the difference between two averages mean? Are two things associated? These are only a few of the questions I address in Part 3, and I discuss the Excel functions and tools that help you answer them.

Part 4: Working with Probability

Probability is the basis for statistical analysis and decision-making. In Part 4, I tell you all about it. I show you how to apply probability, particularly in the area of modeling. Excel provides a rich set of built-in capabilities that help you understand and apply probability. Here's where you find them.

Part 5: The Part of Tens

Part 5 meets two objectives. First, I get to stand on the soapbox and rant about statistical peeves and about helpful hints. The peeves and hints total up to ten. Also, I discuss ten (okay, 12) Excel things I couldn't fit into any other chapter. They come from all over the world of statistics. If it's Excel and statistical, and if you can't find it anywhere else in the book, you'll find it here.

As I said in the first three editions — pretty handy, this Part of Tens.

Appendix A: When Your Worksheet Is a Database

In addition to performing calculations, Excel serves another purpose: recordkeeping. Although it's not a dedicated database, Excel does offer some database functions. Some of them are statistical in nature. I introduce Excel database functions in Appendix A, along with pivot tables that allow you to turn your database inside out and look at your data in different ways.

Appendix B: The Analysis of Covariance

The Analysis of Covariance (ANCOVA) is a statistical technique that combines two other techniques: analysis of variance and regression analysis. If you know how two variables are related, you can use that knowledge in some nifty ways, and this is one of the ways. The kicker is that Excel doesn't have a built-in tool for ANCOVA — but I show you how to use what Excel does have so you can get the job done.

Bonus Appendix B1: When Your Data Live Elsewhere

This appendix is all about importing data into Excel — from the web, from databases, from text, and from PDF documents.

Bonus Appendix B2: Tips for Teachers (and Learners)

Excel is terrific for managing, manipulating, and analyzing data. It's also a great tool for helping people understand statistical concepts. This appendix covers some ways for using Excel to do just that.

Icons Used in This Book

As is the case with all *For Dummies* books, icons appear all over the place. Each one is a little picture in the margin that lets you know something special about the paragraph it's next to.

TIP

This icon points out a hint or a shortcut that can help you in your work and make you an all-around better human being.

REMEMBER

This one points out timeless wisdom to take with you long after you finish this book, young Jedi.

WARNING

Pay attention to this icon. It's a reminder to avoid something that might gum up the works for you.

TECHNICAL STUFF

As I mention earlier, in the section "What You Can Safely Skip," this icon indicates material you can blow right past if statistics and Excel aren't your passion.

Where to Go from Here

You can start the book anywhere, but here are a few hints. Want to learn the foundations of statistics? Turn the page. Introduce yourself to Excel's statistical features? That's Chapter 2. Want to start with graphics? Hit Chapter 3. For anything else, find it in the table of contents or in the index and go for it.

In addition to what you're reading right now, this book also comes with a free, access-anywhere Cheat Sheet that will help you quickly use the tools I discuss. To get this Cheat Sheet, visit `www.dummies.com` and search for "Statistical Analysis with Excel For Dummies Cheat Sheet" in the Search box. And don't forget to check out the bonus content on this book's companion website at `www.dummies.com/go/statisticalanalysiswexcel4e`.

1

Getting Started with Statistical Analysis with Excel: A Marriage Made in Heaven

IN THIS PART . . .

Find out about Excel's statistical capabilities

Explore how to work with populations and samples

Test your hypotheses

Understand errors in decision making

Determine independent and dependent variables

Chapter 1

Evaluating Data in the Real World

The field of statistics is all about decision-making — decision-making based on groups of numbers. Statisticians constantly ask questions: What do the numbers tell us? What are the trends? What predictions can we make? What conclusions can we draw?

To answer these questions, statisticians have developed an impressive array of analytical tools. These tools help us to make sense of the mountains of data that are out there waiting for us to delve into, and to understand the numbers we generate in the course of our own work.

The Statistical (and Related) Notions You Just Have to Know

Because intensive calculation is often part and parcel of the statistician's tool set, many people have the misconception that statistics is about number crunching.

Number crunching is just one small part of the path to sound decisions, however.

By shouldering the number-crunching load, software increases our speed of traveling down that path. Some software packages are specialized for statistical analysis and contain many of the tools that statisticians use. Although not marketed specifically as a statistical package, Excel provides a number of these tools, which is why I wrote this book.

I said that number crunching is a small part of the path to sound decisions. The most important part is the concepts statisticians work with, and that's what I talk about for most of the rest of this chapter.

Samples and populations

On election night, TV commentators routinely predict the outcome of elections before the polls close. Most of the time they're right. How do they do that?

The trick is to interview a sample of voters after they cast their ballots. Assuming the voters tell the truth about whom they voted for, and assuming the sample truly represents the population, network analysts use the sample data to generalize to the population of voters.

This is the job of a statistician — to use the findings from a sample to make a decision about the population from which the sample comes. But sometimes those decisions don't turn out the way the numbers predicted. History buffs are probably familiar with the memorable picture of President Harry Truman holding up a copy of the *Chicago Daily Tribune* with the famous, but wrong, headline "Dewey Defeats Truman" after the 1948 election. Part of the statistician's job is to express how much confidence he or she has in the decision.

Another election-related example speaks to the idea of the confidence in the decision. Pre-election polls (again, assuming a representative sample of voters) tell you the percentage of sampled voters who prefer each candidate. The polling organization adds how accurate it believes the polls are. When you hear a newscaster say something like "accurate to within 3 percent," you're hearing a judgment about confidence.

Here's another example. Suppose you've been assigned to find the average reading speed of all fifth-grade children in the United States but you haven't got the time or the money to test them all. What would you do?

Your best bet is to take a sample of fifth-graders, measure their reading speeds (in words per minute), and calculate the average of the reading speeds in the sample. You can then use the sample average as an estimate of the population average.

Estimating the population average is one kind of *inference* that statisticians make from sample data. I discuss inference in more detail in the upcoming section "Inferential Statistics: Testing Hypotheses."

REMEMBER

Here's some terminology you have to know: Characteristics of a population (like the population average) are called *parameters,* and characteristics of a sample (like the sample average) are called *statistics.* When you confine your field of view to samples, your statistics are *descriptive.* When you broaden your horizons and concern yourself with populations, your statistics are *inferential.*

REMEMBER

And here's a notation convention you have to know: Statisticians use Greek letters (μ, σ, ρ) to stand for parameters, and English letters $\overline{X}$, s, r) to stand for statistics. Figure 1-1 summarizes the relationship between populations and samples, and parameters and statistics.

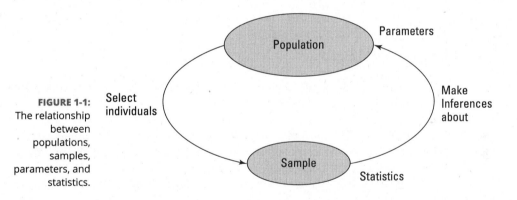

FIGURE 1-1: The relationship between populations, samples, parameters, and statistics.

Variables: Dependent and independent

Simply put, a *variable* is something that can take on more than one value. (Something that can have only one value is called a *constant.*) Some variables you might be familiar with are today's temperature, the Dow Jones Industrial Average, your age, and the value of the dollar against the euro.

Statisticians care about two kinds of variables: *independent* and *dependent.* Each kind of variable crops up in any study or experiment, and statisticians assess the relationship between them.

For example, imagine a new way of teaching reading that's intended to increase the reading speed of fifth-graders. Before putting this new method into schools, it would be a good idea to test it. To do that, a researcher would randomly assign a sample of fifth-grade students to one of two groups: One group receives instruction via the new method, and the other receives instruction via traditional methods. Before and after both groups receive instruction, the researcher measures the reading speeds of all the children in this study. What happens next? I get to that in the upcoming section "Inferential Statistics: Testing Hypotheses."

For now, understand that the independent variable here is Method of Instruction. The two possible values of this variable are New and Traditional. The dependent variable is reading speed — which you might measure in words per minute.

REMEMBER

In general, the idea is to find out if changes in the independent variable are associated with changes in the dependent variable.

REMEMBER

In the examples that appear throughout the book, I show you how to use Excel to calculate various characteristics of groups of scores. Keep in mind that each time I show you a group of scores, I'm really talking about the values of a dependent variable.

Types of data

Data come in four kinds. When you work with a variable, the way you work with it depends on what kind of data it is.

The first variety is called *nominal* data. If a number is a piece of nominal data, it's just a name. Its value doesn't signify anything. A good example is the number on an athlete's jersey. It's just a way of identifying the athlete and distinguishing him or her from teammates. The number doesn't indicate the athlete's level of skill.

Next come ordinal data. *Ordinal* data are all about order, and numbers begin to take on meaning over and above just being identifiers. A higher number indicates the presence of more of a particular attribute than a lower number. One example is the *Mohs scale:* Used since 1822, it's a scale whose values are 1 through 10; mineralogists use this scale to rate the hardness of substances. Diamond, rated at 10, is the hardest. Talc, rated at 1, is the softest. A substance that has a given rating can scratch any substance that has a lower rating.

What's missing from the Mohs scale (and from all ordinal data) is the idea of equal intervals and equal differences. The difference between a hardness of 10 and a hardness of 8 is not the same as the difference between a hardness of 6 and a hardness of 4.

Interval data provide equal differences. Fahrenheit temperatures provide an example of interval data. The difference between 60 degrees and 70 degrees is the same as the difference between 80 degrees and 90 degrees.

Here's something that might surprise you about Fahrenheit temperatures: A temperature of 100 degrees is not twice as hot as a temperature of 50 degrees. For ratio statements (twice as much as, half as much as) to be valid, zero has to mean the complete absence of the attribute you're measuring. A temperature of 0 degrees F doesn't mean the absence of heat — it's just an arbitrary point on the Fahrenheit scale.

The last data type, *ratio* data, includes a meaningful zero point. For temperatures, the Kelvin scale gives ratio data. One hundred degrees Kelvin is twice as hot as 50 degrees Kelvin. This is because the Kelvin zero point is *absolute zero,* where all molecular motion (the basis of heat) stops. Another example is a ruler. Eight inches is twice as long as four inches. A length of zero means a complete absence of length.

REMEMBER

Any of these data types can form the basis for an independent variable or a dependent variable. The analytical tools you use depend on the type of data you're dealing with.

A little probability

When statisticians make decisions, they express their confidence about those decisions in terms of probability. They can never be certain about what they decide. They can only tell you how probable their conclusions are.

So what is probability? The best way to attack this is with a few examples. If you toss a coin, what's the probability that it comes up heads? Intuitively, you know that if the coin is fair, you have a 50–50 chance of heads and a 50–50 chance of tails. In terms of the kinds of numbers associated with probability, that's ½.

How about rolling a die? (That's one member of a pair of dice.) What's the probability that you roll a 3? Hmmm. . . . A die has six faces and one of them is 3, so that ought to be ⅙, right? Right.

Here's one more. You have a standard deck of playing cards. You select one card at random. What's the probability that it's a club? Well . . . a deck of cards has four suits, so that answer is ¼.

I think you're getting the picture. If you want to know the probability that an event occurs, figure out how many ways that event can happen and divide by the total number of events that can happen. In each of the three examples, the event we are interested in (head, 3, or club) only happens one way.

Things can get a bit more complicated. When you toss a die, what's the probability you roll a 3 or a 4? Now you're talking about two ways the event you're interested in can occur, so that's $(1 + 1)/6 = \frac{2}{6} = \frac{1}{3}$. What about the probability of rolling an even number? That has to be 2, 4, or 6, and the probability is $(1 + 1 + 1)/6 = \frac{3}{6} = \frac{1}{2}$.

On to another kind of probability question. Suppose you roll a die and toss a coin at the same time. What's the probability you roll a 3 and the coin comes up heads? Consider all the possible events that could occur when you roll a die and toss a coin at the same time. Your outcome could be a head and 1-6 or a tail and 1-6. That's a total of 12 possibilities. The head-and-3 combination can happen only one way, so the answer is $\frac{1}{12}$.

In general, the formula for the probability that a particular event occurs is

$$\Pr\left(Event\right) = \frac{Number\ of\ ways\ the\ event\ can\ occur}{Total\ number\ of\ possible\ events}$$

I begin this section by saying that statisticians express their confidence about their decisions in terms of probability, which is really why I brought up this topic in the first place. This line of thinking leads me to *conditional* probability — the probability that an event occurs given that some other event occurs. For example, suppose I roll a die, take a look at it (so that you can't see it), and tell you I've rolled an even number. What's the probability that I've rolled a 2? Ordinarily, the probability of a 2 is $\frac{1}{6}$, but I've narrowed the field. I've eliminated the three odd numbers (1, 3, and 5) as possibilities. In this case, only the three even numbers (2, 4, and 6) are possible, so now the probability of rolling a 2 is $\frac{1}{3}$.

Exactly how does conditional probability play into statistical analysis? Read on.

Inferential Statistics: Testing Hypotheses

In advance of doing a study, a statistician draws up a tentative explanation — a *hypothesis* — as to why the data might come out a certain way. After the study is complete and the sample data are all tabulated, he or she faces the essential decision a statistician has to make: whether or not to reject the hypothesis.

That decision is wrapped in a conditional probability question — what's the probability of obtaining the data, given that this hypothesis is correct? Statistical analysis provides tools to calculate the probability. If the probability turns out to be low, the statistician rejects the hypothesis.

Suppose you're interested in whether or not a particular coin is fair — whether it has an equal chance of coming up heads or tails. To study this issue, you'd take the coin and toss it a number of times — say, 100. These 100 tosses make up your sample data. Starting from the hypothesis that the coin is fair, you'd expect that the data in your sample of 100 tosses would show around 50 heads and 50 tails.

If it turns out to be 99 heads and 1 tail, you'd undoubtedly reject the fair coin hypothesis. Why? The conditional probability of getting 99 heads and 1 tail given a fair coin is very low. Wait a second. The coin could still be fair and you just happened to get a 99-1 split, right? Absolutely. In fact, you never really know. You have to gather the sample data (the results from 100 tosses) and make a decision. Your decision might be right, or it might not.

Juries face this dilemma all the time. They have to decide among competing hypotheses that explain the evidence in a trial. (Think of the evidence as data.) One hypothesis is that the defendant is guilty. The other is that the defendant is not guilty. Jury members have to consider the evidence and, in effect, answer a conditional probability question: What's the probability of the evidence given that the defendant is not guilty? The answer to this question determines the verdict.

Null and alternative hypotheses

Consider once again the coin-tossing study I mention in the preceding section. The sample data are the results from the 100 tosses. Before tossing the coin, you might start with the hypothesis that the coin is a fair one so that you expect an equal number of heads and tails. This starting point is called the *null hypothesis.* The statistical notation for the null hypothesis is H_0. According to this hypothesis, any heads-tails split in the data is consistent with a fair coin. Think of it as the idea that nothing in the results of the study is out of the ordinary.

An alternative hypothesis is possible — that the coin isn't a fair one, and it's loaded to produce an unequal number of heads and tails. This hypothesis says that any heads-tails split is consistent with an unfair coin. The alternative hypothesis is called, believe it or not, the *alternative hypothesis.* The statistical notation for the alternative hypothesis is H_1.

With the hypotheses in place, toss the coin 100 times and note the number of heads and tails. If the results are something like 90 heads and 10 tails, it's a good idea to reject H_0. If the results are around 50 heads and 50 tails, don't reject H_0. Similar ideas apply to the reading-speed example I give earlier, in the section "Samples and populations." One sample of children receives reading instruction under a new method designed to increase reading speed, and the other learns via a traditional method. Measure the children's reading speeds before and after instruction, and tabulate the improvement for each child. The null hypothesis, H_o, is that one method isn't different from the other. If the improvements are greater with the new method than with the traditional method — so much greater that it's unlikely that the methods aren't different from one another — reject H_o. If they're not greater, don't reject H_o.

Notice that I *didn't* say "accept H_o." The way the logic works, you *never* accept a hypothesis. You either reject H_o or don't reject H_o.

Here's a real-world example to help you understand this idea. When a defendant goes on trial, he or she is presumed innocent until proven guilty. Think of *innocent* as H_o. The prosecutor's job is to convince the jury to reject H_o. If the jurors reject, the verdict is *guilty.* If they don't reject, the verdict is *not guilty.* The verdict is never *innocent.* That would be like accepting H_o.

Back to the coin-tossing example. Remember I said "around 50 heads and 50 tails" is what you could expect from 100 tosses of a fair coin. What does *around* mean? Also, I said if it's 90-10, reject H_o. What about 85-15? 80-20? 70-30? Exactly how much different from 50-50 does the split have to be for you reject H_o? In the reading-speed example, how much greater does the improvement have to be to reject H_o?

I won't answer these questions now. Statisticians have formulated decision rules for situations like this, and you explore those rules throughout the book.

Two types of error

Whenever you evaluate the data from a study and decide to reject H_o or to not reject H_o, you can never be absolutely sure. You never really know what the true state of the world is. In the context of the coin-tossing example, that means you never know for certain if the coin is fair or not. All you can do is make a decision based on the sample data you gather. If you want to be certain about the coin, you'd have to have the data for the entire population of tosses — which means you'd have to keep tossing the coin until the end of time.

Because you're never certain about your decisions, it's possible to make an error regardless of what you decide. As I mention earlier in this chapter, the coin could be fair and you just happen to get 99 heads in 100 tosses. That's not likely, and that's why you reject H_o. It's also possible that the coin is biased, yet you just happen to toss 50 heads in 100 tosses. Again, that's not likely and you don't reject H_o in that case.

Although not likely, those errors are possible. They lurk in every study that involves inferential statistics. Statisticians have named them *Type I* and *Type II.*

If you reject H_o and you shouldn't, that's a Type I error. In the coin example, that's rejecting the hypothesis that the coin is fair, when in reality it is a fair coin.

If you don't reject H_o and you should have, that's a Type II error. That happens if you don't reject the hypothesis that the coin is fair and in reality it's biased.

How do you know if you've made either type of error? You don't — at least not right after you make your decision to reject or not reject H_o. (If it's possible to know, you wouldn't make the error in the first place!) All you can do is gather more data and see if the additional data are consistent with your decision.

If you think of H_o as a tendency to maintain the status quo and not interpret anything as being out of the ordinary (no matter how it looks), a Type II error means you missed out on something big. Looked at in that way, Type II errors form the basis of many historical ironies.

Here's what I mean: In the 1950s, a particular TV show gave talented young entertainers a few minutes to perform on stage and a chance to compete for a prize. The audience voted to determine the winner. The producers held auditions around the country to find people for the show. Many years after the show went off the air, the producer was interviewed. The interviewer asked him if he had ever turned down anyone at an audition whom he shouldn't have.

"Well," said the producer, "once a young singer auditioned for us and he seemed really odd."

"In what way?" asked the interviewer.

"In a couple of ways," said the producer. "He sang really loud, gyrated his body and his legs when he played the guitar, and he had these long sideburns. We figured this kid would never make it in show business, so we thanked him for showing up, but we sent him on his way."

"Wait a minute — are you telling me you turned down . . .?"

"That's right. We actually said no . . . to Elvis Presley!"

Now *that's* a Type II error.

What's New in Excel 2016?

Microsoft has made a few changes to Excel's *Ribbon* (the tabbed band across the top), reflecting changes in Excel. The most obvious addition is the light bulb, at the top to the right of Add-ins. It's labeled "Tell me what you want to do." This is called the Tell Me box, and it's a new way to connect to Excel Help. Type a phrase like *Insert a chart* into the Tell Me box, and Excel opens a menu whose choices include icons that you click to insert charts and to find help with inserting charts. Figure 1-2 shows this capability.

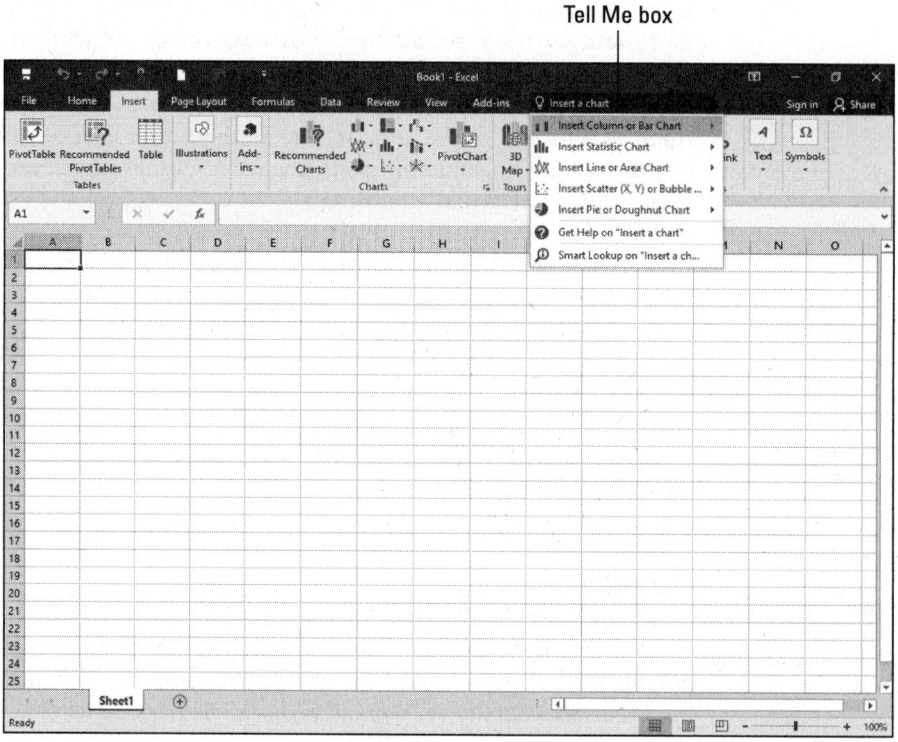

FIGURE 1-2: The interface in Excel 2016, showing the Tell Me box.

Sadly, this feature is not part of Excel 2016 for the Mac. This is the case for a number of other capabilities, too (like a couple I mention in the next paragraph). Overall, however, Mac users will find greater consistency across platforms than in previous editions.

REMEMBER

Figure 1-2 shows the Insert tab, which incorporates a couple of changes in the Charts area. One addition is a set of Statistical Charts (which are not in the Mac version). Another is 3D Map, the new and improved Power View (which first appeared in Excel 2013 and will not be appearing in a Mac near you). I discuss these features in Chapter 3.

What's Old in Excel 2016?

Each tab on the Ribbon presents groups of icon-labeled command buttons separated into categories. When you're trying to figure out the capability a particular button activates, you can move the cursor to the button (without clicking) and helpful information pops up.

Clicking a button typically opens a whole category of possibilities. Buttons that do this are called *category buttons*.

Microsoft has developed shorthand for describing a mouse-click on a command button on the Ribbon, and I use that shorthand throughout this book. The shorthand is

Tab | Command Button

To indicate clicking on the Insert tab's Recommended Charts category button, for example, I write

Insert | Recommended Charts

When I click that button (with some data-containing cells selected), the Insert Chart dialog box, shown in Figure 1-3, appears.

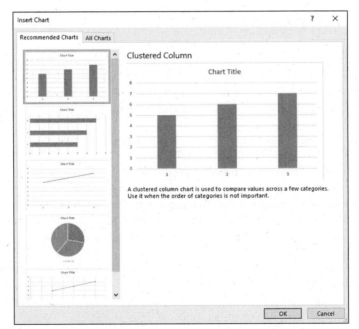

FIGURE 1-3:
Clicking Insert |
Recommended
Charts opens
this box.

Notice that its Recommended Charts tab is open. Clicking the All Charts tab (which is not in the Mac version) changes the box to what you see in Figure 1-4, a gallery of all possible Excel charts.

Chart is Excel's name for *graph*.

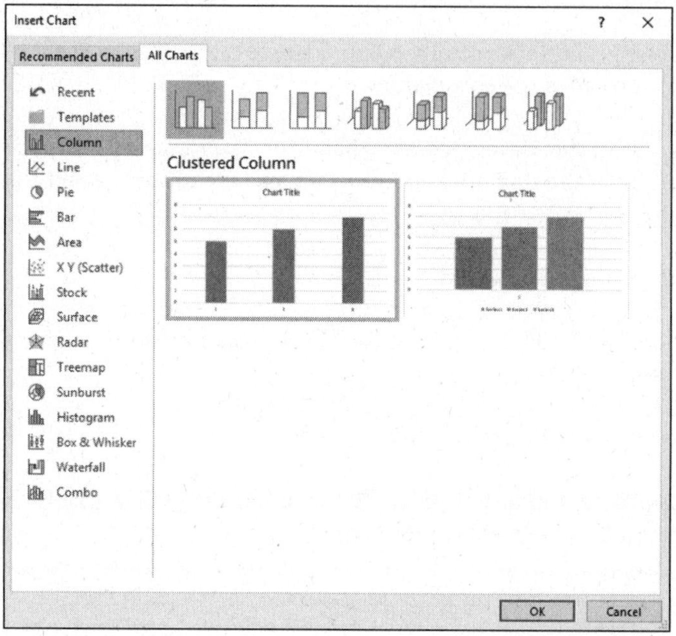

FIGURE 1-4:
The All Charts tab
in the Insert
Chart dialog box.

Incidentally, the All Charts tab shows five of the six charts new in Excel 2016: Waterfall, Treemap, Sunburst, Histogram, and Box & Whisker. (Pareto, the sixth new chart, is buried a bit deeper.) The last three are called "statistical charts. I cover statistical charts (and others) in Chapter 3.

To find the bulk of Excel's statistical functionality, select

Formulas | More Functions | Statistical

This is an extension of the shorthand. It means, "Select the Formulas tab, click the More Functions button, and then select the Statistical Functions choice from the pop-up menu that opens." Figure 1-5 shows what I mean.

In Chapter 2, I show you how to make the Statistical Functions menu more accessible.

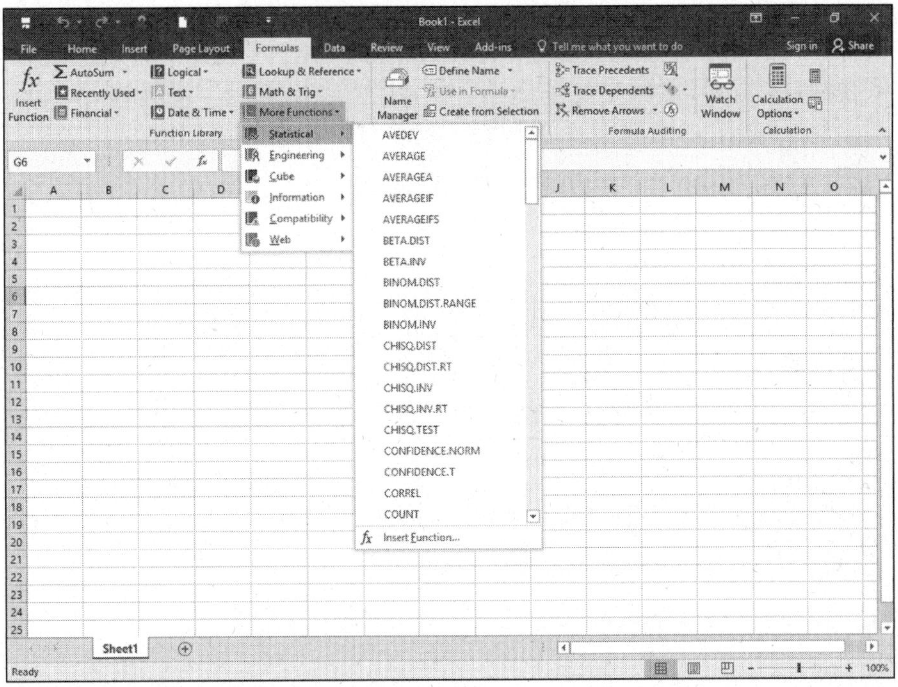

FIGURE 1-5:
Accessing the
Statistical
Functions menu.

In the 2010 version, Microsoft changed the way Excel names its functions. The objective was to make a function's purpose as obvious as possible from its name. Excel also changed some of the programming behind these functions to make them more accurate.

Excel 2016 continues this naming style, and maintains the older statistical functions (pre-2010 vintage, and one – FORECAST – from 2013) for compatibility with older versions of Excel. So if you're creating a spreadsheet for users of older Excel versions, use the older functions.

You won't find them on the Statistical Functions menu. They have their own menu. To find it, select Formulas | More Functions | Compatibility.

I provide Table 1-1 to help you transition from older Excel versions. The table lists the old functions, their replacements, and the chapter in which I discuss the new function.

The table shows that the FORECAST function has morphed into five functions in Excel 2016: FORECAST.LINEAR, FORECAST.ETS, FORECAST.ETS.CONFINT, FORECAST.ETS.SEASONALITY, and FORECAST.ETS.STAT. Along with Excel's new one-click forecasting capability, I cover these functions in Chapter 16.

TABLE 1-1 **Older Excel Statistical Functions, Their Replacements, and the Chapter That Deals with the New Function**

Old Function	New Function	Chapter
BETADIST	BETA.DIST	19
BETAINV	BETA.INV	19
BINOMDIST	BINOM.DIST	18
CRITBINOM	BINOM.INV	18
CHIDIST	CHISQ.DIST.RT	10
CHIINV	CHISQ.INV.RT	10
CHITEST	CHISQ.TEST	20
CONFIDENCE	CONFIDENCE.NORM	9
COVAR	COVARIANCE.P	15
EXPONDIST	EXPON.DIST	19
FDIST	F.DIST.RT	11
FINV	F.INV.RT	11
FTEST	F.TEST	11
FORECAST	FORECAST.LINEAR, FORECAST.ETS, FORECAST.ETS.CONFINT, FORECAST.ETS.SEASONALITY, FORECAST.ETS.STAT	16
GAMMADIST	GAMMA.DIST	19
GAMMAINV	GAMMA.INV	19
HYPGEOMDIST	HYPGEOM.DIST	18
LOGNORMDIST	LOGNORM.DIST	22
LOGINV	LOGNORM.INV	22
MODE	MODE.SNGL, MODE.MULT	4
NEGBINOMDIST	NEGBINOM.DIST	18
NORMDIST	NORM.DIST	8
NORMINV	NORM.INV	8
NORMSDIST	NORM.S.DIST	8

Old Function	New Function	Chapter
NORMSINV	NORM.S.INV	8
PERCENTILE	PERCENTILE.INC	6
PERCENTRANK	PERCENTRANK.INC	6
POISSON	POISSON.DIST	19
QUARTILE	QUARTILE.INC	6
RANK	RANK.EQ	6
STDEVP	STDEV.P	5
STDEV	STDEV.S	5
TDIST	T.DIST.2T	10
TDIST	T.DIST.RT	10
TINV	T.INV.2T	9
TTEST	T.TEST	11
VARP	VAR.P	5
VAR	VAR.S	5
WEIBULL	WEIBULL.DIST	22
ZTEST	Z.TEST	10

The most important addition in Excel 2016 is on the Macintosh side: After a long absence, the Analysis ToolPak returns to Excel 2016 for the Mac. Available in all Windows versions of Excel, the Analysis ToolPak is a free add-in that supplies analytic tools often found in dedicated statistical software packages. In previous Mac versions, intrepid users accessed a similar set of tools by downloading a third-party application that did not integrate with Excel in the same way as the Analysis ToolPak.

Mac users are a hearty lot, however, and they'll be happy with this change in Excel 2016. (Have I done enough . . . Apple-polishing? Sorry.)

I cover the Analysis ToolPak in Chapter 2.

Knowing the Fundamentals

Although I'm assuming you're not new to Excel, I think it's wise to take a little time and space to discuss a few fundamental Excel principles that figure prominently in statistical work. Knowing these fundamentals helps you work efficiently with Excel formulas.

Autofilling cells

The first fundamental feature is autofill, Excel's capability for repeating a calculation throughout a worksheet. Insert a formula into a cell, and you can drag that formula into adjoining cells.

Figure 1-6 is a worksheet of expenditures for R&D in science and engineering at colleges and universities for the years shown. The data, taken from a U.S. National Science Foundation report, are in millions of dollars. Column H holds the total for each field, and Row 11 holds the total for each year. (More about column I in a moment.)

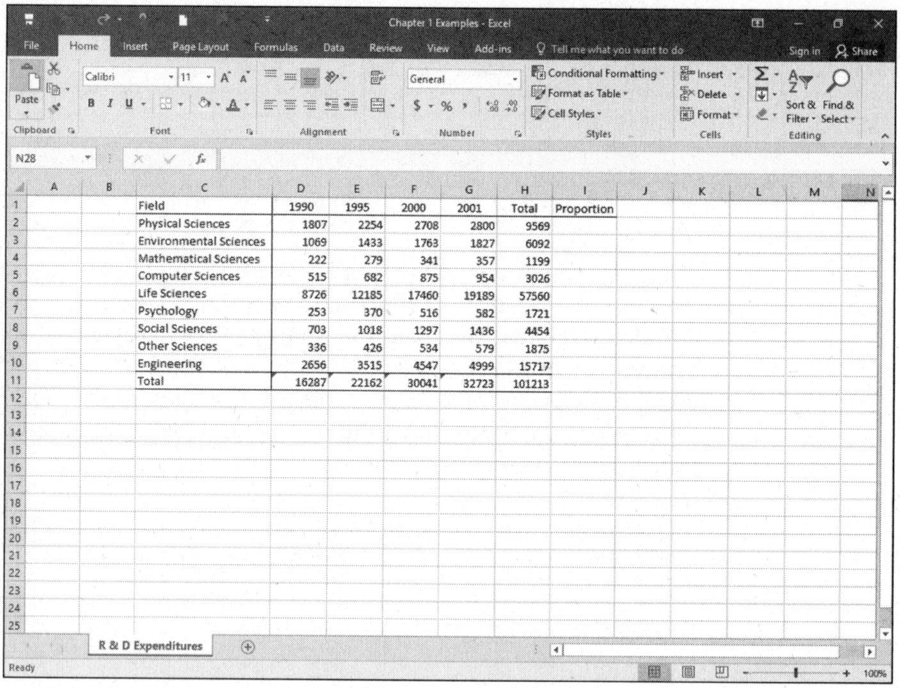

FIGURE 1-6: Expenditures for R&D in science and engineering.

	A	B	C	D	E	F	G	H	I
1			Field	1990	1995	2000	2001	Total	Proportion
2			Physical Sciences	1807	2254	2708	2800	9569	
3			Environmental Sciences	1069	1433	1763	1827	6092	
4			Mathematical Sciences	222	279	341	357	1199	
5			Computer Sciences	515	682	875	954	3026	
6			Life Sciences	8726	12185	17460	19189	57560	
7			Psychology	253	370	516	582	1721	
8			Social Sciences	703	1018	1297	1436	4454	
9			Other Sciences	336	426	534	579	1875	
10			Engineering	2656	3515	4547	4999	15717	
11			Total	16287	22162	30041	32723	101213	

I started with column H blank and with row 11 blank. How did I get the totals into column H and row 11?

If I want to create a formula to calculate the first row total (for Physical Sciences), one way (among several) is to enter

```
= D2 + E2 + F2 + G2
```

into cell H2. (A formula always begins with an equal sign: =.) Press Enter and the total appears in H2.

Now, to put that formula into cells H3 through H10, the trick is to position the cursor on the lower-right corner of H2 until a plus sign (+) appears, hold down the left mouse button, and drag the mouse through the cells. That plus sign is called the cell's *fill handle*.

When you finish dragging, release the mouse button and the row totals appear. This saves huge amounts of time because you don't have to reenter the formula eight times.

Same thing with the column totals. One way to create the formula that sums up the numbers in the first column (1990) is to enter

```
=D2 + D3 + D4 + D5 + D6 + D7 + D8 + D9 + D10
```

into cell D11. Position the cursor on D11's fill handle, drag through row 11 and release in column H, and you autofill the totals into E11 through H11.

Dragging isn't the only way to do it. Another way is to select the array of cells you want to autofill (including the one that contains the formula) and click

```
Home | Fill
```

Where's Fill? On the Home tab, in the Editing area, you see a down arrow. That's Fill. Clicking Fill opens the Fill pop-up menu (see Figure 1-7). Select Down and you accomplish the same thing as dragging and dropping.

Still another way is to select Series from the Fill pop-up menu. Doing this opens the Series dialog box (see Figure 1-8). In this dialog box, select the AutoFill radio button and click OK, and you're all set. This method takes one more step, but the Series dialog box is a bit more compatible with earlier versions of Excel.

I bring this up because statistical analysis often involves repeating a formula from cell to cell. The formulas are usually more complex than the ones in this section, and you might have to repeat them many times, so it pays to know how to autofill.

FIGURE 1-7:
The Fill pop-up
menu.

↓	Down
→	Fill Down (Ctrl+D)
↑	Up
←	Left
	Across Worksheets...
	Series...
	Justify
	Flash Fill

FIGURE 1-8:
The Series
dialog box.

Series   ? ×

Series in
● Rows
○ Columns

Type
○ Linear
○ Growth
○ Date
● AutoFill

Date unit
● Day
○ Weekday
○ Month
○ Year

☐ Trend

Step value: 1   Stop value:

OK   Cancel

TIP

A quick way to autofill is to click in the first cell in the series, move the cursor to that cell's lower-right corner until the autofill handle appears, and double-click. This works in both PC and Mac.

Referencing cells

Another important fundamental principle is the way Excel references worksheet cells. Consider again the worksheet in Figure 1-6. Each autofilled formula is slightly different from the original. This, remember, is the formula in cell H2:

```
= D2 + E2 + F2 + G2
```

After autofill, the formula in H3 is

```
= D3 + E3 + F3 + G3
```

and the formula in H4 is — well, you get the picture.

This is perfectly appropriate. You want the total in each row, so Excel adjusts the formula accordingly as it automatically inserts it into each cell. This is called *relative referencing* — the reference (the cell label) gets adjusted relative to where it is in the worksheet. Here, the formula directs Excel to total up the numbers in the cells in the four columns immediately to the left.

Now for another possibility. Suppose you want to know each row total's proportion of the grand total (the number in H11). That should be straightforward, right? Create a formula for I2, and then autofill cells I3 through I10.

Similar to the earlier example, you start by entering this formula into I2:

```
=H2/H11
```

Press Enter and the proportion appears in I2. Position the cursor on the fill handle, drag through column I, release in I10, and — D'oh! Figure 1-9 shows the unhappy result — the extremely ugly #/DIV0! in I3 through I10. What's the story?

	A	B	C	D	E	F	G	H	I	J	K	L
1			Field	1990	1995	2000	2001	Total	Proportion			
2			Physical Sciences	1807	2254	2708	2800	9569	0.0945432			
3			Environmental Sciences	1069	1433	1763	1827	6092	#DIV/0!			
4			Mathematical Sciences	222	279	341	357	1199	#DIV/0!			
5			Computer Sciences	515	682	875	954	3026	#DIV/0!			
6			Life Sciences	8726	12185	17460	19189	57560	#DIV/0!			
7			Psychology	253	370	516	582	1721	#DIV/0!			
8			Social Sciences	703	1018	1297	1436	4454	#DIV/0!			
9			Other Sciences	336	426	534	579	1875	#DIV/0!			
10			Engineering	2656	3515	4547	4999	15717	#DIV/0!			
11			Total	16287	22162	30041	32723	101213				
12												
13												
14												

The story is this: Unless you tell it not to, Excel uses relative referencing when you autofill. So the formula inserted into I3 is not

```
=H3/H11
```

Instead, it's

```
=H3/H12
```

Why does H11 become H12? Relative referencing assumes that the formula means "Divide the number in the cell by whatever number is nine cells south of here in the same column." Because H12 has nothing in it, the formula is telling Excel to divide by zero, which is a no-no.

The idea is to tell Excel to divide all the numbers by the number in H11, not by "whatever number is nine cells south of here." To do this, you work with absolute referencing. You show absolute referencing by adding $ signs to the cell ID. The correct formula for I2 is

```
= H2/$H$11
```

This line tells Excel to not adjust the column and to not adjust the row when you autofill. Figure 1-10 shows the worksheet with the proportions, and you can see the correct formula in the formula bar (the area above the worksheet and below the Ribbon).

FIGURE 1-10: Autofill, based on absolute referencing.

Field	1990	1995	2000	2001	Total	Proportion
Physical Sciences	1807	2254	2708	2800	9569	0.0945432
Environmental Sciences	1069	1433	1763	1827	6092	0.0601899
Mathematical Sciences	222	279	341	357	1199	0.0118463
Computer Sciences	515	682	875	954	3026	0.0298973
Life Sciences	8726	12185	17460	19189	57560	0.5687016
Psychology	253	370	516	582	1721	0.0170037
Social Sciences	703	1018	1297	1436	4454	0.0440062
Other Sciences	336	426	534	579	1875	0.0185253
Engineering	2656	3515	4547	4999	15717	0.1552864
Total	16287	22162	30041	32723	101213	

Formula bar: I10 =H10/$H$11

TIP

To convert a relative reference into absolute reference format, select the cell address (or addresses) you want to convert and press the F4 key. F4 is a toggle that switches among relative reference (H11, for example), absolute reference for both the row and column in the address ($H$11), absolute reference for the row-part only (H$11), and absolute reference for the column-part only ($H11).

In Excel 2016 for the Mac, toggle a relative reference into an absolute reference by holding down the fn key when you press F4. Another Mac shortcut for this is Command + T.

What's New in This Edition?

One prominent new feature in this edition is my emphasis on graphs of distributions. In my experience, graphing a distribution helps you understand it. Because some distributions (t, Chi-Square, and F) form the basis of inferential statistics and other distributions (Poisson) are important in modeling, I felt it important to emphasize their visualization. These visualizations appear in Chapters 8, 10, 11, and 19.

Speaking of visualization, I cover some existing chart types for the first time in this edition: Bubble, Stock, Surface, and Radar. They're in Chapter 3, along with the new charts I mention earlier.

In the previous edition, I added an online appendix on an analysis-of-variance design — mixed-model ANOVA — that doesn't appear in the first two editions. In this edition, the material appears in Chapter 13. Because this is a widely used design, I thought it wise to include it in a chapter rather than in an online appendix.

The mixed-model ANOVA combines a Between-Groups variable and a Repeated Measure. If you have no idea what the preceding sentence means, read Chapter 12. Anyway, Excel doesn't have a tool for working with this design, but in Chapter 13 I show you an Excel-based workaround that enables you to compute this analysis.

Chapter 16 is completely new. As I point out earlier, Excel has expanded its forecasting capabilities. Five new worksheet functions replace the old FORECAST function, and Excel has added one-click forecasting from historical data. This merits an entirely new chapter on time series.

Chapter 17 is also completely new. Its subject matter — nonparametric statistics — is an important branch of statistics. This is another area that has no dedicated Excel tools. After I discuss each subtopic, I show you how to apply Excel.

In the third edition, the section "For Mac Users" appears in many of the chapters. The absence of the Analysis ToolPak in Excel 2011 for the Mac (and the need for a third-party app to fill the void) necessitated this strategy. With the return of the Analysis ToolPak to Excel 2016 for the Mac, those sections are no longer necessary.

Chapter 2

Understanding Excel's Statistical Capabilities

n this chapter, I introduce you to Excel's statistical functions and data analysis tools. If you've used Excel, and I'm assuming you have, you're aware of Excel's extensive functionality, of which statistical capabilities are a subset. Into each worksheet cell you can enter a piece of data, instruct Excel to carry out calculations on data that reside in a set of cells, or use one of Excel's worksheet functions to work on data. Each worksheet function is a built-in formula that saves you the trouble of having to direct Excel to perform a sequence of calculations. As newbies and veterans know, formulas are the "business end" of Excel. The data analysis tools go beyond the formulas. Each tool provides a set of informative results.

Getting Started

Many of Excel's statistical features are built into its worksheet functions. In previous versions (pre-2003), you accessed the worksheet functions by using the Excel Insert Function button, labeled with the symbol *fx*. Clicking this button opens the Insert Function dialog box, which presents a list of Excel's functions and the capability to search for Excel functions. (On the Mac, this button opens the Formula Builder, which is pretty much the same thing.) Although Excel 2016 provides easier ways to access the worksheet functions, this latest version preserves this button and offers additional ways to open the Insert Function dialog box. I discuss all of this in more detail in a moment.

Figure 2-1 shows the two locations of the Insert Function button and the Formula bar. Along with one Insert Function button, the Formula bar is to the right of the Name box. All three are just below the Ribbon.

Insert Function Button

Name Box   Function Library   Formula Bar

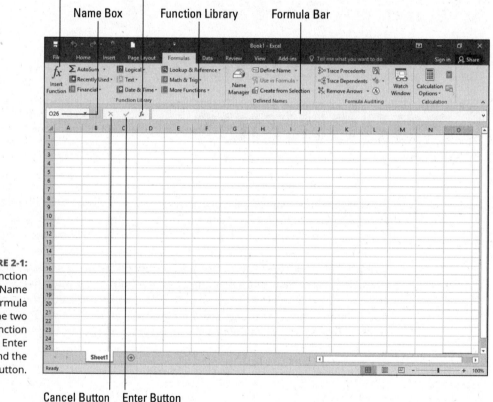

FIGURE 2-1:
The Function Library, the Name box, the Formula bar, the two Insert Function buttons, the Enter button, and the Cancel button.

Cancel Button   Enter Button

Near the Name box, just to the left of the Insert Function button, are an X and a check mark. The X is the Cancel button, and the check mark is the Enter button. Clicking the Enter button is like pressing the Enter key on the keyboard: It tells Excel to perform a computation you type into a cell. Clicking the Cancel button removes anything you've typed into a cell, if you haven't already entered it.

Inside the Ribbon, on the Formulas tab, is the Function Library. Mac users see a similar layout in Excel 2016 for the Mac.

The Formula bar is sort of a clone of a cell you select: Information entered into the Formula bar goes into the selected cell, and information entered into the selected cell appears in the Formula bar.

Figure 2-1, shown earlier, shows Excel with the Formulas tab open. You can see the other location for the Insert Function button. Labeled *fx*, it's on the extreme left end of the Ribbon, in the Function Library area. As I mention earlier in this section, when you click the Insert Function button, you open the Insert Function dialog box. (See Figure 2-2.)

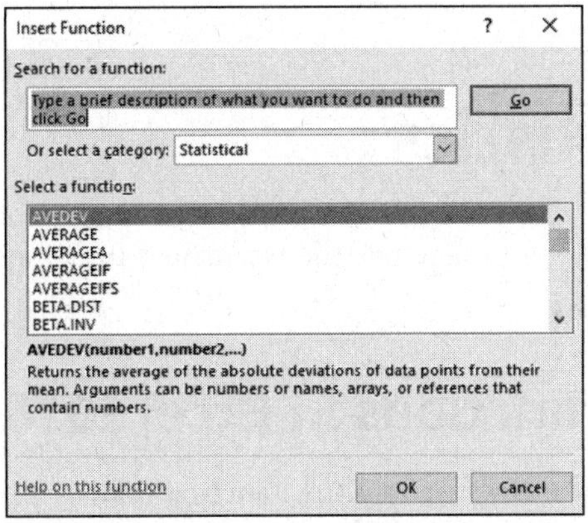

FIGURE 2-2:
The Insert Function dialog box.

This dialog box enables you to find a function that fits your needs by either typing a search term or by scrolling through a list of Excel functions.

In addition to clicking the Insert Function button next to the Formula bar, you can open the Insert Function dialog box by selecting

Formulas | Insert Function

REMEMBER

Because of the way pre-Ribbon versions of Excel were organized, the Insert Function dialog box was extremely useful. In Excel 2016, however, it's mostly helpful if you're not sure which function to use or where to find it.

The Function Library presents the categories of formulas you can use and makes it convenient for you to access them. Clicking a category button in this area opens a menu of functions in that category.

Most of the time, I work with statistical functions that are easily accessible from the Statistical Functions menu. Sometimes I work with math functions on the Math & Trig Functions menu. (You see a couple of these functions later in this chapter.) In Chapter 5, I show you how to use a couple of logic functions.

TIP

The final selection on each category menu (like the Statistical Functions menu) is Insert Function. Selecting this option is still another way to open the Insert Function dialog box. (The Mac version refers to this dialog box as the Formula Builder.)

The Name box is sort of a running record of what you do in the worksheet. Select a cell, and the cell's address appears in the Name box. Click the Insert Function button, and the name of the function you selected most recently appears in the Name box.

In addition to the statistical functions, Excel provides a number of data analysis tools that you access from the Data tab's Analysis area.

Setting Up for Statistics

In this section, I show you how to use the worksheet functions and the analysis tools.

Worksheet functions in Excel 2016

As I point out in the preceding section, the Function Library area of the Formulas tab shows all categories of worksheet functions.

The steps in using a worksheet function are

1. **Type your data into a data array and select a cell for the result.**

2. **Select the appropriate formula category and choose a function from its pop-up menu.**

   Doing this opens the Function Arguments dialog box.

3. **In the Function Arguments dialog box, type the appropriate values for the function's arguments.**

Argument is a term from mathematics. It has nothing to do with debates, fights, or confrontations. In mathematics, an *argument* is a value on which a function does its work.

4. **Click OK to put the result into the selected cell.**

Yes, that's all there is to it.

To give you an example, I explore a function that typifies how Excel's worksheet functions work. This function, SUM, adds up the numbers in cells you specify and returns the sum in still another cell that you specify. Although adding numbers together is an integral part of statistical number-crunching, SUM is not in the Statistical category. It is, however, a typical worksheet function, and it shows a familiar operation.

Here, step by step, is how to use SUM:

1. **Enter your numbers into an array of cells and select a cell for the result.**

   In this example, I've entered **45**, **33**, **18**, **37**, **32**, **46**, and **39** into cells C2 through C8, respectively, and selected C9 to hold the sum.

2. **Select the appropriate formula category and choose the function from its pop-up menu.**

   This step opens the Function Arguments dialog box.

   I selected Formulas | Math & Trig and scrolled down to find and choose SUM.

3. **In the Function Arguments dialog box, enter the appropriate values for the arguments.**

   Excel guesses that you want to sum the numbers in cells C2 through C8 and identifies that array in the Number1 box. Excel doesn't keep you in suspense: The Function Arguments dialog box shows the result of applying the function. In this example, the sum of the numbers in the array is 250. (See Figure 2-3.)

4. **Click OK to put the sum into the selected cell.**

Note a couple of points. First, as Figure 2-3 shows, the Formula bar holds

```
=SUM(C2:C8)
```

This formula indicates that the value in the selected cell equals the sum of the numbers in cells C2 through C8.

TIP

After you get familiar with a worksheet function and its arguments, you can bypass the menu and type the function directly into the cell or into the Formula bar, beginning with an equal sign (=). When you do, Excel opens a helpful menu as you type the formula. (See Figure 2-4.) The menu shows possible formulas beginning with the letter(s) you type, and you can select one by double-clicking it.

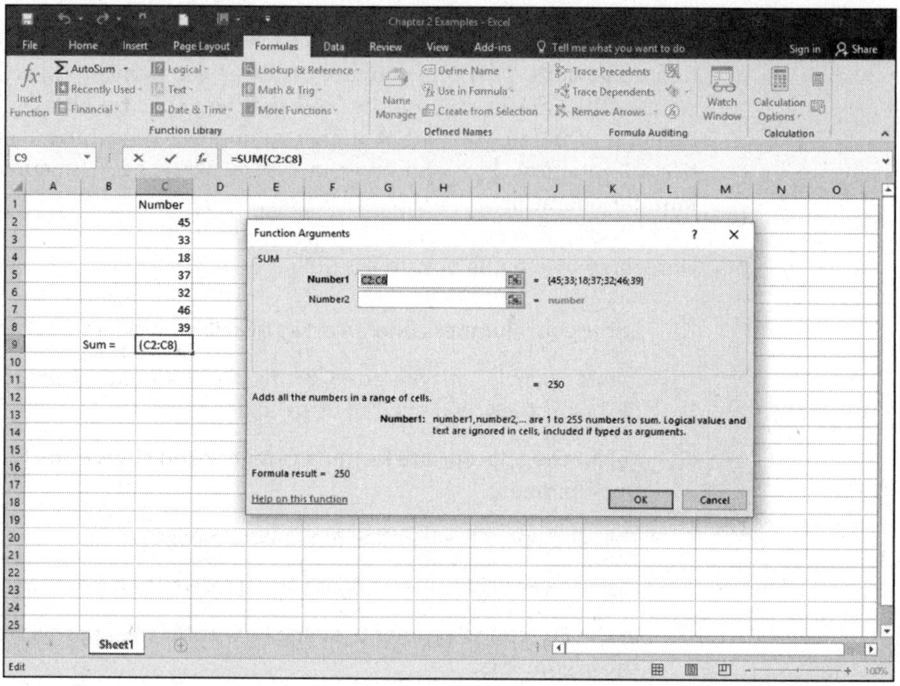

FIGURE 2-3:
Using SUM.

Another noteworthy point is the set of boxes in the Function Arguments dialog box, shown in Figure 2-3. In the figure, you see just two boxes: Number1 and Number2. The data array appears in Number1. So what's Number2 for?

The Number2 box allows you to include an additional argument in the sum. And it doesn't end there. Click in the Number2 box, and the Number3 box appears. Click in the Number3 box, and the Number4 box appears — and on and on. The limit is 255 boxes, with each box corresponding to an argument. A value can be another array of cells anywhere in the worksheet, a number, an arithmetic expression that evaluates to a number, a cell ID, or a name that you have attached to a range of cells. (Regarding that last one: Read the upcoming section "What's in a name? An array of possibilities.") As you type values, the SUM dialog box shows the updated sum. Clicking OK puts the updated sum into the selected cell.

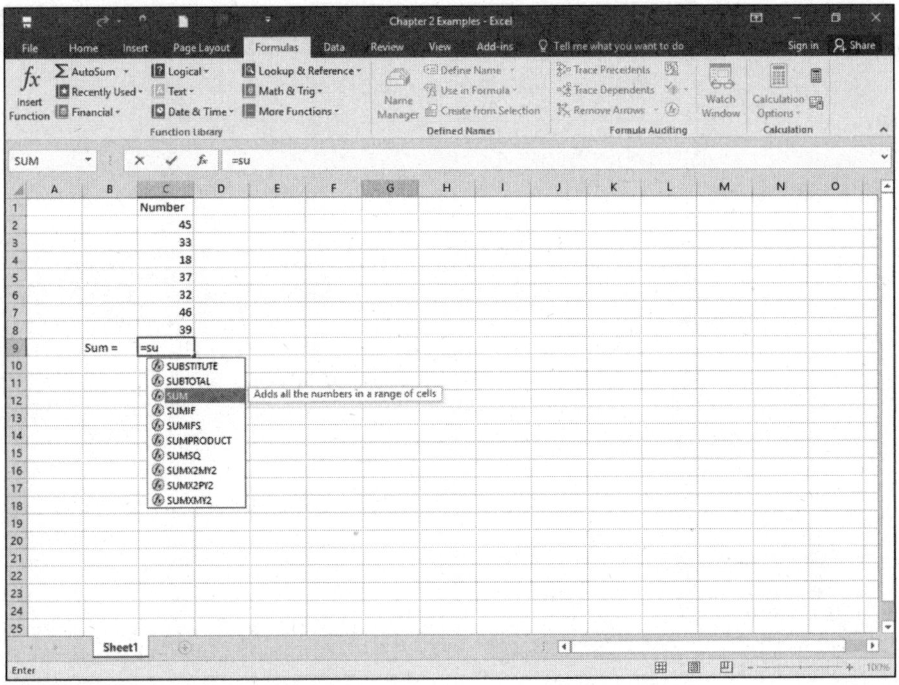

FIGURE 2-4:
As you type a
formula, Excel
opens a helpful
menu.

REMEMBER

You won't find this multiargument capability on every worksheet function. Some are designed to work with just one argument. For the ones that work with multiple arguments, however, you can incorporate data that reside all over the worksheet. Figure 2-5 shows a worksheet with a Function Arguments dialog box that includes data from two arrays of cells, two arithmetic expressions, and one cell. Notice the format of the function in the Formula bar — a comma separates successive arguments.

TIP

If you select a cell in the same column as your data and just below the last data cell, Excel correctly guesses the data array that you want to work on. Excel doesn't always guess what you want to do with that array, however. Sometimes when Excel does guess, its guess is incorrect. When either of those things happens, it's up to you to enter the appropriate values into the Function Arguments dialog box.

Quickly accessing statistical functions

In this section, I show you how to create a shortcut to Excel's statistical functions.

You can get to Excel's statistical functions by selecting

Formulas | More Functions | Statistical

and then choosing from the resulting pop-up menu. (See Figure 2-6.)

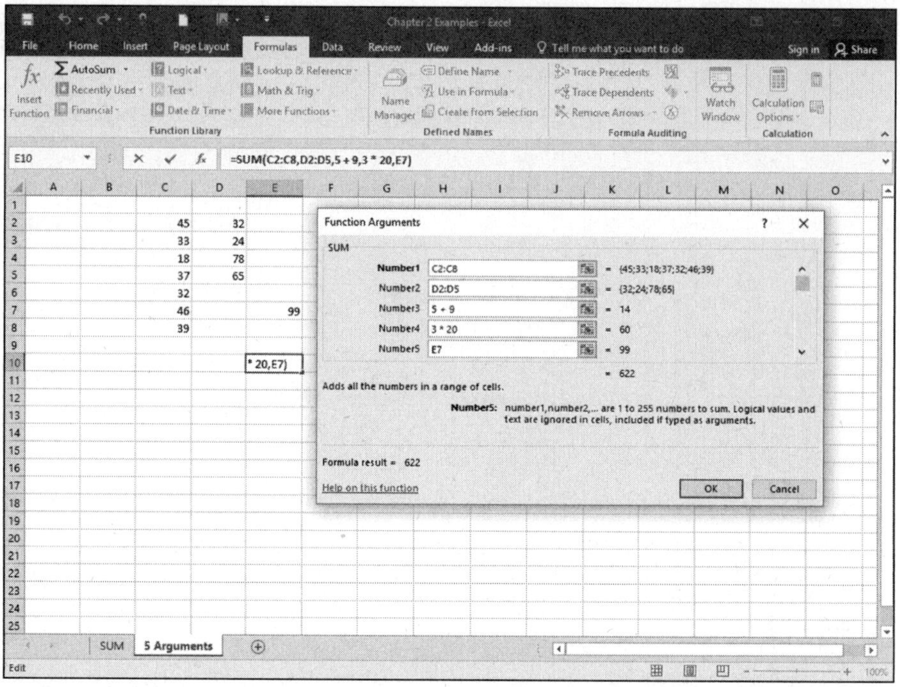

FIGURE 2-5:
Using SUM with
five arguments.

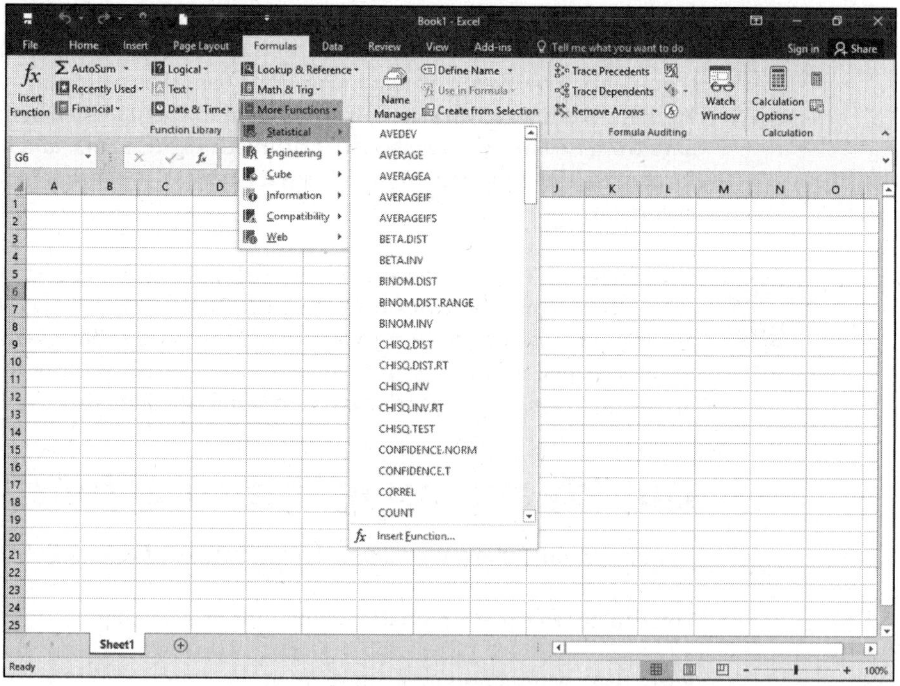

FIGURE 2-6:
Accessing Excel's
Statistical
functions.

Although Excel has buried the statistical functions several layers deep, you can use a handy technique to make them as accessible as any of the other categories: You add them to the Quick Access toolbar in the upper-left corner. (Every Office application has one, unless you're a Mac user — in which case, no Office application has one. So the next steps are unavailable on the Mac. Sorry.)

To do this, select

Formulas | More Functions

and right-click Statistical. From the pop-up menu, pick the first option, Add to Quick Access Toolbar. (See Figure 2-7.) Doing this adds a button to the Quick Access toolbar. Clicking the new button's down arrow opens the pop-up menu of statistical functions. (See Figure 2-8.)

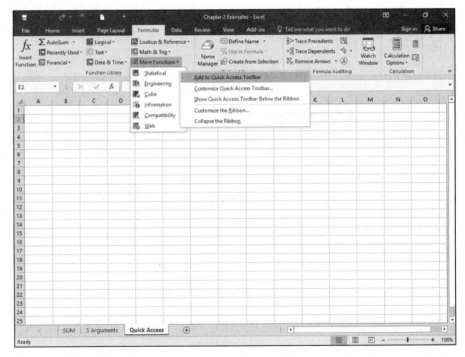

FIGURE 2-7:
Adding the statistical functions to the Quick Access toolbar.

From now on, when I deal with a statistical function, I assume that you've created this shortcut so that you can quickly open the menu of statistical functions. The next section provides an example.

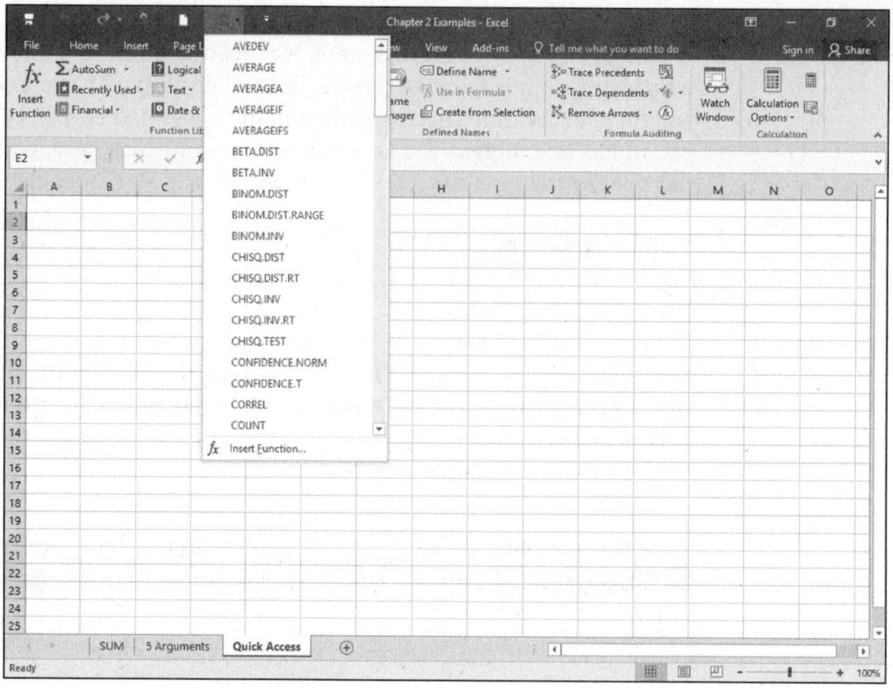

FIGURE 2-8:
Accessing the Statistical Functions menu from the Quick Access toolbar.

Array functions

Most of Excel's built-in functions are formulas that calculate a single value (like a sum) and put that value into a worksheet cell. Excel has another type of function. It's called an *array function* because it calculates multiple values and puts those values into an array of cells rather than into a single cell.

A good example of an array function is FREQUENCY (and it's an Excel statistical function, too). Its job is to summarize a group of scores by showing how the scores fall into a set of intervals that you specify. For example, given these scores

77, 45, 44, 61, 52, 53, 68, 55

and these intervals

50, 60, 70, 80

FREQUENCY shows how many are less than or equal to 50 (2, in this example), how many are greater than 50 and less than or equal to 60 (that would be 3), and so on. The number of scores in each interval is called a *frequency*. A table of the intervals and the frequencies is called a *frequency distribution*.

Here's an example of how to use FREQUENCY:

1. Enter the scores into an array of cells.

Figure 2-9 shows a group of scores in cells B2 through B16.

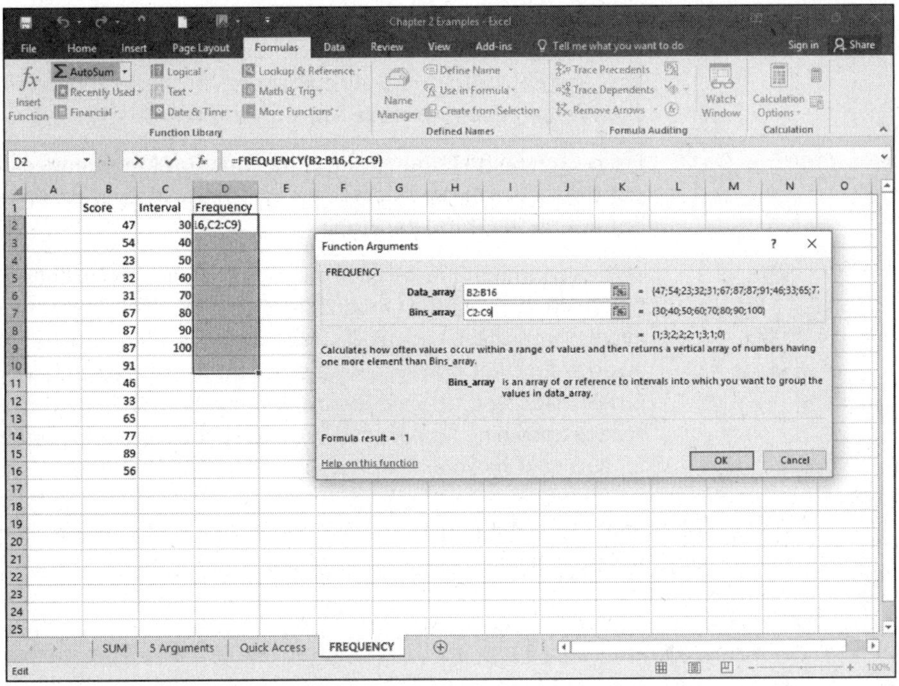

FIGURE 2-9:
Working with
FREQUENCY.

2. Enter the intervals into an array.

I've put the intervals in C2 through C9.

3. Select an array for the frequencies.

I've put Frequency as the label at the top of column D, so I select D2 through D10 for the resulting frequencies. Why the extra cell? FREQUENCY returns a vertical array that has one more cell than the frequencies array.

4. From the Statistical Functions menu, select FREQUENCY to open the Function Arguments dialog box.

I use the shortcut I installed on the Quick Access toolbar to open this menu and select FREQUENCY.

5. **In the Function Arguments dialog box, enter the appropriate values for the arguments.**

I begin with the Data_array box. In this box, I enter the cells that hold the scores. In this example, that's B2:B16. I'm assuming you know Excel well enough to know how to do this in several ways.

Next, I identify the intervals array. FREQUENCY refers to intervals as *bins* and holds the intervals in the Bins_array box. For this example, C2:C9 goes into the Bins_array box. After I identify both arrays, the Insert Function dialog box shows the frequencies inside a pair of curly brackets: {}.

6. **Press Ctrl+Shift+Enter to close the Function Arguments dialog box and put the values in the selected array. On the Mac, press Ctrl+Shift+Return or Command+Shift+Return.**

WARNING

This is *very* important. Because the dialog box has an OK button (a Done button on the Mac), the tendency is to click OK, thinking that it puts the results into the worksheet. Clicking OK doesn't get the job done when you work with an array function, however. Always use the keystroke combination Ctrl+Shift+Enter (Ctrl+Shift+Return or Command+Shift+Return on the Mac; but see the upcoming Tip paragraphs) to close the Function Arguments dialog box for an array function.

After you close the Function Arguments dialog box, the frequencies go into the appropriate cells, as Figure 2-10 shows.

	A	B	C	D	E	F	G
		Score	Interval	Frequency			
2		47	30	1			
3		54	40	3			
4		23	50	2			
5		32	60	2			
6		31	70	2			
7		67	80	1			
8		87	90	3			
9		87	100	1			
10		91		0			
11		46					
12		33					
13		65					
14		77					
15		89					
16		56					

D2 — fx {=FREQUENCY(B2:B16,C2:C9)}

FIGURE 2-10: The finished frequencies.

Note the formula in the Formula bar:

```
{= FREQUENCY(B2:B16,C2:C9)}
```

The curly brackets are Excel's way of telling you that this is an array function.

REMEMBER

I'm not one to repeat myself, but in this case I'll make an exception: As I said in Step 6, press Ctrl+Shift+Enter (Ctrl+Shift+Return or Command+Shift+Return on the Mac) whenever you work with an array function. Keep this in mind because the Arguments Function dialog box doesn't provide any reminders. If you click OK after you enter the arguments into an array function, you'll be very frustrated. Trust me.

TIP

Weird behavior on the Mac: Before I press Ctrl+Shift+Return or Command+Shift+Return, I have to click in the Formula bar. Otherwise, the values don't appear in the target array.

TIP

Here's a cleaner way to do all this on the Mac: Instead of Ctrl+Shift+Enter or Command+Shift+Enter, hold down the Ctrl and Shift keys (or the Command and Shift keys) and click the onscreen Enter button (the check mark to the left of the Formula bar). So it's Ctrl+Shift+Click the Enter button. Just holding down the Command key and clicking the Enter button works, too.

What's in a name? An array of possibilities

As you get more into Excel's statistical features, you work increasingly with formulas that have multiple arguments. Oftentimes, these arguments refer to arrays of cells, as in the preceding examples.

If you attach meaningful names to these arrays, it helps you keep straight what you're doing. Also, if you return to a worksheet after not working on it for a while, meaningful array names can help you quickly get back into the swing of things. Another benefit: If you have to explain your worksheet and its formulas to others, meaningful array names are tremendously helpful.

Excel gives you an easy way to attach a name to a group of cells. In Figure 2-11, column C is named Revenue_Millions, indicating "revenue in millions of dollars." As it stands, that just makes it a bit easier to read the column. If I explicitly tell Excel to treat Revenue_Millions as the name of the array of cells C2 through C13, however, I can use Revenue_Millions whenever I refer to that array of cells.

Why did I use Revenue_Millions and not Revenue (Millions) or Revenue In Millions or Revenue: Millions? Because Excel doesn't like blank spaces or symbols in its names, that's why. In fact, here are four rules to follow when you supply a name for a range of cells. The name

>> Must begin with an alphabetic character — a letter rather than a number or a punctuation mark.

	A	B	C
1	Year	Region	Revenue_Millions
2	2006	North	20
3	2006	South	22
4	2006	East	19
5	2006	West	25
6	2007	North	26
7	2007	South	28
8	2007	East	21
9	2007	West	27
10	2008	North	32
11	2008	South	29
12	2008	East	25
13	2008	West	31

FIGURE 2-11:
Defining names
for arrays of cells.

>> Must be unique within the worksheet.

>> Cannot contain spaces or symbols (as I just mentioned) — use an underscore to denote a space between words in the name.

>> Cannot duplicate any cell reference in the worksheet.

Here's how to define a name:

1. Put a descriptive name at the top of a column (or to the left of a row) you want to name.

Figure 2-10, shown earlier, shows this.

2. Select the range of cells you want to name.

For this example, that's cells C2 through C13. Why not include C1? I explain in a second.

3. Right-click the selected range.

This step opens the pop-up menu shown in Figure 2-12.

4. From this pop-up menu, select Define Name.

This selection opens the New Name dialog box. (See Figure 2-13.) As you can see, Excel knows that Revenue_Millions is the name of the array and that Revenue_Millions refers to cells C2 through C13. When presented with a selected range of cells to name, Excel looks for a nearby name — just above a column or just to the left of a row. If no name is present, you get to supply one in the New Name dialog box. (The New Name dialog box is also accessible by choosing Formulas | Define Name.)

WARNING

When you select a range of cells, like a column, with a name at the top, you can include the cell with the name in it and Excel attaches the name to the range. *I strongly advise against doing this, however.* Why? If I select C1 through C13, the name Revenue_Millions refers to cells C1 through C13, not C2 through C13. In that case, the first value in the range is text and the others are numbers.

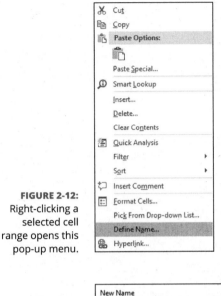

FIGURE 2-12:
Right-clicking a
selected cell
range opens this
pop-up menu.

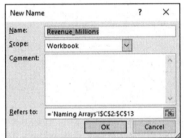

FIGURE 2-13:
The New Name
dialog box.

For a formula such as SUM (or SUMIF or SUMIFS, which I discuss next), this doesn't make a difference: In those formulas, Excel just ignores values that aren't numbers. If you have to use the whole array in a calculation, however, it makes a *huge* difference: Excel thinks the name is part of the array and tries to use it in the calculation. You see this in the next section, on creating your own array formulas.

5. Click OK.

Excel attaches the name to the range of cells.

Now I have the convenience of using the name in a formula. Here, selecting a cell (like C14) and entering the SUM formula directly into C14 opens the boxes shown in Figure 2-14.

As the figure shows, the boxes open as you type. Selecting Revenue_Millions and pressing the Tab key fills in the formula in a way that Excel understands. You have to supply the close parenthesis (see Figure 2-15) and press Enter to see the result.

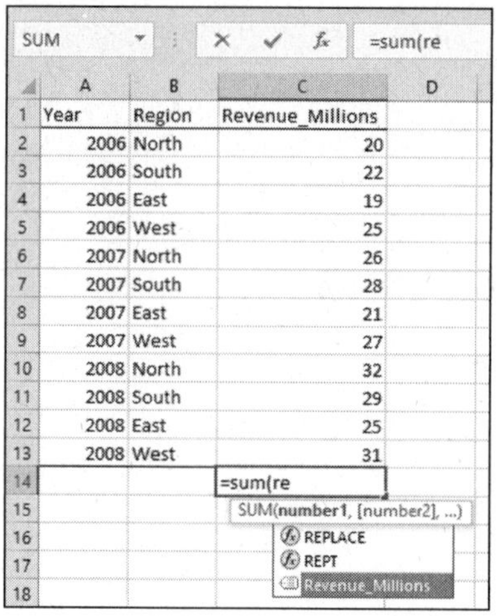

FIGURE 2-14:
Entering a
formula directly
into a cell opens
these boxes.

Using the named array, then, the formula is

```
=SUM(Revenue_Millions)
```

which is more descriptive than

```
=SUM(C2:C13)
```

A couple of other formulas show just how convenient this naming capability can be. These formulas, SUMIF and SUMIFS, add a set of numbers if specific conditions in one cell range (SUMIF) or in more than one cell range (SUMIFS) are met.

To take full advantage of naming, I name both column A (Year) and column B (Region) in the same way I named column C.

WARNING

When you define a name for a cell range like B2:B13 in this example, beware: Excel can be a bit quirky when the cells hold names. Excel might guess that the name in the uppermost cell is the name you want to assign to the cell range. In this case, Excel guesses *North* for the name rather than *Region.* If that happens, you make the change in the New Name dialog box.

To keep track of the names in a worksheet, select

Formulas | Name Manager

to open the Name Manager box, shown in Figure 2-16. The nearby buttons in the Defined Names area of the Ribbon are also useful.

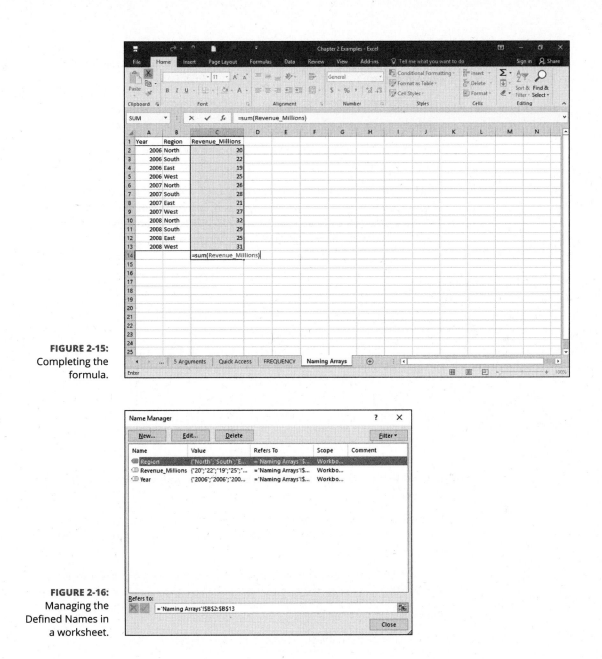

FIGURE 2-15:
Completing the
formula.

FIGURE 2-16:
Managing the
Defined Names in
a worksheet.

Next, I sum the data in column C, but only for the North region. That is, I consider a cell in column C only if the corresponding cell in column B contains *North*. To do this, I follow these steps:

1. **Select a cell for the formula result.**

My selection here is C15.

2. **Select the appropriate formula category and choose a function from its pop-up menu.**

This opens the Function Arguments dialog box. I selected

Formulas | Math & Trig

and scrolled down the menu to find and choose SUMIF. This selection opens the Function Arguments dialog box, shown in Figure 2-17.

SUMIF has three arguments. The first, Range, is the range of cells to evaluate for the condition to include in the sum (North, South, East, or West, in this example). The second, Criteria, is the specific value in the range (North, for this example). The third, Sum_range, holds the values I sum.

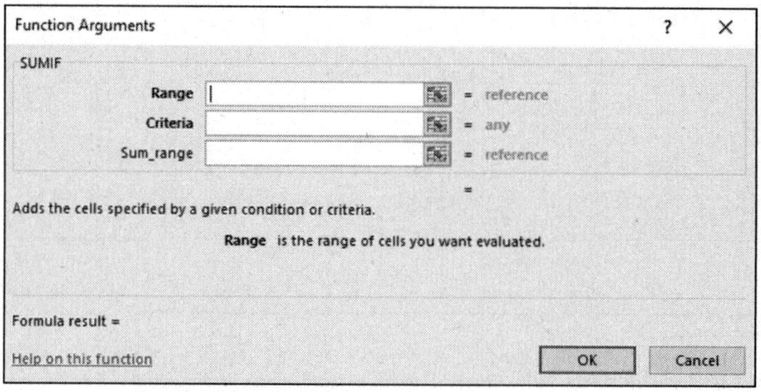

FIGURE 2-17:
The Function Arguments dialog box for SUMIF.

3. **In the Function Arguments dialog box, enter the appropriate values for the arguments.**

Here's where another Defined Names button comes in handy. In that Ribbon area, click the down arrow next to Use in Formula to open the drop-down list shown in Figure 2-18.

Selecting from this list fills in the Function Arguments dialog box, as shown in Figure 2-19. I had to type North into the Criteria box. Excel adds the double quotes.

4. **Click OK.**

The result appears in the selected cell. In this example, it's 78.

In the Formula bar,

```
=SUMIF(Region,"North", Revenue_Millions)
```

appears. I can type it exactly that way into the Formula bar, without the dialog box or the drop-down list. When I don't use the dialog box, I have to supply the double-quotes around the criteria.

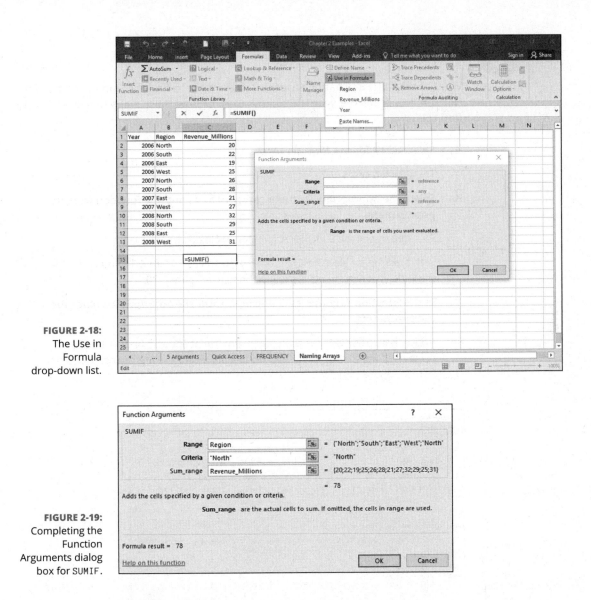

FIGURE 2-18:
The Use in
Formula
drop-down list.

FIGURE 2-19:
Completing the
Function
Arguments dialog
box for SUMIF.

The formula in the Formula bar is easier to understand than

```
= SUMIF(B2:B13,"North", C2:C13)
```

isn't it?

Incidentally, the same cell range can be both the Range and the Sum_range. For example, to sum just the cells for which Revenue_Millions is less than 25, that's

```
=SUMIF(Revenue_Millions, "< 25", Revenue_Millions)
```

The second argument (Criteria) is always in double quotes.

What about SUMIFS? That one is useful if you want to find the sum of revenues for North but only for the years 2006 and 2007. Follow these steps to use SUMIFS to find this sum:

1. **Select a cell for the formula result.**

   The selected cell is C17.

2. **Select the appropriate formula category and choose a function from its pop-up menu.**

   This step opens the Function Arguments dialog box.

   In this example, select SUMIFS from the Formulas | Math & Trig menu to open the Functions Arguments dialog box shown in Figure 2-20.

3. **In the Function Arguments dialog box, enter the appropriate values for the arguments.**

   Notice that, in SUMIFS, the Sum Range argument appears first. In SUMIF, however, it appears last. The appropriate values for the arguments appear in Figure 2-20.

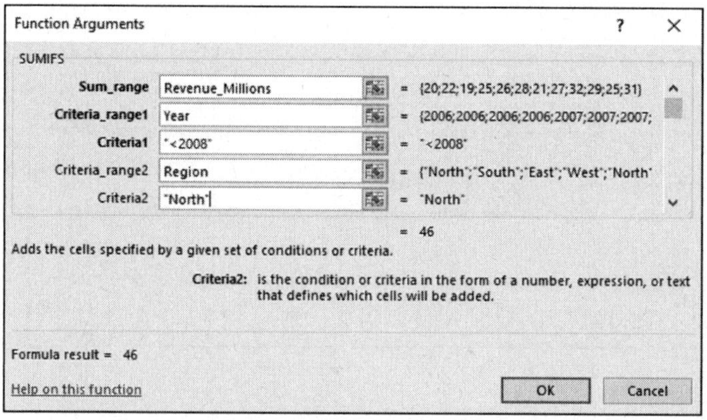

FIGURE 2-20:
The completed Function Arguments dialog box for SUMIFS.

4. **The formula in the Formula bar is**

   ```
   =SUMIFS(Revenue_Millions,Year,"<2008",Region,"North")
   ```

5. **Click OK.**

   The answer, 46, appears in the selected cell.

With unnamed arrays, the formula would have been

```
=SUMIFS(C2:C13,A2:A13,"<2008",B2:B13,"North")
```

which seems much harder to comprehend.

WARNING

A defined name involves absolute referencing. (See Chapter 1.) Therefore, if you try to autofill from a named array, you'll be in for an unpleasant surprise: Rather than autofill a group of cells, you'll copy a value over and over again.

Here's what I mean. Suppose you assign the name Series_1 to A2:A11 and Series_2 to B2:B11. In A12, you calculate SUM(Series_1). Because you're clever, you figure you'll just drag the result from A12 to B12 to calculate SUM(Series_2). What do you find in B12? SUM(Series_1), that's what.

TIP

Excel does not treat array names as case-sensitive. If your named array is Test, for example, SUM(Test), SUM(test), and SUM(tEST) all give you the same result.

Creating your own array formulas

In addition to Excel's built-in array formulas, you can create your own. To help things along, you can incorporate named arrays.

Figure 2-21 shows two named arrays, X and Y, in columns C and D, respectively. X refers to C2 through C5 (*not* C1 through C5), and Y refers to D2 through D5 (*not* D1 through D5). XY is the column header for column F. Each cell in column F will store the product of the corresponding cell in column C and the corresponding cell in column D.

▲	A	B	C	D	E	F
1			X	Y		XY
2			12	8		
3			14	9		
4			15	10		
5			16	11		
6						
7						

An easy way to enter the products, of course, is to set F2 equal to C2*E2 and then autofill the remaining applicable cells in column F.

Just to illustrate array formulas, though, follow these steps to work on the data in the worksheet. (Refer to Figure 2-21.)

1. **Select the array that will hold the answers to the array formula.**

   That would be F2 through F5 — or F2:F5, in Excel-speak. (Figure 2-21 shows the array selected.)

2. **Into the selected array, type the formula.**

   The formula here is =X * Y

3. **Press Ctrl+Shift+Enter (not Enter). On the Mac, that's Ctrl+Shift+Return or Command+Shift+Return.**

   The answers appear in F2 through F5, as Figure 2-22 shows. Note the formula {=X*Y}

   in the Formula bar. As I told you earlier, the curly brackets indicate an array formula.

F2			✕ ✓ f_x	{=X*Y}		
	A	B	C	D	E	F
1			X	Y		XY
2			12	8		96
3			14	9		126
4			15	10		150
5			16	11		176
6						
7						

FIGURE 2-22: The results of the array formula {=X * Y}.

Another thing I mention earlier in this chapter: When you name a range of cells, make sure that the named range does *not* include the cell with the name in it. If it does, an array formula like {=X * Y} tries to multiply the letter X by the letter Y to produce the first value, which is impossible and results in the exceptionally ugly #VALUE! error.

The weird Mac behavior I mention earlier with regard to the FREQUENCY array formula does not occur in a homemade array formula — it's not necessary to click the Formula bar before pressing the keystroke combination.

TIP

Command+clicking the Enter button (the check mark next to the Formula bar) works in this context, too.

TIP

Using data analysis tools

Excel 2016 has a set of sophisticated tools for data analysis. They reside in the Analysis ToolPak. Table 2-1 lists the tools I cover. (The one I don't cover, Fourier Analysis, is extremely technical.) Some of the terms in the table may be unfamiliar to you, so I define them throughout this book.

TABLE 2-1   ## Excel's Data Analysis Tools

Tool	What It Does
Anova: Single Factor	Analysis of variance for two or more samples.
Anova: Two Factor with Replication	Analysis of variance with two independent variables, and multiple observations in each combination of the levels of the variables.
Anova: Two Factor without Replication	Analysis of variance with two independent variables, and one observation in each combination of the levels of the variables. It's also a Repeated Measures Analysis of variance.
Correlation	With more than two measurements on a sample of individuals, calculates a matrix of correlation coefficients for all possible pairs of the measurements.
Covariance	With more than two measurements on a sample of individuals, calculates a matrix of covariances for all possible pairs of the measurements.
Descriptive Statistics	Generates a report of central tendency, variability, and other characteristics of values in the selected range of cells.
Exponential Smoothing	In a sequence of values, calculates a prediction based on a preceding set of values and on a prior prediction for those values.
F-Test Two Sample for Variances	Performs an F-test to compare two variances.
Histogram	Tabulates individual and cumulative frequencies for values in the selected range of cells.
Moving Average	In a sequence of values, calculates a prediction which is the average of a specified number of preceding values.
Random Number Generation	Provides a specified amount of random numbers generated from one of seven possible distributions.
Rank and Percentile	Creates a table that shows the ordinal rank and the percentage rank of each value in a set of values.
Regression	Creates a report of the regression statistics based on linear regression through a set of data containing one dependent variable and one or more independent variables.
Sampling	Creates a sample from the values in a specified range of cells.
t-Test: Two Sample	Three t-test tools that test the difference between two means. One assumes equal variances in the two samples. Another assumes unequal variances in the two samples. The third assumes matched samples.
z-Test: Two Sample for Means	Performs a two-sample z-test to compare two means when the variances are known.

The ToolPak is an add-in. To use it, you first have to load it into Excel. To start (in the Windows version), click

File | Options   (Do *not* click File | Add-ins.)

Doing this opens the Excel Options dialog box. Then follow these steps:

1. **In the Excel Options dialog box, select Add-Ins.**

   Oddly enough, this step opens a list of add-ins.

   Near the bottom of the list, you see a drop-down list labeled Manage.

2. **From this list, select Excel Add-Ins, if it's not already selected.**

3. **Click Go.**

   This opens the Add-Ins dialog box. (See Figure 2-23.)

4. **Select the check box next to Analysis ToolPak, select the check box next to Solver Add-in, and then click OK.**

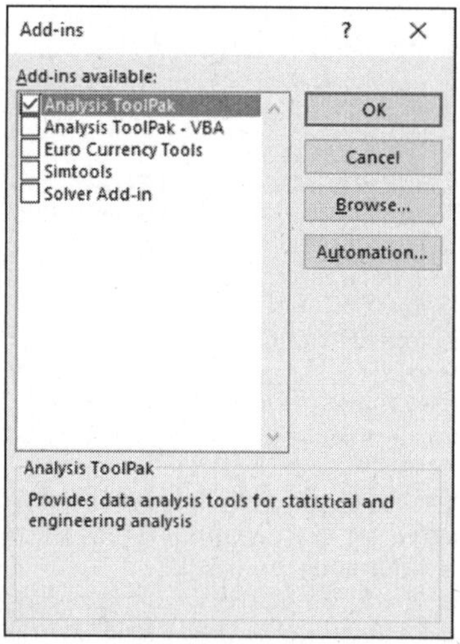

FIGURE 2-23:
The Add-Ins
dialog box.

When Excel finishes loading the ToolPak and the Solver, you'll find a Data Analysis button and a Solver button in the Analysis area of the Data tab.

The installation procedure for the Analysis ToolPak on the Mac is much simpler than the one for Windows.

To begin, click

Tools | Add-Ins

Figure 2-24 shows this menu choice.

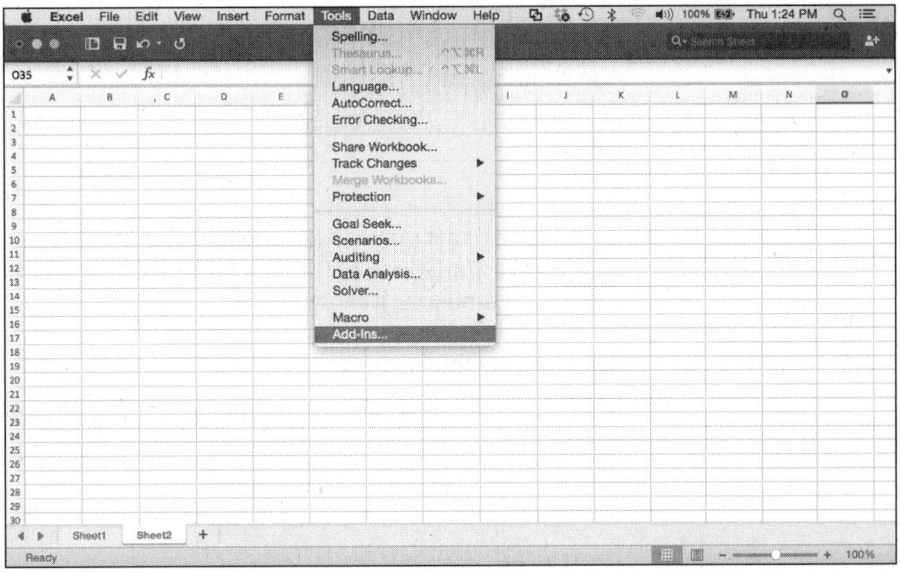

FIGURE 2-24:
The Tools |
Add-Ins menu
choice on the
Mac.

Doing so opens the Add-Ins dialog box (see Figure 2-25). Select the check box next to Analysis ToolPak. Then click OK, and that's it. The ToolPak then appears as a choice on the Tools menu.

Here are the general steps for using a ToolPak data analysis tool:

1. **Enter your data into an array.**

2. **Click Data | Data Analysis to open the Data Analysis dialog box.**

3. **In the Data Analysis dialog box, select the data analysis tool you want to work with.**

4. **Click OK (or just double-click the selection) to open the dialog box for the selected tool.**

5. **In the tool's dialog box, enter the appropriate information.**

   I know this step is vague, but each tool is different.

6. **Click OK to close the dialog box and see the results.**

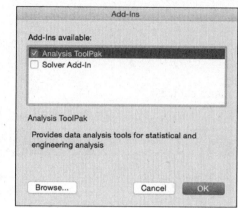

FIGURE 2-25:
The Add-Ins
dialog box
on the Mac.

Here's an example to get you accustomed to using these tools. In this example, I put the Descriptive Statistics tool through its paces. This tool calculates a number of statistics that summarize a set of scores.

1. **Enter your data into an array.**

   Figure 2-26 shows an array of numbers in cells B2 through B9, with a column header in B1.

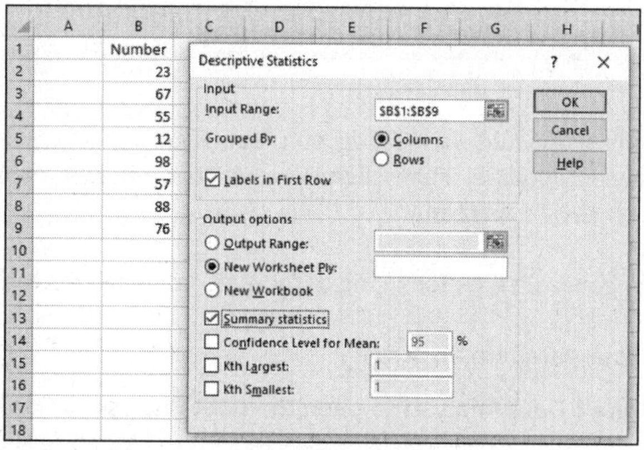

FIGURE 2-26:
Working with the
Descriptive
Statistics tool.

2. **Click Data | Data Analysis to open the Data Analysis dialog box.**

3. **Click Descriptive Statistics and click OK (or just double-click Descriptive Statistics) to open the Descriptive Statistics dialog box.**

4. **Identify the data array.**

In the Input Range box, enter the cells that hold the data. In this example, that's B1 through B9. The easiest way to do this is to move the cursor to the top cell (B1), press the Shift key, and click in the bottom cell (B9). That puts the absolute reference format $B$1:$B$9 into input range.

5. **Select the Columns radio button to indicate that the data are organized by columns.**

6. **Select the Labels in First Row check box because the input range includes the column heading.**

7. **Select the New Worksheet Ply radio button, if it isn't already selected.**

   This step tells Excel to create a new tabbed sheet within the current worksheet, and to send the results to the newly created sheet.

8. **Select the Summary Statistics check box and leave the others deselected.**

9. **Click OK.**

   The new tabbed sheet (ply) opens, displaying statistics that summarize the data. Figure 2-27 shows the new ply, after you widen Column A.

	A	B
1	Number	
2		
3	Mean	59.5
4	Standard Error	10.55428
5	Median	62
6	Mode	#N/A
7	Standard Deviation	29.85202
8	Sample Variance	891.1429
9	Kurtosis	-0.66894
10	Skewness	-0.50676
11	Range	86
12	Minimum	12
13	Maximum	98
14	Sum	476
15	Count	8

FIGURE 2-27:
The output of the Descriptive Statistics tool.

For now, I won't tell you the meaning of each individual statistic in the Summary Statistics display. I leave that for Chapter 7, when I delve more deeply into descriptive statistics.

Accessing Commonly Used Functions

Need quick access to a few commonly used statistical functions? You can get to AVERAGE, MIN (minimum value in a selected cell range) and MAX (maximum value in a selected range) by clicking the down arrow next to the AutoSum button on the left side of the Formulas tab. Clicking this down arrow also gets you to the Mathematical functions SUM and COUNT NUMBERS (counts the numerical values in a cell range).

The AutoSum button is labeled Σ. Figure 2-28 shows you not only exactly where it is but also the menu opened by its down arrow.

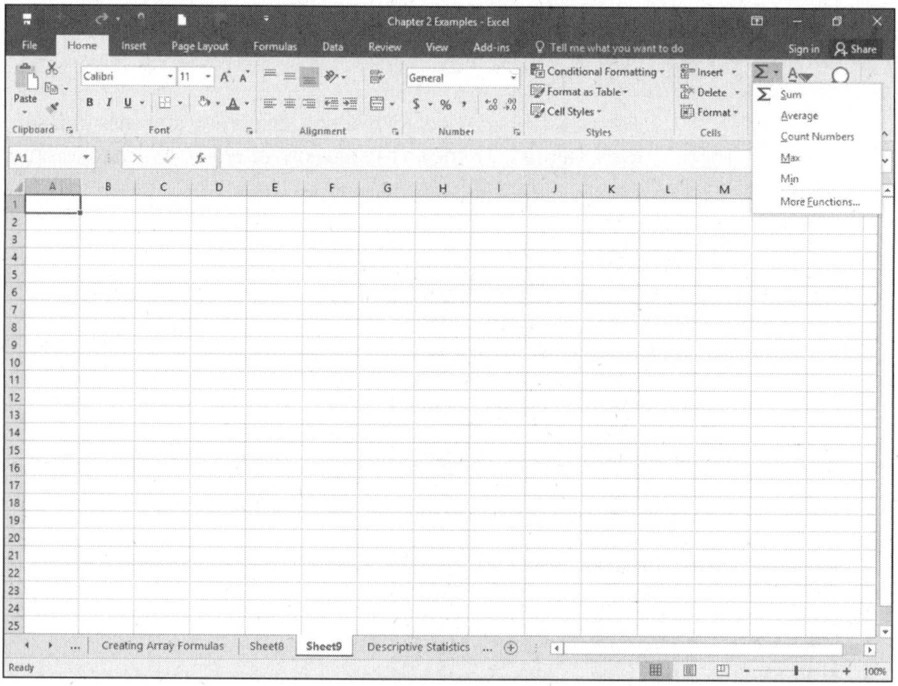

FIGURE 2-28:
The Home | Σ button and the menu its down arrow opens.

By the way, if you just click the button

Formulas | Σ

and not the down arrow, you get SUM.

The last selection on that menu is yet another way to open the Insert Function dialog box.

One nice thing about using this menu — it eliminates a step: When you select a function, you don't have to select a cell for the result. Just select the cell range and the function inserts the value in a cell immediately after the range.

2

Describing Data

IN THIS PART . . .

Summarize and describe data

Work with Excel graphics

Determine central tendency and variability

Work with standard scores

Understand and visualize normal distributions

Chapter 3

Show and Tell: Graphing Data

The visual presentation of data is extremely important in statistics. Visual presentation enables you to discern relationships and trends you might not see if you look only at numbers. Visual presentation helps in another way: It's valuable for presenting ideas to groups and making them understand your point of view.

Graphs come in many varieties. In this chapter, I explore the types of graphs you use in statistics and explain when it's advisable to use them. I also show you how to use Excel to create those graphs.

Why Use Graphs?

Suppose you have to make a pitch to a Congressional committee about commercial space revenues in the early 1990s.

Which would you rather present: the data in Table 3-1 or the graph in Figure 3-1, which shows the same data? (The data, by the way, is from the U.S. Department of Commerce, via the Statistical Abstract of the U.S.)

TABLE 3-1

U.S. Commercial Space Revenues from 1990 through 1994 (in Millions of Dollars)

Industry	1990	1991	1992	1993	1994
Commercial Satellites Delivered	1,000	1,300	1,300	1,100	1,400
Satellite Services	800	1,200	1,500	1,850	2,330
Satellite Ground Equipment	860	1,300	1,400	1,600	1,970
Commercial Launches	570	380	450	465	580
Remote Sensing Data	155	190	210	250	300
Commercial R&D Infrastructure	0	0	0	30	60
Total	3,385	4,370	4,860	5,295	6,640

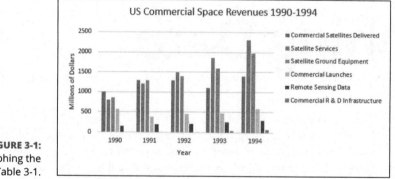

FIGURE 3-1: Graphing the data in Table 3-1.

Which one would have a greater and more lasting impact? Although the table is certainly informative, most people would argue that the graph gets the point across better and more memorably. (Eyes that glaze over when looking at numbers often shine brighter when looking at pictures.)

The graph shows you trends you might not see as quickly on the table. (Satellite services rose fastest. Commercial launches, not so much.) Bottom line: Tables are good; graphs are better.

Graphs help bring concepts to life that might otherwise be difficult to understand. In fact, I do that throughout the book. I illustrate points by ... well ... illustrating points!

Some Fundamentals

First of all, Excel uses the word *chart* instead of *graph*. Like the graph, er, chart in Figure 3-1, most chart formats have a horizontal axis and a vertical axis. Several other formats (pie, treemap, and sunburst), which I show you later in this chapter, do not. Neither the radar chart nor the box-and-whisker chart (which also appear in this chapter) has a horizontal axis.

By convention, the horizontal axis is also called the *x-axis*, and the vertical axis is also called the *y-axis*.

Also, by convention, what goes on the horizontal axis is called the *independent variable*, and what goes on the vertical axis is called the *dependent variable*. One of Excel's chart formats reverses that convention, and I bring that to your attention when I cover it. Just to give you a heads-up, Excel calls that reversed-axis format a *bar chart*. You might have seen the chart shown in Figure 3-1 referred to as a bar chart. So have I. (Actually, I've seen it referred to as a bar *graph*, but never mind that.) Excel calls Figure 3-1 a *column* chart, so I say *columns* from now on.

Getting back to *independent* and *dependent*, these terms imply that changes in the vertical direction depend (at least partly) on changes in the horizontal direction.

Another fundamental principle of creating a chart: Don't wear out the viewer's eyes! If you put too much into a chart in the way of information or special effects, you defeat the whole purpose of the chart.

For example, in Figure 3-1, I had to make some choices about filling in the columns. Color-coded columns would have been helpful, but the page you're looking at shows only black, white, and shades of gray.

A lot of Chart creation skill comes with experience, and you just have to use your judgment. In this case, my judgment came into play with the horizontal gridlines. In most charts, I prefer not to have them. Here, they seem to add structure and help the viewer figure out the dollar value associated with each column. But then again, that's just my opinion.

Excel's Graphics (Chartics?) Capabilities

As I mention in the preceding section, the chart in Figure 3-1 is a column chart. It's one of many types of charts you can create with Excel. Of all the graphics possibilities Excel provides, however, only a few are useful for statistical work. Those are the ones I cover in this chapter.

In addition to the column chart, I show you how to create pie charts, bar charts, line charts, and scatter plots. I also cover an exciting new capability called Power View.

Inserting a Chart

When you create a chart, you *insert* it into a spreadsheet. This immediately clues you in that all chart creation tools are in the Charts area of the Insert tab. (See Figure 3-2.)

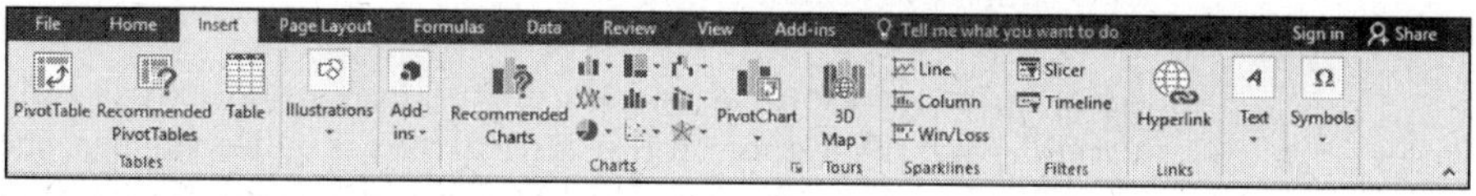

FIGURE 3-2:
The Charts area of the Insert tab.

To insert a chart, follow these steps:

1. **Enter your data into a worksheet.**

2. **Select the data that go into the chart.**

3. **In the Charts area of the Insert tab, select Recommended Charts.**

    The Insert Chart dialog box opens. This dialog box presents Excel's best guesses for the kind of chart that captures your data. Choose one, and Excel creates a chart in the worksheet.

4. **Modify the chart.**

    Click on the chart, and Excel adds a Design tab and a Layout tab to the Ribbon. These tabs allow you to make all kinds of changes to the chart. You can also click on a chart element (like an axis or a data point) to open a *task pane* on the right side of the screen. The task pane enables you to modify the element. If you keep the task pane open and click on another element, the task pane changes to accommodate the newly clicked element and the possible modifications you can make.

It's really that simple. (Charts seem to get easier with each new version of Excel.) The next section shows what I mean.

By the way, here's one more important concept about Excel graphics. In Excel, a chart is *dynamic*. This means that after you create a chart, changing its worksheet data results in an immediate change in the chart.

In this example, and in all the ones to follow, Step 3 is always

Insert | Recommended Charts

You can, however, directly access a chart type without Excel's recommendations. Each chart type occupies a place on the Insert tab. You can also access each chart from the All Charts tab in the Recommended Charts dialog box.

Becoming a Columnist

In this section, I show you how to create the spiffy graph shown earlier, in Figure 3-1. Follow these steps:

1. **Enter your data into a worksheet.**

   Figure 3-3 shows the data from Table 3-1 entered into a worksheet.

FIGURE 3-3: Table 3-1 data, entered into a worksheet.

▲	A	B	C	D	E	F
1	Industry	1990	1991	1992	1993	1994
2	Commercial Satellites Delivered	1000	1300	1300	1100	1400
3	Satellite Services	800	1200	1500	1850	2300
4	Satellite Ground Equipment	860	1300	1400	1600	1970
5	Commercial Launches	570	380	450	465	580
6	Remote Sensing Data	155	190	210	250	300
7	Commercial R & D Infrastructure	0	0	0	30	60
8	Total	3385	4370	4860	5295	6610
9						

2. **Select the data that go into the chart.**

   I selected A1:F7. The selection includes the labels for the axes but doesn't include row 8, which holds the column totals.

3. **In the Charts area of the Insert tab, select Recommended Charts.**

   Selecting Insert | Charts | Recommended Charts opens the Insert Chart dialog box, shown in Figure 3-4. I scrolled down the recommended charts in the left column and selected Excel's fifth recommendation. (Apparently, Excel's tastes are a bit different from mine. Perhaps in a future version, Excel and I will see eye to eye.) This type of chart is called Clustered Column.

4. **Modify the chart.**

   Figure 3-5 shows the resulting chart, as well as the Design tab and the Format tab. These tabs combine to form Chart Tools. As you can see, I have to do some modifying. Why? Excel has guessed wrong about how I want to design the chart. It looks okay, but it will look better (to my eye) if I relocate the legend (the part below the x-axis that shows what all the colors mean). As Figure 3-1 shows, I prefer the legend on the right side of the chart.

To make the modification, I double-click on the legend. This opens the Format Legend pane. (See Figure 3-5.) I select the Top Right radio button to reposition the legend.

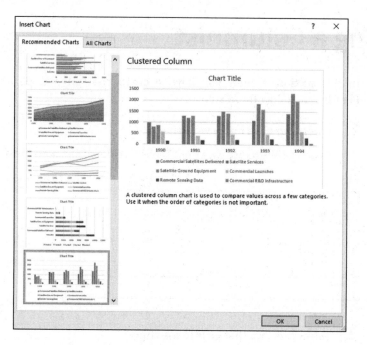

FIGURE 3-4:
The Insert Chart
dialog box.

Some work remains. For some reason, Excel creates the chart without a line for the y-axis, and with a light gray line for the x-axis. Also, the axes aren't labeled yet, and the graph has no title.

I start by formatting the axes. When I click on the y-axis, *Format Legend* changes to *Format Axis.* Figure 3-6 shows this pane after selecting Axis Options and then Line. I worked with the Color button to change the color of the y-axis. In the same way, I can select the x-axis and then repeat the same steps to change the color of the x-axis.

Next, I add the axis titles and the chart title. To do this, I move the cursor inside the chart and click. A set of buttons appears to the right of the chart. One of them, labeled with a plus sign, is called the Chart Elements button. Click this button and, on the pop-up menu that appears, select the check box next to Axis Titles. Figure 3-7 shows the Chart Elements button and the Axis Titles check box selected. Choosing an axis in the pop-up menu adds a text box with placeholder text to that axis.

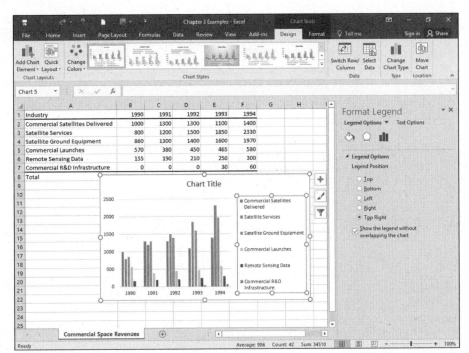

FIGURE 3-5:
The Format Legend pane.

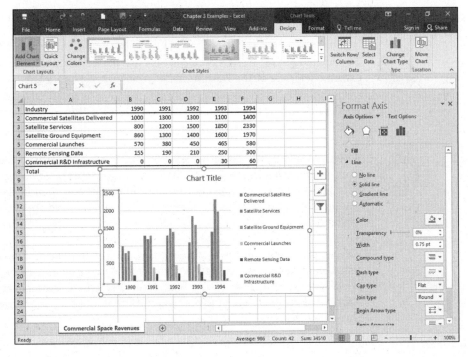

FIGURE 3-6:
The Format Axis pane, with Axis Options and Line selected.

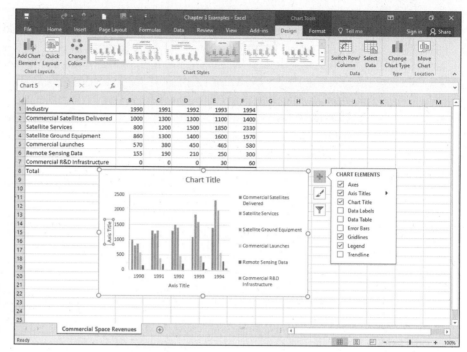

FIGURE 3-7:
The Chart Elements button, with Axis Titles selected.

Use the title textboxes to add the titles and finish off the chart to make it look like the chart in Figure 3-1.

TIP

To add elements to a chart, you can also use the Add Chart Elements button on the extreme left side of the Design tab.

For a quick way to add the chart title, just click the title in the chart and type a new title.

TIP

When you add a title (whether axis or chart), you can either select the title and start typing or highlight the title before you start typing. If you type without highlighting, the new title appears in the Formula bar and then in the title area after you press Enter. If you highlight before you type, the title appears in the title area as you type.

You can preview a chart in a couple of ways. In the Insert Chart dialog box, clicking each recommended chart previews how your data looks in each type of chart. Each preview appears in the dialog box. After you create your chart, mousing over alternatives in the Design tab previews different looks for your chart. Each preview temporarily changes your chart.

That set of buttons headed by the plus sign provides many useful shortcuts. The paintbrush button presents a variety of color schemes and styles for your chart. The filter button allows you to delete selected elements from the chart and gives a shortcut for opening the Select Data Source dialog box (which I use in the later section "Drawing the Line.")

Stacking the Columns

If I had selected Excel's seventh recommended chart, I would have created a set of columns that presents the same information in a slightly different way. This type of chart is called Stacked Columns. Each column represents the total of all the data series at a point on the x-axis. Each column is divided into segments and each segment's size is proportional to how much it contributes to the total. Figure 3-8 shows this.

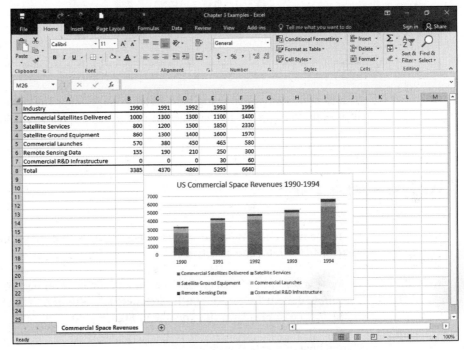

FIGURE 3-8:
A stacked column chart of the data in Table 3-1.

I inserted each graph into the worksheet. Excel also allows you to move a graph to a separate page in the workbook. Select Design | Move Chart (it's on the extreme right side of the Design tab) to open the Move Chart dialog box. Select the New Sheet radio button to add a worksheet and move the chart there. Figure 3-9 shows how the chart looks in its own page. As you can see in Figure 3-9, I relocated the legend from Figure 3-8.

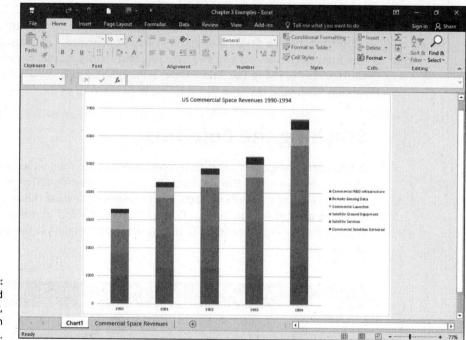

FIGURE 3-9:
The Stacked
Column chart,
in its own
worksheet.

This is a nice way of showing percentage changes over the course of time. If you just want to focus on percentages in one year, the next type of graph is more effective.

Slicing the Pie

On to the next chart type. To show the percentages that make up one total, a pie chart gets the job done effectively.

Suppose you want to focus on U.S. commercial space revenues for 1994 — the last column of data in Table 3-1. You'll catch people's attention if you present the data in the form of a pie chart, like the one in Figure 3-10.

Here's how to create this chart:

1. Enter your data into a worksheet.

It's pretty easy. I've already done this.

2. Select the data that go into the chart.

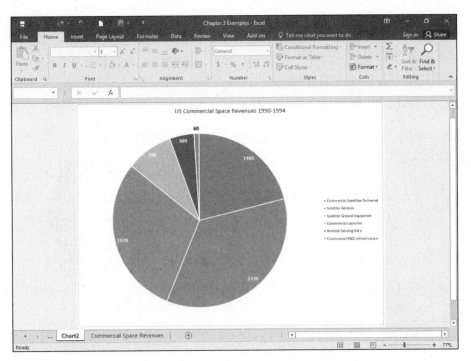

FIGURE 3-10:
A pie chart of the
last column of
data in Table 3-1.

I want the names in column A and the data in column F. The trick is to select column A (cells A2 through A7) in the usual way and then press and hold the Ctrl key. While holding this key, drag the cursor from F2 through F7. Voilà — two non-adjoining columns are selected.

3. **Select Insert | Recommended Charts and pick Pie Chart from the list on the left side of the screen.**

4. **Modify the chart.**

   Figure 3-11 shows the initial pie chart (after I added the title) on its own page. To get it to look like Figure 3-10, I had to do a lot of modifying. First, I formatted the legend as in the preceding example.

   The numbers inside the slices are called data labels. To add them, I select the chart (not just one slice) and then click the Chart Elements button. I then check the box next to Data Labels.

   To change the font color of the labels, click one of the data labels and select Text Options in the Format Data Labels pane that appears. Select the Solid Fill radio button and change the color from black to white. Press Ctrl+B to make the font bold. For the data label (60) that's outside the pie, you can select it individually and change its font color back to black.

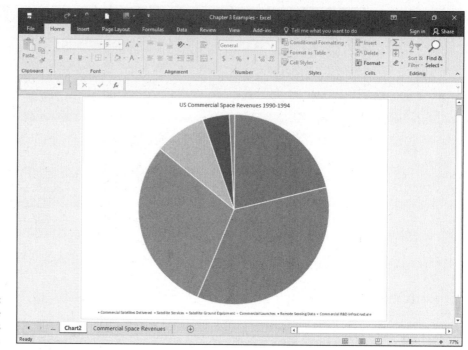

FIGURE 3-11:
The initial pie chart on its own page.

Whenever you set up a pie chart, always keep the following in mind . . .

A word from the wise

The late, great social commentator, raconteur, and former baseball player Yogi Berra once went to a restaurant and ordered a whole pizza.

"How many slices should I cut," asked the waitress, "four or eight?"

"Better make it four," said Yogi. "I'm not hungry enough to eat eight."

Yogi's insightful analysis leads to a useful guideline about pie charts: They're more digestible if they have fewer slices. If you cut a pie chart too fine, you're likely to leave your audience with information overload.

TIP

When you create a chart for a presentation (as in PowerPoint), include the data labels. They often clarify important points and trends for your audience.

(That Yogi anecdote appears in the previous three editions of this book. Did it really happen? We can't be sure. As Mr. Berra once famously said: "Half the lies they tell about me aren't true.")

Drawing the Line

In the preceding example, I focus on one column of data from Table 3-1. In this example, I focus on one *row*. The idea is to trace the progress of one space-related industry across the years 1990–94. In this example, I graph the revenues from Satellite Services. The final product, shown on its own page, is shown in Figure 3-12.

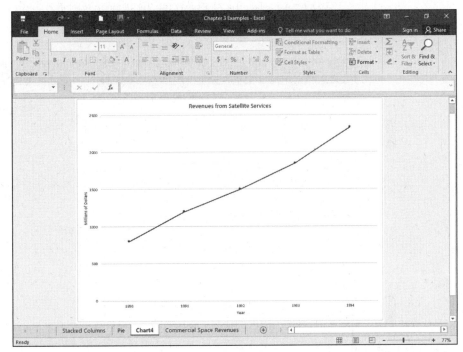

FIGURE 3-12:
A line chart of the
second row of
data in Table 3-1.

A line chart is a good way to show change over time, when you aren't dealing with many data series. If you try to graph all six industries on one line chart, it begins to look like spaghetti.

How do you create a chart like Figure 3-12? Follow along:

1. **Enter your data into a worksheet.**

   Once again, it's already done.

2. **Select the data that go into the chart.**

   For this example, that's cells A3 through F3. Yes, I include the label.

Whoa! Did I forget something? What about that little trick I showed you earlier, where you hold down the Ctrl key and select additional cells? Couldn't I do that and select the top row of years for the *x*-axis?

Nope. Not this time. If I do that, Excel thinks 1990, 1991, 1992, 1993, and 1994 are just another series of data points to plot on the graph. I show you another way to put those years on the *x*-axis.

3. Click Insert | Recommended Charts, and select a chart type.

This time, I select the All Charts tab, pick Line in the left column, and choose Line with Markers from the options. Figure 3-13 shows the result.

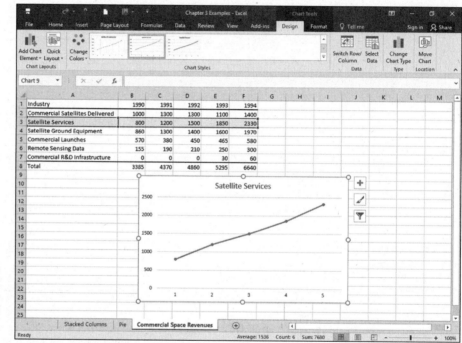

4. Modify the chart.

The line on the chart might be a little hard to see. Clicking the line and then selecting Design | Change Colors gives a set of colors for the line. I chose black.

Next, I added the titles for the chart and for the axes. The easiest way to change the title (which starts out as the label I selected along with the data) is to click the title and type the change.

To add the axis titles, I clicked the Chart Elements button (labeled with a plus sign) and selected the check box next to Axis Titles on the pop-up menu.

(Refer to Figure 3-7.) I then clicked an axis title, highlighted the text, and typed the new title.

I still have to put the years on the *x*-axis. To do this, I right-clicked inside the chart to open the pop-up menu shown in Figure 3-14.

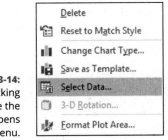

FIGURE 3-14:
Right-clicking
inside the
chart opens
this menu.

Choosing Select Data from this menu opens the Select Data Source dialog box. (See Figure 3-15.) In the box labeled Horizontal (Category) Axis Labels, clicking the Edit button opens the Axis Labels dialog box (see Figure 3-16). A blinking cursor in the Axis Label Range box shows it's ready for business. Selecting cells B1 through F1 and clicking OK sets the range and closes this dialog box. Clicking OK closes the Select Data Source dialog box and puts the years on the *x*-axis.

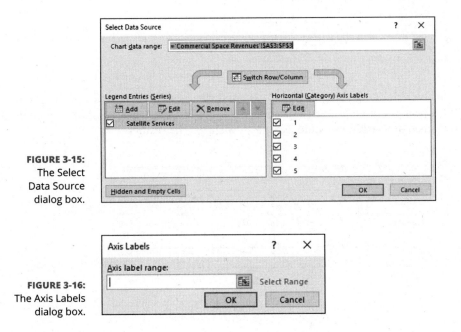

FIGURE 3-15:
The Select
Data Source
dialog box.

FIGURE 3-16:
The Axis Labels
dialog box.

Adding a Spark

The brainchild of Edward Tufte (also known as "the daVinci of data"), a *sparkline* is a tiny chart you can integrate into text or a table to quickly illustrate a trend. It's designed to be the size of a word. In fact, Tufte refers to sparklines as *datawords*.

Three types of sparklines are available: One is a line chart; another is a column chart. The third is a special type of column chart that sports fans will enjoy. It shows wins and losses.

To show you what these sparklines look like, I apply the first two to the Table 3-1 data. First, I insert two columns between Column A and Column B. Then in the new (blank) Column B, I select cell B2. Then I select

Insert | Sparklines | Line

to open the Create Sparklines dialog box. (See Figure 3-17.)

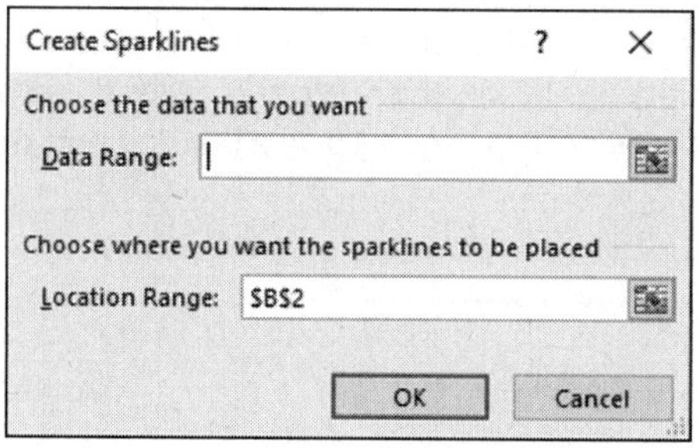

FIGURE 3-17:
The Create
Sparklines
dialog box.

In the Data Range box, I enter D2:H2 and clicked OK. Then I autofill the column. I repeat these steps for Column C, except this time I use Sparklines | Column instead of Sparklines | Line. Figure 3-18 shows the results.

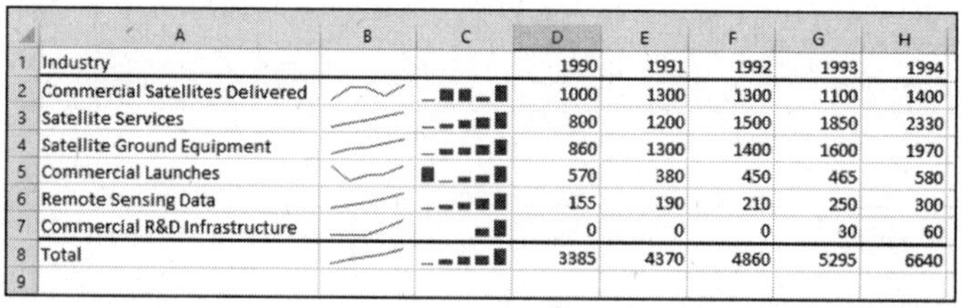

FIGURE 3-18:
Line sparklines
and column
sparklines for the
data in Table 3-1.

	A	B	C	D	E	F	G	H
1	Industry			1990	1991	1992	1993	1994
2	Commercial Satellites Delivered			1000	1300	1300	1100	1400
3	Satellite Services			800	1200	1500	1850	2330
4	Satellite Ground Equipment			860	1300	1400	1600	1970
5	Commercial Launches			570	380	450	465	580
6	Remote Sensing Data			155	190	210	250	300
7	Commercial R&D Infrastructure			0	0	0	30	60
8	Total			3385	4370	4860	5295	6640
9								

If you absolutely must show a table in a presentation, sparklines would be a welcome addition. If I were presenting this table, I would include the column sparklines.

How else would you use a sparkline? Figure 3-19 shows two column sparklines integrated into a Word document. It takes a little maneuvering to copy and paste properly, and you have to paste the sparkline as a picture. I think you'll agree the results are worth the effort.

In the first half of the 1990's, commercial launch revenue started strong, went through a slump, and then recovered nicely. Overall, US commercial space revenues showed steady growth in the years 1990-1994.

The Wins Losses sparkline nicely summarizes a sports team's progress throughout a season. Created with the Wins Losses button in the Sparklines area, the sparklines in Figure 3-20 represent the monthly records of the teams in Major League Baseball's National League East Division in 2015.

FIGURE 3-20:
Wins Losses
sparklines for the
2015 National
League East
Division,
featuring the
National League
Champion New
York Mets.

National League East	Sparkline	April	May	June	July	August	September
New York Mets		1	-1	-1	1	1	1
Washington Nationals		-1	1	1	-1	-1	0
Miami Marlins		-1	-1	-1	-1	-1	1
Atlanta Braves		-1	1	-1	-1	-1	-1
Philadelphia Phillies		-1	-1	-1	1	-1	-1

In the data, 1 represents a winning record for the month (more wins than losses), −1 represents a losing record, and 0 means the team won as many games as they lost. I didn't include October, because each team played only four regular-season games that month. (They played 22 to 28 games a month between April and September.) In the sparkline, a winning month appears as a marker above the line, a losing record appears as a marker below the line, and a breakeven record is a blank.

Note that the Division champion (and National League champion) New York Mets was the only team to string together three winning months. (Yes, I know they went on to lose the World Series. Don't remind me. You're better than that.)

TIP

To delete a sparkline, skip the usual method. Instead, right-click it and select Sparklines from the pop-up menu. You see a choice that allows you to clear the sparkline.

Passing the Bar

Excel's bar chart is a column chart laid on its side. This is the one that reverses the horizontal-vertical convention. Here, the vertical axis holds the independent variable, and it's referred to as the x-axis. The horizontal axis is the y-axis and it tracks the dependent variable.

When would you use a bar chart? This type of chart fits the bill when you want to make a point about reaching a goal, or about the inequities in attaining one.

Table 3-2 shows the data on home Internet usage. The data, from the U.S. Census Bureau (via the U.S. Statistical Abstract), are for the year 2013. *Percent* means the percentage of people in each income group.

TABLE 3-2

Use of the Internet at Home (2013)

Household Income	Percent
Less than $25,000	48.4
$25,000 to $49,999	69.0
$50,000 to $99,999	84.9
$100,000 to $149,999	92.7
$150,000 and more	94.9

The numbers in the table show a clear trend. Casting them into a bar chart shows the trend even more clearly, as you can see in Figure 3-21.

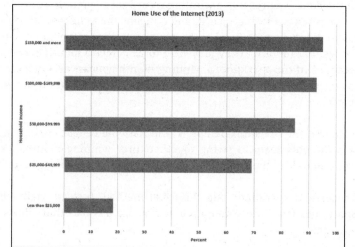

FIGURE 3-21:
A bar chart of the data in Table 3-2.

To create this graph, follow these steps:

1. **Enter your data into a worksheet.**

   Figure 3-22 shows the data entered into a worksheet.

	A	B
4	Household Income	Percent
5	Less than $25,000	18.4
6	$25,000-$49,999	69
7	$50,000-$99.999	84.9
8	$100,000-$149,999	92.7
9	$150,000 and more	94.9
10		

FIGURE 3-22:
Table 3-2 data in
a worksheet.

2. **Select the data that go into the chart.**

   For this example, the data are cells A1 through B8.

3. **Select Insert | Recommended Charts and choose the chart you like from the list on the left side of the screen.**

   I selected the first option: Clustered Bar. Figure 3-23 shows the result.

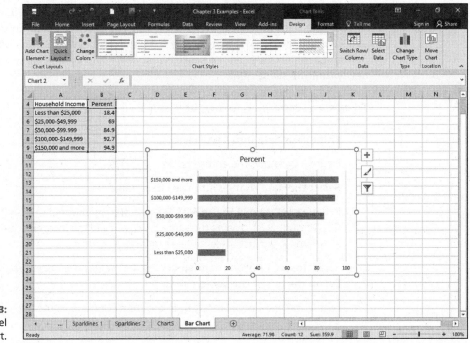

FIGURE 3-23:
The initial Excel
bar chart.

4. **Modify the chart.**

   The first modification is to change the chart title. One way to do this is to click the current title and type the new title. Next, I add the axis titles. To do this, I select the Chart Elements button (that button labeled with a plus sign). Selecting the Axis Labels check box on the menu that appears adds generic axis titles, which I changed. Finally, I bold the font on the axis titles as well as the axis numbers. The easiest way to do that is to select an element and press Ctrl+B.

The Plot Thickens

You use an important statistical technique called *linear regression* to determine the relationship between one variable, *x*, and another variable, *y*. For more information on linear regression, see Chapter 14.

The basis of the technique is a graph that shows individuals measured on both *x* and *y*. The graph represents each individual as a point. Because the points seem to scatter around the graph, the graph is called a *scatterplot*.

Suppose you're trying to find out how well a test of aptitude for sales predicts salespeople's productivity. You administer the test to a sample of salespersons and you tabulate how much money they make in commissions over a 2-month period. Each person's pair of scores (test score and commissions) locates him or her within the scatterplot.

To create a scatterplot, follow these steps:

1. **Enter your data into a worksheet.**

   Figure 3-24 shows the entered data.

2. **Select the data that go into the chart.**

   In the background of Figure 3-25, you can see the selected cells — B2 through C21. (Including B1 creates the same chart, but with an incorrect title.) The cells in Column A are just placeholders that organize the data.

3. **Select Insert | Recommended Charts and select the chart type from the list on the left of the screen.**

   I chose the first option, resulting in the chart shown in Figure 3-25.

	A	B	C
1	Salesperson	Aptitude Score	Commissions (Thousands of Dollars)
2	1	54	65
3	2	34	45
4	3	23	39
5	4	46	36
6	5	34	45
7	6	47	50
8	7	51	76
9	8	54	62
10	9	35	49
11	10	45	50
12	11	40	48
13	12	39	48
14	13	35	47
15	14	56	61
16	15	22	38
17	16	58	64
18	17	42	54
19	18	33	50
20	19	39	45
21	20	50	62
22			

FIGURE 3-24:
Your scatterplot data.

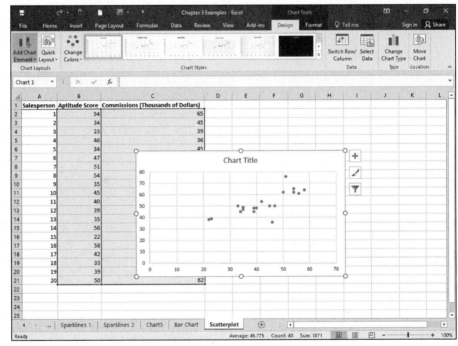

FIGURE 3-25:
The initial scatterplot.

4. Modify the chart.

I clicked the generic chart title and typed a new title. Next, I clicked the Chart Elements tool (labeled with a plus sign) and used the resulting menu to add generic axis titles to the chart. I then typed new titles. Finally, I selected each axis title and typed Ctrl+B to turn the font bold. I did that for the chart title, too. The result is the scatterplot in Figure 3-26.

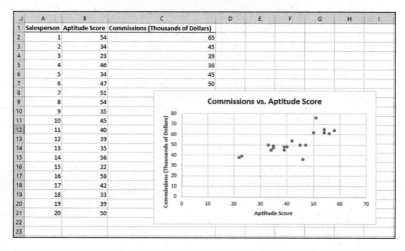

FIGURE 3-26: The almost-finished scatterplot.

For the other graphs, that would just about do it, but this one's special. Right-clicking any of the points in the scatterplot opens the pop-up menu shown in Figure 3-27.

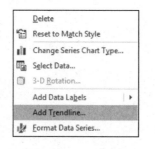

FIGURE 3-27: Right-clicking any point on the scatterplot opens this menu.

Selecting Add Trendline opens the Format Trendline panel. (See Figure 3-28.) I selected the Linear radio button (the default) and clicked the two check boxes at the bottom. (You have to scroll down to see them.) They're labeled Display Equation on Chart and Display R-Squared Value on Chart.

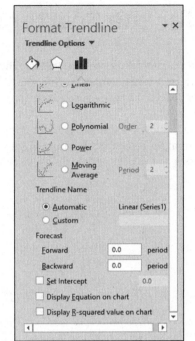

FIGURE 3-28:
The Format
Trendline panel.

Clicking the Close button closes the Format Trendline panel. A couple of additional items are now on the scatterplot, as Figure 3-29 shows. A line passes through the points. Excel refers to it as a *trendline,* but it's more accurately called a *regression line.* A couple of equations are there, too. (For clarity, I dragged them from their original locations.) What do they mean? What are those numbers all about?

Read Chapter 14 to find out.

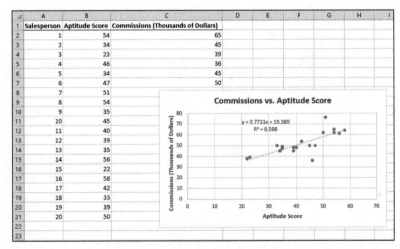

FIGURE 3-29:
The scatterplot,
with additional
information.

Finding Another Use for the Scatter Chart

In addition to the application in the preceding section, you use the scatter chart to create something like a line chart. The conventional line chart works when the values on the x-axis are equally spaced, as is the case for the data in Table 3-1.

Suppose your data look like the values in Figure 3-30. Veterans of earlier Excel versions (Excel 2010 and before) might remember having to figure out that a scatter chart with lines and markers was the best way to visualize these data.

	A	B
1	x	y
2	10	12
3	20	16
4	50	22
5	100	75
6	200	112
7		

FIGURE 3-30: These data suggest a line chart, but the x-values are not equally spaced.

Excel 2016 figures this out for you. Selecting the data and then Insert | Recommended Charts presents the Scatter with Straight Lines and Markers as the first option — although Excel labels it simply as Scatter. (See Figure 3-31.) This puts you on the road to the appropriate chart.

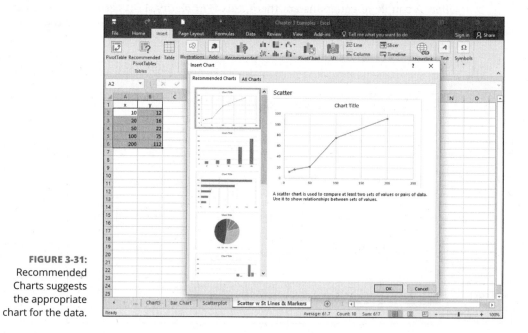

FIGURE 3-31: Recommended Charts suggests the appropriate chart for the data.

TIP

In Chapters 8, 10, 11, and 19, I show you still another use for the scatter chart. In those chapters, I apply Scatter with Smooth Lines. Stay tuned.

Tasting the Bubbly

A *bubble chart* is a way to visualize three dimensions in a two-dimensional chart. Each data point appears as a circle, or "bubble," in the chart. The bubble's position along the x and y axes represent two dimensions, and the size of the bubble represents the third.

Figure 3-32 shows data I use in Chapter 14 to discuss multiple regression. The data are for the 20 students listed in Column A. Column B shows SAT data, column C shows high school averages, and column D shows college grade point averages (GPA).

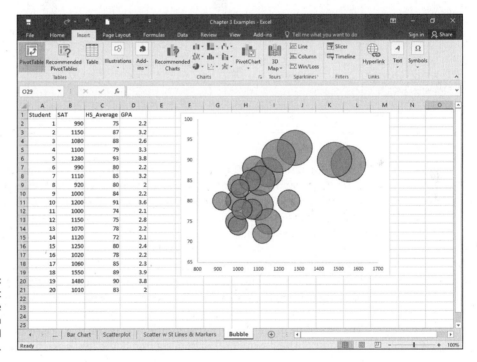

FIGURE 3-32:
A bubble chart
shows three
dimensions in a
two-dimensional
chart.

In the accompanying bubble chart, SAT is on the *x*-axis, the high school average is on the *y*-axis, and the width of the bubbles represents college GPA.

I selected cells B2 through D21, and the bubble chart is the sixth choice in Recommended Charts. I reformatted the axes and the bubbles a bit to make everything stand out more clearly.

Taking Stock

If you're keeping tabs on all the companies in your diversified stock portfolio, the Stock chart is the one for you.

Figure 3-33 shows the prices for Google stock for January 5–13, 2016. (The data are freely available at www.google.com/finance/historical?q=NASDAQ:GOOG.)

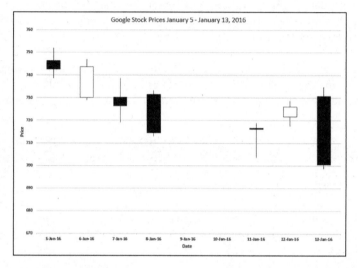

FIGURE 3-33:
A Stock chart
showing Google
stock prices
January 5–13,
2016.

Each data point in the Stock chart is a box with a line extending upward and a line extending downward. The upper and lower bounds of the box represent the opening and closing prices for a particular date — note that I did not say *respectively*. That's because sometimes the opening price is higher than the closing price, and sometimes vice versa.

How do you know which is which? If the box is empty, the opening price is the lower bound (and the stock posted a gain for the day). If the box is filled, the opening price is the upper bound (and the stock posted a loss).

The endpoint of the upward-extending line is the high price for the day, and the endpoint of the downward-extending line is the low price for the day.

Notice that Excel fills in the x-axis with empty dates (days when the stock market was closed.)

To create the chart, follow these steps:

1. **Enter your data into a worksheet.**

Figure 3-34 shows the data in the worksheet.

	A	B	C	D	E
1	Date	Open	High	Low	Close
2	13-Jan-16	730.85	734.74	698.61	700.56
3	12-Jan-16	721.68	728.75	717.32	726.07
4	11-Jan-16	716.61	718.86	703.54	716.03
5	8-Jan-16	731.45	733.23	713	714.47
6	7-Jan-16	730.31	738.5	719.06	726.39
7	6-Jan-16	730	747.18	728.92	743.62
8	5-Jan-16	746.45	752	738.64	742.58

FIGURE 3-34:
The data for
the Google
stock chart.

2. **Select the data that go into the chart.**

For this example, that's cells A1 through E8. I include the labels.

3. **Click Insert | Recommended Charts, and select the chart type.**

Curiously, Excel does not recommend the Stock chart. So I select the All Charts
tab, pick Stock in the left column, and choose Open-High-Low-Close from the
options. Figure 3-35 shows the result.

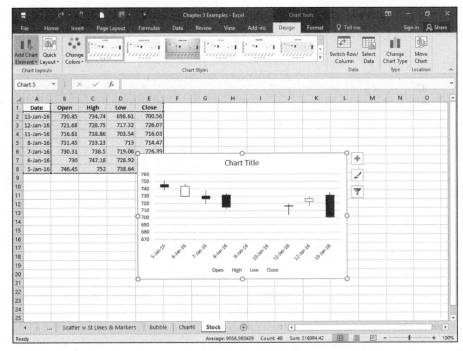

FIGURE 3-35:
Creating an
Open-High-Low-
Close Stock chart.

4. Modify the chart.

I clicked the generic chart title and typed a new title. Next, I clicked the Chart Elements tool (labeled with a plus sign) and used it to add generic axis titles to the chart. I then typed new titles to replace the generic ones. Finally, I selected each axis title and pressed Ctrl+B to turn the font bold. I did that for the chart title, too.

Scratching the Surface

The *Surface chart* is a 3-dimensional way to show the results of combining one variable with another. The spreadsheet in Figure 3-36 shows study time (in hours) combined with the number of breaks. The number in each cell is the score on an exam.

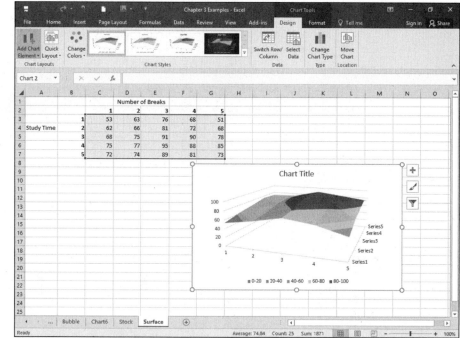

FIGURE 3-36:
Creating a
Surface chart.

In the accompanying Surface chart, study time is on the *x*-axis (the one that shows *Series 1* through *Series 5*), the number of breaks is on the *y*-axis, and performance (the exam score) is on the z-axis. Colored bands (not easily discernible on the gray-scale illustration) indicate score intervals.

I selected the data in cells C3 through G7 and then picked Surface from the All Charts tab. The first option results in the Surface chart shown in the figure.

On the Radar

The Radar chart plots the values of each of a set of categories on a set of concentric rings. The values appear along an axis that starts at the center and ends on the outer ring.

In Figure 3-37, the categories are Madison, Wisconsin, and Jacksonville, Florida. The values are the monthly mean high temperatures in each city (from http:// usclimatedata.com). As you might expect, the chart shows that for every month, the mean high temperature in Jacksonville is higher than in Madison.

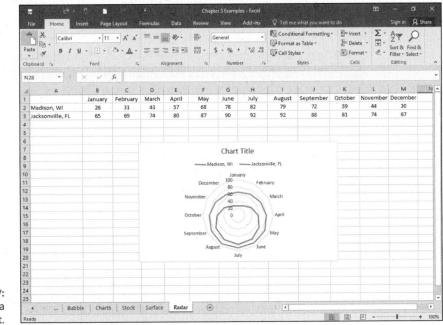

FIGURE 3-37:
Creating a
Radar chart.

I selected cells A1 through M3 and then selected Radar from the All Charts tab to create this particular chart.

WARNING

Sorry, Mac users: The remaining charts, and 3D Maps, are not part of Excel 2016 for the Mac.

Growing a Treemap and Bursting Some Sun

A *treemap* is a type of hierarchical chart that shows patterns in data. Rectangles represent tree branches, and smaller rectangles represent subbranches.

In Figure 3-38, the data in the spreadsheet are research-and-development expenditures in three U.S. federal agencies in 2010. (Source: www.census.gov/library/publications/2011/compendia/statab/131ed/science-technology.html) Each agency is the highest level in the hierarchy (tree branch), and the area is the next level (subbranch). To make the treemap shown in the figure, I selected cells A1 through C8 and picked Tree Map from the Recommended Charts.

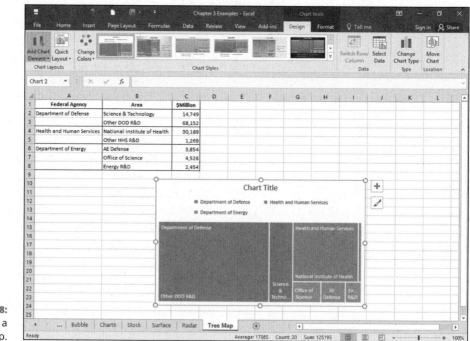

FIGURE 3-38:
Creating a treemap.

Note that the treemap doesn't show the dollar figures, but represents them as proportions of area.

The Sunburst chart illustrates the same type of data as the treemap. Figure 3-39 shows the Sunburst chart for the data in Figure 3-38. The highest level in the hierarchy is in the inner ring; the sublevels are in the outer ring. Like the treemap, the Sunburst chart doesn't show the dollar figures, but represents them as proportions. I created this one by selecting cells A1 through C8, and selecting Sunburst from Recommended Charts.

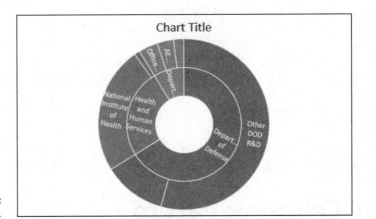

FIGURE 3-39:
A Sunburst chart.

Building a Histogram

Histograms have always been part of Excel. You can use the ToolPak Histogram tool to create one, or you can use the Frequency function along with the Column chart. Excel 2016 gives you the ability to do the latter just by selecting a data array and then inserting the Histogram chart.

The data in Figure 3-40 are the SAT scores for the 20 students in Figure 3-32. To create the accompanying histogram, I selected cells C2 through C21 and selected Histogram from All Charts. As you can see, Excel takes a guess about the interval size (210, in this case). To change this, double-click the x-axis and change Bin Width in the Format Axis panel.

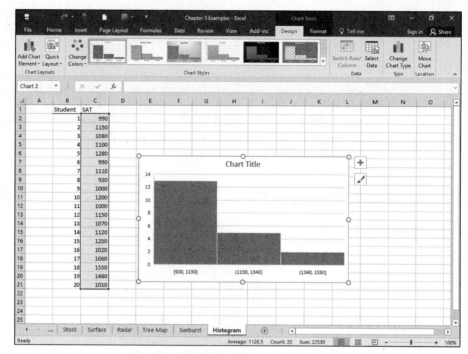

FIGURE 3-40:
Creating a
histogram.

Ordering Columns: Pareto

The *Pareto chart* is a combination of a column chart and a line chart. The column part is special: Columns appear in decreasing order of magnitude. The line represents cumulative percentage.

Figure 3-41 shows what I mean. The data are the number of scientists (x 1000) working in the indicated industries in 2006. (Source: www.census.gov/library/publications/2011/compendia/statab/131ed/science-technology.html)

The columns in the Pareto chart represent the industries arranged in decreasing order, and the line shows the cumulative percentage of each industry, as per the percentage *y*-axis on the right.

To create with this chart, I selected cells A2 through B10, and Pareto from Recommended Charts.

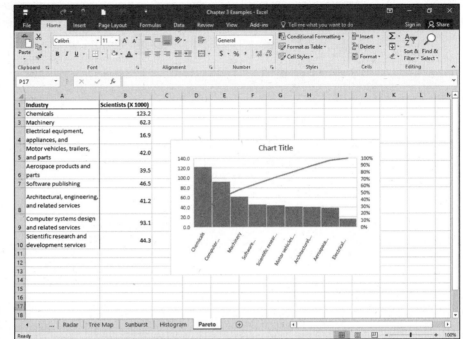

FIGURE 3-41:
Creating a
Pareto chart.

Of Boxes and Whiskers

The Box-&-Whisker chart is valuable for statistical work. Vaguely similar in appearance to a Stock chart, each data point is a box with an upward extension and a downward extension. That's where the similarity ends.

In the spreadsheet in Figure 3-42, the data are the number of Internet connections in the eight districts of the fictional Farchadat County for 2014-2016. I created the chart by selecting cells B2 through D9, and Box & Whiskers from All Charts.

As you can see, each extension looks like an uppercase "T." Those are the "whiskers." Each box and its whiskers summarize an array of data. The lower and upper bounds of the box are the 25th and 75th percentile of the data. (For more on working with percentiles, see Chapter 6). A horizontal line inside the box indicates the median (a/k/a, the 50th percentile). An "X" inside the box indicates the mean. The end of the upward whisker is the highest value and the end of the downward whisker is the lowest value.

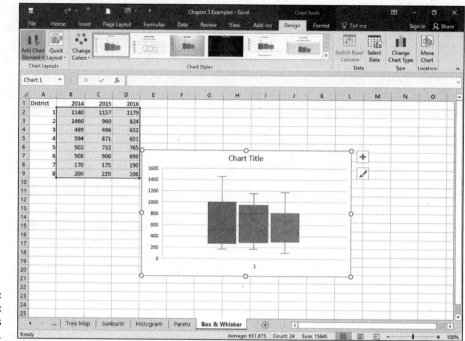

FIGURE 3-42:
Creating a Box
and Whiskers
chart.

If you add each data array individually to the Box & Whisker chart (instead of all at once), each box shows all the points in the data array. To get this done, choose the Box & Whisker chart before you select any data. Then, to add an array individually, right-click on the chart and choose Select Data from the pop-up menu that appears. That will get you started.

Excel refers to these last three charts as "statistical charts."

TIP

3D Maps

Added as Power View to Excel 2013, 3D Maps is the current incarnation. As its name implies, 3D Maps adds three-dimensional visualization. In this section, I show you how to use 3D Maps to create a globe with data on numerous countries.

Figure 3-43 shows part of a spreadsheet with data on life expectancy at birth, expected years of schooling, and mean years of schooling for 188 countries. (Source: http://hdr.undp.org/en/composite/HDI.)

	Country	Life expectancy at birth	Expected years of schooling	Mean years of schooling
1				
2	Norway	81.6	17.5	12.6
3	Australia	82.4	20.2	13.0
4	Switzerland	83.0	15.8	12.8
5	Denmark	80.2	18.7	12.7
6	Netherlands	81.6	17.9	11.9
7	Germany	80.9	16.5	13.1
8	Ireland	80.9	18.6	12.2
9	United States	79.1	16.5	12.9
10	Canada	82.0	15.9	13.0
11	New Zealand	81.8	19.2	12.5
12	Singapore	83.0	15.4	10.6
13	Hong Kong, China (SAR)	84.0	15.6	11.2
14	Liechtenstein	80.0	15.0	11.8
15	Sweden	82.2	15.8	12.1
16	United Kingdom	80.7	16.2	13.1
17	Iceland	82.6	19.0	10.6
18	Korea (Republic of)	81.9	16.9	11.9
19	Israel	82.4	16.0	12.5
20	Luxembourg	81.7	13.9	11.7
21	Japan	83.5	15.3	11.5
22	Belgium	80.8	16.3	11.3
23	France	82.2	16.0	11.1
24	Austria	81.4	15.7	10.8

FIGURE 3-43: Life expectancy, expected years of schooling, and mean years of schooling for 188 countries.

I use 3D Maps to create a three-dimensional globe that shows these countries and their associated statistics. The globe comes courtesy of Microsoft's Bing search engine, so an active Internet connection is necessary.

To create the globe, follow these steps:

1. Enter the data into a worksheet.

2. Select the data, including the column headers.

3. Click Insert | 3D Maps | Open 3D Maps.

After a few seconds (be patient!), the page in Figure 3-44 opens.

4. Drag fields (column header names) to the Layer pane.

I dragged Life Expectancy at Birth, Expected Years of Schooling, and Mean Years of Schooling into the Height box. Figure 3-45 shows the result. You can see the data added to the globe, as stacked columns in the center of each country.

5. Reveal the globe.

Close the pane on the left and the pane on the right, leaving the globe pane open, as shown in Figure 3-46.

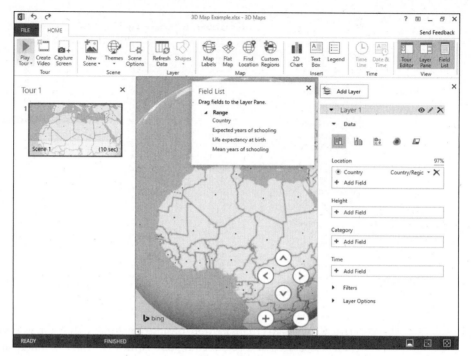

FIGURE 3-44:
This screen opens
when you select
Open 3D Maps.

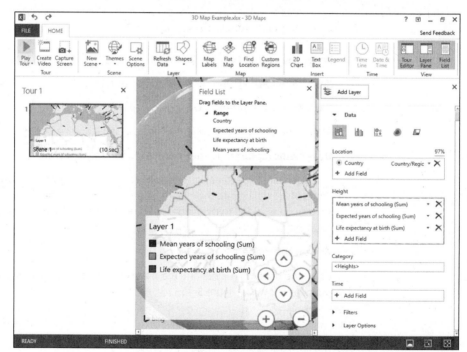

FIGURE 3-45:
The globe, with
data added as
stacked columns.

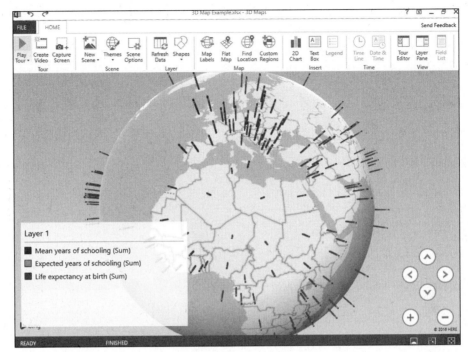

FIGURE 3-46:
The finished globe.

A stationary 3D globe wouldn't be very useful, as many of the countries would be hidden from view. The onscreen controls (and judicious clicking) enable you to rotate the globe and expand or contract it. You can also change colors of the columns and reorient them.

TIP

3D Maps is not just for international mapping — you can create maps on a much smaller scale.

Chapter 4

Finding Your Center

S tatisticians deal with groups of numbers. They often find it helpful to use a single number to summarize a group of numbers. Where would a single summary number come from?

The best bet is to find a number that's somewhere in the middle and use that number to stand for the whole group. If you look at a group of numbers and try to find one that's somewhere in the middle, you're dealing with that group's *central tendency*. Like good ice cream, central tendency comes in several flavors.

Means: The Lore of Averages

Just about everyone uses averages. The statistical term for an average is *mean*. Sometime in your life, you've undoubtedly calculated one. The mean is a quick way of characterizing your grades, your money, or perhaps your performance in some task or sport over time.

Another reason for calculating means concerns the kind of work that scientists do. Typically, a scientist applies some kind of procedure to a small sample of people or things and measures the results in some way. He or she uses the results from the sample to estimate the effects of the procedure on the population that produced the sample. As it happens, the mean of the sample is the best estimate of the population mean.

Calculating the mean

You probably don't need me to tell you how to calculate a mean, but I'm going to do it anyway. Then I show you the statistical formula. My goal is to help you understand statistical formulas in general and then set you up for how Excel calculates means.

A *mean* is just the sum of a bunch of numbers divided by the amount of numbers you added up. Here's an example. Suppose you measure the reading speeds of six children in words per minute and you find that their speeds are

56, 78, 45, 49, 55, 62

The average reading speed of these six children is

$$\frac{56 + 78 + 45 + 49 + 55 + 62}{6} = 57.5$$

That is, the mean of this sample is 57.5 words per minute.

A first try at a formula might be

$$\text{Mean} = \frac{\text{Sum of Numbers}}{\text{Amount of Numbers You Added Up}}$$

This is unwieldy as formulas go, so statisticians use abbreviations. A commonly used abbreviation for *number* is X. A typical abbreviation for the phrase *Amount of Numbers You Added Up* is N. With these abbreviations, the formula becomes

$$\text{Mean} = \frac{\text{Sum of } X}{N}$$

Another abbreviation, used throughout statistics, stands for *Sum of.* It's the upper-case Greek letter for S. It's pronounced "sigma," and it looks like this: Σ. Here's the formula with the sigma:

$$\text{Mean} = \frac{\Sigma X}{N}$$

What about *mean?* Statisticians abbreviate that, too. M would be a good abbreviation, and some statisticians use it, but most use $\bar{X}$ (pronounced "X bar") to represent the mean. Here's the formula:

$$\bar{X} = \frac{\Sigma X}{N}$$

Is that it? Well . . . not quite. English letters, like $\bar{X}$, represent characteristics of samples. For characteristics of populations, the abbreviations are Greek letters. For the population mean, the abbreviation is the Greek equivalent of *M*, which is μ

(pronounced like "you" but with *m* in front of it). The formula for the population mean, then, is

$$\mu = \frac{\sum X}{N}$$

AVERAGE and AVERAGEA

Excel's AVERAGE worksheet function calculates the mean of a set of numbers. Figure 4-1 shows the data and Function Arguments dialog box for AVERAGE.

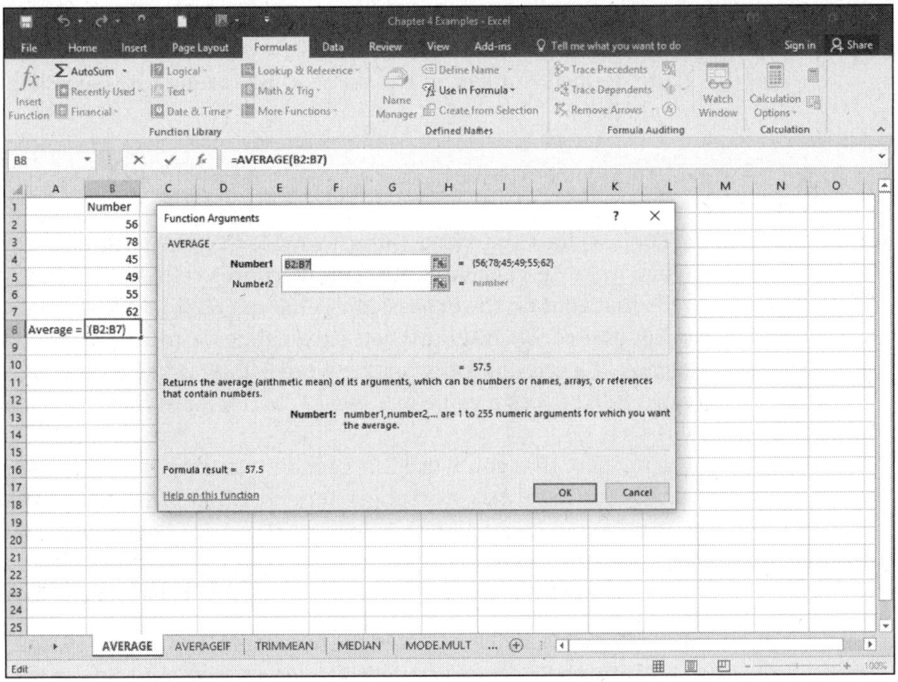

FIGURE 4-1:
Working with
AVERAGE.

Here are the steps:

1. **In your worksheet, enter your numbers into an array of cells and select the cell where you want AVERAGE to place the result.**

   For this example, I entered 56, 78, 45, 49, 55, and 62 into cells B2 through B7, and I selected B8 for the result.

2. **From the Statistical Functions menu, choose AVERAGE to open the AVERAGE Function Arguments dialog box.**

3. **In the Function Arguments dialog box, enter the values for the arguments.**

   If the array of number-containing cells isn't already in the Number1 box, enter it into that box. The mean (57.5, for this example) appears in this dialog box.

4. **Click OK to close the AVERAGE Function Arguments dialog box.**

   This puts the mean into the cell selected in the worksheet. In this example, that's B8.

As you can see in Figure 4-1, the formula in the Formula bar is

```
=AVERAGE(B2:B7)
```

Had I defined Number as the name of B2 through B7 (see Chapter 2), the formula would be

```
=AVERAGE(Number)
```

AVERAGEA does the same thing as AVERAGE, but with one important difference: When AVERAGE calculates a mean, it ignores cells that contain text and it ignores cells that contain the expressions TRUE or FALSE. AVERAGEA takes text and expressions into consideration when it calculates a mean. As far as AVERAGEA is concerned, if a cell holds text or the word FALSE, it has a value of 0. If a cell holds the word TRUE, it has a value of 1. AVERAGEA includes these values in the mean.

I'm not sure that you'll use this capability during everyday statistical work (I never have), but Excel has worksheet functions like AVERAGEA, VARA, and STDEVA, and I want you to know how they operate. Here are the steps for AVERAGEA:

1. **Type the numbers into the worksheet and select a cell for the result.**

   For this example, I entered the numbers 56, 78, 45, 49, 55, and 62 in cells B2 through B7 and selected B9. This leaves B8 blank. I did this because I'm going to put different values into B8 and show you the effect on AVERAGEA.

2. **From the Statistical Functions menu, select AVERAGEA to open the AVERAGEA Function Arguments dialog box.**

3. **In the Function Arguments dialog box, enter the values for the arguments.**

   This time I entered B2:B8 into the Number1 box. The mean (57.5) appears in this dialog box. AVERAGEA ignores blank cells, just as AVERAGE does.

4. **Click OK to close the Function Arguments dialog box, and the answer appears in the selected cell.**

Now for some experimentation. In B8, if I type xxx, the mean in B9 changes from 57.5 to 49.28571. Next, typing TRUE into B8 changes the mean in B9 to 49.42857. Finally, after I type FALSE into B8, the mean changes to 49.28571.

Why the changes? AVERAGEA evaluates a text string like xxx as zero. Thus, the average in this case is based on seven numbers (not six), one of which is zero. AVERAGEA evaluates the value TRUE as 1. So the average with TRUE in B8 is based on seven numbers, one of which is 1.00. AVERAGEA evaluates FALSE as zero, and calculates the same average as when B8 holds xxx.

AVERAGEIF and AVERAGEIFS

The two functions AVERAGEIF and AVERAGEIFS calculate average conditionally. AVERAGEIF includes numbers in the average if a particular condition is met. AVERAGEIFS includes numbers in the average if more than one condition is met.

To show you how these two functions work, I set up the worksheet in Figure 4-2. The entries represent the data from a fictional psychology experiment. In this experiment, a person sits in front of a screen and a color-filled shape appears. The color is either red or green, and the shape is either a square or a circle. The combination for each trial is random, and all combinations appear an equal number of times. In the lingo of the field, each appearance of a color-filled shape is a *trial.* So the worksheet shows the outcomes of 16 trials.

	A	B	C	D
1	Trial	Color	Shape	RT_msec
2	1	Red	Circle	410
3	2	Red	Square	334
4	3	Green	Square	335
5	4	Green	Circle	336
6	5	Red	Square	398
7	6	Red	Circle	450
8	7	Green	Circle	440
9	8	Green	Square	467
10	9	Green	Circle	445
11	10	Red	Square	296
12	11	Green	Square	378
13	12	Red	Circle	496
14	13	Red	Circle	544
15	14	Green	Square	468
16	15	Red	Square	577
17	16	Green	Circle	448
18				
19			Average Overall =	426.375
20			Average Circle =	446.125
21			Av Green Square =	412

FIGURE 4-2: Data from 16 trials of a fictional psychology experiment.

The person sitting in front of the screen presses a button as soon as he or she sees the shape. Column D (labeled RT msec) presents one person's reaction time in milliseconds (thousandths of a second) for each trial. Columns B and C show the characteristics of the shape presented on that trial. For example, row 2 tells you that on the first trial, a red circle appeared and the person responded in 410 msec (milliseconds).

For each column, I defined the name in the top cell of the column to refer to the data in that column. (If you don't remember how to do that, read Chapter 2.)

I've calculated three averages. The first, Average Overall (in cell D19), is just

```
=AVERAGE(RT_msec)
```

What about the other two? Cell D20 holds the average of trials that displayed a circle. That's what I mean by a conditional average: It's the average of trials that meet the condition Shape = Circle.

Figure 4-3 shows the completed Function Arguments dialog box for AVERAGEIF. The formula created after clicking OK is

```
=AVERAGEIF(Shape,"Circle",RT_msec)
```

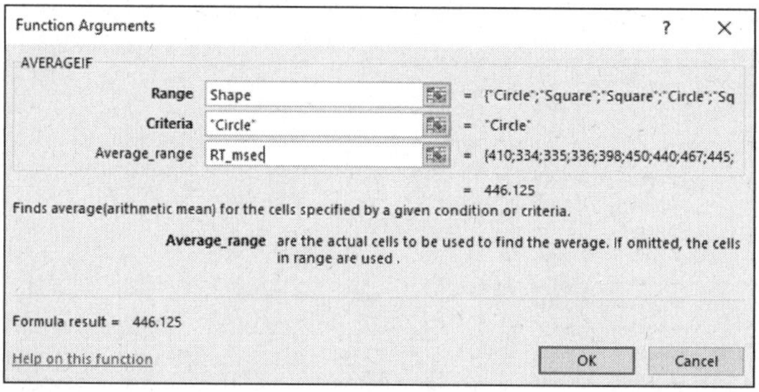

FIGURE 4-3:
The completed dialog box for AVERAGEIF.

What the dialog box and the formula are telling you is this: Excel includes a cell in column D (RT_msec) in the average if the corresponding cell in column B (Shape) holds the value "Circle." If not, the cell is not included.

To create this formula, follow these steps:

1. **Type the numbers into the worksheet and select a cell for the result.**

    The cell I selected is D20.

2. **From the Statistical Functions menu, select AVERAGEIF to open the AVERAGEIF Function Arguments dialog box.**

3. **In the Function Arguments dialog box, enter the values for the arguments.**

   For AVERAGEIF in this example, the Range is Shape, the Criteria is "Circle" (Excel types the double quotes), and the Average_range is RT_msec.

4. **Click OK to close the Function Arguments dialog box, and the answer appears in the selected cell.**

Some more information on AVERAGEIF: To find the average of the first eight trials, the formula is

```
=AVERAGEIF(Trial,"<9",RT_msec)
```

To find the average of reaction times faster than 400 msec, the formula is

```
=AVERAGEIF(RT_msec,"<400",RT_msec)
```

REMEMBER

For each of these last two, the operator "<" precedes the numeric value. If you try to somehow set it up so that the value precedes the operator, the formula won't work.

What about the average for Green Squares in cell D21? Figure 4-4 shows the completed dialog box for AVERAGEIFS, which can work with more than one criterion. The formula for calculating the average of trials on which Color = Green and Shape = Square is

```
=AVERAGEIFS(RT_msec,Color,"Green",Shape,"Square")
```

Function Arguments	? ×

AVERAGEIFS

Average_range	RT_msec		= {410;334;335;336;398;450;440;467;445;
Criteria_range1	Color		= {"Red";"Red";"Green";"Green";"Red";"R
Criteria1	"Green"		= "Green"
Criteria_range2	Shape		= {"Circle";"Square";"Square";"Circle";"Sq
Criteria2	"Square"		= "Square"

= 412

Finds average(arithmetic mean) for the cells specified by a given set of conditions or criteria.

Criteria2: is the condition or criteria in the form of a number, expression, or text that defines which cells will be used to find the average.

Formula result = 412

Help on this function   OK   Cancel

FIGURE 4-4: The completed dialog box for AVERAGEIFS.

Notice that RT_msec is the first argument in AVERAGEIFS but the last argument in AVERAGEIF.

To create this formula, follow these steps:

1. **Type the numbers into the worksheet and select a cell for the result.**

   The cell I selected is D21.

2. **From the Statistical Functions menu, select AVERAGEIFS to open the AVERAGEIFS Function Arguments dialog box.**

3. **In the Function Arguments dialog box, enter the values for the arguments.**

   For AVERAGEIFS in this example, the Average_range is RT_msec. Criteria_range1 is "Color" and Criteria1 is "Green." Criteria_range2 is Shape, the Criteria is "Square." (Excel types the double quotes.)

4. **Click OK to close the Function Arguments dialog box, and the answer appears in the selected cell.**

Given what you just saw, you may be wondering why it's necessary for Excel to have both AVERAGEIF and AVERAGEIFS. After all,

```
=AVERAGEIF(Shape,"Circle",RT_msec)
```

gives the same answer as

```
=AVERAGEIFS(RT_msec, Shape,"Circle")
```

So why two functions? Short answer: I don't know. Long answer: I don't know.

TRIMMEAN

In a retake on a famous quote about statistics, someone said "There are three kinds of liars: liars, darned liars, and statistical outliers." An *outlier* is an extreme value in a set of scores — so extreme, in fact, that the person who gathered the scores believes that something is amiss.

One example of outliers involves psychology experiments that measure a person's time to make a decision. Measured in thousandths of a second, these reaction times depend on the complexity of the decision. The more complex the decision, the longer the reaction time.

Typically, a person in this kind of experiment goes through many experimental trials — one decision per trial. A trial with an overly fast reaction time (way below the average) might indicate that the person made a quick guess without really considering what he or she was supposed to do. A trial with a very slow reaction time (way above the average) might mean that the person wasn't paying attention at first and then buckled down to the task at hand.

Either kind of outlier can get in the way of conclusions based on averaging the data. For this reason, it's often a good idea to eliminate them before you calculate the mean. Statisticians refer to this as *trimming the mean*, and Excel's TRIMMEAN function does this.

Here's how you use TRIMMEAN:

1. Type the scores into a worksheet and select a cell for the result.

For this example, I put these numbers into cells B2 through B11:

500, 280, 550, 540, 525, 595, 620, 1052, 591, 618

These scores might result from a psychology experiment that measures reaction time in thousandths of a second (milliseconds). I selected B12 for the result.

2. From the Statistical Functions menu, select TRIMMEAN to open the TRIMMEAN Function Arguments dialog box.

3. In the Function Arguments dialog box, type the values for the arguments.

The data array goes into the Array box. For this example, that's B2:B11.

Next, I have to identify the percent of scores I want to trim. In the Percent box, I enter .2. This tells TRIMMEAN to eliminate the extreme 20 percent of the scores before calculating the mean. The *extreme 20 percent* means the highest 10 percent of scores and the lowest 10 percent of scores. Figure 4-5 shows the dialog box, the array of scores, and the selected cell. The dialog box shows the value of the trimmed mean, 567.375.

4. Click OK to close the dialog box, and the answer appears in the selected cell.

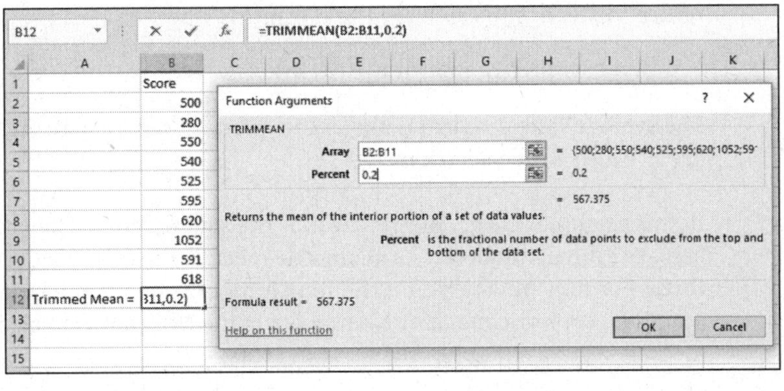

FIGURE 4-5: The TRIMMEAN Function Arguments dialog box, along with the array of cells and the selected cell.

TIP

The label *Percent* is a little misleading here. You have to express the percent as a decimal, so you enter .2 rather than 20 in the Percent box if you want to trim the extreme 20 percent. (Quick question: If you enter 0 in the Percent box, what's the answer equivalent to? Answer: AVERAGE(B2:B11).

REMEMBER

What percentage of scores should you trim? That's up to you. it depends on what you're measuring, how extreme your scores can be, and how well you know the area you're studying. When you do trim scores and report a mean, it's important to let people know that you've done this and to let them know the percentage you've trimmed.

In the upcoming section on the median, I show you another way to deal with extreme scores.

Other means to an end

This section deals with two types of averages that are different from the one you're familiar with. I tell you about them because you might run into them as you go through Excel's statistical capabilities. (How many different kinds of averages are possible? Ancient Greek mathematicians came up with 11!)

Geometric mean

Suppose you have a two-year investment that yields 25 percent the first year and 75 percent the second year. (If you do, I want to know about it!) What's the average annual rate of return?

To answer that question, you might be tempted to find the mean of 25 and 75 (which averages out to 50). But that misses an important point: At the end of the first year, you *multiply* your investment by 1.25 — you don't add 1.25 to it. At the end of the second year, you multiply the first-year result by 1.75.

The regular, everyday, garden-variety mean won't give you the average rate of return. Instead, you calculate the mean this way:

$$\text{Average Rate of Return} = \sqrt{1.25 \times 1.75} = 1.479$$

The average rate of return is about 47.9 percent, not 50 percent. This kind of average is called the *geometric mean.*

In this example, the geometric mean is the square root of the product of two numbers. For three numbers, the geometric mean is the cube root of the product of the three. For four numbers, it's the fourth root of their product, and so on. In general, the geometric mean of N numbers is the Nth root of their product.

The Excel worksheet function GEOMEAN calculates the geometric mean of a group of numbers. Follow the same steps as you would for AVERAGE, but select GEOMEAN from the Statistical Functions menu.

Harmonic mean

Still another mean is something you run into when you have to solve the kinds of problems that live in algebra textbooks.

Suppose, for example, you're in no particular hurry to get to work in the morning, and you drive from your house to your job at the rate of 40 miles per hour. At the end of the day you'd like to get home quickly, so on the return trip (over exactly the same distance) you drive from your job to your house at 60 miles per hour. What is your average speed for the total time you're on the road?

It's not 50 miles per hour, because you're on the road a different amount of time on each leg of the trip. Without going into this in too much detail, the formula for figuring this one out is

$$\frac{1}{\text{Average}} = \frac{1}{2}\left[\frac{1}{40} + \frac{1}{60}\right] = \frac{1}{48}$$

The average here is 48. This kind of average is called a *harmonic mean.* I show it to you for two numbers, but you can calculate it for any amount of numbers. Just put each number in the denominator of a fraction with 1 as the numerator. Mathematicians call this the *reciprocal* of a number. (So ¹⁄₄₀ is the reciprocal of 40.) Add all the reciprocals together and take their average. The result is the reciprocal of the harmonic mean.

In the rare event you ever have to figure out one of these in the real world, Excel saves you from the drudgery of calculation. The worksheet function HARMEAN calculates the harmonic mean of a group of numbers. Follow the same steps as you would for AVERAGE, but on the Statistical Functions menu, select HARMEAN.

For any set of numbers, the harmonic mean is less than the geometric mean, which is less than the mean.

TIP

Medians: Caught in the Middle

The mean is a useful way to summarize a group of numbers. It's sensitive to extreme values, however: If one number is out of whack relative to the others, the mean quickly gets out of whack, too. When that happens, the mean might not be a good representative of the group.

TIP

For example, with these numbers as reading speeds (in words per minute) for a group of children:

56, 78, 45, 49, 55, 62

the mean is 57.5. Suppose the child who reads at 78 words per minute leaves the group and an exceptionally fast reader replaces him. Her reading speed is 180 words per minute. Now the group's reading speeds are

56, 180, 45, 49, 55, 62

The new average is 74.5. It's misleading because — except for the new child — no one else in the group reads nearly that fast. In a case like this, it's a good idea to turn to a different measure of central tendency — the median.

Simply put, the *median* is the middle value in a group of numbers. Arrange the numbers in order, and the median is the value below which half the scores fall and above which half the scores fall.

Finding the median

In our example, the first group of reading speeds (in increasing order) is

45, 49, 55, 56, 62, 78

The median is right in the middle of 55 and 56 — it's 55.5.

What about the group with the new child? That's

45, 49, 55, 56, 62, 180

The median is still 55.5. The extreme value doesn't change the median.

MEDIAN

The worksheet function MEDIAN (you guessed it) calculates the median of a group of numbers. Here are the steps:

1. **Type your data into a worksheet and select a cell for the result.**

   I used 45, 49, 55, 56, 62, 78 for this example, in cells B2 through B7, with cell B8 selected for the median. I arranged the numbers in increasing order, but you don't have to do that to use MEDIAN.

2. From the Statistical Functions menu, select MEDIAN to open the MEDIAN Function Arguments dialog box.

3. In the Function Arguments dialog box, enter the values for the arguments.

The Function Arguments dialog box opens with the data array in the Number1 box. The median appears in that dialog box. (It's 55.5 for this example.) Figure 4-6 shows the dialog box along with the array of cells and the selected cell.

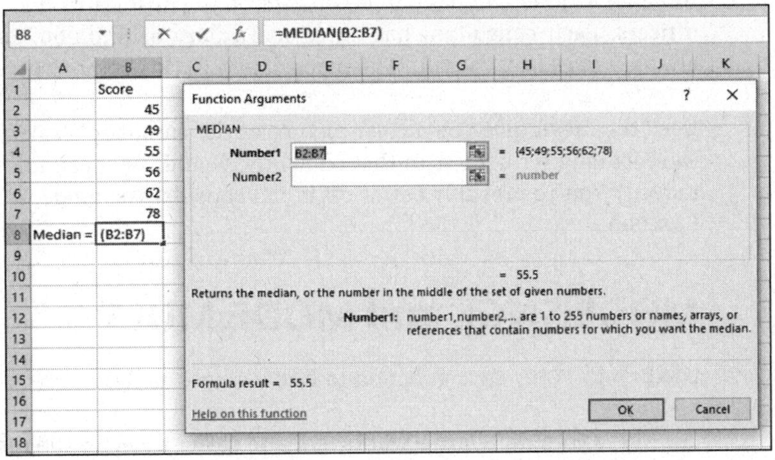

FIGURE 4-6:
The MEDIAN
Function
Arguments
dialog box, along
with the array of
cells and the
selected cell.

4. Click OK to close the dialog box and the answer appears in the selected cell.

As an exercise, replace 78 with 180 in A6, and you'll see that the median doesn't change.

In Appendix C, I explore an application of the median.

Statistics à la Mode

One more measure of central tendency is important. This one is the score that occurs most frequently in a group of scores. It's called the *mode*.

Finding the mode

Nothing is complicated about finding the mode. Look at the scores, find the one that occurs most frequently, and you've found the mode. Two scores tie for that honor? In that case, your set of scores has two modes. (The technical name is *bimodal*.)

Can you have more than two modes? Absolutely.

Suppose every score occurs equally often. When that happens, you have no mode.

Sometimes, the mode is the most representative measure of central tendency. Imagine a small company that consists of 30 consultants and two high-ranking officers. Each consultant has an annual salary of $40,000. Each officer has an annual salary of $250,000. The mean salary in this company is $53,125.

Does the mean give you a clear picture of the company's salary structure? If you were looking for a job with that company, would the mean influence your expectations? You're probably better off if you consider the mode, which in this case is $40,000.

MODE.SNGL and MODE.MULT

Use Excel's MODE.SNGL function to find a single mode:

1. **Type your data into a worksheet and select a cell for the result.**

I use 56, 23, 77, 75, 57, 75, 91, 59, and 75 in this example. The data are in cells B2 through B10, with B11 as the selected cell for the mode.

2. **From the Statistical Functions menu, select MODE.SNGL to open the MODE.SNGL Function Arguments dialog box. (See Figure 4-7.)**

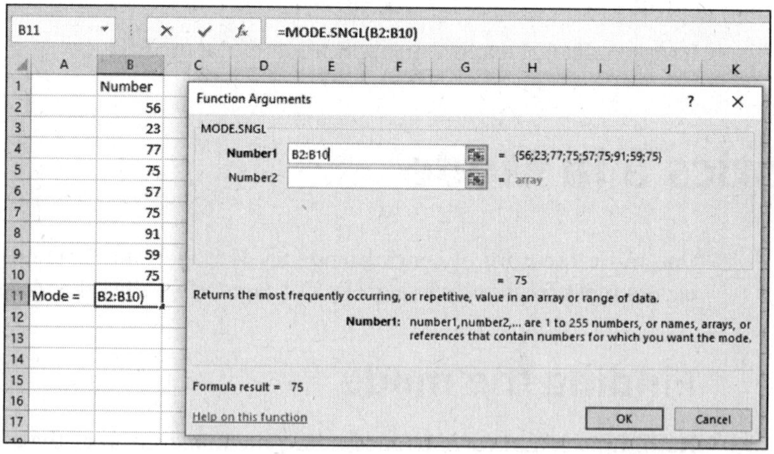

FIGURE 4-7:
The MODE.SNGL
Function
Arguments
dialog box, along
with the array of
cells and the
selected cell.

3. **In the Function Arguments dialog box, type the values for the arguments.**

I entered B2:B10 in the Number1 box and the mode (75 for this example) appears in the dialog box.

4. **Click OK to close the dialog box and the answer appears in the selected cell.**

For a set of numbers that has more than one mode (that is, if it's multimodal), use Excel's MODE.MULT function. This is an array function: It returns (potentially) an array of answers, not just one. You select an array of cells for the results, and when you finish with the dialog box, you press Ctrl+Shift+Enter to populate the array.

Here's an example of MODE.MULT:

1. **Type your data into a worksheet and select a vertical array of cells for the results.**

I typed 57, 23, 77, 75, 57, 75, 91, 57, and 75 into cells B2:B10. I selected B11:B14 for the results. Notice that this set of numbers has two modes: 57 and 75.

2. **From the Statistical Functions menu, select MODE.MULT to open the MODE.MULT Function Arguments dialog box. (See Figure 4-8.)**

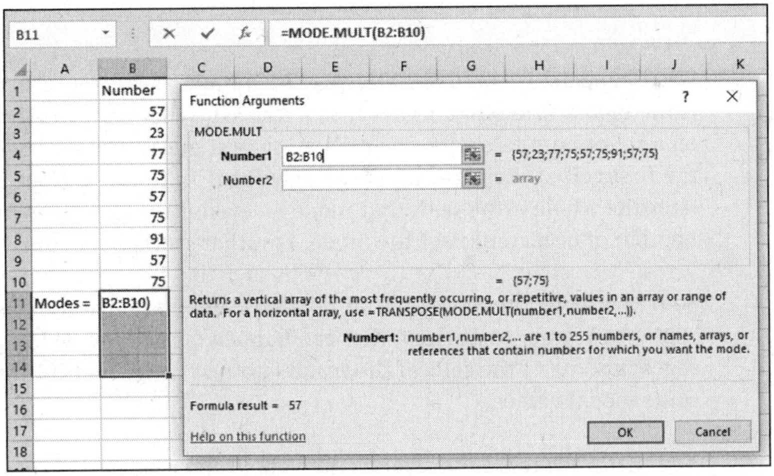

FIGURE 4-8: The MODE.MULT Function Arguments dialog box, along with the array of data cells and the array of cells for the results.

3. In the Function Arguments dialog box, type the values for the arguments.

Important: Do not click OK.

4. Because this is an array function, press Ctrl+Shift+Enter to put MODE. MULT's answers into the selected array.

Nothing in the dialog box even remotely hints that you have to do this.

Figure 4-9 shows what happens after you press Ctrl+Shift+Enter. Because I've allocated four cells for the results and only two modes were in the set of numbers, error messages show up in the remaining two cells.

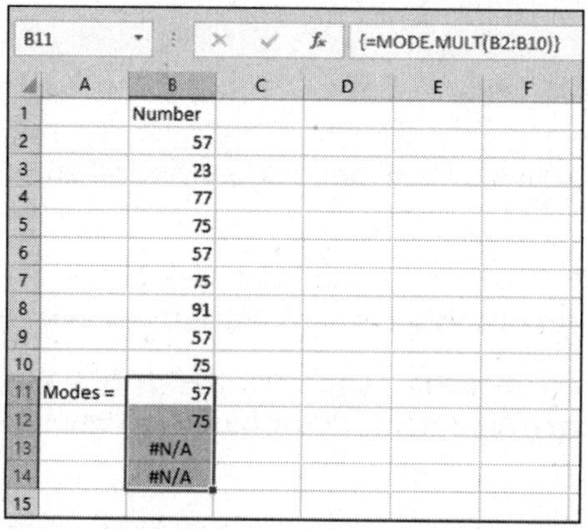

FIGURE 4-9:
The results of
MODE.MULT.
In the Formula
bar, the curly
brackets indicate
an array formula.

What happens if you use MODE.SNGL on a multimodal set of numbers? The result is the modal value that occurs first in the set. What happens if you use MODE.MULT on a set of numbers with one mode? My first guess was that one mode appears in the first cell of the array and error messages in the rest. Nope. MODE.MULT populates the whole array with that mode — even if the array has more cells than the number of occurrences of the mode. Yes, that stumps me, too.

So if you have a long column of numbers and you have to find the mode(s), use MODE.MULT. The worst thing that can happen is that you wind up with error messages in some of the cells of the results array. The trade-off is that you don't miss some modal values.

And that's the most I've ever written about the mode!

Chapter 5

Deviating from the Average

H ere are three pieces of wisdom about statisticians:

Piece of Wisdom #1: "A statistician is a person who stands in a bucket of ice water, sticks their head in an oven and says 'on average, I feel fine.'" (K. Dunning)

Piece of Wisdom #2: "A statistician drowned crossing a stream with an average depth of 6 inches." (Anonymous)

Piece of Wisdom #3: "Three statisticians go deer hunting with bows and arrows. They spot a big buck and take aim. One shoots and his arrow flies off ten feet to the left. The second shoots and his arrow goes ten feet to the right. The third statistician jumps up and down yelling, 'We got him! We got him!'" (Bill Butz, quoted by Diana McLellan in *Washingtonian*)

What's the common theme? Calculating the mean is a great way to summarize a group of numbers, but it doesn't supply all the information you typically need. If you just rely on the mean, you might miss something important.

To avoid missing important information, another type of statistic is necessary — a statistic that measures *variation*. It's a kind of average of how much each number in a group differs from the group mean. Several statistics are available for measuring variation. All of them work the same way: The larger the value of the statistic, the more the numbers differ from the mean. The smaller the value, the less they differ.

Measuring Variation

Suppose you measure the heights of a group of children and you find that their heights (in inches) are

48, 48, 48, 48, and 48

Then you measure another group and find that their heights are

50, 47, 52, 46, and 45

If you calculate the mean of each group, you'll find they're the same — 48 inches. Just looking at the numbers tells you the two groups of heights are different: The heights in the first group are all the same, while the heights in the second vary quite a bit.

Averaging squared deviations: Variance and how to calculate it

One way to show the dissimilarity between the two groups is to examine the deviations in each one. Think of a *deviation* as the difference between a score and the mean of all the scores in a group.

Here's what I'm talking about. Table 5-1 shows the first group of heights and their deviations.

One way to proceed is to average the deviations. Clearly, the average of the numbers in the Deviation column is zero.

TABLE 5-1

The First Group of Heights and Their Deviations

Height	Height-Mean	Deviation
48	48-48	0
48	48-48	0
48	48-48	0
48	48-48	0
48	48-48	0

Table 5-2 shows the second group of heights and their deviations.

TABLE 5-2

The Second Group of Heights and Their Deviations

Height	Height-Mean	Deviation
50	50-48	2
47	47-48	–1
52	52-48	4
46	46-48	–2
45	45-48	–3

What about the average of the deviations in Table 5-2? That's . . . zero!

Hmmm. . . . Now what?

Averaging the deviations doesn't help you see a difference between the two groups, because the average of deviations from the mean in any group of numbers is *always* zero. In fact, veteran statisticians will tell you that's a defining property of the mean.

TIP

The joker in the deck here is the negative numbers. How do statisticians deal with them?

The trick is to use something you might recall from algebra: A minus times a minus is a plus. Sound familiar?

So . . . does this mean that you multiply each deviation times itself, and then average the results? Absolutely. Multiplying a deviation times itself is called *squaring a deviation.* The average of the squared deviations is so important that it has a special name: *variance.*

Table 5-3 shows the group of heights from Table 5-2, along with their deviations and squared deviations.

TABLE 5-3   **The Second Group of Heights and Their Squared Deviations**

Height	Height-Mean	Deviation	Squared Deviation
50	50-48	2	4
47	47-48	-1	1
52	52-48	4	16
46	46-48	-2	4
45	45-48	-3	9

The variance — the average of the squared deviations for this group — is $(4 + 1 + 16 + 4 + 9)/5 = 34/5 = 6.8$. This, of course, is very different from the first group, whose variance is zero.

To develop the variance formula for you and show you how it works, I use symbols to show all this. *X* represents the Height heading in the first column of the table, and $\bar{X}$ represents the mean. Because a deviation is the result of subtracting the mean from each number,

$$\left(X - \bar{X}\right)$$

represents a deviation. Multiplying a deviation by itself? That's just

$$\left(X - \bar{X}\right)^2$$

To calculate variance, you square each deviation, add them up, and find the average of the squared deviations. If *N* represents the amount of squared deviations you have (in this example, five), then the formula for calculating the variance is

$$\frac{\sum\left(X - \bar{X}\right)^2}{N}$$

Σ is the uppercase Greek letter *sigma,* and it stands for "the sum of."

What's the symbol for variance? As I say in Chapter 1, Greek letters represent population parameters, and English letters represent statistics. Imagine that our little group of five numbers is an entire population. Does the Greek alphabet have a letter that corresponds to V in the same way that μ (the symbol for the population mean) corresponds to M?

REMEMBER

As a matter of fact, it doesn't. Instead, you use the *lowercase* sigma! It looks like this: σ. Not only that, but because you're talking about squared quantities, the symbol is σ^2.

So the formula for calculating variance is

$$\sigma^2 = \frac{\sum\left(X - \bar{X}\right)^2}{N}$$

REMEMBER

Variance is large if the numbers in a group vary greatly from their mean. Variance is small if the numbers are very similar to their mean.

The variance you just worked through is appropriate if the group of five measurements is a population. Does this mean that variance for a sample is different? It does, and you see why in a minute. First, I turn your attention back to Excel.

VAR.P and VARPA

Excel's two worksheet functions, VAR.P and VARPA, calculate the population variance.

Start with VAR.P. Figure 5-1 shows the Function Arguments dialog box for VAR.P along with data.

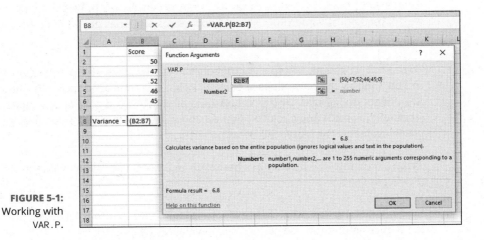

FIGURE 5-1:
Working with
VAR.P.

Here are the steps to follow:

1. **Put your data into a worksheet and select a cell to display the result.**

   Figure 5-1 shows that, for this example, I've put the numbers 50, 47, 52, 46, and 45 into cells B2 through B6 and selected B8 for the result.

2. **From the Statistical Functions menu, select VAR.P to open the VAR.P Function Arguments dialog box.**

3. **In the Function Arguments dialog box, enter the appropriate values for the arguments.**

   I entered B2:B7 in the Number1 field, rather than B2:B6. I did this to show you how VAR.P handles blank cells. The population variance, 6.8, appears in the Function Arguments dialog box.

4. **Click OK to close the dialog box and put the result in the selected cell.**

Had I defined Score as the name of B2:B7 (see Chapter 2), the formula in the formula bar would be

```
=VAR.P(Score)
```

When VAR.P calculates the variance in a range of cells, it only sees numbers. If text, blanks (like B7), or logical values are in some of the cells, VAR.P ignores them.

VARPA, on the other hand, does not. VARPA takes text and logical values into consideration and includes them in its variance calculation. How? If a cell contains text, VARPA sees that cell as containing a value of zero. If a cell contains the logical value FALSE, that's also zero as far as VARPA is concerned. In VARPA's view of the world, the logical value TRUE is one. Those zeros and ones get added into the mix and affect the mean and the variance.

To see this in action, I keep the numbers in cells B2 through B6 and again select cell B8. I follow the same steps as for VAR.P, but this time open the VARPA Function Arguments dialog box. In the Value1 field of the VARPA dialog box, I type B2:B7 (that's B7, *not* B6) and click OK. Cell B8 shows the same result as before because VARPA evaluates the blank cell B7 as no entry.

Typing TRUE into cell B7 changes the result in B8 because VARPA evaluates B7 as 1. (See Figure 5-2.)

Typing FALSE (or any other string of letters except TRUE) into B7 changes the value in B8 once again. In those cases, VARPA evaluates B7 as zero.

B8		▾	⋮	×	✓	f_x	=VARPA(B2:B7)

◢	A	B	C	D	E
1		Score			
2		50			
3		47			
4		52			
5		46			
6		45			
7		TRUE			
8	Variance =	312.4722			
9					

FIGURE 5-2: VARPA evaluates TRUE as 1.0, changing the variance from the value in Figure 5-1.

Sample variance

Earlier, I mention that you use this formula to calculate population variance:

$$\sigma^2 = \frac{\sum(X - \bar{X})^2}{N}$$

I also explain that sample variance is a little different. Here's the difference. If your set of numbers is a sample drawn from a large population, you're probably interested in using the variance of the sample to estimate the variance of the population.

The formula you used for the variance doesn't quite work as an estimate of the population variance. Although the sample mean works just fine as an estimate of the population mean, this doesn't hold true with variance, for reasons *way* beyond the scope of this book.

REMEMBER

How do you calculate a good estimate of the population variance? It's pretty easy. You just use N-1 in the denominator rather than N. (Again, for reasons way beyond this book's scope.)

Also, because you're working with a characteristic of a sample (rather than of a population), you use the English equivalent of the Greek letter — s rather than σ. This means that the formula for the sample variance is

$$s^2 = \frac{\sum(X - \bar{X})^2}{N - 1}$$

The value of s^2, given the squared deviations in the set of five numbers, is

(4 + 1 + 16 + 4 + 9)/4 = 34/4 = 8.5

So, if these numbers

50, 47, 52, 46, and 45

are an entire population, their variance is 6.4. If they're a sample drawn from a larger population, the best estimate of that population's variance is 8.5.

VAR.S and VARA

The worksheet functions VAR.S and VARA calculate the sample variance.

Figure 5-3 shows the Function Arguments dialog box for VAR.S with 50, 47, 52, 46, and 45 entered into cells B2 through B6. Cell B7 is part of the cell range, but I left it empty.

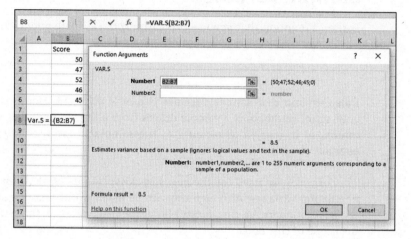

FIGURE 5-3:
Working with
VAR.S.

REMEMBER

The relationship between VAR.S and VARA is the same as the relationship between VAR.P and VARPA: VAR.S ignores cells that contain logical values (TRUE and FALSE) and text. VARA includes those cells. Once again, TRUE evaluates to 1.0, and FALSE evaluates to 0. Text in a cell causes VARA to see that cell's value as 0.

This is why I left B7 blank. If you experiment a bit with VARA and logical values or text in B7, you'll see exactly what VARA does.

Back to the Roots: Standard Deviation

After you calculate the variance of a set of numbers, you have a value whose units are different from your original measurements. For example, if your original measurements are in inches, their variance is in square inches. This is because you square the deviations before you average them.

Often, it's more intuitive if you have a variation statistic that's in the same units as the original measurements. It's easy to turn variance into that kind of statistic. All you have to do is take the square root of the variance.

Like the variance, this square root is so important that it is given a special name: standard deviation.

Population standard deviation

The *standard deviation of a population* is the square root of the population variance. The symbol for the population standard deviation is σ (sigma). Its formula is

$$\sigma = \sqrt{\sigma^2} = \sqrt{\frac{\sum\left(X - \bar{X}\right)^2}{N}}$$

For these measurements (in inches)

50, 47, 52, 46, and 45

the population variance is 6.8 square inches, and the population standard deviation is 2.61 inches (rounded off).

STDEV.P and STDEVPA

The Excel worksheet functions STDEV.P and STDEVPA calculate the population standard deviation. Follow these steps:

1. **Type your data into an array and select a cell for the result.**

2. **In the Statistical Functions menu, select STDEV.P to open the STDEV.P Function Arguments dialog box.**

3. **In the Function Arguments dialog box, type the appropriate values for the arguments.**

   After you enter the data array, the dialog box shows the value of the population standard deviation for the numbers in the data array. Figure 5-4 shows this.

4. **Click OK to close the dialog box and put the result into the selected cell.**

Like VARPA, STDEVPA uses any logical values and text values it finds when it calculates the population standard deviation. TRUE evaluates to 1.0, and FALSE evaluates to 0. Text in a cell gives that cell a value of 0.

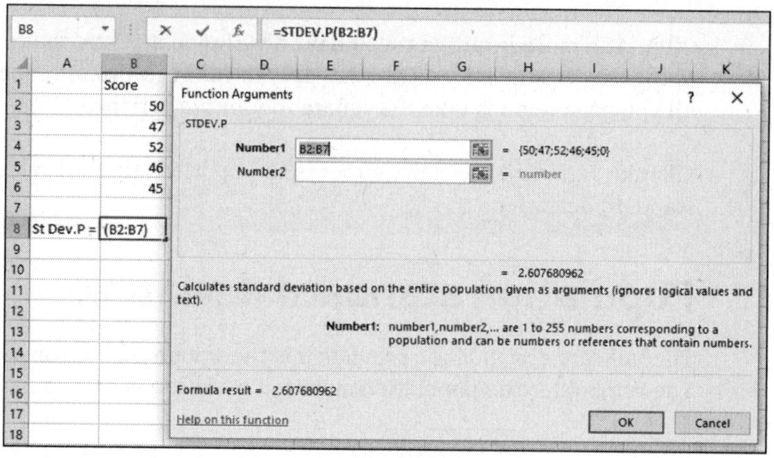

FIGURE 5-4:
The Function
Arguments
dialog box for
STDEV.P, along
with the data.

Sample standard deviation

The *standard deviation of a sample* — an estimate of the standard deviation of a population — is the square root of the sample variance. Its symbol is *s* and its formula is

$$s = \sqrt{s^2} = \sqrt{\frac{\sum\left(X - \bar{X}\right)^2}{N-1}}$$

For these measurements (in inches)

50, 47, 52, 46, and 45

the population variance is 8.4 square inches, and the population standard deviation is 2.92 inches (rounded off).

STDEV.S and STDEVA

The Excel worksheet functions STDEV.S and STDEVA calculate the sample standard deviation. To work with STDEV.S, follow these steps:

1. **Type your data into an array and select a cell for the result.**

2. **In the Statistical Functions menu, select STDEV.S to open the STDEV.S Function Arguments dialog box.**

3. **In the Function Arguments dialog box, type the appropriate values for the arguments.**

With the data array entered, the dialog box shows the value of the population standard deviation for the numbers in the data array. Figure 5-5 shows this.

4. **Click OK to close the dialog box and put the result into the selected cell.**

STDEVA uses text and logical values in its calculations. Cells with text have values of 0, and cells whose values are FALSE also evaluate to 0. Cells that evaluate to TRUE have values of 1.0.

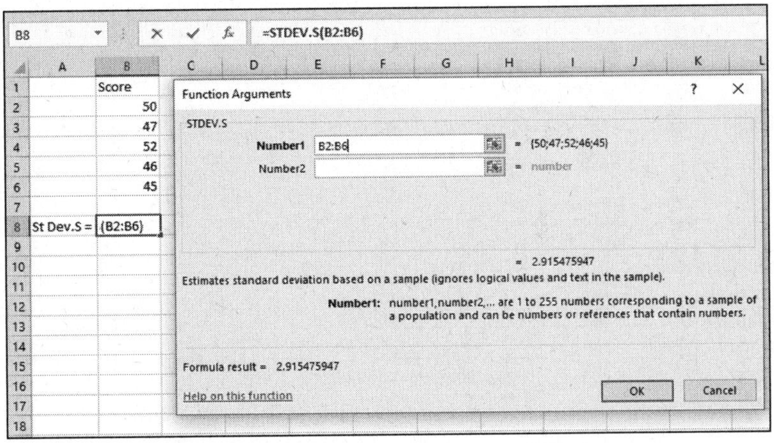

FIGURE 5-5: The Function Arguments dialog box for STDEV.S.

The missing functions: STDEVIF and STDEVIFS

Here's a rule of thumb: Whenever you present a mean, provide a standard deviation. Use AVERAGE and STDEV.S in tandem.

Remember that Excel offers two functions, AVERAGEIF and AVERAGEIFS, for calculating means conditionally. (See Chapter 4.) Two additional functions would have been helpful: STDEVIF and STDEVIFS, for calculating standard deviations conditionally when you calculate means conditionally.

Excel, however, doesn't provide these functions. Instead, I show you a couple of workarounds that enable you to calculate standard deviations conditionally.

The workarounds filter out data that meet a set of conditions, and then calculate the standard deviation of the filtered data. Figure 5-6 shows what I mean. The data are from the fictional psychology experiment I describe in Chapter 4.

Here, once again, is the description:

A person sits in front of a screen and a color-filled shape appears. The color is either red or green and the shape is either a square or a circle. The combination for each trial is random, and all combinations appear an equal number of times. In the lingo of the field, each appearance of a color-filled shape is called a *trial.* So the worksheet shows the outcomes of 16 trials.

	A Trial	B Color	C Shape	D RT_msec	E	F	G	H Circle	I	J	K Green Square
2	1	Red	Circle	410				410			
3	2	Red	Square	334							
4	3	Green	Square	335							335
5	4	Green	Circle	336				336			
6	5	Red	Square	398							
7	6	Red	Circle	450				450			
8	7	Green	Circle	440				440			
9	8	Green	Square	467							467
10	9	Green	Circle	445				445			
11	10	Red	Square	296							
12	11	Green	Square	378							378
13	12	Red	Circle	496				496			
14	13	Red	Circle	544				544			
15	14	Green	Square	468							468
16	15	Red	Square	577							
17	16	Green	Circle	448				448			
18											
19			Average Overall =	426.375			St Dev Circle =	60.42336		St Dev Green Square =	66.44797464
20			Average Circle =	446.125							
21			Av Green Square =	412							

FIGURE 5-6: Filtering data to calculate standard deviation conditionally.

The person sitting in front of the screen presses a button as soon as he or she sees the shape. Column A presents the trial number. Columns B and C show the color and shape, respectively, presented on that trial. Column D (labeled RT_msec) presents one person's reaction time in milliseconds (thousandths of a second) for each trial. For example, row 2 tells you that on the first trial, a red circle appeared and the person responded in 410 msec (milliseconds).

For each column, I define the name in the top cell of the column to refer to the data in that column. (If you don't remember how to do that, read Chapter 2.)

Cell D19 displays the overall average of RT_msec. The formula for that average, of course, is

```
=AVERAGE(RT_msec)
```

Cell D20 shows the average for all trials on which a circle appeared. The formula that calculates that conditional average is

```
=AVERAGEIF(Shape,"Circle",RT_msec)
```

Cell D21 presents the average for trials on which a green square appeared. That formula is

```
=AVERAGEIFS(RT_msec, Color,"Green", Shape,"Square")
```

Columns H and K hold filtered data. Column H shows the data for trials that displayed a circle. Cell H19 presents the standard deviation (STDEV.S) for those trials and is the equivalent of

```
=STDEVIF(Shape,"Circle",RT_msec)
```

if this function existed.

Column K shows the data for trials that displayed a green square. Cell K19 presents the standard deviation (STDEV.S) for those trials, and is the equivalent of

```
=STDEVIFS(RT_msec, Color,"Green",Shape,"Square")
```

if *that* function existed.

How did I filter the data? I let you in on the secret in a moment, but first I have to tell you about . . .

A little logic

In order to proceed, you have to know about two of Excel's logic functions: IF and AND. You access them by clicking

Formulas | Logical Functions

and selecting them from the Logical Functions menu.

IF takes three arguments:

>> A logical condition to be satisfied

>> The action to take if the logical condition is satisfied (that is, if the value of the logical condition is TRUE)

>> An optional argument that specifies the action to take if the logical condition is not satisfied (that is, if the value of the logical condition is FALSE)

Figure 5-7 shows the Function Arguments dialog box for IF.

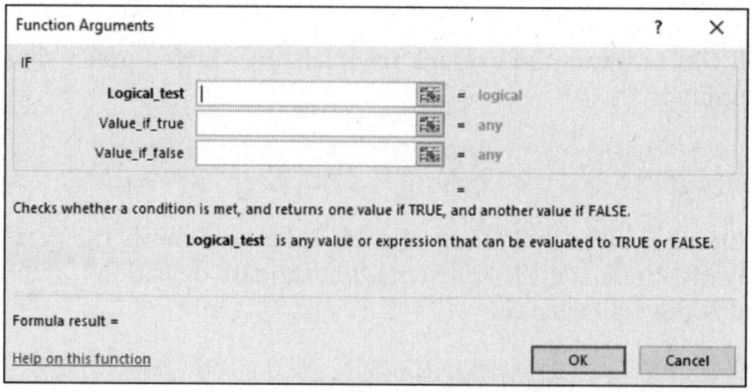

FIGURE 5-7:
The Function
Arguments
dialog box for IF.

AND can take up to 255 arguments. AND checks to see if all of its arguments meet each specified condition — that is, if each condition is TRUE. If they all do, AND returns the value TRUE. If not, AND returns FALSE.

Figure 5-8 shows the Function Arguments dialog box for AND.

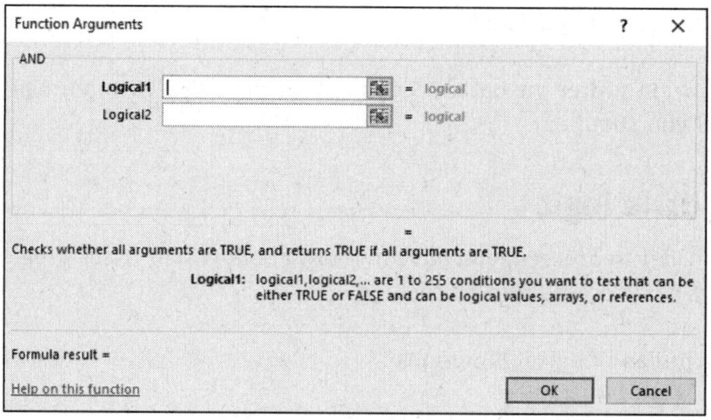

FIGURE 5-8:
The Function
Arguments
dialog box
for AND.

And now, back to the show

In this example, I use IF to set the value of a cell in Column H to the corresponding value in Column D if the value in the corresponding cell in Column C is "Circle". The formula in cell H2 is

```
=IF(C2="Circle",D2," ")
```

If this were a phrase, it would be, "If the value in C2 is 'Circle,' then set the value of this cell to the value in D2. If not, leave this cell blank." Autofilling the next

15 cells of column H yields the filtered data in column H. (Refer to Figure 5-6.) The standard deviation in cell H19 is the value STDEVIF would have provided.

TIP

I could have omitted the third argument (the two double quotes) without affecting the value of the standard deviation. Without the third argument, Excel fills in FALSE for cells that don't meet the condition, instead of leaving them blank.

I use AND along with IF for the cells in column K. Each one holds the value from the corresponding cell in column D if two conditions are true:

>> The value in the corresponding cell in column B is "Green"

>> The value in the corresponding cell in column C is "Square"

The formula for cell K2 is

```
=IF(AND(B2="Green",C2="Square"),D2," ")
```

If *this* were a phrase, it would be, "If the value in B2 is 'Green' and the value in C2 is 'Square,' then set the value of this cell to the value in D2. If not, leave this cell blank." Autofilling the next 15 cells in column K results in the filtered data in column K, as shown in Figure 5-6. The standard deviation in cell K19 is the value STDEVIFS would have provided.

Related Functions

Before you move on, take a quick look at a couple of other variation-related worksheet functions.

DEVSQ

DEVSQ calculates the sum of the squared deviations from the mean (without dividing by N or by $N-1$). For these numbers

50, 47, 52, 46, and 45

that's 34, as Figure 5-9 shows.

Although it's rare to calculate just the sum of squared deviations, I apply this function in Chapter 17.

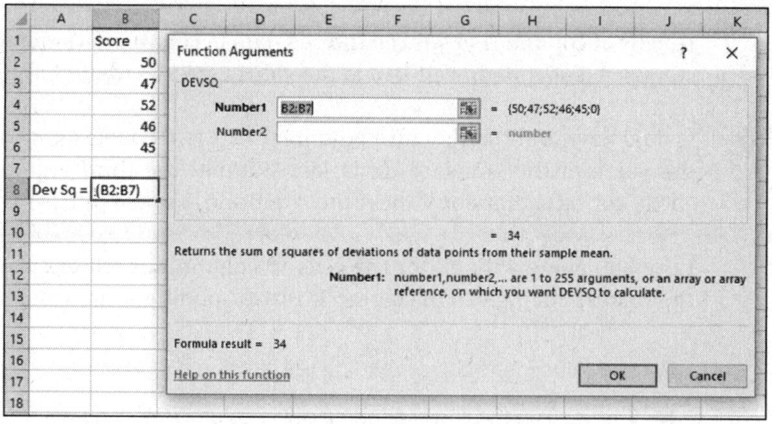

FIGURE 5-9:
The DEVSQ
dialog box.

Average deviation

One more Excel function deals with deviations in a way other than squaring them.

The variance and standard deviation deal with negative deviations by squaring all the deviations before averaging them. How about if you just ignore the minus signs? This is called taking the *absolute value* of each deviation. (That's the way mathematicians say "How about if we just ignore the minus signs?")

If you do that for the heights

50, 47, 52, 46, and 45

you can put the absolute values of the deviations into a table like Table 5-4.

TABLE 5-4

A Group of Numbers and Their Absolute Deviations

Height	Height-Mean	|Deviation|
50	50-48	2
47	47-48	1
52	52-48	4
46	46-48	2
45	45-48	3

REMEMBER

In Table 5-4, notice the vertical lines around *Deviation* in the heading for the third column. Vertical lines around a number symbolize its absolute value. That is, the vertical lines are the mathematical symbol for "How about if we just ignore the minus signs?"

The average of the numbers in the third column is 2.4. This average is called the *average absolute deviation,* and it's a quick and easy way to characterize the spread of measurements around their mean. It's in the same units as the original measurements. So if the heights are in inches, the absolute average deviation is in inches, too.

Like variance and standard deviation, a large average absolute deviation signifies a lot of spread. A small average absolute deviation signifies little spread.

TIP

This statistic is less complicated than variance or standard deviation, but is rarely used. Why? For reasons that are (once again) beyond this book's scope, statisticians can't use it as the foundation for additional statistics you meet later. Variance and standard deviation serve that purpose.

AVEDEV

Excel's AVEDEV worksheet function calculates the average absolute deviation of a group of numbers. Figure 5-10 shows the AVEDEV dialog box, which presents the average absolute deviation for the cells in the indicated range.

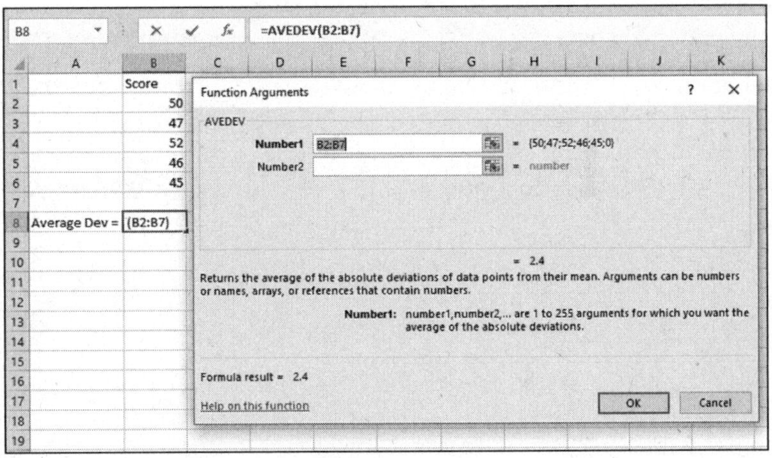

FIGURE 5-10:
The AVEDEV
Function
Arguments
dialog box.

Chapter 6

Meeting Standards and Standings

In my left hand, I hold 15 Argentine pesos. In my right, I hold 100 Colombian pesos. Which is worth more? Both currencies are called *pesos*, right? So shouldn't the 100 be greater than the 15? Not necessarily. *Peso* is just word-magic — a coincidence of names. Each one comes out of a different country, and each country has its own economy.

To compare the two amounts of money, you have to convert each currency into a standard unit. The most intuitive standard for us is our own currency. How much is each amount worth in dollars and cents? As I write this, 15 Argentine pesos are worth $1.05. One hundred Colombian pesos are worth 3 cents.

In this chapter, I show you how to use statistics to create standard units. Standard units show you where a score stands in relation to other scores in a group, and I show you additional ways to determine a score's standing within a group.

Catching Some Zs

As the previous paragraphs, a number in isolation doesn't really tell a story. In order to fully understand what a number means, you have to consider the process that produced it. In order to compare one number to another, they both have to be on the same scale.

In some cases, like currency conversion, it's easy to figure out a standard. In others, like temperature conversion or conversion into the metric system, a formula guides you.

When it's not all laid out for you, you can use the mean and the standard deviation to standardize scores that come from different processes. The idea is to take a set of scores and use its mean as a zero-point and its standard deviation as a unit of measure. Then you compare the deviation of each score from the mean to the standard deviation. You're asking, "How big is a particular deviation relative to (something like) an average of all the deviations?"

To do this, you divide the score's deviation by the standard deviation. In effect, you transform the score into another kind of score. The transformed score is called a *standard score,* or a *z-score.*

REMEMBER

The formula for this is

$$z = \frac{X - \bar{X}}{s}$$

if you're dealing with a sample, and it's

$$z = \frac{X - \mu}{\sigma}$$

if you're dealing with a population. In either case, X represents the score you're transforming into a z-score.

Characteristics of z-scores

A z-score can be positive, negative, or zero. A negative z-score represents a score that's less than the mean, and a positive z-score represents a score that's greater than the mean. When the score is equal to the mean, its z-score is zero.

When you calculate the z-score for every score in the set, the mean of the z-scores is 0, and the standard deviation of the z-scores is 1.

After you do this for several sets of scores, you can legitimately compare a score from one set to a score from another. If the two sets have different means and different standard deviations, comparing without standardizing is like comparing apples with kumquats.

In the examples that follow, I show how to use z-scores to make comparisons.

Bonds versus the Bambino

Here's an important question that often comes up in the context of serious metaphysical discussions: Who is the greatest home run hitter of all time — Barry Bonds or Babe Ruth? Although this is a difficult question to answer, one way to get your hands around it is to look at each player's best season and compare the two. Bonds hit 73 home runs in 2001, and Ruth hit 60 in 1927. On the surface, Bonds appears to be the more productive hitter.

The year 1927 was very different from 2001, however. Baseball (and everything else) went through huge changes in the intervening years, and player statistics reflect those changes. A home run was harder to hit in the 1920s than in the 2000s. Still, 73 versus 60? Hmmm. . . .

Standard scores can help decide whose best season was better. To standardize, I took the top 50 home run hitters of 1927 and the top 50 from 2001. I calculated the mean and standard deviation of each group and then turned Ruth's 60 and Bonds's 73 into z-scores.

The average from 1927 is 12.68 homers with a standard deviation of 10.49. The average from 2001 is 37.02 homers with a standard deviation of 9.64. Although the means differ greatly, the standard deviations are pretty close.

And the z-scores? Ruth's is

$$z = \frac{60 - 12.68}{10.49} = 4.51$$

Bonds' is

$$z = \frac{73 - 37.02}{9.64} = 3.73$$

The clear winner in the z-score best-season home run derby is Babe Ruth. Period.

Just to show you how times have changed, Lou Gehrig hit 47 home runs in 1927 (finishing second to Ruth) for a z-score of 3.27. In 2001, 47 home runs amounted to a z-score of 1.04.

Exam scores

Getting away from sports debates, one practical application of z-scores is the assignment of grades to exam scores. Based on percentage scoring, instructors traditionally evaluate a score of 90 points or higher (out of 100) as an A, 80–89 points as a B, 70–79 points as a C, 60–69 points as a D, and less than 60 points as an F. Then they average scores from several exams to assign a course grade.

Is that fair? Just as a peso from Argentina is worth more than a peso from Colombia, and a home run was harder to hit in 1927 than in 2001, is a "point" on one exam worth the same as a "point" on another? (Like *peso*, isn't that just word-magic?)

Indeed it is. A point on a difficult exam is, by definition, harder to come by than a point on an easy exam. Because points might not mean the same thing from one exam to another, the fairest thing to do is convert scores from each exam into z-scores before averaging them. That way, you're averaging numbers on a level playing field.

In the courses I teach, I do just that. I often find that a lower numerical score on one exam results in a higher z-score than a higher numerical score from another exam. For example, on an exam where the mean is 65 and the standard deviation is 12, a score of 71 results in a z-score of .5. On another exam, with a mean of 69 and a standard deviation of 14, a score of 75 is equivalent to a z-score of .429. (Yes, it's like Ruth's 60 home runs versus Bonds's 73.) Moral of the story: Numbers in isolation tell you very little. You have to understand the process that produces them.

STANDARDIZE

Excel's STANDARDIZE worksheet function calculates z-scores. Figure 6-1 shows a set of exam scores along with their mean and standard deviation. I used AVERAGE and STDEVP to calculate the statistics. The Function Arguments dialog box for STANDARDIZE is also in the figure.

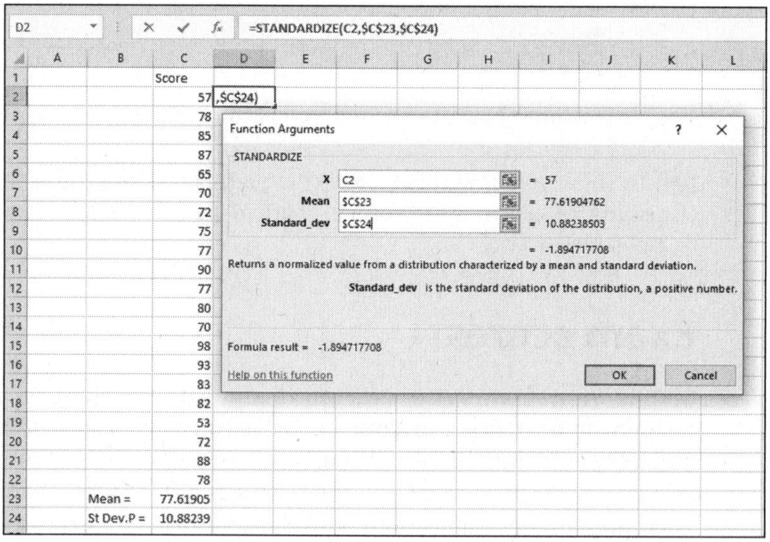

FIGURE 6-1:
Exam scores and the Function Arguments dialog box for STANDARDIZE.

CACHING SOME Z'S

Because negative z-scores might have connotations that are, well, negative, educators sometimes change the z-score when they evaluate students. In effect, they're hiding the z-score, but the concept is the same — standardization with the standard deviation as the unit of measure.

One popular transformation is called the T-score. The T-score eliminates negative scores because a set of T-scores has a mean of 50 and a standard deviation of 10. The idea is to give an exam, grade all the tests, and calculate the mean and standard deviation. Next, turn each score into a z-score. Then follow this formula:

$$T = (z)(10) + 50$$

People who use the T-score often like to round to the nearest whole number.

SAT scores are another transformation of the z-score. (Some refer to the SAT as a C-score.) Under the old scoring system, the SAT has a mean of 500 and a standard deviation of 100. After the exams are graded, and their mean and standard deviation calculated, each exam score becomes a z-score in the usual way. This formula converts the z-score into a SAT score:

$$SAT = (z)(100) + 50$$

Rounding to the nearest whole number is part of the procedure here, too.

The IQ score is still another transformed z. Its mean is 100 and (in the Stanford-Binet version) its standard deviation is 16. What's the procedure for computing an IQ score? You guessed it. In a group of IQ scores, calculate the mean and standard deviation, and then calculate the z-score. Then it's

$$IQ = (z)(16) + 100$$

As with the other two, IQ scores are rounded to the nearest whole number.

Here are the steps:

1. **Enter the data into an array and select a cell.**

   The data are in C2:C22. I selected D2 to hold the z-score for the score in C2. Ultimately, I'll autofill column D and line up all the z-scores next to the corresponding exam scores.

2. **From the Statistical Functions menu, select STANDARDIZE to open the Function Arguments dialog box for STANDARDIZE.**

3. **In the Function Arguments dialog box, enter the appropriate values for the arguments.**

   First, I enter into the X box the cell that holds the first exam score. In this example, that's C2.

   In the Mean box, I enter the cell that holds the mean — C23, for this example. It has to be in absolute reference format, so the entry is $C$23. You can type it that way, or you can select C23 and then highlight the Mean box and press the F4 key.

   In the Standard_dev box, I enter the cell that holds the standard deviation. The appropriate cell in this example is C24. This also has to be in absolute reference format, so the entry is $C$24.

4. **Click OK to close the Function Arguments dialog box and put the z-score for the first exam score into the selected cell.**

To finish up, I position the cursor on the selected cell's autofill handle, hold down the left mouse button, and drag the cursor to autofill the remaining z-scores.

Figure 6-2 shows the autofilled array of z-scores.

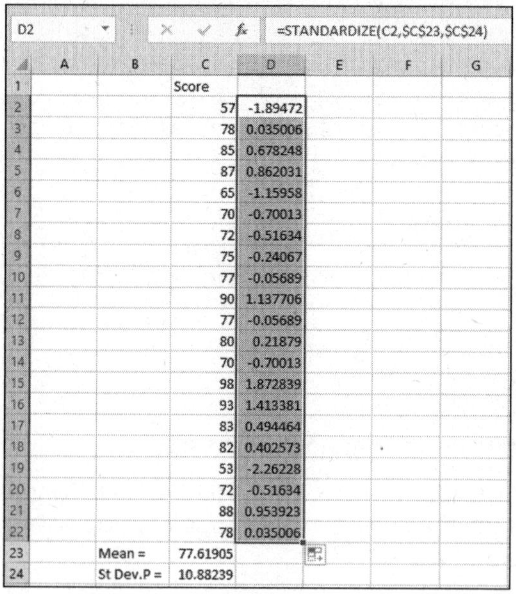

D2 =STANDARDIZE(C2,$C$23,$C$24)

	A	B	C	D	E	F	G
1			Score				
2			57	-1.89472			
3			78	0.035006			
4			85	0.678248			
5			87	0.862031			
6			65	-1.15958			
7			70	-0.70013			
8			72	-0.51634			
9			75	-0.24067			
10			77	-0.05689			
11			90	1.137706			
12			77	-0.05689			
13			80	0.21879			
14			70	-0.70013			
15			98	1.872839			
16			93	1.413381			
17			83	0.494464			
18			82	0.402573			
19			53	-2.26228			
20			72	-0.51634			
21			88	0.953923			
22			78	0.035006			
23		Mean =	77.61905				
24		St Dev.P =	10.88239				

FIGURE 6-2: The autofilled array of z-scores.

Where Do You Stand?

Standard scores are designed to show you how a score stands in relation to other scores in the same group. To do this, they use the standard deviation as a unit of measure.

If you don't want to use the standard deviation, you can show a score's relative standing in a simpler way. You can determine the score's rank within the group: The highest score has a rank of 1, the second highest has a rank of 2, and so on.

RANK.EQ and RANK.AVG

Excel 2016 offers two ranking functions. They differ on how they treat ties. When RANK.EQ encounters tie scores, it assigns all of them the highest rank those scores attain. Therefore, three scores tied for second are all ranked second.

When RANK.AVG encounters ties, it assigns all of them the average of the ranks they attain. With this function, three scores tied for second are all ranked third (the average of ranks 2, 3, and 4).

To give you a better idea of how these two functions work, Figure 6-3 shows the results of applying each function to the scores in column B.

	A	B	C	D
1		Score	RANK.EQ	RANK.AVG
2		45	10	10
3		44	11	11
4		34	12	12
5		23	13	13.5
6		22	15	15
7		48	8	8.5
8		48	8	8.5
9		67	5	5
10		65	6	6
11		78	2	3
12		78	2	3
13		80	1	1
14		78	2	3
15		23	13	13.5
16		54	7	7
17				

FIGURE 6-3:
Applying RANK.EQ and RANK.AVG.

Here are the steps for using RANK.EQ:

1. **Enter the data into an array and select a cell.**

   For this example, I enter the scores into cells B2 through B16 and selected cell C2.

2. **From the Statistical Functions menu, select RANK.EQ to open the Function Arguments dialog box for RANK.EQ.**

3. **In the Function Arguments dialog box, type the appropriate values for the arguments.**

   In the Number box, I enter the cell that holds the score whose rank I want to insert into the selected cell. For this example, that's B2.

   In the Ref box, I enter the array that contains the scores. I entered B2:B16 into the Ref box.

   This part is important. After I insert RANK.EQ into C2, I'm going to drag the cursor through column C and autofill the ranks of the remaining scores. To set up for this, I have to let Excel know I want B2 through B16 to be the array for every score, not just the first one.

   That means the array in the Ref box has to look like this: $B$2:$B$16. I can either add the $ signs manually or highlight the Ref box and then press the F4 key.

   In the Order box, I indicate the order for sorting the scores. To rank the scores in descending order, I can either leave the Order box alone or type 0 (zero) into that box. To rank the scores in ascending order, I type a non-zero value into the Order box. I left this box alone. (See Figure 6-4.)

4. **Click OK to put the rank into the selected cell.**

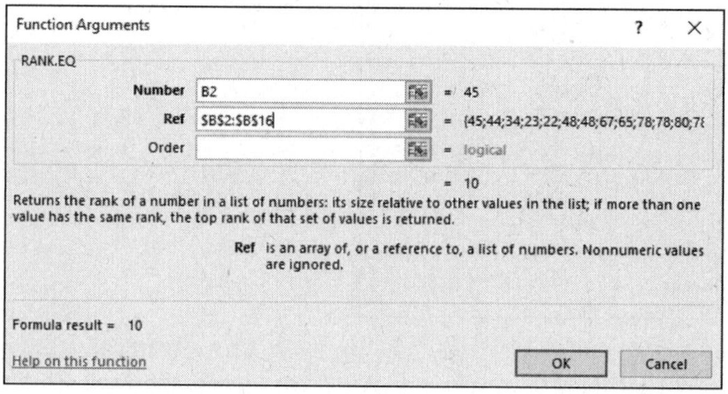

FIGURE 6-4: The Function Arguments dialog box for RANK.EQ.

I then position the cursor on the selected cell's autofill handle, hold down the left mouse button, and drag the cursor to autofill the ranks of the remaining scores. That, of course, is how I completed column C in Figure 6-3.

LARGE and SMALL

You can turn the ranking process inside out by supplying a rank and asking which score has that rank. The worksheet functions LARGE and SMALL handle this from either end. They tell you the fifth largest score or the third smallest score or any other rank you're interested in.

Figure 6-5 shows the Function Arguments dialog box for LARGE. In the Array box, you enter the array of cells that holds the group of scores. In the K box, you enter the position whose value you want to find. To find the seventh largest score in the array, for example, type **7** into the K box.

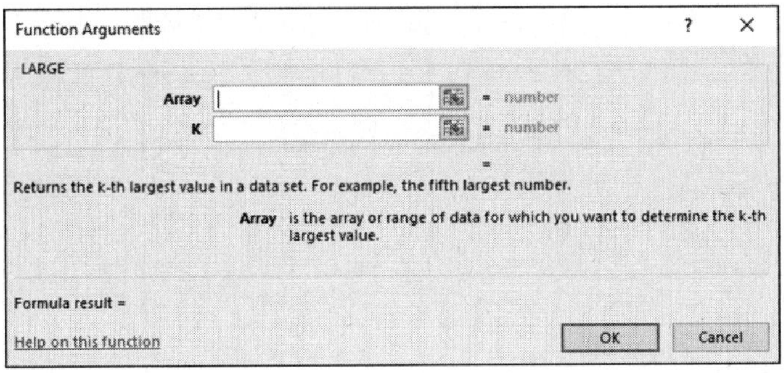

FIGURE 6-5:
The Function
Arguments
dialog box
for LARGE.

SMALL does the same thing, except it finds score positions from the lower end of the group. The Function Arguments dialog box for SMALL also has an Array box and a K box. Entering **7** in this K box returns the seventh lowest score in the array.

PERCENTILE.INC and PERCENTILE.EXC

Closely related to rank is the *percentile,* which represents a score's standing in the group as the percent of scores below it. If you've taken standardized tests like the SAT, you've encountered percentiles. A SAT score in the 80th percentile is higher than 80 percent of the other SAT scores.

Simple, right? Not so fast. The definition of *percentile* is a bit shaky these days. Some define *percentile* as "greater than" (as in the preceding paragraph), some define *percentile* as "greater than or equal to." *Greater than* equates to *exclusive.* *Greater than or equal to* equates to *inclusive.*

For this reason, Excel provides two worksheet formulas for dealing with percentile. PERCENTILE.INC works via "greater than or equal to." PERCENTILE.EXC works with "greater than."

To use either one, you input a range of scores and a percentile. In these formulas, K represents *percentile*. PERCENTILE.INC finds the score that's greater than or equal to that percentile. PERCENTILE.EXC finds the lowest score that's greater than that percentile.

To show you how these two differ, I created the worksheet in Figure 6-6.

	A	B	C	D	E	F	G
1			Score		K	PERCENTILE.INC	PERCENTILE.EXC
2			80		0.95	78.6	#NUM!
3			78		0.90	78	78.8
4			78		0.85	78	78
5			78		0.80	78	78
6			67		0.75	72.5	78
7			65		0.70	66.6	69.2
8			54		0.65	65.2	65.8
9			48		0.60	58.4	60.6
10			48		0.55	52.2	52.8
11			45		0.50	48	48
12			44		0.45	48	48
13			34		0.40	46.8	46.2
14			23		0.35	44.9	44.6
15			23		0.30	44.2	42
16			22		0.25	39	34
17					0.20	31.8	25.2
18					0.15	24.1	23
19					0.10	23	22.6
20					0.05	22.7	#NUM!
21							

FIGURE 6-6: PERCENTILE.INC versus PERCENTILE.EXC.

The scores in column C are the same ones as in the preceding examples in this chapter, rearranged in descending order. K refers to percentiles. Notice that they are in decimal form, so .95 means *95th percentile*. The values in columns F and G are the results of calculating the formulas at the top of each column. The score in each row of those columns refers to the percentile in the same row of column C. So column F shows inclusive percentiles and column G shows exclusive percentiles. I bolded the 75th, 50th, and 25th percentiles to set up the discussion in the upcoming sidebar, "Drawn and quartiled."

Some differences stand out — particularly, the error messages in column G. PERCENTILE.EXC returns an error message if the requested percentile is greater than N/(N + 1), where N is the number of scores. This is the maximum value of K that this formula works with. In this case, the maximum value is .94.

PERCENTILE.EXC also returns an error message if the requested percentile is less than 1/(N + 1). This is the minimum value the formula works with. In this case, that's .06.

Also, as the figure shows, the two formulas locate percentiles differently. For example, the inclusive 70th percentile is somewhere between 65 and 67. PERCENTILE.INC interpolates it at 66.6. (The three ties at 78 pull the interpolation up from 66.) PERCENTILE.EXC extrapolates the exclusive 70th percentile at 69.2, the lowest number greater than that 65–67 neighborhood.

This doesn't mean that the exclusive percentile is always greater than the inclusive version. A couple of entries in columns F and G show that the opposite sometimes happens. Tie scores and where they are play major roles.

I doubt if the difference matters much in practical terms, but that's just my opinion. Bottom line: If you require "greater than or equal to" for your percentile, use INC. If you're looking for just "greater than," use EXC.

Here's how to use PERCENTILE.INC:

1. **Enter your data into a worksheet and select a cell.**

2. **From the Statistics menu, choose PERCENTILE.INC to open the PERCENTILE.INC Function Arguments dialog box.**

3. **In the Function Arguments dialog box, type the appropriate values for the arguments.**

   Figure 6-7 shows the data, the selected cell, and the PERCENTILE.INC Function Arguments dialog box. I typed C2:C16 into the Range box and .75 into the K box.

4. **Click OK to put the percentile into the selected cell.**

Follow similar steps for PERCENTILE.EXC.

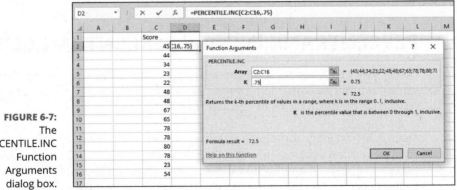

FIGURE 6-7:
The
PERCENTILE.INC
Function
Arguments
dialog box.

TIP

In both the PERCENTILE.INC and the PERCENTILE.EXC dialog boxes, you can enter the percentile into the K as a decimal (.75) or as a percentage (75%). If you do it the second way, you have to include the percent sign.

DRAWN AND QUARTILED

A few specific percentiles are often used to summarize a group of scores: the 25th , the 50th, the 75th, and the 100th percentile (the maximum score). Because they divide a group of scores into fourths, these particular four percentiles are called *quartiles.* Excel's QUARTILE.INC and QUARTILE.EXC formulas calculate them. The INC version calculates inclusively; the EXC version, exclusively. To understand how these formula differ, take a look at the bolded rows in Figure 6-6.

Selecting QUARTILE.INC from the Insert Function dialog box opens the Function Arguments dialog box shown in the figure below. (The dialog box for QUARTILE.EXC looks just like this one.)

The trick is to enter the right kind of numbers into the Quart box — 1 for the 25th percentile, 2 for the 50th, 3 for the 75th, and 4 for the 100th. Entering 0 into the Quart box gives you the lowest score in the group.

PERCENTRANK.INC and PERCENTRANK.EXC

Excel's two PERCENTRANK formulas tell you a given score's percentile. The INC version returns percentile in terms of "greater than or equal to." The EXC version returns percentile in terms of "greater than."

Again, I illustrate the difference with a worksheet that pits one against the other. Figure 6-8 shows scores (in descending order) in column C, inclusive percentile ranks in column D, and exclusive percentile ranks in column E. Note that the inclusive percentile rank of the highest score (80) is 1, and the exclusive percentile rank is 0.937. The inclusive rank of the lowest score (22) is 0, and the exclusive rank is 0.062.

Here are the steps for using PERCENTRANK.INC:

1. **Enter your data into a worksheet and select a cell.**

   From the Statistics menu, choose PERCENTRANK.INC to open the PERCENTRANK.INC Function Arguments dialog box.

	A	B	C	D	E
1			Score	PERCENTRANK.INC	PERCENTRANK.EXC
2			80	1	0.937
3			78	0.785	0.75
4			78	0.785	0.75
5			78	0.785	0.75
6			67	0.714	0.687
7			65	0.642	0.625
8			54	0.571	0.562
9			48	0.428	0.437
10			48	0.428	0.437
11			45	0.357	0.375
12			44	0.285	0.312
13			34	0.214	0.25
14			23	0.071	0.125
15			23	0.071	0.125
16			22	0	0.062
17					

FIGURE 6-8:
PERCENTRANK.INC versus PERCENTRANK.EXC.

2. **In the Function Arguments dialog box, type the appropriate values for the arguments.**

   Figure 6-9 shows the data, the selected cell, and the PERCENTRANK.INC Function Arguments dialog box. I typed C2:C16 into the Range box and C2 into the X box. C2 contains the score whose percent rank I want to calculate. The Significance box is for the amount of significant figures in the answer. Leaving this box vacant returns three significant figures.

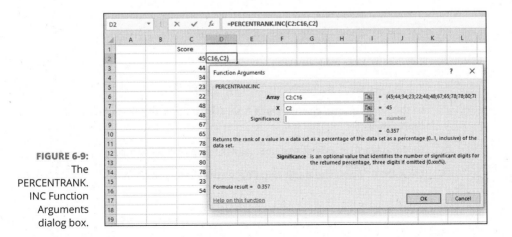

FIGURE 6-9:
The PERCENTRANK.INC Function Arguments dialog box.

3. **Click OK to put the percentile into the selected cell.**

Follow a similar set of steps for PERCENTRANK.EXC.

Data analysis tool: Rank and Percentile

As the name of this section indicates, Excel provides a data analysis tool that calculates ranks and percentiles of each score in a group. The Rank and percentile tool calculates both at the same time, so it saves you some steps versus using the separate worksheet functions. (See Chapter 2 to install Excel's data analysis tools.) In Figure 6-10, I take the exam scores from the z-score example and open the Rank and Percentile dialog box. (*Mac users:* StatPlus does not have this tool.)

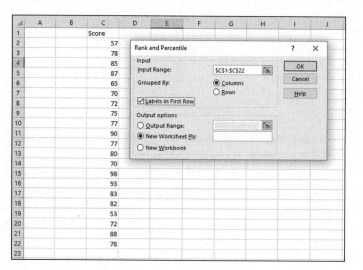

FIGURE 6-10: The Rank and Percentile analysis tool.

Here are the steps for using Rank and Percentile:

1. **Type your data into an array.**

   In this example, the data are in cells C2 through C22.

2. **In the Tools menu, choose Data Analysis to open the Data Analysis dialog box.**

3. **In the Data Analysis dialog box, select Rank and Percentile.**

4. **Click OK to open the Rank and Percentile dialog box.**

5. **In the Rank and Percentile dialog box, enter the data array into the Input Range box. Make sure that it's in absolute reference format.**

   In this example, a label is in the first row (in cell C1). I want the label included in the output, so I enter $C$1:$C$32 in the Input Range box, and I select the Labels in First Row check box.

6. **Select the Columns radio button to indicate that the data are organized by columns.**

7. **Select the New Worksheet Ply radio button to create a new tabbed page in the worksheet, and to send the results to the newly created page.**

8. **Click OK to close the dialog box. Open the newly created page to see the results.**

Figure 6-11 shows the new page with the results. The table orders the scores from highest to lowest, as the Score column shows along with the Rank column. The Point column tells you the score's position in the original grouping. For example, the 98 in cell B2 is the 14th score in the original data. The Percent column gives the percentile for each score, the same way PERCENTILE.INC does.

	A	B	C	D
1	Point	Score	Rank	Percent
2	14	98	1	100.00%
3	15	93	2	95.00%
4	10	90	3	90.00%
5	20	88	4	85.00%
6	4	87	5	80.00%
7	3	85	6	75.00%
8	16	83	7	70.00%
9	17	82	8	65.00%
10	12	80	9	60.00%
11	2	78	10	50.00%
12	21	78	10	50.00%
13	9	77	12	40.00%
14	11	77	12	40.00%
15	8	75	14	35.00%
16	7	72	15	25.00%
17	19	72	15	25.00%
18	6	70	17	15.00%
19	13	70	17	15.00%
20	5	65	19	10.00%
21	1	57	20	5.00%
22	18	53	21	0.00%

FIGURE 6-11: The Output of the Rank and Percentile analysis tool.

Chapter 7
Summarizing It All

Measures of central tendency and variability are excellent ways of summarizing a set of scores. They aren't the only ways, though. Central tendency and variability make up a subset of descriptive statistics. Some descriptive statistics are intuitive — like count, maximum, and minimum. Some are not — like skewness and kurtosis.

In this chapter, I discuss descriptive statistics, and I show you Excel's capabilities for calculating them and visualizing them.

Counting Out

The most fundamental descriptive statistic I can imagine is the number of scores in a set of scores. Excel offers five ways to determine that number. Yes, five ways. Count them.

COUNT, COUNTA, COUNTBLANK, COUNTIF, COUNTIFS

Given an array of cells, COUNT gives you the amount of those cells that contain numerical data. Figure 7-1 shows that I've entered a group of scores, selected a cell to hold COUNT's result, and opened the Function Arguments dialog box for COUNT.

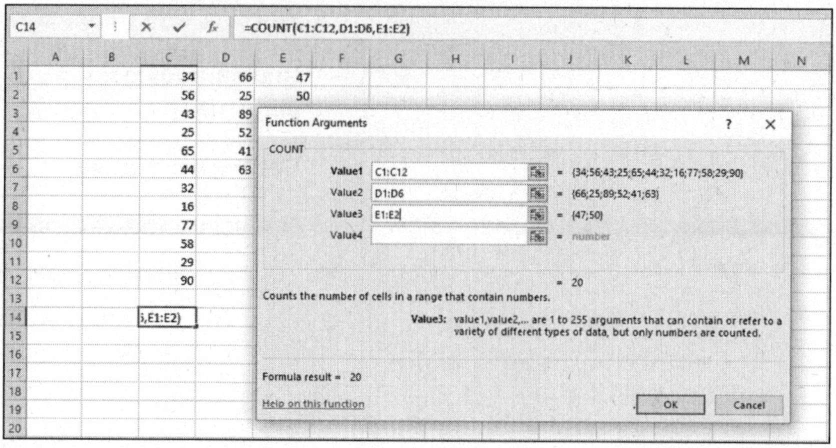

FIGURE 7-1:
The Function Arguments dialog box for COUNT, showing multiple arguments.

Here are the steps:

1. Enter your data into the worksheet and select a cell for the result.

I entered data into columns C, D, and E to show off COUNT's multi-argument capability. I selected cell C14 to hold the count.

2. From the Statistical Functions menu, select COUNT and click OK to open the Function Arguments dialog box for COUNT.

3. In the Function Arguments dialog box, enter the appropriate values for the arguments.

In the Number1 box, I entered one of the data columns for this example, like C1:C12.

I clicked in the Number2 box and entered another data column. I entered D1:D6.

I clicked in the Number3 box and entered the last column, which in this example is E1:E2.

4. Click OK to put the result in the selected cell.

COUNTA works like COUNT, except that its tally includes cells that contain text and logical values in its tally.

COUNTBLANK counts the number of blank cells in an array. In Figure 7-2, I use the numbers from the preceding example, but I extend the array to include cells D7 through D12 and E3 through E12. The array in the Range box is C1:E12. The Argument Functions dialog box for COUNTBLANK shows the number of blank cells (16, for this example).

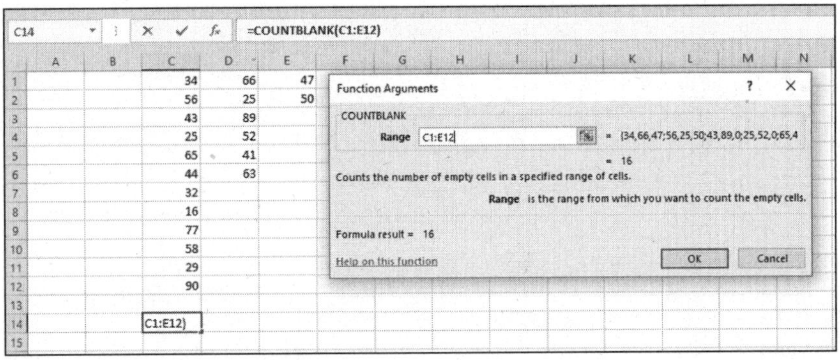

FIGURE 7-2:
COUNTBLANK
tallies the blank
cells in a specified
array.

COUNTIF shows the number of cells whose value meets a specified criterion. Figure 7-3 reuses the data once again, showing the Arguments Function dialog box for COUNTIF. Although the range is C1:E12, COUNTIF doesn't include blank cells.

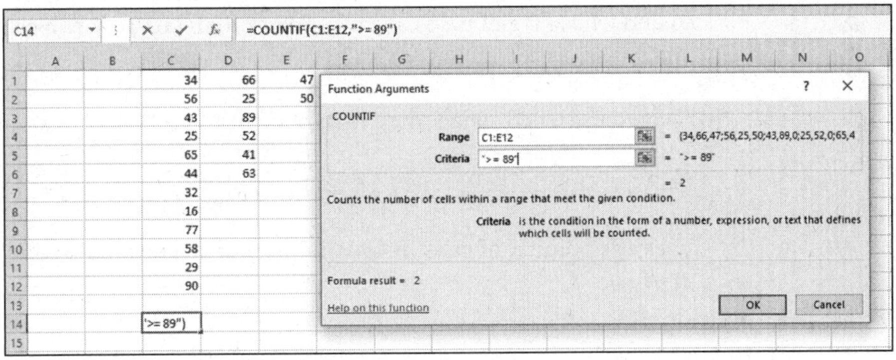

FIGURE 7-3:
COUNTIF tallies
the amount of
cells whose data
meet a specified
criterion.

The criterion I used, >= 89, tells COUNTIF to count only the cells whose values are greater than or equal to 89. For this example, that count is 2.

TIP

This probably won't make much difference as you use the COUNTIF function, but a little quirk of Excel shows up here: If you put double quotes around the criterion, the result appears in the dialog box before you click OK. If you don't, it doesn't. If you click OK without quoting, Excel supplies the quotes and the result appears in the selected cell, and Excel applies the quotes.

COUNTIFS can use multiple criteria to determine the count. If the criteria come from two arrays, they must have the same number of cells. This is because COUNTIFS counts pairs of cells. It includes a pair of cells in the count if one of the cells meets a criterion *and* the other meets a criterion. Take a look at Figure 7-4.

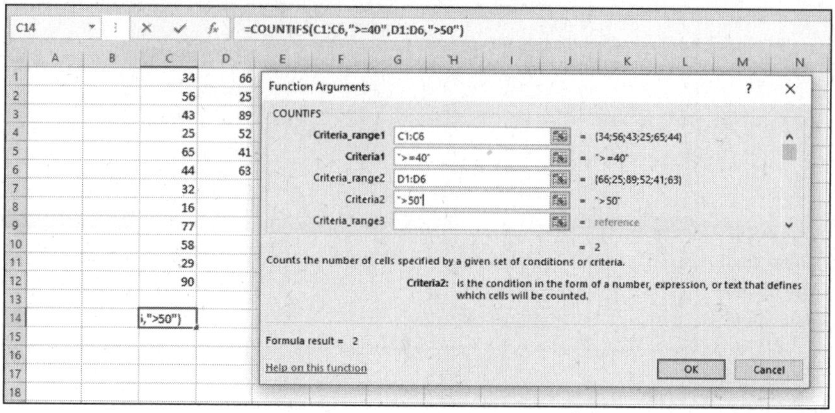

FIGURE 7-4:
Working with
COUNTIFS.

In this example, COUNTIFS operates in C1:C6 and D1:D6. The criterion for the cells in column C is >=40. The criterion for the cells in column D is >50. This means that COUNTIFS counts cell-pairs whose C cell holds a value greater than or equal to 40 and whose D cell holds a value greater than 50. Only two cell-pairs meet these conditions, as the dialog box shows.

You can use a cell range more than once in COUNTIFS. For example,

```
=COUNTIFS(C1:C12,">30",C1:C12,"<60")
```

gives the number of cells in which the value is between 30 and 60 (not including 30 or 60).

The Long and Short of It

Two more descriptive statistics that probably require no introduction are the maximum and the minimum. These, of course, are the largest value and the smallest value in a group of scores.

MAX, MAXA, MIN, and MINA

Excel has worksheet functions that determine a group's largest and smallest values. I show you what MAX is all about. The others work in a similar fashion.

Figure 7-5 reuses the scores from the preceding examples.

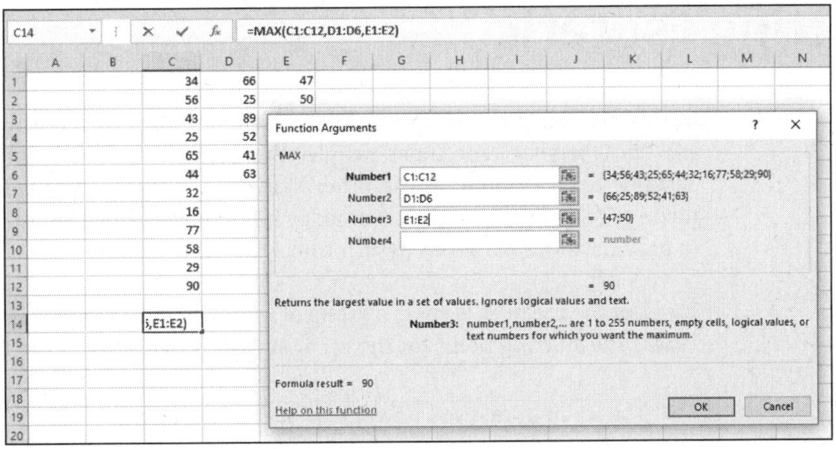

FIGURE 7-5:
The Function
Arguments dialog
box for MAX.

I selected a cell to hold their maximum value and opened the Function Arguments dialog box for MAX. Here are the steps you can follow:

1. **Type your data into the worksheet and select a cell to hold the result.**

   I entered data into columns C, D, and E to show off MAX's multi-argument capability. For this example, I selected cell C14.

2. **From the Statistical Functions menu, select MAX to open the Function Arguments dialog box for MAX.**

3. **In the Function Arguments dialog box, enter the appropriate values for the arguments.**

   In the Number1 box, I entered one of the data columns: C1:C12.

   Clicking the Number2 box creates and opens the Number3 box. In the Number2 box, I entered another array: D1:D6.

   I clicked in the Number3 box and entered the last array: E1:E2.

4. **Click OK to put the result in the selected cell.**

MAX ignores any text or logical values it encounters along the way. MAXA takes text and logical values into account when it finds the maximum. If MAXA encounters the logical value TRUE, it converts that value to 1. MAXA converts FALSE, or any text other than "TRUE", to 0.

MIN and MINA work the same way as MAX and MAXA, except that they find the minimum rather than the maximum. Take care when you use MINA, because the conversions of logical values and text to 0 and 1 influence the result. With the numbers in the preceding example, the minimum is 22. If you enter FALSE or other text into a cell in any of the arrays, MINA gives 0 as the minimum. If you enter TRUE, MINA gives 1 as the minimum.

Getting Esoteric

In this section, I discuss some little-used statistics that are related to the mean and the variance. For most people, the mean and the variance are enough to describe a set of data. These other statistics, *skewness* and *kurtosis*, go just a bit further. You might use them someday if you have a huge set of data and you want to provide some in-depth description.

Think of the mean as *locating* a group of scores by showing you where their center is. This is the starting point for the other statistics. With respect to the mean:

>> The variance tells you how *spread out* the scores are.

>> Skewness indicates how *symmetrically* the scores are distributed.

>> Kurtosis shows you whether or not the scores are distributed with a *peak* in the neighborhood of the mean.

TECHNICAL STUFF

Skewness and kurtosis are related to the mean and variance in fairly involved mathematical ways. The variance involves the sum of squared deviations of scores around the mean. *Skewness* depends on cubing the deviations around the mean before you add them all up. *Kurtosis* takes it all to a higher power — the fourth power, to be exact. I get more specific in the subsections that follow.

SKEW and SKEW.P

Figure 7-6 shows three histograms. The first is symmetric; the other two are not. The symmetry and the asymmetry are reflected in the skewness statistic.

For the symmetric histogram, the skewness is 0. For the second histogram — the one that tails off to the right — the value of the skewness statistic is positive. It's also said to be skewed to the right. For the third histogram (which tails off to the left), the value of the skewness statistic is negative. It's also said to be skewed to the left.

TECHNICAL STUFF

Where do zero, positive, and negative skew come from? They come from this formula:

$$skewness = \frac{\sum\left(X - \bar{X}\right)^3}{(N-1)s^3}$$

In the formula, $\bar{X}$ is the mean of the scores, N is the number of scores, and s is the standard deviation. This formula is for the skewness of a sample. The formula for the skewness in a population uses N rather than N-1.

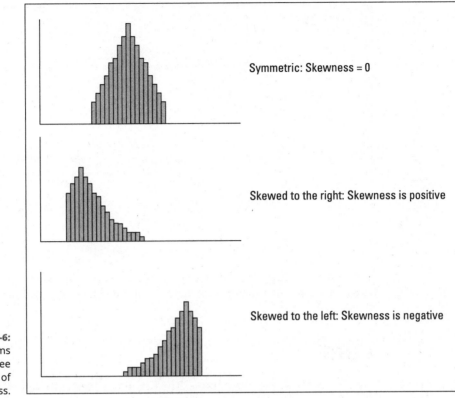

Symmetric: Skewness = 0

Skewed to the right: Skewness is positive

Skewed to the left: Skewness is negative

FIGURE 7-6:
Three histograms
showing three
kinds of
skewness.

I include this formula for completeness. If you're ever concerned with skewness of a sample, you probably won't use this formula anyway because Excel's SKEW function does the work for you.

To use SKEW:

1. **Type your numbers into a worksheet and select a cell for the result.**

   For this example, I've entered scores into the first ten rows of columns B, C, D, and E. (See Figure 7-7.) I selected cell H2 for the result.

2. **From the Statistical Functions menu, select SKEW to open the Function Arguments dialog box for SKEW.**

3. **In the Function Arguments dialog box, type the appropriate values for the arguments.**

   In the Number1 box, enter the array of cells that holds the data. For this example, the array is B1:E10. With the data array entered, the Function Arguments dialog box shows the skewness, which for this example is negative.

4. **Click OK to put the result into the selected cell.**

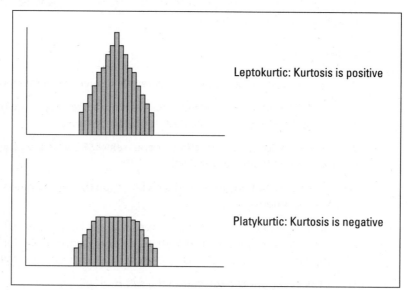

| H2 | | | × | ✓ | *fx* | =SKEW(B1:E10) | | | | | | | | |

	A	B	C	D	E	F	G	H	I	J	K	L	M	N
1		22	20	23	30									
2		26	28	29	24		Skewness =	B1:E10)						
3		23	22	25	13									
4		12	27	28	17									
5		21	19	23	25									
6		26	22	15	18									
7		11	6	21	29									
8		25	24	27	30									
9		10	26	7	19									
10		24	15	14	21									

Function Arguments   ?   ✕

SKEW

Number1 B1:E10 = {22,20,23,30;26,28,29,24;23,22,25,13;1;

Number2 = number

= -0.755562979

Returns the skewness of a distribution: a characterization of the degree of asymmetry of a distribution around its mean.

Number1: number1,number2,... are 1 to 255 numbers or names, arrays, or references that contain numbers for which you want the skewness.

Formula result = -0.755562979

Help on this function   OK   Cancel

FIGURE 7-7:
Using the SKEW function to calculate skewness.

The Function Arguments dialog box for SKEW.P (the skewness of a population) looks the same. As I mention earlier, population skewness incorporates N rather than N–1.

KURT

Figure 7-8 shows two histograms. The first has a peak at its center; the second is flat. The first is said to be *leptokurtic.* its kurtosis is positive. The second is *platykurtic*; its kurtosis is negative.

Leptokurtic: Kurtosis is positive

Platykurtic: Kurtosis is negative

FIGURE 7-8:
Two histograms, showing two kinds of kurtosis.

TECHNICAL STUFF

Negative? Wait a second. How can that be? I mention earlier that kurtosis involves the sum of fourth powers of deviations from the mean. Because four is an even number, even the fourth power of a negative deviation is positive. If you're adding all positive numbers, how can kurtosis ever be negative?

Here's how. The formula for kurtosis is

$$kurtosis = \frac{\sum(X - \bar{X})^2}{(N-1)s^4} - 3$$

where $\bar{X}$ is the mean of the scores, N is the number of scores, and s is the standard deviation.

Uh, why 3? The 3 comes into the picture because that's the kurtosis of something special called the *standard normal distribution*. (I discuss normal distributions at length in Chapter 8.) Technically, statisticians refer to this formula as *kurtosis excess* — meaning that it shows the kurtosis in a set of scores that's in excess of the standard normal distribution's kurtosis. If you're about to ask the question "Why is the kurtosis of the standard normal distribution equal to 3?" don't ask.

This is another formula you'll probably never use because Excel's KURT function takes care of business. Figure 7-9 shows the scores from the preceding example, a selected cell, and the Function Arguments dialog box for KURT.

To use KURT:

1. **Enter your numbers into a worksheet and select a cell for the result.**

For this example, I enter scores into the first ten rows of columns B, C, D, and E. I select cell H2 for the result.

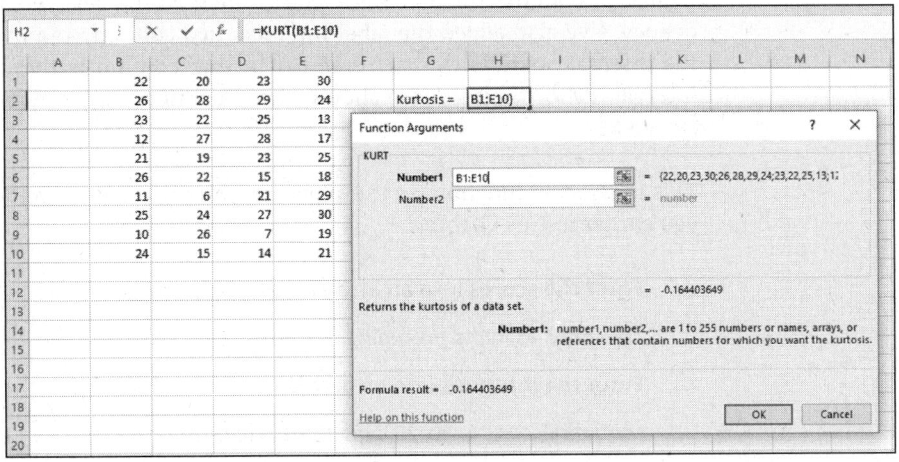

FIGURE 7-9:
Using KURT to calculate kurtosis.

2. **From the Statistical Functions menu, select KURT to open the Function Arguments dialog box for** KURT.

3. **In the Function Arguments dialog box, enter the appropriate values for the arguments.**

   In the Number1 box, I enter the array of cells that holds the data. Here, the array is B1:E10. With the data array entered, the Function Arguments dialog box shows the kurtosis, which for this example is negative.

4. **Click OK to put the result into the selected cell.**

Tuning In the Frequency

Although the calculations for skewness and kurtosis are all well and good, it's helpful to see how the scores are distributed. To do this, you create a *frequency distribution*, a table that divides the possible scores into intervals and shows the number (the frequency) of scores that fall into each interval.

Excel gives you two ways to create a frequency distribution. One is a worksheet, and the other is a data analysis tool.

FREQUENCY

I show you the FREQUENCY worksheet function in Chapter 2 when I introduce array functions. Here, I give you another look. In the upcoming example, I reuse the data from the skewness and kurtosis discussions so that you can see what the distribution of those scores looks like.

Figure 7-10 shows the data once again, along with a selected array, labeled Frequency. I've also added the label Intervals to a column, and in that column I put the interval boundaries. Each number in that column is the upper bound of an interval. The figure also shows the Function Arguments dialog box for FREQUENCY.

This is an array function, so the steps are a bit different from the functions I show you earlier in this chapter:

1. **Enter the scores into an array of cells.**

   The array, as in the preceding examples, is B1:E10.

2. **Enter the intervals into an array.**

   I entered 5, 10, 15, 20, 25, and 30 into G2:G7.

Figure 7-10: showing Excel spreadsheet with FREQUENCY function

The formula bar shows: `=FREQUENCY(B1:E10,G2:G7)`

	A	B	C	D	E	F	G	H	I	J	K	L	M	N
1		22	20	23	30		Interval	Frequency						
2		26	28	29	24		5	0,G2:G7)						
3		23	22	25	13		10							
4		12	27	28	17		15							
5		21	19	23	25		20							
6		26	22	15	18		25							
7		11	6	21	29		30							
8		25	24	27	30									
9		10	26	7	19									
10		24	15	14	21									

Function Arguments dialog box, FREQUENCY:

Data_array: B1:E10 = {22,20,23,30;26,28,29,24;23,22,25,13;...

Bins_array: G2:G7 = {5;10;15;20;25;30}

= {0;3;6;5;15;11;0}

Calculates how often values occur within a range of values and then returns a vertical array of numbers having one more element than Bins_array.

Bins_array is an array of or reference to intervals into which you want to group the values in data_array.

Formula result = 0

Help on this function

FIGURE 7-10:
Finding the
frequencies in an
array of cells.

3. Select an array for the resulting frequencies.

I put Frequency as the label at the top of column H, so I selected H2 through H7 to hold the resulting frequencies.

4. From the Statistical Functions menu, select FREQUENCY to open the Function Arguments dialog box for FREQUENCY.

5. In the Function Arguments dialog box, enter the appropriate values for the arguments.

In the Data_array box, I entered the cells that hold the scores. In this example, that's B1:E10.

FREQUENCY refers to intervals as *bins,* and holds the intervals in the Bins_array box. For this example, G2:G7 goes into the Bins_array box.

After I identified both arrays, the Function Arguments dialog box shows the frequencies inside a pair of curly brackets. Look closely at Figure 7-10 and you see that Excel adds a frequency of zero to the end of the set of frequencies in the third line of the dialog box.

6. Press Ctrl+Shift+Enter to close the Function Arguments dialog box.

Use this keystroke combination because FREQUENCY is an array function.

When you close the Function Arguments dialog box, the frequencies go into the appropriate cells, as Figure 7-11 shows.

If I had assigned the name Data to B1:E10 and the name Interval to G2:G7, and used those names in the Function Arguments dialog box, the resulting formula would have been

TIP

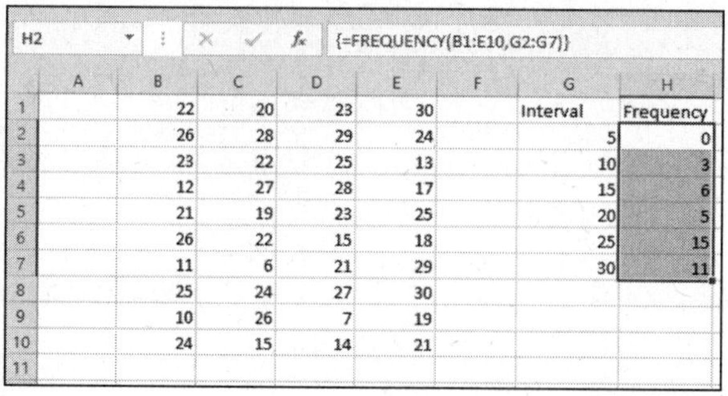

	A	B	C	D	E	F	G	H
1		22	20	23	30		Interval	Frequency
2		26	28	29	24		5	0
3		23	22	25	13		10	3
4		12	27	28	17		15	6
5		21	19	23	25		20	5
6		26	22	15	18		25	15
7		11	6	21	29		30	11
8		25	24	27	30			
9		10	26	7	19			
10		24	15	14	21			
11								

FIGURE 7-11: FREQUENCY's frequencies.

```
=FREQUENCY(Data,Interval)
```

which might be easier to understand than

```
=FREQUENCY(B1:E10,G2:G7)
```

(Don't remember how to assign a name to a range of cells? Take a look at Chapter 2.)

Data analysis tool: Histogram

Here's another way to create a frequency distribution — with the Histogram data analysis tool. To show you that the two methods are equivalent, I use the data from the `FREQUENCY` example. Figure 7-12 shows the data along with the Histogram dialog box.

The steps are listed here:

1. **Enter the scores into an array, and enter intervals into another array.**
2. **Click on Data | Data Analysis to open the Data Analysis dialog box.**
3. **From the Analysis Tools menu, select Histogram to open the Histogram dialog box.**
4. **In the Histogram dialog box, enter the appropriate values.**

   The data are in cells B1 through E10, so B1:E10 goes into the Input Range box. The easiest way to enter this array is to click in B1, press and hold the Shift key, and then click in E10. Excel puts the absolute reference format ($B$1:$E$10) into the Input Range box.

   In the Bin Range box, I enter the array that holds the intervals. In this example, that's G2 through G7. I click in G2, press and hold the Shift key, and then click in G7. The absolute reference format ($G$2:$G$7) appears in the Bin Range box.

5. Select the New Worksheet Ply radio button to create a new tabbed page and to put the results on the new page.

6. Select the Chart Output check box to create a histogram and visualize the results.

7. Click OK to close the dialog box.

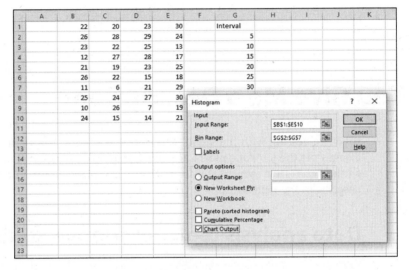

FIGURE 7-12: The Histogram analysis tool.

Figure 7-13 shows Histogram's output. The table matches up with what FREQUENCY produces. Notice that Histogram adds *More* to the Bin column. The size of the histogram is somewhat smaller when it first appears. I used the mouse to stretch the histogram and give it the appearance you see in the figure. The histogram shows that the distribution tails off to the left (consistent with the negative skewness statistic) and seems to not have a distinctive peak (consistent with the negative kurtosis statistic). Notice also the chart toolset (the three icons) that appears to the right of the histogram. The tools enable you to modify the histogram in a variety of ways. (See Chapter 3.)

By the way, the other check box options in the Histogram dialog box are Pareto Chart and Cumulative Percentage. The Pareto Chart option sorts the intervals in order, from highest frequency to lowest, before creating the graph. The Cumulative Percentage option shows the percentage of scores in an interval combined with the percentages in all the preceding intervals. Selecting this check box also puts a cumulative percentage line in the histogram. (You'd have to select both the Pareto Chart option and the Cumulative Percentage option to duplicate the effect of the Pareto chart I describe in Chapter 3.)

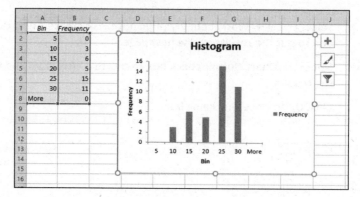

FIGURE 7-13:
The Histogram tool's output (after stretching the chart).

Can You Give Me a Description?

If you're dealing with individual descriptive statistics, the worksheet functions I discuss get the job done nicely. If you want an overall report that presents nearly all the descriptive statistical information in one place, use the Data Analysis tool I describe in the next section.

Data analysis tool: Descriptive Statistics

In Chapter 2, I show you the Descriptive Statistics tool to introduce Excel's data analysis tools. Here's a slightly more complex example. Figure 7-14 shows three columns of scores and the Descriptive Statistics dialog box. I've labeled the columns First, Second, and Third so that you can see how this tool incorporates labels.

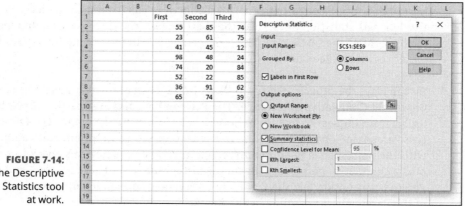

FIGURE 7-14:
The Descriptive Statistics tool at work.

Here are the steps for using this tool:

1. **Enter the data into an array.**

2. **Select Data | Data Analysis to open the Data Analysis dialog box.**

3. **In the Analysis Tools menu, choose Descriptive Statistics to open the Descriptive Statistics dialog box.**

4. **In the Descriptive Statistics dialog box, enter the appropriate values.**

   In the Input Range box, I enter the data. The easiest way to do this is to move the cursor to the upper-left cell (C1), press the Shift key, and click in the lower-right cell (E9). That puts $C$1:$E$9 into Input Range.

5. **Select the Columns radio button to indicate that the data are organized by columns.**

6. **Select the Labels in First Row check box because the input range includes the column headings.**

7. **Select the New Worksheet Ply radio button to create a new tabbed sheet within the current worksheet, and to send the results to the newly created sheet.**

8. **Select the Summary Statistics check box, and leave the others deselected.**

9. **Click OK to close the dialog box.**

   The new tabbed sheet *(ply)* opens, displaying statistics that summarize the data.

   As Figure 7-15 shows, the statistics summarize each column separately. When this page first opens, the columns that show the statistic names are too narrow, so the figure shows what the page looks like after I widen the columns.

	A	B	C	D	E	F
1	First		Second		Third	
2						
3	Mean	55.5	Mean	55.75	Mean	56.875
4	Standard Error	8.343089527	Standard Error	9.497650085	Standard Error	9.990062026
5	Median	53.5	Median	54.5	Median	68
6	Mode	#N/A	Mode	#N/A	Mode	#N/A
7	Standard Deviation	23.59782072	Standard Deviation	26.86341112	Standard Deviation	28.25616241
8	Sample Variance	556.8571429	Sample Variance	721.6428571	Sample Variance	798.4107143
9	Kurtosis	0.288278448	Kurtosis	-1.387273189	Kurtosis	-1.303364816
10	Skewness	0.567053259	Skewness	-0.106049703	Skewness	-0.661035774
11	Range	75	Range	71	Range	73
12	Minimum	23	Minimum	20	Minimum	12
13	Maximum	98	Maximum	91	Maximum	85
14	Sum	444	Sum	446	Sum	455
15	Count	8	Count	8	Count	8
16						

FIGURE 7-15: The Descriptive Statistics tool's output.

The Descriptive Statistics tool gives values for these statistics: Mean, standard error, median, mode, standard deviation, sample variance, kurtosis, skewness, range, minimum, maximum, sum, and count. Except for standard error and range, I discuss all of them.

Range is just the difference between the maximum and the minimum. Standard error is more involved, and I defer the explanation until Chapter 9. For now, I'll just say that standard error is the standard deviation divided by the square root of the sample size and leave it at that.

By the way, one of the check boxes left deselected in the example's Step 6 provides something called the *Confidence Limit of the Mean*, which I also defer until Chapter 9. The remaining two check boxes, Kth Largest and Kth Smallest, work like the functions LARGE and SMALL.

Be Quick About It!

Quick Analysis was a wonderful addition to Excel 2013, but it still hasn't made its way to the Mac. You select a range of data and an icon appears in the lower-right corner of the selection. Clicking the icon (or pressing Ctrl+Q) opens numerous possibilities for visualizing and summarizing the selected data. Mousing over these possibilities gives you a preview of what they look like. Selecting one puts it into your worksheet.

The worksheet in Figure 7-16 shows the percentages by age group that used the indicated media in 2006 (Source: U.S. Statistical Abstract). I selected the data, which caused the Quick Analysis icon to appear. Clicking the icon opened the panel with the options.

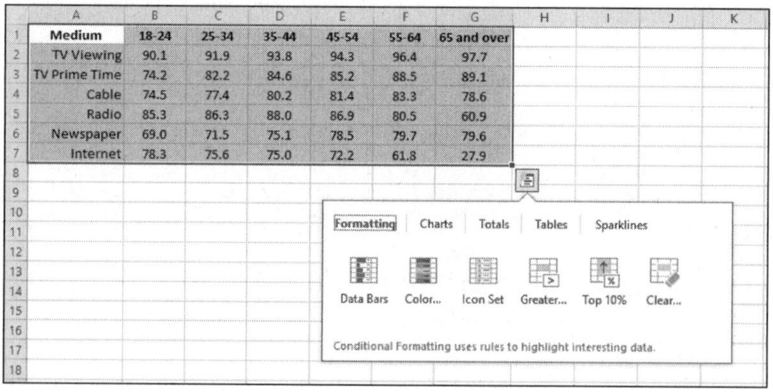

FIGURE 7-16: Selected data, the Quick Analysis icon, and the panel of options for visualizing and summarizing the data.

Figure 7-17 shows what happens when I mouse over FORMATTING | Data Bars.

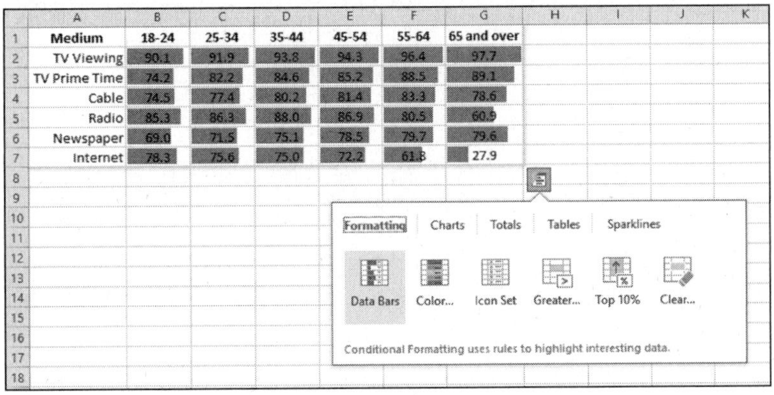

FIGURE 7-17:
Mousing over
FORMATTING |
Data Bars.

Want to see what a column chart looks like? Mouse over CHARTS | Clustered Column. (See Figure 7-18.)

FIGURE 7-18:
Mousing over
CHARTS |
Clustered
Column.

How about inserting the means? That's TOTALS | Average, as in Figure 7-19.

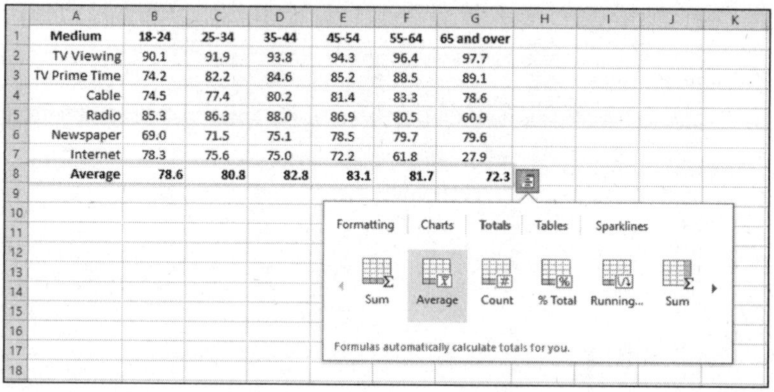

FIGURE 7-19:
Mousing over
TOTALS |
Average.

I could go on all day with this, but I'll just show you a couple more. If you'd like to add some professional-looking table effects to the selection, try TABLES | Table. (See Figure 7-20.)

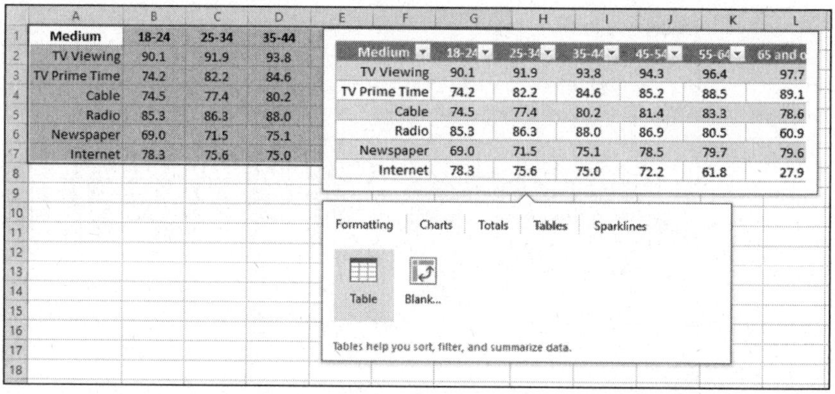

FIGURE 7-20:
Mousing over
TABLES | Table.

I couldn't finish off this topic without taking a look at the sparklines in Quick Analysis. When I mouse over SPARKLINES | Column, the result is Figure 7-21. The columns give a concise look at important age-related trends: Contrast the Internet sparkline with the sparklines for Newspapers and TV.

	A	B	C	D	E	F	G	H	I	J	K
1	**Medium**	**18-24**	**25-34**	**35-44**	**45-54**	**55-64**	**65 and over**				
2	TV Viewing	90.1	91.9	93.8	94.3	96.4	97.7				
3	TV Prime Time	74.2	82.2	84.6	85.2	88.5	89.1				
4	Cable	74.5	77.4	80.2	81.4	83.3	78.6				
5	Radio	85.3	86.3	88.0	86.9	80.5	60.9				
6	Newspaper	69.0	71.5	75.1	78.5	79.7	79.6				
7	Internet	78.3	75.6	75.0	72.2	61.8	27.9				

Formatting | Charts | Totals | Tables | **Sparklines**

Line | Column | Win/Loss

Sparklines are mini charts placed in single cells.

Instant Statistics

Suppose that you're working with a cell range full of data. You might like to quickly know the status of the average and perhaps some other descriptive statistics about the data without going to the trouble of using several statistical functions. You can customize the status bar at the bottom of the worksheet to track these values for you and display them whenever you select the cell range. To do this, right-click the status bar to open the Customize Status Bar menu. (See Figure 7-22.) In the area third from the bottom, selecting all the items displays the values I mention in the preceding section (along with the count of items in the range — numerical and non-numerical).

Figure 7-23 shows these values displayed on the status bar for the cells I selected.

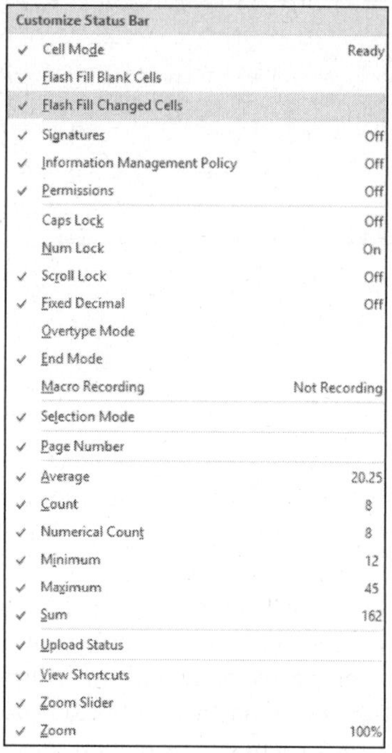

FIGURE 7-22:
The Customize status bar menu.

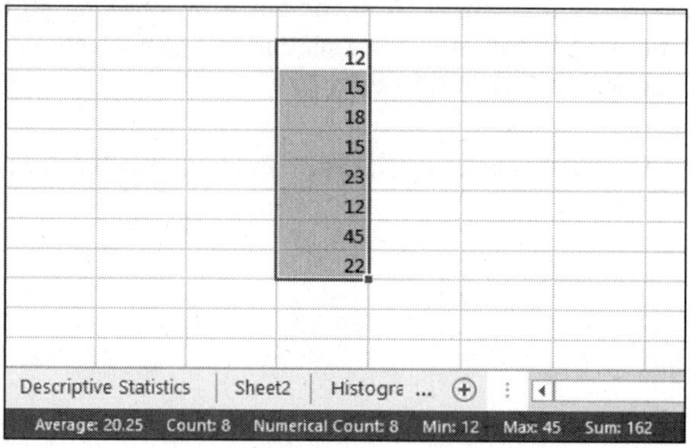

FIGURE 7-23:
Displaying values on the status bar.

Chapter 8
What's Normal?

A main job of statisticians is to estimate population characteristics. The job becomes easier if they can make some assumptions about the populations they study.

One particular assumption works over and over again: A specific attribute, trait, or ability is distributed throughout a population so that most people have an average or near-average amount of the attribute, and progressively fewer people have increasingly extreme amounts of the attribute. In this chapter, I discuss this assumption and what it means for statistics. I also describe Excel functions related to this assumption.

Hitting the Curve

When you measure something in the physical world, like length or weight, you deal with objects you can see and touch. Statisticians, social scientists, market researchers, and businesspeople, on the other hand, often have to measure something they can't see or put their hands around. Traits like intelligence, musical ability, or willingness to buy a new product fall into this category.

These kinds of traits are usually distributed throughout the population so that most people are around the average — with progressively fewer people represented toward the extremes. Because this happens so often, it's become an assumption about how most traits are distributed.

It's possible to capture the most-people-are-about-average assumption in a graphic way. Figure 8-1 shows the familiar *bell curve* that characterizes how a variety of attributes are distributed. The area under the curve represents the population. The horizontal axis represents measurements of the ability under consideration. A vertical line drawn down the center of the curve would correspond to the average of the measurements.

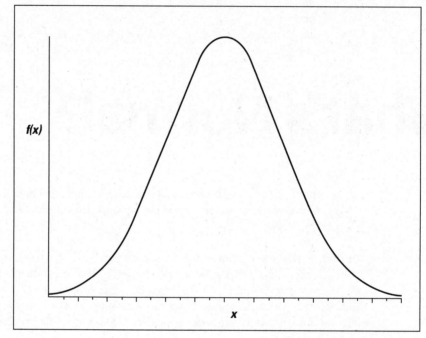

FIGURE 8-1:
The bell curve.

So, if you assume that it's possible to measure a trait like intelligence, and if you assume this curve represents how intelligence is distributed in the population, you can say this: The bell curve shows that most people have about average intelligence, very few have very little intelligence, and very few are geniuses. That seems to fit nicely with our intuitions about intelligence, doesn't it?

Digging deeper

On the horizontal axis of Figure 8-1, you see x, and on the vertical axis, $f(x)$. What do these symbols mean? The horizontal axis, as I mention, represents measurements, so think of each measurement as an x.

The explanation of $f(x)$ is a little more involved. A mathematical relationship between x and $f(x)$ creates the bell curve and enables us to visualize it.

The relationship is rather complex, and I won't burden you with it. Just understand that *f(x)* represents the height of the curve for a specified value of *x*. You supply a value for *x* (and for a couple of other things), and that complex relationship I mentioned returns a value of *f(x)*.

Now for some specifics. The bell curve is formally called the *normal distribution.* The term *f(x)* is called *probability density,* so the normal distribution is an example of a *probability density function.* Rather than give you a technical definition of probability density, I ask you to think of probability density as something that turns the area under the curve into probability. Probability of . . . what? I discuss that in the next section.

Parameters of a normal distribution

People often speak of *the* normal distribution. That's a misnomer. It's really a family of distributions. The members of the family differ from one another in terms of two parameters — yes, *parameters* because I'm talking about populations. Those two parameters are the mean (μ) and the standard deviation (σ). The mean tells you where the center of the distribution is, and the standard deviation tells you how spread out the distribution is around the mean. The mean is in the middle of the distribution. Every member of the normal distribution family is symmetric — the left side of the distribution is a mirror image of the right.

The characteristics of the normal distribution are well known to statisticians. More important, you can apply those characteristics to your work.

How? This brings me back to probability. You can find some useful probabilities if you can do four things:

>> If you can lay out a line that represents the scale of the attribute you're measuring

>> If you can indicate on the line where the mean of the measurements is

>> If you know the standard deviation

>> If you know (or if you can assume) the attribute is normally distributed throughout the population

I'll work with IQ scores to show you what I mean. Scores on the Stanford-Binet IQ test follow a normal distribution. The mean of the distribution of these scores is 100, and the standard deviation is 16. Figure 8-2 shows this distribution.

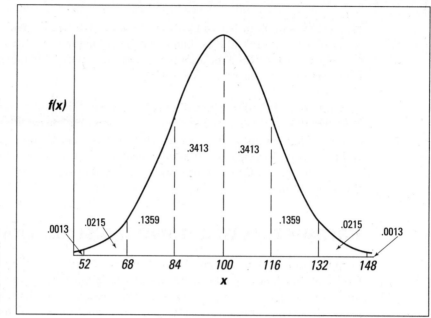

FIGURE 8-2:
The normal
distribution of IQ,
divided into
standard
deviations.

As the figure shows, I've laid out a line for the IQ scale. Each point on the line represents an IQ score. With 100 (the mean) as the reference point, I've marked off every 16 points (the standard deviation). I've drawn a dotted line from the mean up to *f100* (the height of the normal distribution where *x* = 100), and a dotted line from each standard deviation point.

The figure also shows the proportion of area bounded by the curve and the horizontal axis, and by successive pairs of standard deviations. It also shows the proportion beyond three standard deviations on either side (52 and 148). Note that the curve never touches the horizontal. It gets closer and closer, but it never touches. (Mathematicians say the curve is *asymptotic* to the horizontal.)

So, between the mean and one standard deviation — between 100 and 116 — are .3413 (or 34.13 percent) of the scores in the population. Another way to say this: The probability that an IQ score is between 100 and 116 is .3413. At the extremes, in the tails of the distribution, .0013 (.13 percent) of the scores are on each side.

REMEMBER

The proportions in Figure 8-2 hold for every member of the normal distribution family, not just for Stanford-Binet IQ scores. For example, in a sidebar in Chapter 6, I mention SAT scores, which (under the old scoring system) have a mean of 500 and a standard deviation of 100. They're normally distributed, too. That means 34.13 percent of SAT scores are between 500 and 600, 34.13 percent between 400 and 500, and . . . well, you can use Figure 8-2 as a guide for other proportions.

NORM.DIST

Figure 8-2 only shows areas partitioned by scores at the standard deviations. What about the proportion of IQ scores between 100 and 125? Or between 75 and 91? Or greater than 118? If you've ever taken a course in statistics, you might remember homework problems that involve finding proportions of areas under the normal distribution. You might also remember relying on tables of the normal distribution to solve them.

Excel's NORM.DIST worksheet function enables you to find normal distribution areas without relying on tables. NORM.DIST finds a *cumulative area.* You supply a score, a mean, and a standard deviation for a normal distribution, and NORM.DIST returns the proportion of area to the left of the score (also called *cumulative proportion* or *cumulative probability*). For example, Figure 8-2 shows that in the IQ distribution, .8413 of the area is to the left of 116.

How did I get that proportion? All the proportions to the left of 100 add up to .5000. (All the proportions to the right of 100 add up to .5000, too.) Add that .5000 to the .3413 between 100 and 116 and you have .8413.

Restating this another way, the probability of an IQ score less than or equal to 116 is .8413.

In Figure 8-3, I use NORM.DIST to find this proportion. Here are the steps:

1. **Select a cell for NORM.DIST's answer.**

   For this example, I selected C2.

2. **From the Statistical Functions menu, select NORM.DIST to open the Function Arguments dialog box for NORM.DIST.**

3. **In the Function Arguments dialog box, enter the appropriate values for the arguments.**

   In the X box, I entered the score for which I want to find the cumulative area. In this example, that's 116.

   In the Mean box, I entered the mean of the distribution, and in the Standard_ dev box, I enter the standard deviation. Here, the mean is 100 and the standard deviation is 16.

   In the Cumulative box, I entered TRUE. This tells NORM.DIST to find the cumulative area. The dialog box shows the result.

4. **Click OK to see the result in the selected cell.**

Figure 8-3 shows that the cumulative area is .84134476 (in the dialog box). If you enter FALSE in the Cumulative box, NORM.DIST returns the height of the normal distribution at 116.

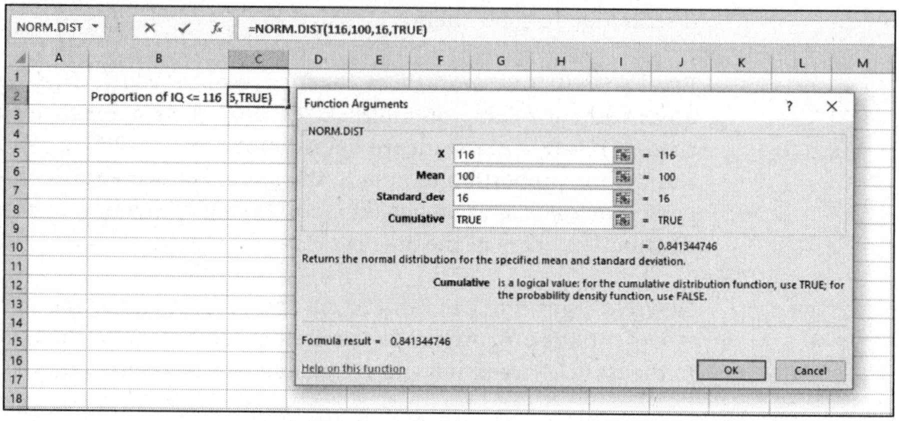

FIGURE 8-3:
Working with
NORM.DIST.

To find the proportion of IQ scores greater than 116, subtract the result from 1.0. (Just for the record, that's .15865524.)

How about the proportion of IQ scores between 116 and 125? Apply NORM.DIST for each score and subtract the results. For this particular example, the formula is

```
=NORM.DIST(125,100,16,TRUE)-NORM.DIST(116,100,16,TRUE)
```

The answer, by the way, is .09957.

NORM.INV

NORM.INV is the flip side of NORM.DIST. You supply a cumulative probability, a mean, and a standard deviation, and NORM.INV returns the score that cuts off the cumulative probability. For example, if you supply .5000 along with a mean and a standard deviation, NORM.INV returns the mean.

This function is useful if you have to calculate the score for a specific percentile in a normal distribution. Figure 8-4 shows the Function Arguments dialog box for NORM.INV with .75 as the cumulative probability, 500 as the mean, and 100 as the standard deviation. Because the SAT follows a normal distribution with 500 as its mean and 100 as its standard deviation, the result corresponds to the score at the 75th percentile for the SAT. (For more on percentiles, see Chapter 6.)

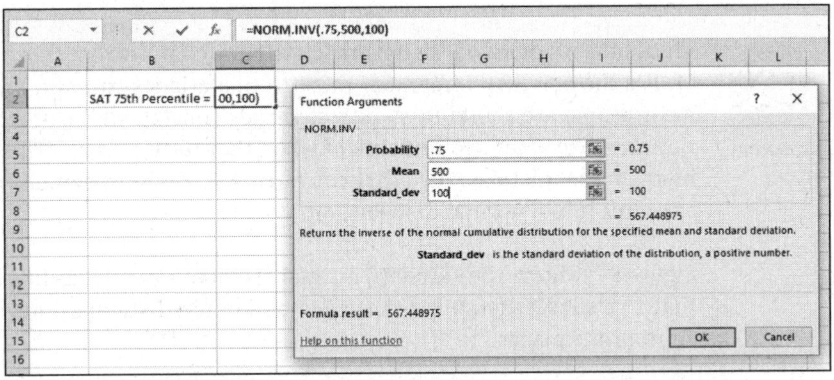

FIGURE 8-4:
Working with
`NORM.INV`.

A Distinguished Member of the Family

To standardize a set of scores so that you can compare them to other sets of scores, you convert each one to a z-score. (See Chapter 6.) The formula for converting a score to a z-score (also known as a *standard score*) is

$$z = \frac{x - \mu}{\sigma}$$

The idea is to use the standard deviation as a unit of measure. For example, the Stanford-Binet version of the IQ test has a mean of 100 and a standard deviation of 16. The Wechsler version has a mean of 100 and a standard deviation of 15. How does a Stanford-Binet score of, say, 110, stack up against a Wechsler score of 110?

An easy way to answer this question is to put the two versions on a level playing field by standardizing both scores.

For the Stanford-Binet:

$$z = \frac{110 - 100}{16} = .625$$

For the Wechsler:

$$z = \frac{110 - 100}{15} = .667$$

So, 110 on the Wechsler is a slightly higher score than 110 on the Stanford-Binet.

Now, if you convert all the scores in a normal distribution (such as either version of the IQ test), you have a normal distribution of z-scores. Any set of z-scores (normally distributed or not) has a mean of 0 and a standard deviation of 1. If a normal distribution has those parameters, it's a *standard normal distribution* — a normal distribution of standard scores.

WARNING

This is the member of the normal distribution family that most people have heard of. It's the one they remember most from statistics courses, and it's the one that most people are thinking about when they (mistakenly) say *the* normal distribution. It's also what people think of when they hear *z-scores*. This distribution leads many to the mistaken idea that converting to z-scores somehow transforms a set of scores into a normal distribution.

Figure 8-5 shows the standard normal distribution. It looks like Figure 8-2, except that I've substituted 0 for the mean and entered standard deviation units in the appropriate places.

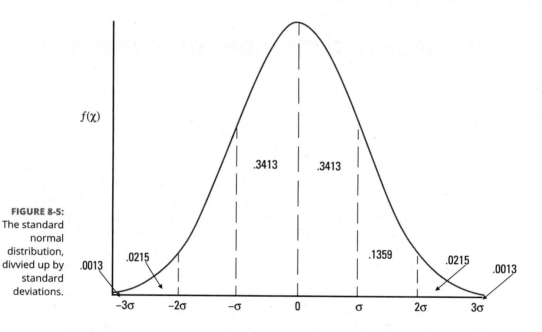

FIGURE 8-5:
The standard normal distribution, divvied up by standard deviations.

In the next two sections, I describe Excel's functions for working with the standard normal distribution.

NORM.S.DIST

NORM.S.DIST is like its counterpart NORM.DIST, except that it's designed for a normal distribution whose mean is 0 and whose standard deviation is 1.00 (that is, a standard normal distribution). You supply a z-score and it returns the area to the left of the z-score — the probability that a z-score is less than or equal to the one you supplied. You also supply either TRUE or FALSE for an argument called Cumulative: TRUE if you're looking for the cumulative probability, FALSE if you're trying to find $f(x)$.

Figure 8-6 shows the Function Arguments dialog box with 1 as the z-score and TRUE in the Cumulative box. The dialog box presents .841344746, the probability that a z-score is less than or equal to 1.00 in a standard normal distribution. Clicking OK puts that result into a selected cell.

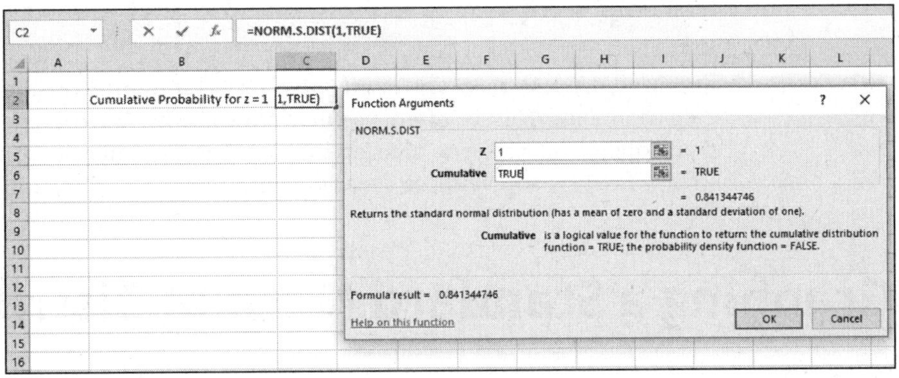

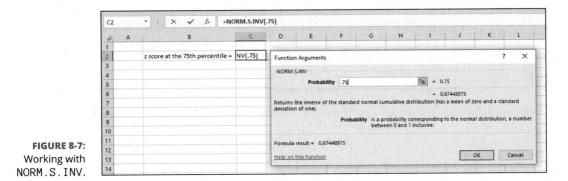

FIGURE 8-6:
Working with
NORM.S.DIST.

NORM.S.INV

NORM.S.INV is the flip side of NORM.S.DIST: You supply a cumulative probability, and NORM.S.INV returns the z-score that cuts off the cumulative probability. For example, if you supply .5000, NORM.S.INV returns 0, the mean of the standard normal distribution.

Figure 8-7 shows the Function Arguments dialog box for NORM.S.INV, with .75 as the cumulative probability. The dialog box shows the answer, .67448975, the z-score at the 75th percentile of the standard normal distribution.

FIGURE 8-7:
Working with
NORM.S.INV.

PHI and GAUSS

These two worksheet functions work with the standard normal distribution. Each takes one argument.

```
=PHI(x)
```

returns the height (that is, the probability density) of the standard normal distribution at x.

```
=GAUSS(x)
```

returns 0.5 less than the cumulative probability of x (in the standard normal distribution). This is often useful if you quickly have to find the cumulative probability on just one side of the distribution and you don't feel like using NORM.S.DIST, supplying all its arguments, and then subtracting 0.5.

Graphing a Standard Normal Distribution

In my experience, graphing a distribution helps you understand it. So, in this section, I walk you through visualizing a standard normal distribution.

The relationship between x and f(x) for the general formula of a normal distribution is, as I mention earlier in this chapter, a pretty complex one. Here's the equation:

$$f(x) = \frac{1}{\sigma\sqrt{2\pi}} e^{\left[\frac{(x-\mu)^2}{2\sigma^2}\right]}$$

If you supply values for μ (the mean), σ (the standard deviation), and x (a score), the equation gives you back a value for f(x) — the height of the normal distribution at x. π and e are important constants in mathematics. π is approximately 3.1416 (the ratio of a circle's circumference to its diameter). e is approximately 2.71828. It's related to something called *natural logarithms* and to a variety of other mathematical concepts. (I tell you more about logarithms and e in Chapter 22, in the section Logarithmica Esoterica.)

In a standard normal distribution, μ = 0 and σ = 1, so the equation becomes

$$f(z) = \frac{1}{\sqrt{2\pi}} e^{\left[\frac{-z^2}{2}\right]}$$

I changed the *x* to *z* because you deal with z-scores in this member of the normal distribution family.

I begin by putting z-scores from −4 to 4 (in steps of .2) in the cells in column B.

Next, in cell C2, I type the standard normal distribution equation as an Excel formula:

```
=((1/SQRT(2*PI()))))*EXP(-(B2^2)/2)
```

`PI()` is an Excel function that gives the value of π. The function `EXP()` raises e to the power indicated by what's in the parentheses that follow it. (Again, see Chapter 22.)

That's the hard, mathy way to do it. The worksheet function `PHI`, which I mention earlier, offers a much easier way to supply the *f(z)* values. If you enter this formula into C2

```
=PHI(B2)
```

you get the same result as typing in the complicated equation.

The next step is to autofill column C.

Then select

Insert | Recommended Charts | All Charts

and choose Scatter with Smooth Lines. You have to do a little more work to get the chart to appear as in Figure 8-8. (See Chapter 3 for more on Excel graphics.) As the accompanying figure shows, this layout nicely traces out the standard normal distribution from z = −4 to z = 4. Figure 8-8 also shows the autofilled values.

Note that the Excel formula shown here in the Formula bar corresponds to the standard normal distribution equation [=((1/SQRT(2*PI()))))*EXP(-(B2^2)/2)] I mention earlier.

I show you all of this because I want you to get accustomed to visualizing important distributions. I do that throughout the rest of the book.

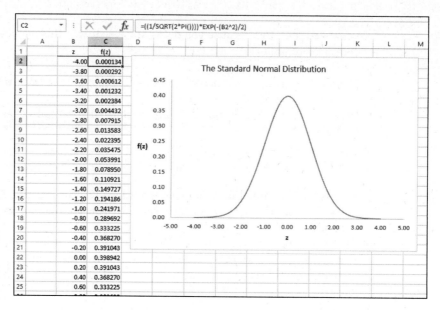

FIGURE 8-8:
The Completed
Graph of the
Standard Normal
Distribution.

3

Drawing Conclusions from Data

IN THIS PART . . .

Create sampling distributions

Figure out confidence limits

Work with t-tests

Work with analysis of variance

Visualize t, chi-square, and F distributions

Understand correlation and regression

Work with time series

Understand non-parametric statistics

Chapter 9

The Confidence Game: Estimation

Populations and samples are pretty straightforward ideas. A *population* is a huge collection of individuals, from which you draw a sample. Assess the members of the sample on some trait or attribute, calculate statistics that summarize that sample, and you're in business.

In addition to summarizing the scores in the sample, you can use the statistics to create estimates of the population parameters. This is no small accomplishment. On the basis of a small percentage of individuals from the population, you can draw a picture of the population.

A question emerges, however: How much confidence can you have in the estimates you create? In order to answer this, you have to have a context in which to place your estimates. How probable are they? How likely is the true value of a parameter to be within a particular lower bound and upper bound?

In this chapter, I introduce the context for estimates, show how that plays into confidence in those estimates, and describe an Excel function that enables you to calculate your confidence level.

Understanding Sampling Distributions

Imagine that you have a population and you draw a sample from this population. You measure the individuals of the sample on a particular attribute and calculate the sample mean. Return the sample members to the population. Draw another sample, assess the new sample's members, and then calculate *their* mean. Repeat this process again and again, always using the same number of individuals as you had in the original sample. If you could do this an infinite amount of times (with the same-size sample each time), you'd have an infinite amount of sample means. Those sample means form a distribution of their own. This distribution is called *the sampling distribution of the mean.*

For a sample mean, this is the context I mention at the beginning of this chapter. Like any other number, a statistic makes no sense by itself. You have to know where it comes from in order to understand it. Of course, a statistic *comes from* a calculation performed on sample data. In another sense, a statistic is part of a sampling distribution.

REMEMBER

In general, *a sampling distribution is the distribution of all possible values of a statistic for a given sample size.*

I italicize that definition for a reason: It's extremely important. After many years of teaching statistics, I can tell you that this concept usually sets the boundary line between people who understand statistics and people who don't.

So . . . if you understand what a sampling distribution is, you'll understand what the field of statistics is all about. If you don't, you won't. It's almost that simple.

If you don't know what a sampling distribution is, statistics will be a cookbook type of subject for you: Whenever you have to apply statistics, you plug numbers into formulas and hope for the best. On the other hand, if you're comfortable with the idea of a sampling distribution, you grasp the big picture of inferential statistics.

To help clarify the idea of a sampling distribution, take a look at Figure 9-1. It summarizes the steps in creating a sampling distribution of the mean.

A sampling distribution — like any other group of scores — has a mean and a standard deviation. The symbol for the mean of the sampling distribution of the mean (yes, I know that's a mouthful) is $\mu_{\bar{x}}$.

REMEMBER

The standard deviation of a sampling distribution is a pretty hot item. It has a special name: *standard error.* For the sampling distribution of the mean, the standard deviation is called *the standard error of the mean.* Its symbol is $\sigma_{\bar{x}}$.

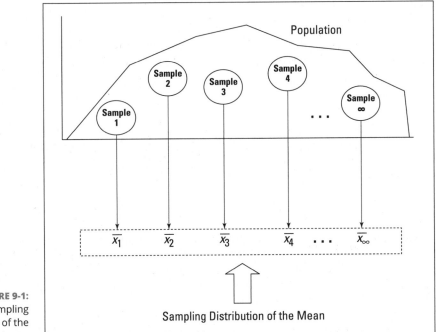

FIGURE 9-1:
The sampling
distribution of the
mean.

Sampling Distribution of the Mean

An EXTREMELY Important Idea: The Central Limit Theorem

The situation I ask you to imagine is one that never happens in the real world. You never take an infinite amount of samples and calculate their means, and you never create a sampling distribution of the mean. Typically, you draw one sample and calculate its statistics.

So if you have only one sample, how can you ever know anything about a sampling distribution — a theoretical distribution that encompasses an infinite number of samples? Is this all just a wild-goose chase?

No, it's not. You can figure out a lot about a sampling distribution because of a great gift from mathematicians to the field of statistics. This gift is called *the Central Limit Theorem.*

REMEMBER

According to the Central Limit Theorem:

>> The sampling distribution of the mean is approximately a normal distribution if the sample size is large enough.

Large enough means about 30 or more.

>> The mean of the sampling distribution of the mean is the same as the population mean.

In equation form, that's

$$\mu_{\bar{x}} = \mu$$

>> The standard deviation of the sampling distribution of the mean (also known as the standard error of the mean) is equal to the population standard deviation divided by the square root of the sample size.

The equation here is

$$\sigma_{\bar{x}} = \sigma \big/ \sqrt{N}$$

Notice that the Central Limit Theorem says nothing about the population. All it says is that if the sample size is large enough, the sampling distribution of the mean is a normal distribution, with the indicated parameters. The population that supplies the samples doesn't have to be a normal distribution for the Central Limit Theorem to hold.

What if the population *is* a normal distribution? In that case, the sampling distribution of the mean is a normal distribution regardless of the sample size.

Figure 9-2 shows a general picture of the sampling distribution of the mean, partitioned into standard error units.

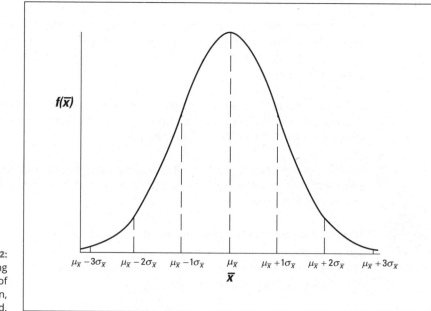

FIGURE 9-2:
The sampling
distribution of
the mean,
partitioned.

$f(\bar{x})$

$\mu_{\bar{x}} - 3\sigma_{\bar{x}}$ $\mu_{\bar{x}} - 2\sigma_{\bar{x}}$ $\mu_{\bar{x}} - 1\sigma_{\bar{x}}$ $\mu_{\bar{x}}$ $\mu_{\bar{x}} + 1\sigma_{\bar{x}}$ $\mu_{\bar{x}} + 2\sigma_{\bar{x}}$ $\mu_{\bar{x}} + 3\sigma_{\bar{x}}$

$\bar{x}$

(Approximately) simulating the Central Limit Theorem

It almost doesn't sound right. How can a population that's not normally distributed result in a normally distributed sampling distribution?

To give you an idea of how the Central Limit Theorem works, I created a simulation. This simulation creates something like a sampling distribution of the mean for a very small sample, based on a population that's not normally distributed. As you'll see, even though the population is not a normal distribution, and even though the sample is small, the sampling distribution of the mean looks quite a bit like a normal distribution.

Imagine a huge population that consists of just three scores — 1, 2, and 3 — and each one is equally likely to appear in a sample. (That kind of population is definitely *not* a normal distribution.) Imagine also that you can randomly select a sample of three scores from this population. Table 9-1 shows all possible samples and their means.

TABLE 9-1 **All Possible Samples of Three Scores (and Their Means) from a Population Consisting of the Scores 1, 2, and 3**

Sample	Mean	Sample	Mean	Sample	Mean
1,1,1	1.00	2,1,1	1.33	3,1,1	1.67
1,1,2	1.33	2,1,2	1.67	3,1,2	2.00
1,1,3	1.67	2,1,3	2.00	3,1,3	2.33
1,2,1	1.33	2,2,1	1.67	3,2,1	2.00
1,2,2	1.67	2,2,2	2.00	3,2,2	2.33
1,2,3	2.00	2,2,3	2.33	3,2,3	2.67
1,3,1	1.67	2,3,1	2.00	3,3,1	2.33
1,3,2	2.00	2,3,2	2.33	3,3,2	2.67
1,3,3	2.33	2,3,3	2.67	3,3,3	3.00

If you look closely at the table, you can almost see what's about to happen in the simulation. The sample mean that appears most frequently is 2.00. The sample means that appear least frequently are 1.00 and 3.00. Hmmm. . . .

In the simulation, I randomly select a score from the population and then randomly select two more. That group of three scores is a sample. Then I calculate the mean of that sample. I repeat this process for a total of 60 samples, resulting in 60 sample means. Finally, I graph the distribution of the sample means.

What does the simulated sampling distribution of the mean look like? Figure 9-3 shows a worksheet that answers this question.

In the worksheet, each row is a sample. The columns labeled x1, x2, and x3 show the three scores for each sample. Column E shows the average for the sample in each row. Column G shows all the possible values for the sample mean, and column H shows how often each mean appears in the 60 samples. Columns G and H, and the graph, show that the distribution has its maximum frequency when the sample mean is 2.00. The frequencies tail off as the sample means get further and further away from 2.00.

The point of all this is that the population looks nothing like a normal distribution and the sample size is very small. Even under those constraints, the sampling distribution of the mean based on 60 samples begins to look very much like a normal distribution.

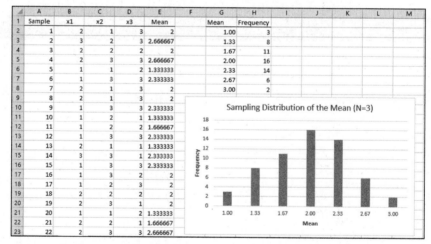

FIGURE 9-3:
Simulating the sampling distribution of the mean (*N*=3) from a population consisting of the scores 1, 2, and 3. The simulation consists of 60 samples.

What about the parameters the Central Limit Theorem predicts for the sampling distribution? Start with the population. The population mean is 2.00 and the population standard deviation is .67. (This kind of population requires some slightly fancy mathematics for figuring out the parameters. The math is a little beyond where we are, so I'll leave it at that.)

On to the sampling distribution. The mean of the 60 means is 1.98, and their standard deviation (an estimate of the standard error of the mean) is .48. Those numbers closely approximate the Central Limit Theorem–predicted parameters for the sampling distribution of the mean, 2.00 (equal to the population mean) and .47 (the standard deviation, .67, divided by the square root of 3, the sample size).

In case you're interested in doing this simulation, here are the steps:

1. **Select a cell for your first randomly selected number.**

   I selected cell B2.

2. **Use the worksheet function RANDBETWEEN to select 1, 2, or 3.**

   This simulates drawing a number from a population consisting of the numbers 1, 2, and 3 where you have an equal chance of selecting each number. You can either select FORMULAS | Math & Trig | RANDBETWEEN and use the Function Arguments dialog box or just type

   ```
   =RANDBETWEEN(1,3)
   ```

   in B2 and press Enter. The first argument is the smallest number RANDBETWEEN returns, and the second argument is the largest number.

3. **Select the cell to the right of the original cell and pick another random number between 1 and 3. Do this again for a third random number in the cell to the right of the second one**.

   The easiest way to do this is to autofill the two cells to the right of the original cell. In my worksheet, those two cells are C2 and D2.

4. **Consider these three cells to be a sample, and calculate their mean in the cell to the right of the third cell.**

   The easiest way to do this is just type

   ```
   =AVERAGE(B2:D2)
   ```

   in cell E2 and press Enter.

5. **Repeat this process for as many samples as you want to include in the simulation. Have each row correspond to a sample.**

   I used 60 samples. The quick and easy way to get this done is to select the first row of three randomly selected numbers and their mean and then autofill the remaining rows. The set of sample means in column E is the simulated sampling distribution of the mean. Use AVERAGE and STDEV.P to find its mean and standard deviation.

To see what this simulated sampling distribution looks like, use the array function FREQUENCY on the sample means in column E. Follow these steps:

1. **Enter the possible values of the sample mean into an array.**

   I used column G for this. I expressed the possible values of the sample mean in fraction form (3/3, 4/3, 5/3, 6/3, 7/3, 8/3, and 9/3) as I entered them into the cells G2 through G8. Excel converts them to decimal form. Make sure those cells are in Number format.

2. **Select an array for the frequencies of the possible values of the sample mean.**

   I used column H to hold the frequencies, selecting cells H2 through H8.

3. **From the Statistical Functions menu, select FREQUENCY to open the Function Arguments dialog box for FREQUENCY.**

4. **In the Function Arguments dialog box, enter the appropriate values for the arguments.**

   In the Data_array box, I entered the cells that hold the sample means. In this example, that's E2:E61.

5. **Identify the array that holds the possible values of the sample mean.**

   FREQUENCY holds this array in the Bins_array box. For my worksheet, G2:G8 goes into the Bins_array box. After you identify both arrays, the Function Arguments dialog box shows the frequencies inside a pair of curly brackets. (See Figure 9-4.)

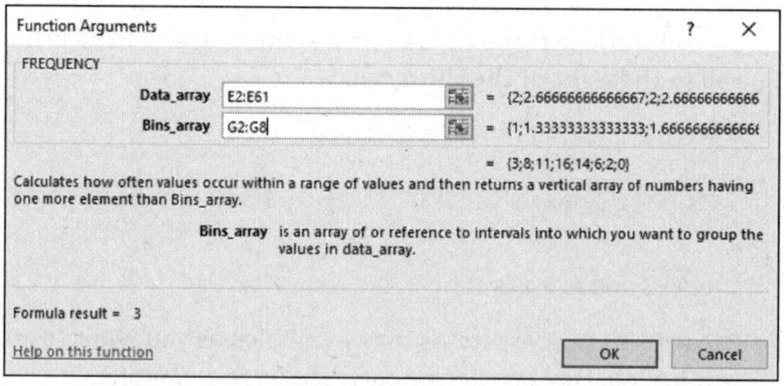

FIGURE 9-4: The Function Arguments dialog box for FREQUENCY in the simulated sampling distribution worksheet.

6. **Press Ctrl+Shift+Enter to close the Function Arguments dialog box and show the frequencies.**

   Use this keystroke combination because FREQUENCY is an array function. (For more on FREQUENCY, see Chapter 7.)

Finally, with H2:H8 highlighted, select

Insert | Recommended Charts

and choose the Clustered Column layout to produce the graph of the frequencies, which I modified to produce what you see in the figure. (See Chapter 3 for more on Excel charts.) Your graph will probably look somewhat different from mine, because you'll likely wind up with different random numbers than I did.

By the way, Excel repeats the random selection process whenever you do something that causes Excel to recalculate the worksheet. The effect is that the numbers can change as you work through this. (That is, you rerun the simulation.) For example, if you go back and autofill one of the rows again, the numbers change and the graph changes.

The Limits of Confidence

I tell you about sampling distributions because they help you answer the question I pose at the beginning of this chapter: How much confidence can you have in the estimates you create?

The idea is to calculate a statistic and then use that statistic to establish upper and lower bounds for the population parameter with, say, 95 percent confidence. You can do this only if you know the sampling distribution of the statistic and the standard error. In the next section, I show how to do this for the mean.

Finding confidence limits for a mean

The FarBlonJet Corporation manufactures navigation systems. (Corporate motto: "If you travel, get FarBlonJet.") They've developed a new battery to power their portable model. To help market their system, FarBlonJet wants to know how long, on average, each battery lasts before it burns out.

They'd like to estimate that average with 95 percent confidence. They test a sample of 100 batteries and find that the sample mean is 60 hours, with a standard deviation of 20 hours. The Central Limit Theorem, remember, says that with a large enough sample (30 or more), the sampling distribution of the mean approximates a normal distribution. The standard error of the mean (the standard deviation of the sampling distribution of the mean) is

$$\sigma_{\bar{x}} = \sigma \Big/ \sqrt{N}$$

The sample size, N, is 100. What about σ? That's unknown, so you have to estimate it. If you know σ, that would mean you know μ, and establishing confidence limits would be unnecessary.

The best estimate of σ is the standard deviation of the sample. In this case, that's 20. This leads to an estimate of the standard error of the mean

$$s_{\bar{x}} = \frac{s}{\sqrt{N}} = \frac{20}{\sqrt{100}} = \frac{20}{10} = 2$$

The best estimate of the population mean is the sample mean, 60. Armed with this information — estimated mean, estimated standard error of the mean, normal distribution — you can envision the sampling distribution of the mean, which is shown in Figure 9-5. Consistent with Figure 9-2, each standard deviation is a standard error of the mean.

Now that you have the sampling distribution, you can establish the 95 percent confidence limits for the mean. Starting at the center of the distribution, how far out to the sides do you have to extend until you have 95 percent of the area under the curve? (For more on area under a normal distribution and what it means, see Chapter 8.)

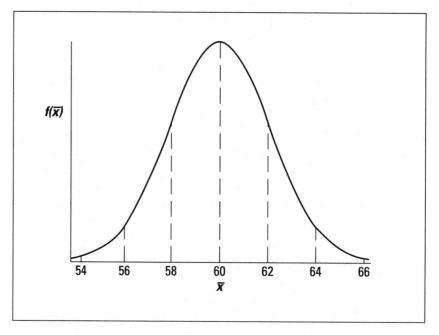

FIGURE 9-5:
The sampling distribution of the mean for the FarBlonJet battery.

One way to answer this question is to work with the standard normal distribution and find the z-score that cuts off 47.5 percent on the right side and 47.5 percent on the left side. (Yes, Chapter 8 again.) The one on the right is a positive z-score, and the one on the left is a negative z-score. Then multiply each z-score by the standard error. Add each result to the sample mean to get the upper confidence limit and the lower confidence limit.

It turns out that the z-score is 1.96 for the boundary on the right side of the standard normal distribution, and −1.96 for the boundary on the left. You can calculate those values (difficult), get them from a table of the standard normal distribution that you typically find in a statistics textbook (easier), or use the Excel worksheet function I describe in the next section to do all the calculations (much easier). The point is that the upper bound in the sampling distribution is 63.92 ($60 + 1.96s_{\bar{x}}$), and the lower bound is 56.08 ($60 - 1.96s_{\bar{x}}$). Figure 9-6 shows these bounds on the sampling distribution.

This means you can say with 95 percent confidence that the FarBlonJet battery lasts, on the average, between 56.08 hours and 63.92 hours. Want a narrower range? You can either reduce your confidence level (to, say, 90 percent) or test a larger sample of batteries.

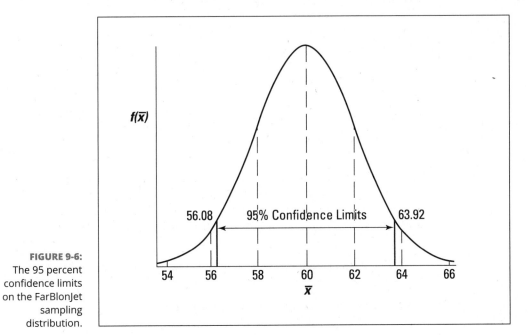

FIGURE 9-6: The 95 percent confidence limits on the FarBlonJet sampling distribution.

CONFIDENCE.NORM

The CONFIDENCE.NORM worksheet function does the lion's share of the work in constructing confidence intervals. You supply the confidence level, the standard deviation, and the sample size. CONFIDENCE.NORM returns the result of multiplying the appropriate z-score by the standard error of the mean. To determine the upper bound of the confidence limit, you add that result to the sample mean. To determine the lower bound, you subtract that result from the sample mean.

To show you how it works, I walk you through the FarBlonJet batteries example again. Here are the steps:

1. **Select a cell.**

2. **From the Statistical Functions menu, select CONFIDENCE.NORM to open the Function Arguments dialog box for CONFIDENCE.NORM. (See Figure 9-7.)**

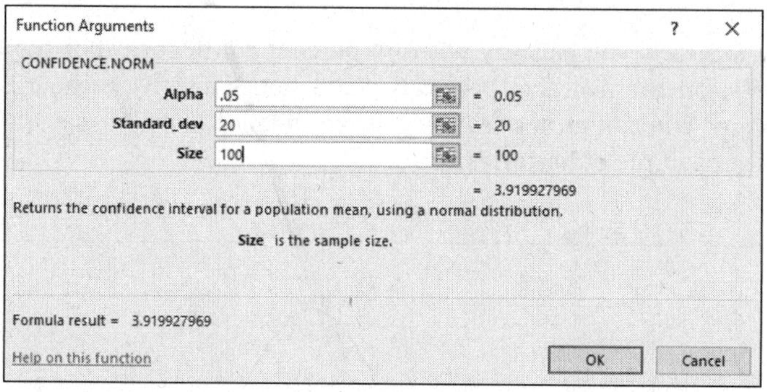

FIGURE 9-7:
The Function Arguments dialog box for CONFIDENCE. NORM.

3. **In the Function Arguments dialog box, enter the appropriate arguments.**

   The Alpha box holds the result of subtracting the desired confidence level from 1.00.

   Yes, that's a little confusing. Instead of typing .95 for the 95 percent confidence limit, I have to type .05. Think of it as the percentage of area *beyond* the confidence limits rather than the area *within* the confidence limits. And why is it labeled *Alpha?* I get into that in Chapter 10.

   The Size box holds the number of individuals in the sample. The example specifies 100 batteries tested. After I type that number, the answer (3.919928) appears in the dialog box.

4. **Click OK to put the answer into your selected cell.**

To finish things off, I add the answer to the sample mean (60) to determine the upper confidence limit (63.92) and subtract the answer from the mean to determine the lower confidence limit (56.08).

Fit to a t

The Central Limit Theorem specifies (approximately) a normal distribution for large samples. Many times, however, you don't have the luxury of large sample sizes, and the normal distribution isn't appropriate. What do you do?

For small samples, the sampling distribution of the mean is a member of a family of distributions called the *t-distribution*. The parameter that distinguishes members of this family from one another is called *degrees of freedom*.

TIP

Think of *degrees of freedom* as the denominator of your variance estimate. For example, if your sample consists of 25 individuals, the sample variance that estimates population variance is

$$s^2 = \frac{\sum(x - \bar{x})^2}{N - 1} = \frac{\sum(x - \bar{x})^2}{25 - 1} = \frac{\sum(x - \bar{x})^2}{24}$$

The number in the denominator is 24, and that's the value of the degrees of freedom parameter. In general, degrees of freedom (df) = $N-1$ (N is the sample size) when you use the t-distribution the way I'm about to in this section.

Figure 9-8 shows two members of the t-distribution family (df =3 and df = 10), along with the normal distribution for comparison. As the figure shows, the greater the df, the more closely t approximates a normal distribution.

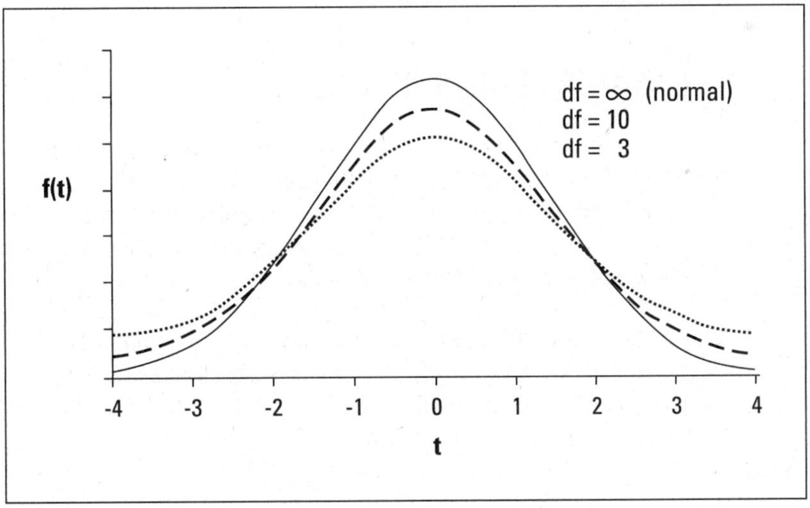

FIGURE 9-8:
Some members of the t-distribution family.

So, to determine the 95 percent confidence level if you have a small sample, work with the member of the t-distribution family that has the appropriate df. Find the value that cuts off 47.5 percent of the area on the right side of the distribution and 47.5 percent of the area on the left side of the distribution. The one on the right is a positive value, and the one on the left is negative. Then multiply each value by the standard error. Add each result to the mean to get the upper confidence limit and the lower confidence limit.

In the FarBlonJet batteries example, suppose the sample consists of 25 batteries, with a mean of 60 and a standard deviation of 20. The estimate for the standard error of the mean is

$$s_{\bar{x}} = s / \sqrt{N} = 20 / \sqrt{25} = 20 / 5 = 4$$

The df = $N - 1$ = 24. The value that cuts off 47.5 percent of the area on the right of this distribution is 2.064, and on the left it's −2.064. As I mention earlier, you can calculate these values (difficult), look them up in a table that's in statistics textbooks (easier), or use the Excel function I describe in the next section (much easier).

The point is that the upper confidence limit is 68.256 ($60 + 2.064s_{\bar{x}}$) and the lower confidence limit is 51.744 ($60 - 2.064s_{\bar{x}}$). With a sample of 25 batteries, you can say with 95 percent confidence that the average life of a FarBlonJet battery is between 51.744 hours and 68.256 hours. Notice that with a smaller sample, the range is wider for the same level of confidence that I use in the preceding example.

CONFIDENCE.T

Excel's CONFIDENCE.T worksheet function works just like CONFIDENCE.NORM, except it works with the *t* distribution rather than the normal distribution. Use it when your data doesn't satisfy the requirements for normal distribution. Its Function Arguments dialog box looks exactly like the dialog box for CONFIDENCE. NORM, and you follow the same steps.

For the second FarBlonJet example (mean = 60, standard deviation = 20, and sample size = 25), CONFIDENCE.T returns 8.256. I add this value to 60 to calculate the upper confidence limit (68.256), and subtract this value from 60 to calculate the lower confidence limit (51.744).

Chapter 10

One-Sample Hypothesis Testing

Whatever your occupation, you often have to assess whether something out of the ordinary has happened. Sometimes you start with a sample from a population about whose parameters you know a great deal. You have to decide whether that sample is like the rest of the population or whether it's different.

Measure that sample and calculate its statistics. Finally, compare those statistics with the population parameters. Are they the same? Are they different? Does the sample represent something that's off the beaten path? Proper use of statistics helps you decide.

Sometimes you don't know the parameters of the population you're dealing with. Then what? In this chapter, I discuss statistical techniques and worksheet functions for dealing with both cases.

Hypotheses, Tests, and Errors

A *hypothesis* is a guess about the way the world works. It's a tentative explanation of some process, whether that process is natural or artificial. Before studying and measuring the individuals in a sample, a researcher formulates hypotheses that predict what the data should look like.

Generally, one hypothesis predicts that the data won't show anything new or interesting. Dubbed the *null hypothesis* (abbreviated H0), this hypothesis holds that if the data deviate from the norm in any way, that deviation is due strictly to chance. Another hypothesis, the *alternative hypothesis* (abbreviated H_1), explains things differently. According to the alternative hypothesis, the data show something important.

After gathering the data, it's up to the researcher to make a decision. The way the logic works, the decision centers around the null hypothesis. The researcher must decide to either reject the null hypothesis or to not reject the null hypothesis. *Hypothesis testing* is the process of formulating hypotheses, gathering data, and deciding whether to reject or not reject the null hypothesis.

REMEMBER

Nothing in the logic involves *accepting* either hypothesis. Nor does the logic entail any decisions about the alternative hypothesis. It's all about rejecting or not rejecting H_0.

Regardless of the reject-don't-reject decision, an error is possible. One type of error occurs when you believe that the data show something important and you reject H_0, and in reality the data are due just to chance. This is called a *Type I* error. At the outset of a study, you set the criteria for rejecting H_0. In so doing, you set the probability of a Type I error. This probability is called *alpha* (α).

The other type of error occurs when you don't reject H_0 and the data are really due to something out of the ordinary. For one reason or another, you happened to miss it. This is called a *Type II* error. Its probability is called *beta* (β). Table 10-1 summarizes the possible decisions and errors.

TABLE 10-1   ## Decisions and Errors in Hypothesis Testing

		"True State" of the World	
		H_0 is True	H_1 is True
	Reject H_0	Type I Error	Correct Decision
Decision			
	Do Not Reject H_0	Correct Decision	Type II Error

Note that you never know the true state of the world. All you can ever do is measure the individuals in a sample, calculate the statistics, and make a decision about H_0.

Hypothesis Tests and Sampling Distributions

In Chapter 9, I discuss sampling distributions. A sampling distribution, remember, is the set of all possible values of a statistic for a given sample size.

Also in Chapter 9, I discuss the Central Limit Theorem. This theorem tells you that the sampling distribution of the mean approximates a normal distribution if the sample size is large (for practical purposes, at least 30). This holds whether or not the population is normally distributed. If the population is a normal distribution, the sampling distribution is normal for any sample size. Two other points from the Central Limit Theorem:

>> The mean of the sampling distribution of the mean is equal to the population mean.

The equation for this is

$$\mu_{\bar{x}} = \mu$$

>> The standard error of the mean (the standard deviation of the sampling distribution) is equal to the population standard deviation divided by the square root of the sample size.

This equation is

$$\sigma_{\bar{x}} = \sigma \big/ \sqrt{N}$$

The sampling distribution of the mean figures prominently into the type of hypothesis testing I discuss in this chapter. Theoretically, when you test a null hypothesis versus an alternative hypothesis, each hypothesis corresponds to a separate sampling distribution.

Figure 10-1 shows what I mean. The figure shows two normal distributions. I placed them arbitrarily. Each normal distribution represents a sampling distribution of the mean. The one on the left represents the distribution of possible sample means if the null hypothesis is truly how the world works. The one on the right represents the distribution of possible sample means if the alternative hypothesis is truly how the world works.

Of course, when you do a hypothesis test, you never know which distribution produces the results. You work with a sample mean — a point on the horizontal axis. It's your job to decide which distribution the sample mean is part of. You set up a *critical value* — a decision criterion. If the sample mean is on one side of the critical value, you reject H_0. If not, you don't.

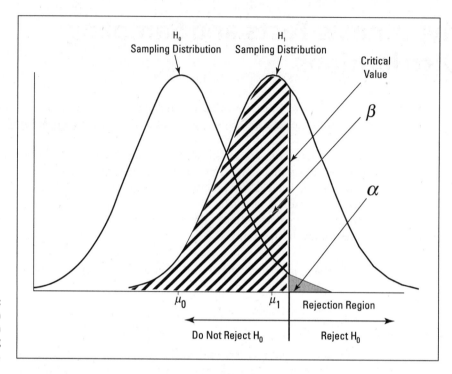

FIGURE 10-1:
H_0 and H_1 each
correspond to a
sampling
distribution.

In this vein, the figure also shows α and β. These, as I mention earlier, are the probabilities of decision errors. The area that corresponds to α is in the H_0 distribution. I shaded it in dark gray. It represents the probability that a sample mean comes from the H_0 distribution, but it's so extreme that you reject H_0.

REMEMBER

Where you set the critical value determines α. In most hypotheses testing, you set α at .05. This means that you're willing to tolerate a Type I error (incorrectly rejecting H_0) 5 percent of the time. Graphically, the critical value cuts off 5 percent of the area of the sampling distribution. By the way, if you're talking about the 5 percent of the area that's in the right tail of the distribution (refer to Figure 10-1), you're talking about the upper 5 percent. If it's the 5 percent in the left tail you're interested in, that's the lower 5 percent.

The area that corresponds to β is in the H_1 distribution. I shaded it in light gray. This area represents the probability that a sample mean comes from the H_1 distribution, but it's close enough to the center of the H_0 distribution that you don't reject H_0. You don't get to set β. The size of this area depends on the separation between the means of the two distributions, and that's up to the world we live in — not up to you.

These sampling distributions are appropriate when your work corresponds to the conditions of the Central Limit Theorem: if you know the population you're working with is a normal distribution or if you have a large sample.

Catching Some Z's Again

Here's an example of a hypothesis test that involves a sample from a normally distributed population. Because the population is normally distributed, any sample size results in a normally distributed sampling distribution. Because it's a normal distribution, you use z-scores in the hypothesis test:

$$z = \frac{\bar{x} - \mu}{\sigma / \sqrt{N}}$$

One more "because": Because you use the z-score in the hypothesis test, the z-score here is called the *test statistic.*

Suppose you think that people living in a particular ZIP code have higher-than-average IQs. You take a sample of 16 people from that ZIP code, give them IQ tests, tabulate the results, and calculate the statistics. For the population of IQ scores, $\mu = 100$ and $\sigma = 16$ (for the Stanford–Binet version).

The hypotheses are

$H_0: \mu_{ZIP\ code} \leq 100$

$H_1: \mu_{ZIP\ code} > 100$

Assume $\sigma = .05$. That's the shaded area in the tail of the H_0 distribution in Figure 10-1.

Why the $\leq$ in H_0? You use that symbol because you'll only reject H_0 if the sample mean is larger than the hypothesized value. Anything else is evidence in favor of not rejecting H_0.

Suppose the sample mean is 107.75. Can you reject H_0?

The test involves turning 107.75 into a standard score in the sampling distribution of the mean:

$$z = \frac{\bar{x} - \mu}{\sigma / \sqrt{N}} = \frac{107.75 - 100}{\left(16 / \sqrt{16}\right)} = \frac{7.75}{\left(16 / 4\right)} = \frac{7.75}{4} = 1.94$$

Is the value of the test statistic large enough to enable you to reject H_0 with $\alpha = .05$? It is. The critical value — the value of z that cuts off 5 percent of the area in a standard normal distribution — is 1.645. (After years of working with the standard normal distribution, I happen to know this. Read Chapter 8, find out about Excel's NORM.S.INV function, and you can have information like that at your fingertips, too.) The calculated value, 1.94, exceeds 1.645, so it's in the rejection region. The decision is to reject H_0.

This means that if H_0 is true, the probability of getting a test statistic value that's at least this large is less than .05. That's strong evidence in favor of rejecting H_0. In statistical parlance, any time you reject H_0 the result is said to be "statistically significant."

This type of hypothesis testing is called *one-tailed* because the rejection region is in one tail of the sampling distribution.

A hypothesis test can be one-tailed in the other direction. Suppose you have reason to believe that people in that ZIP code had lower-than-average IQs. In that case, the hypotheses are

$H_0: \mu_{\text{ZIP code}} \geq 100$

$H_1: \mu_{\text{ZIP code}} < 100$

For this hypothesis test, the critical value of the test statistic is -1.645 if $\alpha = .05$.

A hypothesis test can be *two-tailed*, meaning that the rejection region is in both tails of the H_0 sampling distribution. That happens when the hypotheses look like this:

$H_0: \mu_{\text{ZIP code}} = 100$

$H_1: \mu_{\text{ZIP code}} \neq 100$

In this case, the alternative hypothesis just specifies that the mean is different from the null-hypothesis value, without saying whether it's greater or whether it's less. Figure 10-2 shows what the two-tailed rejection region looks like for $\alpha = .05$. The 5 percent is divided evenly between the left tail (also called the lower tail) and the right tail (the upper tail).

For a standard normal distribution, incidentally, the z-score that cuts off 2.5 percent in the right tail is 1.96. The z-score that cuts off 2.5 percent in the left tail is -1.96. (Again, I happen to know these values after years of working with the standard normal distribution.) The z-score in the preceding example, 1.94, does not exceed 1.96. The decision, in the two-tailed case, is to *not* reject H_0.

TIP

This brings up an important point: A one-tailed hypothesis test can reject H_0, while a two-tailed test on the same data might not. A two-tailed test indicates that you're looking for a difference between the sample mean and the null-hypothesis mean, but you don't know in which direction. A one-tailed test shows that you have a pretty good idea of how the difference should come out. For prac-tical purposes, this means you should try to have enough knowledge to be able to specify a one-tailed test.

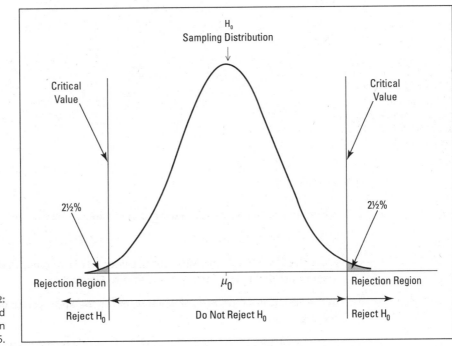

FIGURE 10-2:
The two-tailed rejection region for α = .05.

Z.TEST

Excel's Z.TEST worksheet function does the calculations for hypothesis tests involving z-scores in a standard normal distribution. You provide sample data, a null-hypothesis value, and a population standard deviation. Z.TEST returns the probability in one tail of the H_0 sampling distribution.

This is a bit different from the way things work when you apply the formulas I just showed you. The formula calculates a z-score. Then it's up to you to see where that score stands in a standard normal distribution with respect to probability. Z.TEST eliminates the middleman (the need to calculate the z-score) and goes right to the probability.

Figure 10-3 shows the data and the Function Arguments dialog box for Z.TEST. The data are IQ scores for 16 people in the ZIP code example in the preceding sec-tion. That example, remember, tests the hypothesis that people in a particular ZIP code have a higher-than-average IQ.

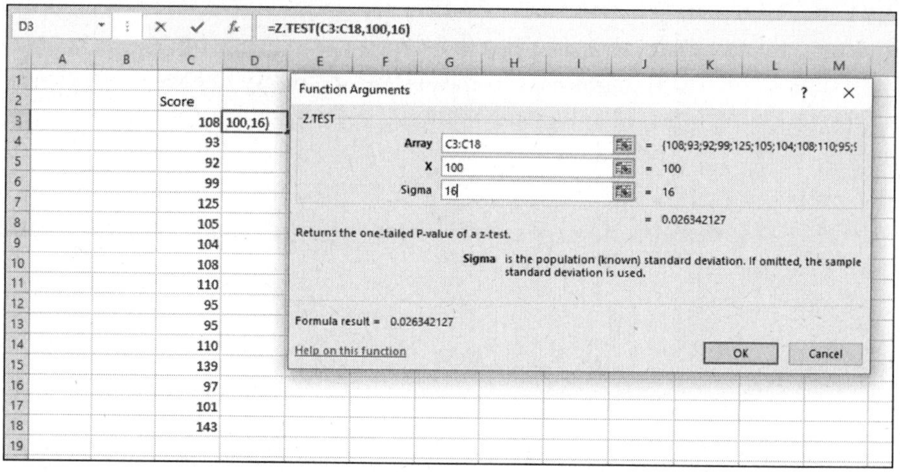

FIGURE 10-3:
Data and the
Function
Arguments dialog
box for Z . TEST.

Here are the steps:

1. **Enter your data into an array of cells and select a cell for the result.**

   The data in this example are in cells C3 through C18. I selected D3 for the result.

2. **From the Statistical Functions menu, select Z.TEST to open the Function Arguments dialog box for Z . TEST. (Refer to Figure 10-3.)**

3. **In the Function Arguments dialog box, enter the appropriate values for the arguments.**

   For this example, the Array is C3:C18. In the X box, I type the mean. That's 100, the mean of IQ scores in the population. In the Sigma box, I type 16, the population standard deviation of IQ scores. The answer (0.026342) appears in the dialog box.

4. **Click OK to put the answer into the selected cell.**

With $\alpha = .05$ and a one-tailed test ($H_1: \mu > 100$), the decision is to reject H_0, because the answer (0.026) is less than .05. Note that with a two-tailed test ($H_1: \mu \neq 100$), the decision is to not reject H_0. That's because 2×0.026 is greater than .05 — just barely greater (.052) — but if you draw the line at .05, you cannot reject H_0.

t for One

In the preceding example, I work with IQ scores. The population of IQ scores is a normal distribution with a well-known mean and standard deviation. This enables me to work with the Central Limit Theorem and describe the sampling distribution of the mean as a normal distribution. I then am able to use z as the test statistic.

In the real world, however, you typically don't have the luxury of working with such well-defined populations. You usually have small samples, and you're typically measuring something that isn't as well known as IQ. The bottom line is that you often don't know the population parameters, nor do you know whether or not the population is normally distributed.

When that's the case, you use the sample data to estimate the population standard deviation, and you treat the sampling distribution of the mean as a member of a family of distributions called the *t*-distribution. You use t as a test statistic. In Chapter 9, I introduce this distribution, and mention that you distinguish members of this family by a parameter called *degrees of freedom* (df).

The formula for the test statistic is

$$t = \frac{\bar{x} - \mu}{s / \sqrt{N}}$$

Think of df as the denominator of the estimate of the population variance. For the hypothesis tests in this section, that's $N-1$, where N is the number of scores in the sample. The higher the df, the more closely the *t*-distribution resembles the normal distribution.

Here's an example. FarKlempt Robotics, Inc., markets microrobots. They claim their product averages four defects per unit. A consumer group believes this average is higher. The consumer group takes a sample of nine FarKlempt microrobots and finds an average of seven defects, with a standard deviation of 3.16. The hypothesis test is

$H_0: \mu \leq 4$

$H_1: \mu > 4$

$\alpha = .05$

The formula is

$$t = \frac{\bar{x} - \mu}{s / \sqrt{N}} = \frac{7 - 4}{\left(3.16 / \sqrt{9}\right)} = \frac{3}{\left(3.16 / 3\right)} = 2.85$$

Can you reject H_0? The Excel function in the next section tells you.

T.DIST, T.DIST.RT, and T.DIST.2T

The T.DIST family of worksheet functions indicates whether or not your calcu-lated t value is in the region of rejection. With T.DIST, you supply a value for t, a value for df, and a value for an argument called Cumulative. The T.DIST returns the probability of obtaining a t value at least as high as yours if H_0 is true. If that probability is less than your α, you reject H_0.

The steps are:

1. **Select a cell to store the result.**

2. **From the Statistical Functions menu, select T.DIST to open the Function Arguments dialog box for** T.DIST. **(See Figure 10-4.)**

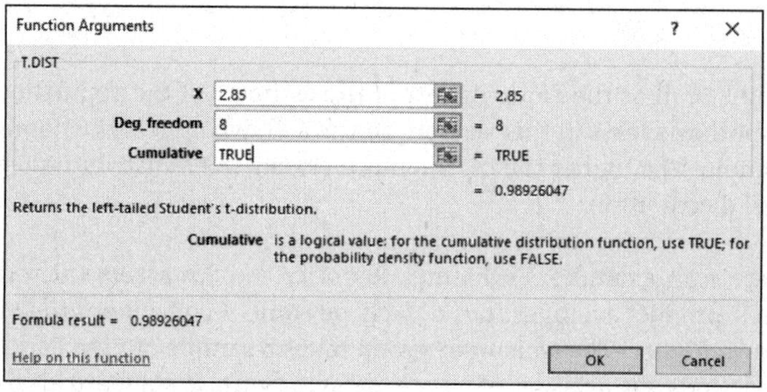

FIGURE 10-4:
The Function Arguments dialog box for T.DIST.

3. **In the Function Arguments dialog box, enter the appropriate values for the arguments.**

The calculated t value goes in the X box. For this example, the calculated t value is 2.85.

Enter the degrees of freedom in the Deg_freedom box. For this example, that value is 8 (9 scores – 1).

The Cumulative box takes either TRUE or FALSE. I type TRUE in this box to give the probability of getting a value of X or less in the t-distribution with the indicated degrees of freedom. Excel refers to this as the *left-tailed* distribution. Entering FALSE gives the height of the t-distribution at X. I use this option later in this chapter, when I create a chart of a t-distribution. Otherwise, I don't know why you would ever type FALSE into this box.

After I type TRUE, the answer (.98926047) appears in the dialog box.

4. **Click OK to close the dialog box and put the answer in the selected cell.**

The value in the dialog box in Figure 10-4 is greater than .95, so the decision is to reject H_0.

You might find T.DIST.RT to be a bit more straightforward, at least for this example. Its Function Arguments dialog box is just like the one in Figure 10-4, but without the Cumulative box. This function returns the probability of getting a value of X or greater in the t-distribution. RT in the function name stands for *right tail*. For this example, the function returns .01073953. Because this value is less than .05, the decision is to reject H_0.

T.DIST.2T gives the two-tailed probability. Its Function Arguments dialog box *is* just like the one for T.DIST.RT. It returns the probability to the right of X in the t-distribution plus the probability to the left of −X in the distribution.

T.INV and T.INV.2T

The T.INV family is the flip side of the T.DIST family. Give T.INV a probability and degrees of freedom, and it returns the value of t that cuts off that probability to its left. To use T.INV:

1. **Select a cell to store the result.**

2. **From the Statistical Functions menu, select T.INV to open the Function Arguments dialog box for T.INV. (See Figure 10-5.)**

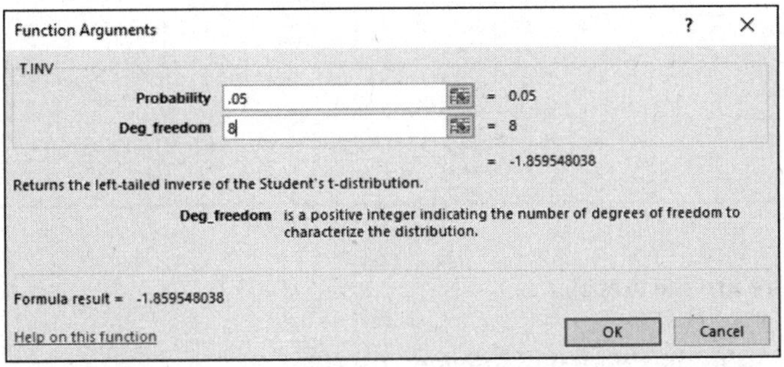

FIGURE 10-5:
The T.INV
Function
Arguments
dialog box.

3. **In the Function Arguments dialog box, enter the appropriate values for the arguments.**

I typed **.05** into the Probability box and **8** into the Deg_freedom box. The answer (−1.859548038) appears in the dialog box.

4. **Click OK to close the dialog box and put the answer in the selected cell.**

T.INV.2T has an identical Function Arguments dialog box. Given Probability and Deg_freedom, this function cuts the probability in half. It returns the value of *t* in the right tail that cuts off half the probability. What about the other half? That would be the same numerical value multiplied by –1. That negative value of *t* cuts off the other half of the probability in the left tail of the distribution.

Visualizing a t-Distribution

As I mention in Chapter 8, visualizing a distribution often helps you understand it. It's easy, and it's instructive. Figure 10-6 shows how to do it for a *t*-distribution. The function you use is T.DIST, with the FALSE option in the Cumulative box.

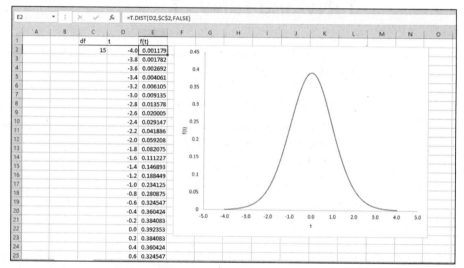

FIGURE 10-6:
Visualizing a
t-distribution.

Here are the steps:

1. **Put the degrees of freedom in a cell.**

   I put 15 into cell C2.

2. **Create a column of values for the statistic.**

   In cells D2 through D42, I put the values –4 to 4 in increments of .2.

3. **In the first cell of the adjoining column, put the value of the probability density for the first value of the statistic.**

   Because I'm graphing a *t*-distribution, I use T.DIST in cell E2. For the value of X, I click cell D2. For df, I click C2 and press the F4 key to anchor this selection. In the Cumulative box, I type FALSE to return the height of the distribution for this value of t. Then I click OK.

4. **Autofill the column with the values.**

5. **Create the chart.**

   Highlight both columns. On the Insert tab, in the Charts area, select Scatter with Smooth Lines.

6. **Modify the chart.**

   The chart appears with the *y*-axis down the middle. Click on the *x*-axis to open the Format Axis panel. Under Axis Options, in the Vertical Axis Crosses area, click the radio button next to Axis Value and type **-5** into the box. You can then click inside the chart to make the Chart Elements tool (the plus sign) appear and use it to add the axis titles (t and f(t)). I also delete the chart title and the gridlines, but that's a matter of personal taste. And I like to stretch out the chart.

7. **Manipulate the chart.**

   To help you get a feel for the distribution, try different values for df and see how the changes affect the chart.

Testing a Variance

So far, I mention one-sample hypothesis testing for means. You can also test hypotheses about variances.

This topic sometimes comes up in the context of manufacturing. Suppose Far-Klempt Robotics, Inc., produces a part that has to be a certain length with a very small variability. You can take a sample of parts, measure them, find the sample variability, and perform a hypothesis test against the desired variability.

The family of distributions for the test is called *chi-square*. Its symbol is χ^2. I won't go into all the mathematics. I'll just tell you that, once again, df is the parameter that distinguishes one member of the family from another. Figure 10-7 shows two members of the chi-square family.

The formula for this test statistic is

$$\chi^2 = \frac{(N-1)s^2}{\sigma^2}$$

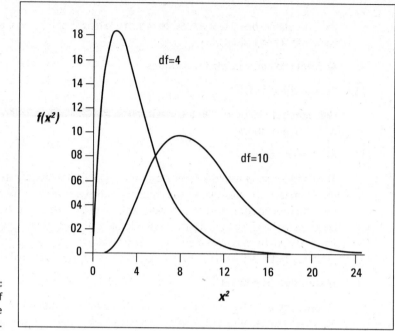

FIGURE 10-7:
Two members of
the chi-square
family.

N is the number of scores in the sample, s^2 is the sample variance, and σ^2 is the population variance specified in H_0.

With this test, you have to assume that what you're measuring has a normal distribution.

Suppose the process for the FarKlempt part has to have at most a standard deviation of 1.5 inches for its length. (Notice I use *standard deviation*. This allows me to speak in terms of inches. If I use *variance*, the units would be square inches.) After measuring a sample of 26 parts, you find a standard deviation of 1.8 inches.

The hypotheses are

H_0: $\sigma^2 \leq 2.25$ (remember to square the "at-most" standard deviation of 1.5 inches)

H_1: $\sigma^2 > 2.25$

$\alpha = .05$

Working with the formula,

$$\chi^2 = \frac{(N-1)s^2}{\sigma^2} = \frac{(26-1)(1.8)^2}{(1.5)^2} = \frac{(25)(3.24)}{2.25} = 36$$

can you reject H_0? Read on.

CHISQ.DIST and CHISQ.DIST.RT

After calculating a value for your chi-square test statistic, you use the `CHSQ.DIST` worksheet function to make a judgment about it. You supply the chi-square value and the df. Just like in `T.DIST`, you supply either `TRUE` or `FALSE` for Cumulative. If you type `TRUE`, `CHISQ.DIST` tells you the probability of obtaining a value at most that high if H_0 is true. (This is the left-tail probability.) If that probability is greater than $1-\alpha$, reject H_0.

To show you how it works, I apply the information from the example in the preceding section. Follow these steps:

1. **Select a cell to store the result.**

2. **From the Statistical Functions menu, select CHISQ.DIST to open the Function Arguments dialog box for `CHISQ.DIST`. (See Figure 10-8.)**

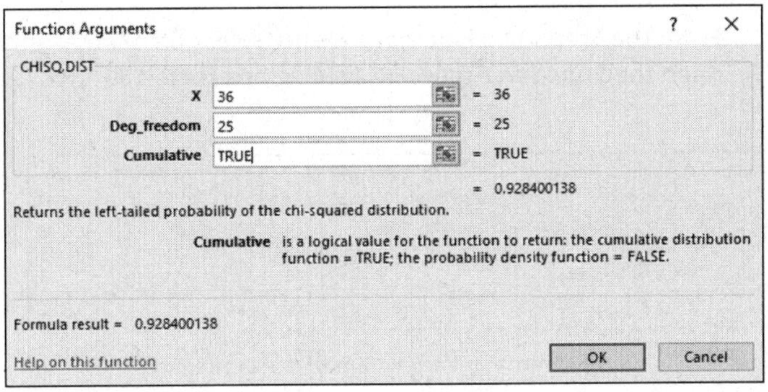

FIGURE 10-8: The Function Arguments dialog box for `CHISQ.DIST`.

3. **In the Function Arguments dialog box, type the appropriate values for the arguments.**

In the X box, I typed the calculated chi-square value. For this example, that value is 36.

In the Deg_freedom box, I typed the degrees of freedom. For this example, that's 25 (26 – 1).

In the Cumulative box, I typed `TRUE`. This returns the left-tailed probability — the probability of obtaining at most the value I typed in the X box. If I type `FALSE`, CHISQ.DIST returns the height of the chi-square distribution at X. This is helpful if you're graphing out the chi-square distribution, which I do later in this chapter, but otherwise not so much.

After you type `TRUE`, the dialog box shows the probability of obtaining at most this value of chi-square if H_0 is true.

4. **Click OK to close the dialog box and put the answer in the selected cell.**

The value in the dialog box in Figure 10-8 is greater than 1-.05, so the decision is to not reject H_0. (Can you conclude that the process is within acceptable limits of variability? See the nearby sidebar "A point to ponder.")

`CHISQ.DIST.2T` works like `CHISQ.DIST`, except its Function Arguments dialog box has no Cumulative box. Supply a value for chi-square and degrees of freedom, and it returns the right-tail probability — the probability of obtaining a chi-square at least as high as the value you type into X.

CHISQ.INV and CHISQ.INV.RT

The `CHISQ.INV` family is the flip side of the `CHISQ.DIST` family. You supply a probability and df, and `CHISQ.INV` tells you the value of chi-square that cuts off the probability in the left tail of the chi-square distribution. Follow these steps:

1. **Select a cell to store the result.**

2. **From the Statistical Functions menu, select CHISQ.INV and click OK to open the Function Arguments dialog box for** `CHISQ.INV`. **(See Figure 10-9.)**

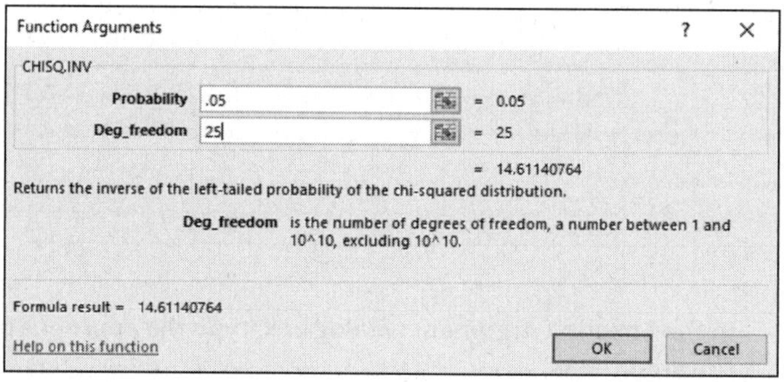

FIGURE 10-9:
The Function Arguments dialog box for `CHISQ.INV`.

3. **In the Function Arguments dialog box, enter the appropriate values for the arguments.**

   In the Probability box, I typed .05, the probability I'm interested in for this example.

   In the Deg_freedom box, I typed the degrees of freedom. The value for degrees of freedom in this example is 25 (26 – 1). After I type the df, the dialog box shows the value (14.61140764) that cuts off the lower 5 percent of the area in this chi-square distribution.

4. **Click OK to close the dialog box and put the answer in the selected cell.**

A POINT TO PONDER

Retrace the preceding example. FarKlempt Robotics wants to show that its manufacturing process is within acceptable limits of variability. The null hypothesis says, in effect, that the process is acceptable. The data do not present evidence for rejecting H_0. The value of the test statistic just misses the critical value. Does that mean the manufacturing process is within acceptable limits? Statistics are an aid to common sense, not a substitute. If the data are just barely within acceptability, that should set off alarms.

Usually, you try to reject H_0. This is a rare case when not rejecting H_0 is more desirable, because nonrejection implies something positive — the manufacturing process is working properly. Can you still use hypothesis testing techniques in this situation?

Yes, you can — with a notable change: Rather than a small value of α, like .05, you choose a large value, like .20. This stacks the deck *against* not rejecting H_0 — small values of the test statistic can lead to rejection. If α is .20 in this example, the critical value is 30.6752. (Use CHISQ.INV.RT to verify that.) Because the obtained value, 36, is higher than this critical value, the decision with this α is to reject H_0.

Using a high α is not often done. When the desired outcome is to *not* reject H_0, I strongly advise using it.

The CHISQ.INV.RT Function Arguments dialog box is identical to the CHISQ.INV dialog box. The RT version returns the chi-square value that cuts off the right-tail probability. This is useful if you want to know the value that you have to exceed in order to reject H_0. For this example, I typed .05 and 25 as the arguments to this function. The returned answer was 37.65248413. The calculated value, 36, didn't miss by much. A miss is still a miss (to paraphrase "As Time Goes By") and you cannot reject H_0.

Visualizing a Chi-Square Distribution

To help you understand chi-square distributions, I show you how to create a chart for one. The function you use is CHISQ.DIST, with the FALSE option in the Cumulative box. Figure 10-10 shows what the numbers and the finished product look like.

Here are the steps:

1. **Put the degrees of freedom in a cell.**

   I put 8 into cell C2.

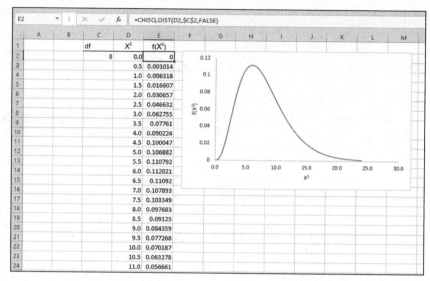

FIGURE 10-10:
Visualizing a
chi-square
distribution.

2. **Create a column of values for the statistic.**

In cells D2 through D50, I put the values 0 to 24 in increments of .5

3. **In the first cell of the adjoining column, put the value of the probability density for the first value of the statistic.**

Because I'm graphing a chi-square distribution, I use CHISQ.DIST in cell E2. For the value of X, I clicked cell D2. For df, I click C2 and press the F4 key to anchor this selection. In the Cumulative box, I type FALSE to return the height of the distribution for this value of χ^2. Then I click OK.

4. **Autofill the column with the values.**

5. **Create the chart.**

Highlight both columns. On the Insert tab, in the Charts area, select Scatter with Smooth Lines.

6. **Modify the chart.**

I click inside the chart to make the Chart Elements Tool (the plus sign) appear and use it to add the axis titles (χ^2 and $f(\chi^2)$). I delete the chart title and the gridlines, but that's a matter of personal taste. I also like to stretch the chart out.

7. **Manipulate the chart.**

To help you get a feel for the distribution, try different values for df, and see how the changes affect the chart.

Chapter 11

Two-Sample Hypothesis Testing

I n business, in education, and in scientific research, the need often arises to compare one sample with another. Sometimes the samples are independent, and sometimes they're matched in some way. Each sample comes from a separate population. The objective is to decide whether or not these populations are different from one another.

Usually, this involves tests of hypotheses about population means. You can also test hypotheses about population variances. In this chapter, I show you how to carry out these tests. I also discuss useful worksheet functions and data analysis tools that help you get the job done.

Hypotheses Built for Two

As in the one-sample case (refer to Chapter 10), hypothesis testing with two samples starts with a null hypothesis (H_0) and an alternative hypothesis (H_1). The null hypothesis specifies that any differences you see between the two samples are due strictly to chance. The alternative hypothesis says, in effect, that any differences you see are real and not due to chance.

It's possible to have a *one-tailed test,* in which the alternative hypothesis specifies the direction of the difference between the two means, or a *two-tailed test,* in which the alternative hypothesis does not specify the direction of the difference.

For a one-tailed test, the hypotheses look like this:

$H_0: \mu_1 - \mu_2 = 0$

$H_1: \mu_1 - \mu_2 > 0$

or like this:

$H_0: \mu_1 - \mu_2 = 0$

$H_1: \mu_1 - \mu_2 < 0$

For a two-tailed test, the hypotheses are

$H_0: \mu_1 - \mu_2 = 0$

$H_1: \mu_1 - \mu_2 \neq 0$

The zero in these hypotheses is the typical case. It's possible, however, to test for any value — just substitute that value for zero.

To carry out the test, you first set α, the probability of a Type I error that you're willing to live with (see Chapter 10). Then you calculate the mean and standard deviation of each sample, subtract one mean from the other, and use a formula to convert the result into a test statistic. Next, compare the test statistic to a sampling distribution of test statistics. If it's in the rejection region that α specifies (see Chapter 10), reject H_0. If not, don't reject H_0.

Revisited

In Chapter 9, I introduce the idea of a sampling distribution — a distribution of all possible values of a statistic for a particular sample size. In that chapter, I describe the sampling distribution of the mean. In Chapter 10, I show its connection with one-sample hypothesis testing.

For two-sample hypothesis testing, another sampling distribution is necessary. This one is *the sampling distribution of the difference between means.*

The sampling distribution of the difference between means is the distribution of all possible values of differences between pairs of sample means with the sample sizes held constant from pair to pair. (Yes, that's a mouthful.) *Held constant from pair to pair* means that the first sample in the pair always has the same size, and the second sample in the pair always has the same size. The two sample sizes are not necessarily equal.

Within each pair, each sample comes from a different population. All the samples are independent of one another, so that picking individuals for one sample has no effect on picking individuals for another.

Figure 11-1 shows the steps in creating this sampling distribution. This is something you never do in practice. It's all theoretical. As the figure shows, the idea is to take a sample out of one population and a sample out of another, calculate their means, and subtract one mean from the other. Return the samples to the populations, and repeat over and over and over. The result of the process is a set of differences between means. This set of differences is the sampling distribution.

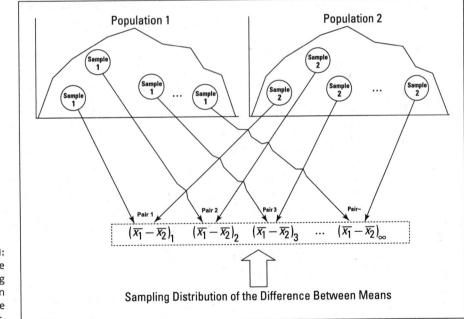

FIGURE 11-1:
Creating the sampling distribution of the difference between means.

Applying the Central Limit Theorem

Like any other set of numbers, this sampling distribution has a mean and a standard deviation. As is the case with the sampling distribution of the mean (see Chapters 9 and 10), the Central Limit Theorem applies here.

According to the Central Limit Theorem, if the samples are large, the sampling distribution of the difference between means is approximately a normal distribution. If the populations are normally distributed, the sampling distribution is a normal distribution even if the samples are small.

The Central Limit Theorem also has something to say about the mean and standard deviation of this sampling distribution. Suppose the parameters for the first population are μ_1 and σ_1, and the parameters for the second population are μ_2 and σ_2. The mean of the sampling distribution is

$$\mu_{\bar{x}_1 - \bar{x}_2} = \mu_1 - \mu_2$$

The standard deviation of the sampling distribution is

$$\sigma_{\bar{x}_1 - \bar{x}_2} = \sqrt{\frac{\sigma_1^2}{N_1} + \frac{\sigma_2^2}{N_2}}$$

N_1 is the number of individuals in the sample from the first population, and N_2 is the number of individuals in the sample from the second.

This standard deviation is called *the standard error of the difference between means.*

Figure 11-2 shows the sampling distribution along with its parameters, as specified by the Central Limit Theorem.

Z's once more

Because the Central Limit Theorem says that the sampling distribution is approximately normal for large samples (or for small samples from normally distributed populations), you use the z-score as your test statistic. Another way to say "Use the z-score as your test statistic" is "Perform a z-test." Here's the formula:

$$z = \frac{(\bar{x}_1 - \bar{x}_2) - (\mu_1 - \mu_2)}{\sigma_{\bar{x}_1 - \bar{x}_2}}$$

The term $(\mu_1 - \mu_2)$ represents the difference between the means in H_0.

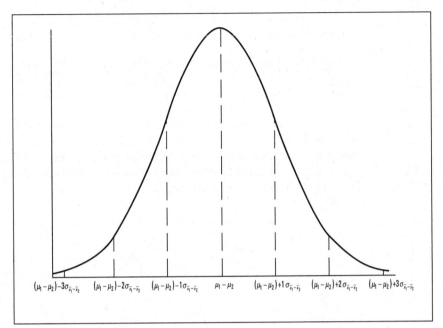

FIGURE 11-2:
The sampling
distribution of the
difference
between means
according to the
Central Limit
Theorem.

$$(\mu_1-\mu_2)-3\sigma_{\bar{x}_1-\bar{x}_2} \quad (\mu_1-\mu_2)-2\sigma_{\bar{x}_1-\bar{x}_2} \quad (\mu_1-\mu_2)-1\sigma_{\bar{x}_1-\bar{x}_2} \quad \mu_1-\mu_2 \quad (\mu_1-\mu_2)+1\sigma_{\bar{x}_1-\bar{x}_2} \quad (\mu_1-\mu_2)+2\sigma_{\bar{x}_1-\bar{x}_2} \quad (\mu_1-\mu_2)+3\sigma_{\bar{x}_1-\bar{x}_2}$$

This formula converts the difference between sample means into a standard score. Compare the standard score against a standard normal distribution — a normal distribution with $\mu = 0$ and $\sigma = 1$. If the score is in the rejection region defined by α, reject H_0. If it's not, don't reject H_0.

You use this formula when you know the value of σ_1^2 and σ_2^2.

Here's an example. Imagine a new training technique designed to increase IQ. Take a sample of 25 people and train them under the new technique. Take another sample of 25 people and give them no special training. Suppose that the sample mean for the new technique sample is 107, and for the no-training sample it's 101.2. The hypothesis test is

$H_0: \mu_1 - \mu_2 = 0$

$H_1: \mu_1 - \mu_2 > 0$

I'll set α at .05.

The IQ is known to have a standard deviation of 16, and I assume that standard deviation would be the same in the population of people trained on the new technique. Of course, that population doesn't exist. The assumption is that if it did, it should have the same value for the standard deviation as the regular population of IQ scores. Does the mean of that (theoretical) population have the same value as the regular population? H_0 says it does. H_1 says it's larger.

The test statistic is

$$z = \frac{(\bar{x}_1 - \bar{x}_2) - (\mu_1 - \mu_2)}{\sigma_{\bar{x}_1 - \bar{x}_2}} = \frac{(\bar{x}_1 - \bar{x}_2) - (\mu_1 - \mu_2)}{\sqrt{\frac{\sigma_1^2}{N_1} + \frac{\sigma_2^2}{N_2}}} = \frac{(107 - 101.2)}{\sqrt{\frac{16^2}{25} + \frac{16^2}{25}}} = \frac{5.8}{4.53} = 1.28$$

With $\alpha = .05$, the critical value of z — the value that cuts off the upper 5 percent of the area under the standard normal distribution — is 1.645. (You can use the worksheet function NORM.S.INV from Chapter 8 to verify this.) The calculated value of the test statistic is less than the critical value, so the decision is to not reject H_0. Figure 11-3 summarizes this.

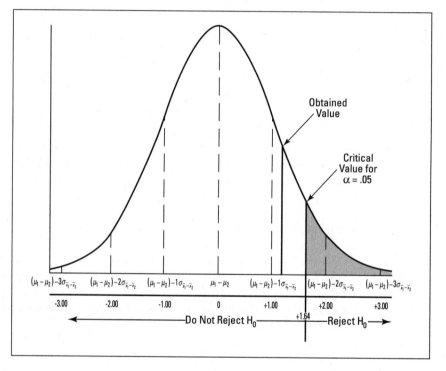

FIGURE 11-3:
The sampling
distribution
of the difference
between means,
along with the
critical value for
$\alpha = .05$ and the
obtained value of
the test statistic
in the IQ
example.

Data analysis tool: z-Test: Two Sample for Means

Excel provides a data analysis tool that makes it easy to do tests like the one in the IQ example. It's called z-Test: Two Sample for Means. Figure 11-4 shows the dialog box for this tool along with sample data that correspond to the IQ example.

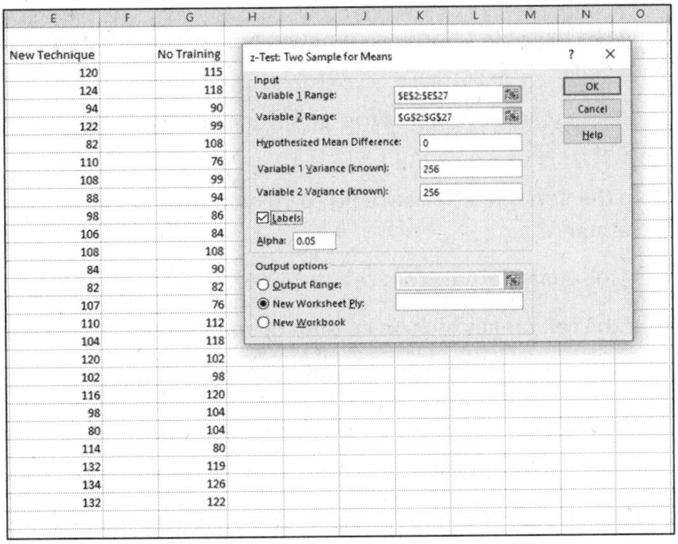

FIGURE 11-4:
The z-Test data analysis tool and data from two samples.

To use this tool, follow these steps:

1. **Type the data for each sample into a separate data array.**

   For this example, the data in the New Technique sample are in column E, and the data for the No Training sample are in column G.

2. **Select DATA | Data Analysis to open the Data Analysis dialog box.**

3. **In the Data Analysis dialog box, scroll down the Analysis Tools list and select z-Test: Two Sample for Means.**

4. **Click OK to open the z-Test: Two Sample for Means dialog box. (Refer to Figure 11-4.)**

5. **In the Variable 1 Range box, enter the cell range that holds the data for one of the samples.**

   For the example, the New Technique data are in $E$2:$E$27. (Note the $ signs for absolute referencing.)

6. **In the Variable 2 Range box, enter the cell range that holds the data for the other sample.**

   The No Training data are in $G$2:$G$27.

7. **In the Hypothesized Mean Difference box, type the difference between $\mu 1$ and $\mu 2$ that H_0 specifies.**

   In this example, that difference is 0.

8. **In the Variable 1 Variance (known) box, type the variance of the first sample.**

The standard deviation of the population of IQ scores is 16, so this variance is $16^2 = 256$.

9. **In the Variable 2 Variance (known) box, type the variance of the second sample.**

In this example, the variance is also 256.

10. **If the cell ranges include column headings, select the Labels check box.**

I included the headings in the ranges, so I selected the box.

11. **The Alpha box has 0.05 as a default.**

I used the default value, consistent with the value of α in this example.

12. **In the Output Options, select a radio button to indicate where you want the results.**

I selected New Worksheet Ply to put the results on a new page in the work-sheet.

13. **Click OK.**

Because I selected New Worksheet Ply, a newly created page opens with the results.

Figure 11-5 shows the tool's results, after I expanded the columns. Rows 4, 5, and 7 hold values you input into the dialog box. Row 6 counts the number of scores in each sample.

	A	B	C	D
1	z-Test: Two Sample for Means			
2				
3		New Technique	No Training	
4	Mean	107	101.2	
5	Known Variance	256	256	
6	Observations	25	25	
7	Hypothesized Mean Difference	0		
8	z	1.281631041		
9	P(Z<=z) one-tail	0.099986053		
10	z Critical one-tail	1.644853627		
11	P(Z<=z) two-tail	0.199972106		
12	z Critical two-tail	1.959963985		
13				

FIGURE 11-5:
Results of the
z-Test data
analysis tool.

The value of the test statistic is in cell B8. The critical value for a one-tailed test is in B10, and the critical value for a two-tailed test is in B12.

Cell B9 displays the proportion of area that the test statistic cuts off in one tail of the standard normal distribution. Cell B11 doubles that value — it's the proportion of area cut off by the positive value of the test statistic (in the tail on the right side of the distribution) plus the proportion cut off by the negative value of the test statistic (in the tail on the left side of the distribution).

t for Two

The example in the preceding section involves a situation you rarely encounter — known population variances. If you know a population's variance, you're likely to know the population mean. If you know the mean, you probably don't have to perform hypothesis tests about it.

Not knowing the variances takes the Central Limit Theorem out of play. This means that you can't use the normal distribution as an approximation of the sampling distribution of the difference between means. Instead, you use the t-distribution, a family of distributions I introduce in Chapter 9 and apply to one-sample hypothesis testing in Chapter 10. The members of this family of distributions differ from one another in terms of a parameter called *degrees of freedom* (df). Think of df as the denominator of the variance estimate you use when you calculate a value of t as a test statistic. Another way to say "Calculate a value of t as a test statistic" is "Perform a t-test."

Unknown population variances lead to two possibilities for hypothesis testing. One possibility is that although the variances are unknown, you have reason to assume they're equal. The other possibility is that you cannot assume they're equal. In the subsections that follow, I discuss these possibilities.

Like peas in a pod: Equal variances

When you don't know a population variance, you use the sample variance to estimate it. If you have two samples, you average (sort of) the two sample variances to arrive at the estimate.

REMEMBER

Putting sample variances together to estimate a population variance is called *pooling*. With two sample variances, here's how you do it:

$$s_p^{\ 2} = \frac{(N_1 - 1)s_1^2 + (N_2 - 1)s_2^2}{(N_1 - 1) + (N_2 - 1)}$$

In this formula, $s_p^{\ 2}$ stands for the pooled estimate. Notice that the denominator of this estimate is $(N_1 - 1) + (N_2 - 1)$. Is this the df? Absolutely!

The formula for calculating t is

$$t = \frac{(\bar{x}_1 - \bar{x}_2) - (\mu_1 - \mu_2)}{s_p\sqrt{\dfrac{1}{N_1} + \dfrac{1}{N_2}}}$$

On to an example. FarKlempt Robotics is trying to choose between two machines to produce a component for its new microrobot. Speed is of the essence, so the company has each machine produce ten copies of the component and they time each production run. The hypotheses are

$H_0: \mu_1 - \mu_2 = 0$

$H_1: \mu_1 - \mu_2 \neq 0$

They set α at .05. This is a two-tailed test because they don't know in advance which machine might be faster.

Table 11-1 presents the data for the production times in minutes.

TABLE 11-1 **Sample Statistics from the FarKlempt Machine Study**

	Machine 1	Machine 2
Mean Production Time	23.00	20.00
Standard Deviation	2.71	2.79
Sample Size	10	10

The pooled estimate of σ^2 is

$$s_p{}^2 = \frac{(N_1 - 1)s_1^2 + (N_2 - 1)s_2^2}{(N_1 - 1) + (N_2 - 1)} = \frac{(10-1)(2.71)^2 + (10-1)(2.79)^2}{(10-1) + (10-1)}$$

$$= \frac{(9)(2.71)^2 + (9)(2.79)^2}{(9) + (9)} = \frac{66 + 70}{18} = 7.56$$

The estimate of σ is 2.75, the square root of 7.56.

The test statistic is

$$t = \frac{(\bar{x}_1 - \bar{x}_2) - (\mu_1 - \mu_2)}{s_p\sqrt{\dfrac{1}{N_1} + \dfrac{1}{N_2}}} = \frac{(23 - 20)}{2.75\sqrt{\dfrac{1}{10} + \dfrac{1}{10}}} = \frac{3}{1.23} = 2.44$$

For this test statistic, df = 18, the denominator of the variance estimate. In a t-distribution with 18 df, the critical value is 2.10 for the right-side (upper) tail and −2.10 for the left-side (lower) tail. If you don't believe me, apply $\texttt{T.INV.2T}$ (see Chapter 10). The calculated value of the test statistic is greater than 2.10, so the decision is to reject H_0. The data provide evidence that Machine 2 is significantly faster than Machine 1. (You can use the word *significant* whenever you reject H_0.)

Like p's and q's: Unequal variances

The case of unequal variances presents a challenge. As it happens, when variances are not equal, the t-distribution with $(N_1-1) + (N_2-1)$ degrees of freedom is not as close an approximation to the sampling distribution as statisticians would like.

Statisticians meet this challenge by reducing the degrees of freedom. To accomplish the reduction, they use a fairly involved formula that depends on the sample standard deviations and the sample sizes.

Because the variances aren't equal, a pooled estimate is not appropriate. So you calculate the t-test in a different way:

$$t = \frac{(\bar{x}_1 - \bar{x}_2) - (\mu_1 - \mu_2)}{\sqrt{\dfrac{s_1^2}{N_1} + \dfrac{s_2^2}{N_2}}}$$

You evaluate the test statistic against a member of the t-distribution family that has the reduced degrees of freedom.

T.TEST

The worksheet function $\texttt{T.TEST}$ eliminates the muss, fuss, and bother of working through the formulas for the t-test.

Figure 11-6 shows the data for the FarKlempt machines example I show you earlier in the chapter. The figure also shows the Function Arguments dialog box for $\texttt{T.TEST}$.

Follow these steps:

1. **Type the data for each sample into a separate data array and select a cell for the result.**

   For this example, the data for the Machine 1 sample are in column B and the data for the Machine 2 sample are in column D.

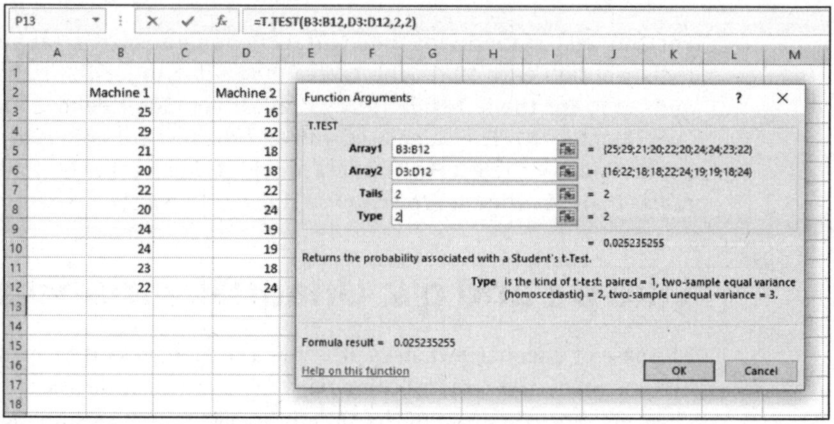

FIGURE 11-6:
Working with
T.TEST.

2. **From the Statistical Functions menu, select T.TEST to open the Function Arguments dialog box for T.TEST.**

3. **In the Function Arguments dialog box, enter the appropriate values for the arguments.**

   In the Array1 box, enter the sequence of cells that holds the data for one of the samples.

   In this example, the Machine 1 data are in B3:B12.

   In the Array2 box, enter the sequence of cells that holds the data for the other sample.

   The Machine 2 data are in D3:D12.

   The Tails box indicates whether this is a one-tailed test or a two-tailed test. In this example, it's a two-tailed test, so I typed 2 in this box.

   The Type box holds a number that indicates the type of t-test. The choices are 1 for a paired test (which you find out about in an upcoming section), 2 for two samples assuming equal variances, and 3 for two samples assuming unequal variances. I typed 2.

   With values supplied for all the arguments, the dialog box shows the probability associated with the t value for the data. It does not show the value of t.

4. **Click OK to put the answer in the selected cell.**

The value in the dialog box in Figure 11-6 is less than .05, so the decision is to reject H_0.

By the way, for this example, typing 3 into the Type box (indicating unequal variances) results in a very slight adjustment in the probability from the equal variance test. The adjustment is small because the sample variances are almost equal and the sample sizes are the same.

Data analysis tool: t-Test: Two Sample

Excel provides data analysis tools that carry out t-tests. One tool works for the equal variance cases, and another for the unequal variances case. As you'll see, when you use these tools, you end up with more information than T.TEST gives you.

Here's an example that applies the equal variances t-test tool to the data from the FarKlempt machines example. Figure 11-7 shows the data along with the dialog box for t-Test: Two-Sample Assuming Equal Variances.

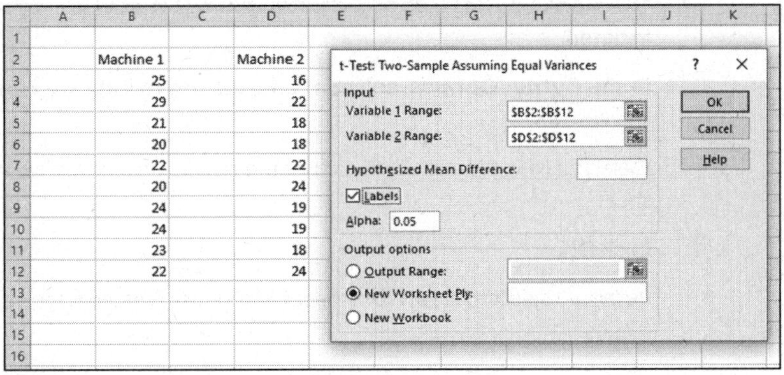

FIGURE 11-7: The equal variances t-Test data analysis tool and data from two samples.

To use this tool, follow these steps:

1. **Type the data for each sample into a separate data array.**

For this example, the data in the Machine 1 sample are in column B and the data for the Machine 2 sample are in column D.

2. **Select DATA | Data Analysis to open the Data Analysis dialog box.**

3. **In the Data Analysis dialog box, scroll down the Analysis Tools list and select t-Test: Two Sample Assuming Equal Variances.**

4. **Click OK to open this tool's dialog box.**

This is the dialog box in Figure 11-7.

5. **In the Variable 1 Range box, enter the cell range that holds the data for one of the samples.**

For the example, the Machine 1 data are in $B$2:$B$12, including the column heading. (Note the $ signs for absolute referencing.)

6. **In the Variable 2 Range box, enter the cell range that holds the data for the other sample.**

The Machine 2 data are in $D$2:$D$12, including the column heading.

7. **In the Hypothesized Mean Difference box, type the difference between μ1 and μ2 that H_0 specifies.**

In this example, that difference is 0.

8. **If the cell ranges include column headings, select the Labels check box.**

I included the headings in the ranges, so I selected the box.

9. **The Alpha box has 0.05 as a default. Change that value if you're so inclined.**

10. **In the Output Options, select a radio button to indicate where you want the results.**

I selected New Worksheet Ply to put the results on a new page in the worksheet.

11. **Click OK.**

Because I selected New Worksheet Ply, a newly created page opens with the results.

Figure 11-8 shows the tool's results, after I expanded the columns. Rows 4 through 7 hold sample statistics. Cell B8 shows the H_0-specified difference between the population means, and B9 shows the degrees of freedom.

	A	B	C
1	t-Test: Two-Sample Assuming Equal Variances		
2			
3		Machine 1	Machine 2
4	Mean	23	20
5	Variance	7.333333333	7.777777778
6	Observations	10	10
7	Pooled Variance	7.555555556	
8	Hypothesized Mean Difference	0	
9	df	18	
10	t Stat	2.44046765	
11	P(T<=t) one-tail	0.012617628	
12	t Critical one-tail	1.734063607	
13	P(T<=t) two-tail	0.025235255	
14	t Critical two-tail	2.10092204	
15			

FIGURE 11-8:
Results of the Equal Variances t-Test data analysis tool.

The remaining rows provide t-related information. The calculated value of the test statistic is in B10. Cell B11 gives the proportion of area that the positive value of the test statistic cuts off in the upper tail of the t-distribution with the indicated df. Cell B12 gives the critical value for a one-tailed test: That's the value that cuts off the proportion of the area in the upper tail equal to α.

Cell B13 doubles the proportion in B11. This cell holds the proportion of area from B11 added to the proportion of area that the negative value of the test statistic cuts off in the lower tail. Cell B14 shows the critical value for a two-tailed test: That's the positive value that cuts off $\alpha/2$ in the upper tail. The corresponding negative value (not shown) cuts off $\alpha/2$ in the lower tail.

The samples in the example have the same number of scores and approximately equal variances, so applying the unequal variances version of the t-Test tool to that data set won't show much of a difference from the equal variances case.

Instead I created another example, summarized in Table 11-2. The samples in this example have different sizes and widely differing variances.

TABLE 11-2   ## Sample Statistics for the Unequal Variances t-Test Example

	Sample 1	Sample 2
Mean	100.125	67.00
Variance	561.84	102.80
Sample Size	8	6

To show you the difference between the equal variances tool and the unequal variances tool, I ran both on the data and put the results side by side. Figure 11-9 shows the results from both tools. To run the Unequal Variances tool, you complete the same steps as for the Equal Variances version, with one exception: In the Data Analysis Tools dialog box, you select t-Test: Two Sample Assuming Unequal Variances.

Figure 11-9 shows one obvious difference between the two tools: The Unequal Variances tool shows no pooled estimate of σ^2, because the t-test for that case doesn't use one. Another difference is in the df. As I point out earlier, in the unequal variances case, you reduce the df based on the sample variances and the sample sizes. For the equal variances case, the df in this example is 12, and for the unequal variances case, it's 10.

The effects of these differences show up in the remaining statistics. The t values, critical values, and probabilities are different.

FIGURE 11-9:
Results of the
Equal Variances
t-Test data
analysis tool and
the Unequal
Variances t-Test
data analysis tool
for the data
summarized in
Table 11-2.

	A	B	C	D	E	F	G
1	t-Test: Two-Sample Assuming Unequal Variances				t-Test: Two-Sample Assuming Equal Variances		
2							
3		Sample 1	Sample 2			Sample 1	Sample 2
4	Mean	100.125	67		Mean	100.125	67
5	Variance	561.8392857	102.8		Variance	561.8393	102.8
6	Observations	8	6		Observations	8	6
7	Hypothesized Mean Difference	0			Pooled Variance	370.5729	
8	df	10			Hypothesized Mean Difference	0	
9	t Stat	3.543982028			df	12	
10	P(T<=t) one-tail	0.002660663			t Stat	3.186219	
11	t Critical one-tail	1.812461123			P(T<=t) one-tail	0.003915	
12	P(T<=t) two-tail	0.005321326			t Critical one-tail	1.782288	
13	t Critical two-tail	2.228138852			P(T<=t) two-tail	0.00783	
14					t Critical two-tail	2.178813	
15							

A Matched Set: Hypothesis Testing for Paired Samples

In the hypothesis tests I describe so far, the samples are independent of one another. Choosing an individual for one sample has no bearing on the choice of an individual for the other.

Sometimes, the samples are matched. The most obvious case is when the same individual provides a score under each of two conditions — as in a before–after study. For example, suppose ten people participate in a weight–loss program. They weigh in before they start the program and again after one month on the program. The important data is the set of before–after differences. Table 11-3 shows the data.

TABLE 11-3   Data for the Weight-Loss Example

Person	Weight Before Program	Weight After One Month	Difference
1	198	194	4
2	201	203	-2
3	210	200	10
4	185	183	2
5	204	200	4
6	156	153	3
7	167	166	1
8	197	197	0

Person	Weight Before Program	Weight After One Month	Difference
9	220	215	5
10	186	184	2
Mean			2.9
Standard Deviation			3.25

The idea is to think of these differences as a sample of scores, and treat them as you would in a one-sample t-test. (See Chapter 10.)

You carry out a test on these hypotheses:

$H_0: \mu_d \leq 0$

$H_1: \mu_d > 0$

The d in the subscripts stands for difference. Set $\alpha = .05$.

The formula for this kind of t-test is

$$t = \frac{\bar{d} - \mu_d}{s_d}$$

In this formula, $\bar{d}$ is the mean of the differences. To find $s_{\bar{d}}$, you calculate the standard deviation of the differences and divide by the square root of the number of pairs:

$$s_{\bar{d}} = \frac{s}{\sqrt{N}}$$

The df is N–1.

From Table 11-3,

$$t = \frac{\bar{d} - \mu_d}{s_d} = \frac{2.9}{\left(3.25 / \sqrt{10}\right)} = 2.82$$

With df = 9 (Number of pairs − 1), the critical value for $\alpha = .05$ is 2.26. (Use T.INV to verify.) The calculated value exceeds this value, so the decision is to reject H_0.

TIP

If you're looking at this test and thinking, "Hmmm. . . looks just like a one-sample t-test, but the one sample consists of the differences between pairs," you've pretty much got it.

T.TEST for matched samples

Earlier, I describe the worksheet function T.TEST and show you how to use it with independent samples. This time, I use it for the matched samples weight–loss example. Figure 11-10 shows the Function Arguments dialog box for T.TEST along with data from the weight–loss example.

Here are the steps to follow:

1. **Enter the data for each sample into a separate data array and select a cell.**

   For this example, the data for the Before sample are in column B and the data for the After sample are in column C.

2. **From the Statistical Functions menu, select T.TEST to open the Function Arguments dialog box for T.TEST.**

3. **In the Function Arguments dialog box, enter the appropriate values for the arguments.**

   In the Array1 box, type the sequence of cells that holds the data for one of the samples. In this example, the Before data are in B3:B12.

   In the Array2 box, type the sequence of cells that holds the data for the other sample.

   The After data are in C3:C12.

   The Tails box indicates whether this is a one-tailed test or a two-tailed test. In this example, it's a one-tailed test, so I type 1 in the Tails box.

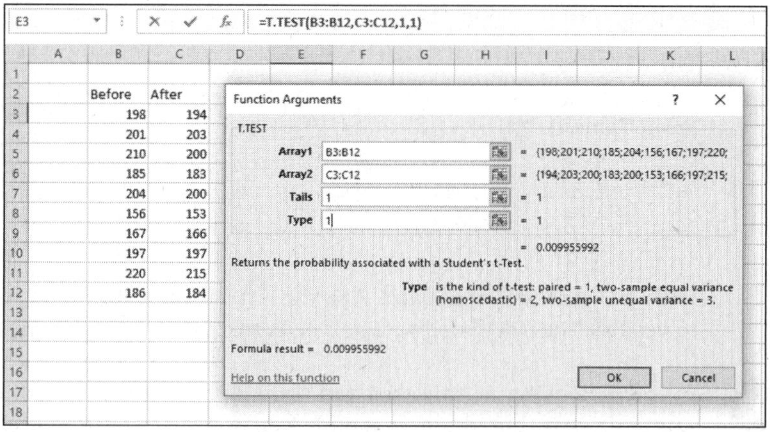

FIGURE 11-10:
The Function Arguments dialog box for T.TEST along with matched sample data.

The Type box holds a number that indicates the type of *t*-test to perform. The choices are 1 for a paired test, 2 for two samples assuming equal variances, and 3 for two samples assuming unequal variances. I typed 1.

With values supplied for all the arguments, the dialog box shows the probability associated with the *t* value for the data. It does not show the value of *t*.

4. **Click OK to put the answer in the selected cell.**

The value in the dialog box in Figure 11-10 is less than .05, so the decision is to reject H_0.

If I assign the column headers in Figure 11-10 as names for the respective arrays, the formula in the Formula bar can be

```
=T.TEST(Before,After,1,1)
```

That format might be easier to explain if you had to show the worksheet to someone. (If you don't remember how to define a name for a cell range, refer to Chapter 2.)

Data analysis tool: t-Test: Paired Two Sample for Means

Excel provides a data analysis tool that takes care of just about everything for matched samples. It's called t-test: Paired Two Sample for Means. In this section, I use it on the weight-loss data.

Figure 11-11 shows the data along with the dialog box for t-Test: Paired Two Sample for Means.

Here are the steps to follow:

1. **Enter the data for each sample into a separate data array.**

   For this example, the data in the Before sample are in column B and the data for the After sample are in column C.

2. **Select Data | Data Analysis to open the Data Analysis dialog box.**

3. **In the Data Analysis dialog box, scroll down the Analysis Tools list, and select t-Test: Paired Two Sample for Means.**

4. **Click OK to open this tool's dialog box.**

   This is the dialog box in Figure 11-11.

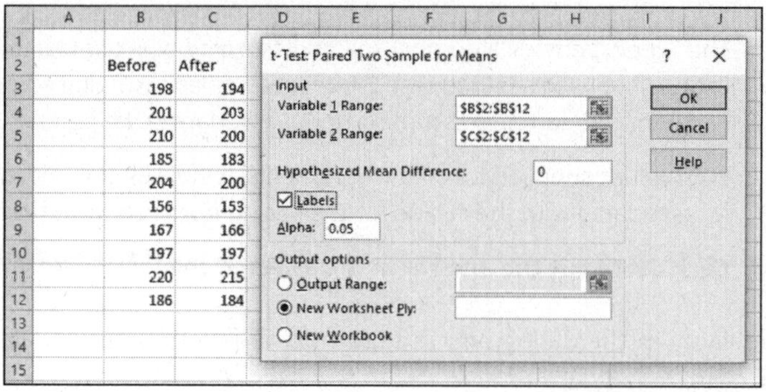

FIGURE 11-11:
The Paired Two
Sample t-Test
data analysis tool
and data from
matched
samples.

5. **In the Variable 1 Range box, enter the cell range that holds the data for one of the samples.**

For the example, the Before data are in $B$2:$B$12, including the heading. (Note the $ signs for absolute referencing.)

6. **In the Variable 2 Range box, enter the cell range that holds the data for the other sample.**

The After data are in $C$2:$C$12, including the heading.

7. **In the Hypothesized Mean Difference box, type the difference between μ_1 and μ_2 that H_0 specifies.**

In this example, that difference is 0.

8. **If the cell ranges include column headings, select the Labels check box.**

I included the headings in the ranges, so I selected the check box.

9. **The Alpha box has 0.05 as a default. Change that value if you want to use a different α.**

10. **In the Output Options, select a radio button to indicate where you want the results.**

I selected New Worksheet Ply to put the results on a new page in the worksheet.

11. **Click OK.**

Because I selected New Worksheet Ply, a newly created page opens with the results.

Figure 11-12 shows the tool's results, after I expanded the columns. Rows 4 through 7 hold sample statistics. The only item that's new is the number in cell B7, the Pearson Correlation Coefficient. This is a number between −1 and +1 that indicates the strength of the relationship between the data in the first sample and the data in the second.

	A	B	C
1	t-Test: Paired Two Sample for Means		
2			
3		*Before*	*After*
4	Mean	192.4	189.5
5	Variance	377.6	342.9444444
6	Observations	10	10
7	Pearson Correlation	0.986507688	
8	Hypothesized Mean Difference	0	
9	df	9	
10	t Stat	2.824139508	
11	P(T<=t) one-tail	0.009955992	
12	t Critical one-tail	1.833112933	
13	P(T<=t) two-tail	0.019911984	
14	t Critical two-tail	2.262157163	
15			

FIGURE 11-12:
Results of the
Paired Two
Sample t-Test
data analysis tool.

If this number is close to 1 (as in the example), high scores in one sample are associated with high scores in the other, and low scores in one are associated with low scores in the other. If the number is close to −1, high scores in the first sample are associated with low scores in the second, and low scores in the first are associated with high scores in the second.

If the number is close to zero, scores in the first sample are unrelated to scores in the second. Because the two samples consist of scores on the same people, you expect a high value. (I describe this topic in much greater detail in Chapter 15.)

Cell B8 shows the H_0-specified difference between the population means, and B9 shows the degrees of freedom.

The remaining rows provide t-related information. The calculated value of the test statistic is in B10. Cell B11 gives the proportion of area the positive value of the test statistic cuts off in the upper tail of the t-distribution with the indicated df. Cell B12 gives the critical value for a one-tailed test: That's the value that cuts off the proportion of the area in the upper tail equal to α.

Cell B13 doubles the proportion in B11. This cell holds the proportion of area from B11 added to the proportion of area that the negative value of the test statistic cuts off in the lower tail. Cell B13 shows the critical value for a two-tailed test: That's the positive value that cuts off $\alpha/2$ in the upper tail. The corresponding negative value (not shown) cuts off $\alpha/2$ in the lower tail.

Testing Two Variances

The two-sample hypothesis testing I describe thus far pertains to means. It's also possible to test hypotheses about variances.

In this section, I extend the one-variance manufacturing example I use in Chapter 10. FarKlempt Robotics, Inc., produces a part that has to be a certain length with a very small variability. The company is considering two machines to produce this part, and it wants to choose the one that results in the least variability. FarKlempt Robotics takes a sample of parts from each machine, measures them, finds the variance for each sample, and performs a hypothesis test to see if one machine's variance is significantly greater than the other's.

The hypotheses are

$$H_{0:}\ \sigma_1^2 = \sigma_2^2$$

$$H_{1:}\ \sigma_1^2 \neq \sigma_2^2$$

As always, an α is a must. As usual, I set it to .05.

When you test two variances, you don't subtract one from the other. Instead, you divide one by the other to calculate the test statistic. Sir Ronald Fisher is a famous statistician who worked out the mathematics and the family of distributions for working with variances in this way. The test statistic is named in his honor. It's called an *F-ratio* and the test is the *F test.* The family of distributions for the test is called the *F-distribution.*

Without going into all the mathematics, I'll just tell you that, once again, df is the parameter that distinguishes one member of the family from another. What's different about this family is that two variance estimates are involved, so each member of the family is associated with two values of df, rather than one as in the *t*-test. Another difference between the *F*-distribution and the others you've seen is that the *F* cannot have a negative value. Figure 11-13 shows two members of the *F*-distribution family.

The test statistic is

$$F = \frac{\text{larger } s^2}{\text{smaller } s^2}$$

Suppose FarKlempt Robotics produces 10 parts with Machine 1 and finds a sample variance of .60 square inches. It produces 15 parts with Machine 2 and finds a sample variance of .44 square inches. Can the company reject H_0?

Calculating the test statistic,

$$F = \frac{.60}{.44} = 1.36$$

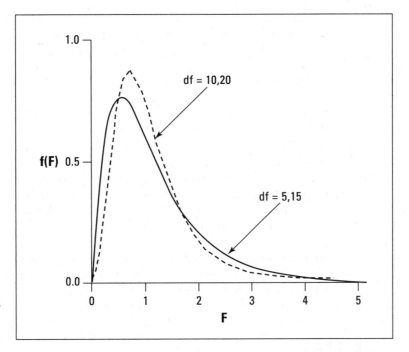

FIGURE 11-13:
Two members of
the *F*-distribution
family.

The df's are 9 and 14: The variance estimate in the numerator of the *F* ratio is based on 10 cases, and the variance estimate in the denominator is based on 15 cases.

When the df's are 9 and 14 and it's a two-tailed test at α = .05, the critical value of *F* is 3.21. (In a moment, I show you an Excel function that finds the value for you.) The calculated value is less than the critical value, so the decision is to not reject H_0.

REMEMBER

It makes a difference which df is in the numerator and which df is in the denominator. The *F*-distribution for df = 9 and df = 14 is different from the *F*-distribution for df = 14 and df = 9. For example, the critical value in the latter case is 3.98, not 3.21.

Using F in conjunction with t

One use of the *F*-distribution is in conjunction with the *t*-test for independent samples. Before you do the *t*-test, you use *F* to help decide whether to assume equal variances or unequal variances in the samples.

In the equal variances t-test example I show you earlier, the standard deviations are 2.71 and 2.79. The variances are 7.34 and 7.78. The F-ratio of these variances is

$$F = \frac{7.78}{7.34} = 1.06$$

Each sample is based on ten observations, so df = 9 for each sample variance. An F-ratio of 1.06 cuts off the upper 47 percent of the F-distribution whose df are 9 and 9, so it's safe to use the equal-variances version of the t-test for these data.

In the sidebar at the end of Chapter 10, I mention that on rare occasions a high α is a good thing. When H_0 is a desirable outcome and you'd rather not reject it, you stack the deck against rejecting by setting α at a high level so that small differences cause you to reject H_0.

This is one of those rare occasions. It's more desirable to use the equal variances t-test, which typically provides more degrees of freedom than the unequal variances t-test. Setting a high value of α (.20 is a good one) for the F-test enables you to be confident when you assume equal variances.

F.TEST

The worksheet function F.TEST calculates an F-ratio on the data from two samples. It doesn't return the F-ratio. Instead, it provides the two-tailed probability of the calculated F-ratio under H_0. This means that the answer is the proportion of area to the right of the F-ratio, and to the left of the reciprocal of the F-ratio (1 divided by the F-ratio).

Figure 11-14 presents the data for the FarKlempt machines example I just summarized for you. The figure also shows the Function Arguments dialog box for F.TEST.

Follow these steps:

1. **Enter the data for each sample into a separate data array and select a cell for the answer.**

   For this example, the data for the Machine 1 sample are in column B and the data for the Machine 2 sample are in column D.

2. **From the Statistical Functions menu, select F.TEST to open the Function Arguments dialog box for** F.TEST.

3. **In the Function Arguments dialog box, enter the appropriate values for the arguments.**

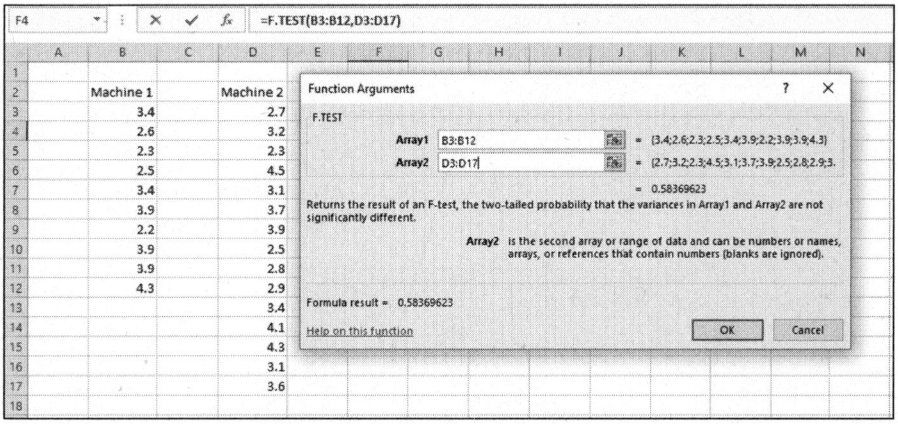

FIGURE 11-14:
Working with
F.TEST.

In the Array1 box, enter the sequence of cells that holds the data for the sample with the larger variance. In this example, the Machine 1 data are in B3:B12.

In the Array2 box, enter the sequence of cells that holds the data for the other sample. The Machine 2 data are in D3:D17.

With values entered for all the arguments, the answer appears in the dialog box.

4. **Click OK to put the answer in the selected cell.**

The value in the dialog box in Figure 11-14 is greater than .05, so the decision is to not reject H_0. Figure 11-15 shows the area that the answer represents.

Had I assigned names to those two arrays, the formula in the Formula bar could have been

```
=F.TEST(Machine_1,Machine_2)
```

If you don't know how to assign names to arrays, see Chapter 2. In that chapter, you also find out why I inserted an underscore into each name.

F.DIST and F.DIST.RT

You use the worksheet function F.DIST or the function F.DIST.RT to decide whether or not your calculated F-ratio is in the region of rejection. For F.DIST, you supply a value for F, a value for each df, and a value (TRUE or FALSE) for an argument called Cumulative. If the value for Cumulative is TRUE, F.DIST returns the probability of obtaining an F-ratio of at most as high as yours if H_0 is true. (Excel calls this the *left-tail* probability.) If that probability is greater than 1- α, you reject H_0. If the value for Cumulative is FALSE, F.DIST returns the height of the F-distribution at your value of F. I use this option later in this chapter to create a chart of the F-distribution.

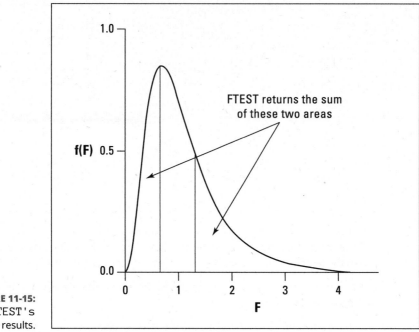

FIGURE 11-15:
F.TEST's
results.

F.DIST.RT returns the probability of obtaining an F-ratio at least as high as yours if H_0 is true. (Excel calls this the *right-tail* probability.) If that value is less than α, reject H_0. In practice, F.DIST.RT is more straightforward.

Here, I apply F.DIST.RT to the preceding example. The F-ratio is 1.36, with 9 and 14 df.

The steps are:

1. **Select a cell for the answer.**

2. **From the Statistical Functions menu, select F.DIST.RT to open the Function Arguments dialog box for F.DIST.RT. (See Figure 11-16.)**

3. **In the Function Arguments dialog box, enter the appropriate values for the arguments.**

   In the X box, type the calculated F. For this example, the calculated F is 1.36.

   In the Deg_freedom1 box, type the degrees of freedom for the variance estimate in the numerator of the F. The degrees of freedom for the numerator in this example is 9 (10 scores – 1).

   In the Deg_freedom2 box, I type the degrees of freedom for the variance estimate in the denominator of the F.

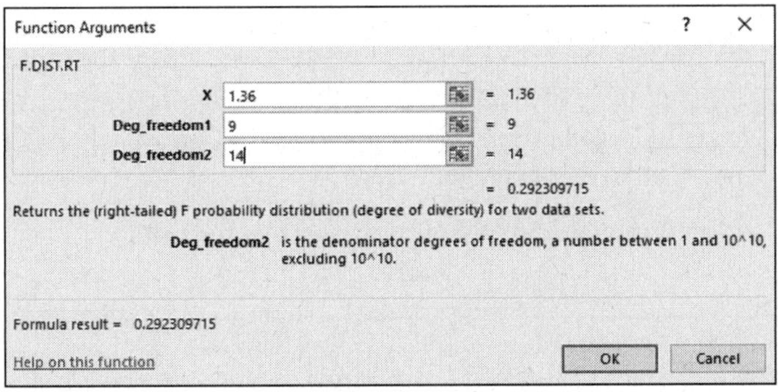

FIGURE 11-16:
The Function
Arguments
dialog box for
F.DIST.RT.

The degrees of freedom for the denominator in this example is 14 (15 scores – 1).

With values entered for all the arguments, the answer appears in the dialog box.

4. **Click OK to close the dialog box and put the answer in the selected cell.**

The value in the dialog box in Figure 11-16 is greater than .05, so the decision is to not reject H_0.

F.INV and F.INV.RT

The F.INV worksheet functions are the reverse of the F.DIST functions. F.INV finds the value in the *F*-distribution that cuts off a given proportion of the area in the lower (left) tail. F.INV.RT finds the value that cuts off a given proportion of the area in the upper (right) tail. You can use F.INV.RT to find the critical value of *F*.

Here, I use F.INV.RT to find the critical value for the two-tailed test in the Far-Klempt machines example:

1. **Select a cell for the answer.**

2. **From the Statistical Functions menu, select F.INV.RT to open the Function Arguments dialog box for FINV.RT.**

3. **In the Function Arguments dialog box, enter the appropriate values for the arguments.**

   In the Probability box, enter the proportion of area in the upper tail. In this example, that's .025 because it's a two-tailed test with $\alpha = .05$.

   In the Deg_freedom1 box, type the degrees of freedom for the numerator. For this example, df for the numerator = 9.

In the Deg_freedom2 box, type the degrees of freedom for the denominator. For this example, df for the denominator = 14.

With values entered for all the arguments, the answer appears in the dialog box. (See Figure 11-17.)

4. **Click OK to put the answer into the selected cell.**

Data analysis tool: F-test: Two Sample for Variances

Excel provides a data analysis tool for carrying out an F-test on two sample variances. I apply it here to the sample variances example I've been using. Figure 11-18 shows the data, along with the dialog box for F–Test: Two–Sample for Variances.

To use this tool, follow these steps:

1. **Enter the data for each sample into a separate data array.**

   For this example, the data in the Machine 1 sample are in column B and the data for the Machine 2 sample are in column D.

2. **Select Data | Data Analysis to open the Data Analysis dialog box.**

3. **In the Data Analysis dialog box, scroll down the Analysis Tools list and select F-Test Two Sample For Variances.**

4. **Click OK to open this tool's dialog box.**

   This is the dialog box shown in Figure 11-18.

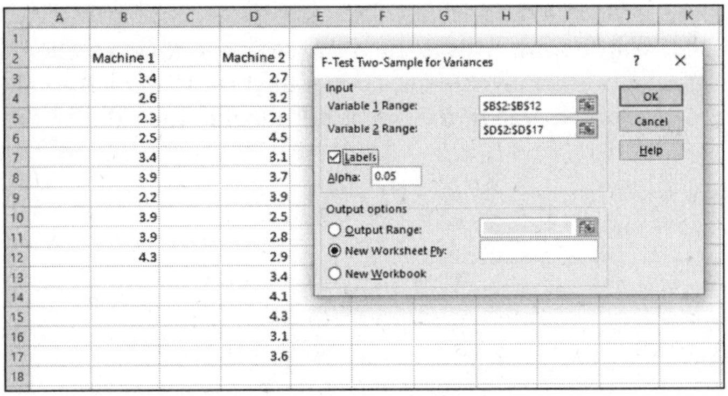

FIGURE 11-18:
The F-Test data
analysis tool and
data from two
samples.

5. **In the Variable 1 Range box, enter the cell range that holds the data for the first sample.**

For the example, the Machine 1 data are in $B$2:$B$12, including the heading. (Note the $ signs for absolute referencing.)

6. **In the Variable 2 Range box, enter the cell range that holds the data for the second sample.**

The Machine 2 data are in $D$2:$D$17, including the heading.

7. **If the cell ranges include column headings, select the Labels check box.**

I included the headings in the ranges, so I selected the box.

8. **The Alpha box has 0.05 as a default. Change that value for a different α.**

The Alpha box provides a one-tailed alpha. I want a two-tailed test, so I changed this value to .025.

9. **In the Output Options, select a radio button to indicate where you want the results.**

I selected New Worksheet Ply to put the results on a new page in the work-sheet.

10. **Click OK.**

Because I selected New Worksheet Ply, a newly created page opens with the results.

Figure 11-19 shows the tool's results, after I expanded the columns. Rows 4 through 6 hold sample statistics. Cell B7 shows the degrees of freedom.

The remaining rows present F-related information. The calculated value of F is in B8. Cell B9 gives the proportion of area the calculated F cuts off in the upper tail of the *F*-distribution. This is the right-side area shown earlier in Figure 11-15. Cell B10 gives the critical value for a one-tailed test: That's the value that cuts off the proportion of the area in the upper tail equal to the value in the Alpha box.

	A	B	C	D
1	F-Test Two-Sample for Variances			
2				
3		Machine 1	Machine 2	
4	Mean	3.24	3.34	
5	Variance	0.600444444	0.441142857	
6	Observations	10	15	
7	df	9	14	
8	F	1.361111111		
9	P(F<=f) one-tail	0.291848115		
10	F Critical one-tail	3.209300341		
11				

FIGURE 11-19: Results of the F-Test data analysis tool.

Visualizing the F-Distribution

The *F*-distribution is extremely important in statistics, as you'll see in the next chapter. In order to increase your understanding of this distribution, I show you how to graph it. Figure 11-20 shows the numbers and the finished product.

Here are the steps:

1. **Put the degrees of freedom in cells.**

   I put 10 into cell B1, and 15 in cell B2.

2. **Create a column of values for the statistic.**

   In cells D2 through D42, I put the values 0 through 8 in increments of .2

3. **In the first cell of the adjoining column, put the value of the probability density for the first value of the statistic.**

   Because I'm graphing an *F*-distribution, I use F.DIST in cell E2. For the value of X, I click cell D2. For df1, I click B1 and press the F4 key to anchor this selection. For df2, I click B2 and press the F4 key. In the Cumulative box, I type FALSE to return the height of the distribution for this value of t. Then I click OK.

4. **Autofill the column with the values.**

5. **Create the chart.**

   Highlight both columns. On the Insert tab, in the Charts area, select Scatter with Smooth Lines.

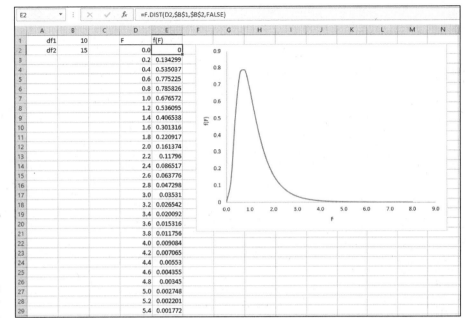

FIGURE 11-20:
Visualizing the
F-distribution.

6. **Modify the chart.**

   I click inside the chart to open the Chart Elements tool (the plus sign) and use it to add the axis titles (F and f(F)). I also delete the chart title and the gridlines, but that's a matter of personal taste. And I like to stretch out the chart.

7. **Manipulate the chart.**

   To help you get a feel for the distribution, try different values for the df and see how the changes affect the chart.

Chapter 12

Testing More Than Two Samples

S tatistics would be limited if you could only make inferences about one or two samples. In this chapter, I discuss the procedures for testing hypotheses about three or more samples. I show what to do when samples are independent of one another, and what to do when they're not. In both cases, I discuss what to do after you test the hypotheses.

I also introduce Excel data analysis tools that do the work for you. Although these tools aren't at the level you'd find in a dedicated statistical package, you can combine them with Excel's standard features to produce some sophisticated analyses.

Testing More Than Two

Imagine this situation. Your company asks you to evaluate three different methods for training its employees to do a particular job. You randomly assign 30 employees to one of the three methods. Your plan is to train them, test them, tabulate the results, and make some conclusions. Before you can finish the study, three people leave the company — one from the Method 1 group and two from the Method 3 group.

Table 12-1 shows the data.

TABLE 12-1 **Data from Three Training Methods**

	Method 1	Method 2	Method 3
	95	83	68
	91	89	75
	89	85	79
	90	89	74
	99	81	75
	88	89	81
	96	90	73
	98	82	77
	95	84	
		80	
Mean	93.44	85.20	75.25
Variance	16.28	14.18	15.64
Standard Deviation	4.03	3.77	3.96

Do the three methods provide different results, or are they so similar that you can't distinguish among them? To decide, you have to carry out a hypothesis test:

H_0: $\mu_1 = \mu_2 = \mu_3$

H_1: Not H_0

with $\alpha = .05$.

A thorny problem

Sounds pretty easy, particularly if you've read Chapter 11. Take the mean of the scores from Method 1, the mean of the scores from Method 2, and do a t-test to see if they're different. Follow the same procedure for Method 1 versus Method 3, and for Method 2 versus Method 3. If at least one of those t-tests shows a significant difference, reject H_0. Nothing to it, right? Wrong. If your α is .05 for each t-test, you're setting yourself up for a Type I error with a probability higher than you planned on. The probability that at least one of the three t-tests results in a significant difference is way above .05. In fact, it's .14, which is way beyond acceptable. (The mathematics behind calculating that number is a little involved, so I won't elaborate.)

With more than three samples, the situation gets even worse. Four groups require six t-tests, and the probability that at least one of them is significant is .26. Table 12-2 shows what happens with increasing numbers of samples.

TABLE 12-2   **The Incredible Increasing Alpha**

Number of Samples t	Number of Tests	Pr (At Least One Significant t)
3	3	.14
4	6	.26
5	10	.40
6	15	.54
7	21	.66
8	28	.76
9	36	.84
10	45	.90

Carrying out multiple t-tests is clearly not the answer. So what do you do?

A solution

It's necessary to take a different approach. The idea is to think in terms of variances rather than means.

I'd like you to think of variance in a slightly different way. The formula for estimating population variance, remember, is

$$s^2 = \frac{\sum(x - \bar{x})^2}{N - 1}$$

Because the variance is almost a mean of squared deviations from the mean, statisticians also refer to it as *Mean Square.* In a way, that's an unfortunate nickname: It leaves out "deviation from the mean," but there you have it.

The numerator of the variance — excuse me, Mean Square — is the sum of squared deviations from the mean. This leads to another nickname, *Sum of Squares*. The denominator, as I say in Chapter 10, is *degrees of freedom* (df). So, the slightly different way to think of variance is

$$\text{Mean Square} = \frac{\text{Sum of Squares}}{\text{df}}$$

You can abbreviate this as

$$\text{MS} = \frac{\text{SS}}{\text{df}}$$

Now, on to solving the thorny problem. One important step is to find the Mean Squares hiding in the data. Another is to understand that you use these Mean Squares to estimate the variances of the populations that produced these samples. In this case, assume those variances are equal, so you're really estimating one variance. The final step is to understand that you use these estimates to test the hypotheses I show you at the beginning of the chapter.

Three different Mean Squares are inside the data in Table 12-1. Start with the whole set of 27 scores, forgetting for the moment that they're divided into three groups. Suppose you want to use those 27 scores to calculate an estimate of the population variance. (A dicey idea, but humor me.) The mean of those 27 scores is 85. I'll call that mean the *grand mean* because it's the average of everything.

So the Mean Square would be

$$\frac{(95-85)^2 + (91-85)^2 + \ldots + (73-85)^2 + (77-85)^2}{(27-1)} = 68.08$$

The denominator has 26 (27 − 1) degrees of freedom. I refer to that variance as the *total variance,* or in the new way of thinking about this, the MS_{Total}. It's often abbreviated as MS_{T}.

Here's another variance to consider. In Chapter 11, I describe the *t*-test for two samples with equal variances. For that test, you put the two sample variances together to create a *pooled* estimate of the population variance. The data in Table 12-1 provide three sample variances for a pooled estimate: 16.28, 14.18, and 15.64. Assuming these numbers represent equal population variances, the pooled estimate is

$$s_p^2 = \frac{(N_1-1)s_1^2 + (N_2-1)s_2^2 + (N_3-1)s_3^2}{(N_1-1) + (N_2-1) + (N_3-1)}$$

$$= \frac{(9-1)(16.28) + (10-1)(14.18) + (8-1)(15.64)}{(9-1) + (10-1) + (8-1)} = 15.31$$

Because this pooled estimate comes from the variance within the groups, it's called MS_{Within}, or MS_W.

One more Mean Square to go — the variance of the sample means around the grand mean. In this example, that means the variance in these numbers: 93.44, 85.20, and 75.25 — sort of. I said "sort of" because these are means, not scores. When you deal with means, you have to take into account the number of scores that produced each mean. To do that, you multiply each squared deviation by the number of scores in that sample.

So this variance is

$$\frac{(9)(93.44-85)^2+(10)(85.20-85)^2+(8)(75.25-85)^2}{3-1}=701.34$$

The df for this variance is 2 (the number of samples − 1).

Statisticians, not known for their crispness of usage, refer to this as the variance *between* sample means. (*Among* is the correct word when you're talking about more than two items.) This variance is known as $MS_{Between}$, or MS_B.

So you now have three estimates of population variance: MS_T, MS_W, and MS_B. What do you do with them?

Remember that the original objective is to test a hypothesis about three means. According to H_0, any differences you see among the three sample means are due strictly to chance. The implication is that the variance among those means is the same as the variance of any three numbers selected at random from the population.

If you could somehow compare the variance among the means (that's MS_B, remember) with the population variance, you could see if that holds up. If only you had an estimate of the population variance that's independent of the differences among the groups, you'd be in business.

Ah . . . but you do have that estimate. You have MS_W, an estimate based on pooling the variances within the samples. Assuming those variances represent equal population variances, this is a pretty solid estimate. In this example, it's based on 24 degrees of freedom.

The reasoning now becomes: If MS_B is about the same as MS_W, you have evidence consistent with H_0. If MS_B is significantly larger than MS_W, you have evidence that's inconsistent with H_0. In effect, you transform these hypotheses:

$H_0: \mu_1 = \mu_2 = \mu_3$

H_1: Not H_0

into these

$$H_0: \sigma_B^2 \le \sigma_W^2$$

$$H_1: \sigma_B^2 > \sigma_W^2$$

Rather than multiple *t*-tests among sample means, you perform a test of the difference between two variances.

What is that test? In Chapter 11, I show you the test for hypotheses about two variances. It's called the *F*-test. To perform this test, you divide one variance by the other. You evaluate the result against a family of distributions called the *F*-distribution. Because two variances are involved, two values for degrees of freedom define each member of the family.

For this example, *F* has df = 2 (for the MS_B) and df = 24 (for the MS_W). Figure 12-1 shows what this member of the *F* family looks like. For our purposes, it's the distribution of possible *F* values if H_0 is true. (Refer to "Visualizing the F-Distribution" in Chapter 11.)

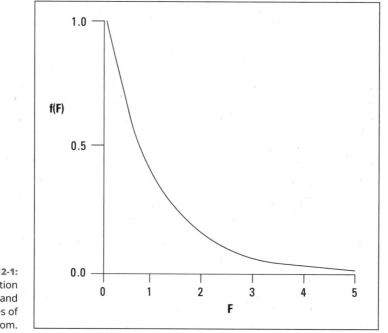

FIGURE 12-1:
The *F*-distribution
with 2 and
24 degrees of
freedom.

The test statistic for the example is

$$F = \frac{701.34}{15.31}$$

What proportion of area does this value cut off in the upper tail of the F-distribution? From Figure 12-1, you can see that this proportion is microscopic, as the values on the horizontal axis only go up to 5. (And the proportion of area beyond 5 is tiny.) It's way less than .05.

This means that it's highly unlikely that differences among the means are due to chance. It means that you reject H_0.

REMEMBER

This whole procedure for testing more than two samples is called the *analysis of variance,* often abbreviated as ANOVA. In the context of an ANOVA, the denominator of an F-ratio has the generic name *error term.* The independent variable is sometimes called a *factor.* So this is a single-factor (or one-factor) ANOVA.

In this example, the factor is Training Method. Each instance of the independent variable is called a *level.* The independent variable in this example has three levels.

More complex studies have more than one factor, and each factor can have many levels.

Meaningful relationships

Take another look at the Mean Squares in this example, each with its Sum of Squares and degrees of freedom. Before, when I calculated each Mean Square for you, I didn't explicitly show you each Sum of Squares, but here I include them:

$$MS_B = \frac{SS_B}{df_B} = \frac{1402.68}{2} = 701.34$$

$$MS_W = \frac{SS_W}{df_W} = \frac{367.32}{24} = 15.31$$

$$MS_T = \frac{SS_T}{df_T} = \frac{1770}{26} = 68.08$$

Start with the degrees of freedom: $df_B = 2$, $df_W = 24$, and $df_T = 26$. Is it a coincidence that they add up? Hardly. It's always the case that

$$df_B + df_W = df_T$$

How about those Sums of Squares?

$$1402.68 + 367.32 = 1770$$

Again, this is no coincidence. In the analysis of variance, this always happens:

$$SS_B + SS_W = SS_T$$

In fact, statisticians who work with the analysis of variance speak of partitioning (read "breaking down into non-overlapping pieces") the SS_T into one portion for the SS_B and another for the SS_W, and partitioning the df_T into one amount for the df_B and another for the df_W.

After the F-test

The F-test enables you to decide whether or not to reject H_0. After you decide to reject, then what? All you can say is that somewhere within the set of means, something is different from something else. The F-test doesn't specify what those "somethings" are.

Planned comparisons

In order to get more specific, you have to do some further tests. Not only that, you have to plan those tests in advance of carrying out the ANOVA.

What are those tests? Given what I mention earlier, this might surprise you: t-tests. While this might sound inconsistent with the increased alpha of multiple t-tests, it's not. If an analysis of variance enables you to reject H_0, then it's okay to use t-tests to turn the magnifying glass on the data and find out where the differences are. And as I'm about to show you, the t-test you use is slightly different from the one I discuss in Chapter 11.

These post-ANOVA t-tests are called *planned comparisons*. Some statisticians refer to them as *a priori tests*. I illustrate by following through with the example. Suppose before you gathered the data, you had reason to believe that Method 1 would result in higher scores than Method 2, and that Method 2 would result in higher scores than Method 3. In that case, you plan in advance to compare the means of those samples in the event your ANOVA-based decision is to reject H_0.

The formula for this kind of t-test is

$$t = \frac{\bar{x}_1 - \bar{x}_2}{\sqrt{MS_W\left[\frac{1}{N_1} + \frac{1}{N_2}\right]}}$$

It's a test of

$H_0: \mu_1 \leq \mu_2$

$H_1: \mu_1 > \mu_2$

MS_W takes the place of the pooled estimate s_p^2 I show you in Chapter 11. In fact, when I introduced MS_W, I showed how it's just a pooled estimate that can incorporate variances from more than two samples. The df for this t-test is df_W, rather than $(n_1 - 1) + (n_2 - 1)$.

For this example, the Method 1 versus Method 2 comparison is

$$t = \frac{\bar{x}_1 - \bar{x}_2}{\sqrt{MS_W\left[\dfrac{1}{N_1} + \dfrac{1}{N_2}\right]}} = \frac{93.44 - 85.2}{\sqrt{15.31\left[\dfrac{1}{9} + \dfrac{1}{10}\right]}} = 4.59$$

With df = 24, this value of t cuts off a miniscule portion of area in the upper tail of the t-distribution. The decision is to reject H_0.

The planned comparison t-test formula I show you matches up with the t-test for two samples. You can write the planned comparison t-test formula in a way that sets up additional possibilities. Start by writing the numerator

$$\bar{x}_1 - \bar{x}_2$$

a bit differently:

$$(+1)\bar{x}_1 + (-1)\bar{x}_2$$

The +1 and −1 are *comparison coefficients.* I refer to them, in a general way, as c_1 and c_2. In fact, c_3 and $\bar{x}_3$ can enter the comparison, even if you're just comparing $\bar{x}_1$ with $\bar{x}_2$:

$$(+1)\bar{x}_1 + (-1)\bar{x}_2 + (0)\bar{x}_3$$

The important thing is that the coefficients add up to zero.

Here's how the comparison coefficients figure into the planned comparison t-test formula for a study that involves three samples:

$$t = \frac{c_1\bar{x}_1 + c_2\bar{x}_2 + c_3\bar{x}_3}{\sqrt{MS_W\left[\dfrac{c_1^2}{N_1} + \dfrac{c_2^2}{N_2} + \dfrac{c_3^2}{N_3}\right]}}$$

Applying this formula to Method 2 versus Method 3:

$$t = \frac{c_1\bar{x}_1 + c_2\bar{x}_2 + c_3\bar{x}_3}{\sqrt{MS_W\left[\dfrac{c_1^2}{N_1} + \dfrac{c_2^2}{N_2} + \dfrac{c_3^2}{N_3}\right]}} = \frac{(0)(93.44) + (+1)(85.2) + (-1)(75.25)}{\sqrt{15.31\left[\dfrac{0^2}{9} + \dfrac{1^2}{10} + \dfrac{(-1)^2}{8}\right]}} = 5.36$$

The value for t indicates the results from Method 2 are significantly higher than the results from Method 3.

You can also plan a more complex comparison — say, Method 1 versus the average of Method 2 and Method 3. Begin with the numerator. That would be

$$\bar{x}_1 - \frac{\left(\bar{x}_2 + \bar{x}_3\right)}{2}$$

With comparison coefficients, you can write this as

$$\left(+1\right)\bar{x}_1 + \left(-\frac{1}{2}\right)\bar{x}_2 + \left(-\frac{1}{2}\right)\bar{x}_3$$

If you're more comfortable with whole numbers, you can write it as:

$$\left(+2\right)\bar{x}_1 + \left(-1\right)\bar{x}_2 + \left(-1\right)\bar{x}_3$$

Plugging these whole numbers into the formula gives you

$$t = \frac{c_1\bar{x}_1 + c_2\bar{x}_2 + c_3\bar{x}_3}{\sqrt{MS_W\left[\dfrac{c_1^2}{N_1} + \dfrac{c_2^2}{N_2} + \dfrac{c_3^2}{N_3}\right]}} = \frac{\left(2\right)\left(93.44\right) + \left(-1\right)\left(85.2\right) + \left(-1\right)\left(75.25\right)}{\sqrt{15.31\left[\dfrac{2^2}{9} + \dfrac{\left(-1\right)^2}{10} + \dfrac{\left(-1\right)^2}{8}\right]}} = 9.97$$

Again, strong evidence for rejecting H_0.

Unplanned comparisons

Things would get boring if your post-ANOVA testing is limited to comparisons you have to plan in advance. Sometimes you want to snoop around your data and see if anything interesting reveals itself. Sometimes something jumps out at you that you didn't anticipate.

When this happens, you can make comparisons you didn't plan on. These comparisons are called *a posteriori tests, post hoc tests,* or *simply unplanned comparisons.* Statisticians have come up with a wide variety of these tests, many of them with exotic names and many of them dependent on special sampling distributions.

The idea behind these tests is that you pay a price for not having planned them in advance. That price has to do with stacking the deck against rejecting H_0 for the particular comparison.

Of all the unplanned tests available, the one I like best is a creation of famed statistician Henry Scheffé. As opposed to esoteric formulas and distributions, you start with the test I already showed you, and then add a couple of easy-to-do extras.

The first extra is to understand the relationship between t and F. I've shown you the F-test for three samples. You can also carry out an F-test for two samples. That F-test has $df_B = 1$ and $df_W = (N_1 - 1) + (N_2 - 1)$. The df for the t-test, of course, is $(N_1 - 1) + (N_2 - 1)$. Hmmm . . . seems like they should be related somehow.

They are. The relationship between the two-sample t and the two-sample F is

$$F = t^2$$

Now I can tell you the steps for performing Scheffé's test:

1. **Calculate the planned comparison t-test.**

2. **Square the value to create F.**

3. **Find the critical value of F for df_B and df_W at $\alpha = .05$ (or whatever α you choose).**

4. **Multiply this critical F by the number of samples – 1.**

   The result is your critical F for the unplanned comparison. I'll call this F'.

5. **Compare the calculated F to F'.**

   If the calculated F is greater, reject H_0 for this test. If it's not, don't reject H_0 for this test.

Imagine that in the example, you didn't plan in advance to compare the mean of Method 1 with the mean of Method 3. (In a study involving only three samples, that's hard to imagine, I grant you.) The t-test is

$$t = \frac{c_1 \bar{x}_1 + c_2 \bar{x}_2 + c_3 \bar{x}_3}{\sqrt{MS_W \left[\frac{c_1^2}{N_1} + \frac{c_2^2}{N_2} + \frac{c_3^2}{N_3} \right]}} = \frac{(+1)(93.44) + (0)(85.2) + (-1)(75.25)}{\sqrt{15.31 \left[\frac{1^2}{9} + \frac{0^2}{10} + \frac{(-1)^2}{8} \right]}} = 9.57$$

Squaring this result gives

$$F = t^2 = (9.57)^2 = 91.61$$

For F with 2 and 24 df and $\alpha = .05$, the critical value is 3.403. (You can look that up in a table in a statistics textbook or you can use the worksheet function F.INV.RT.) So

$$F' = (3-1)F = (2)(3.403) = 6.806$$

Because the calculated F, 91.61, is greater than F', the decision is to reject H_0. You have evidence that Method 1's results are different from Method 3's results.

Data analysis tool: Anova: Single Factor

The calculations for the ANOVA can get intense. Excel has a data analysis tool that does the heavy lifting. It's called Anova: Single Factor. Figure 12-2 shows this tool along with the data for the preceding example.

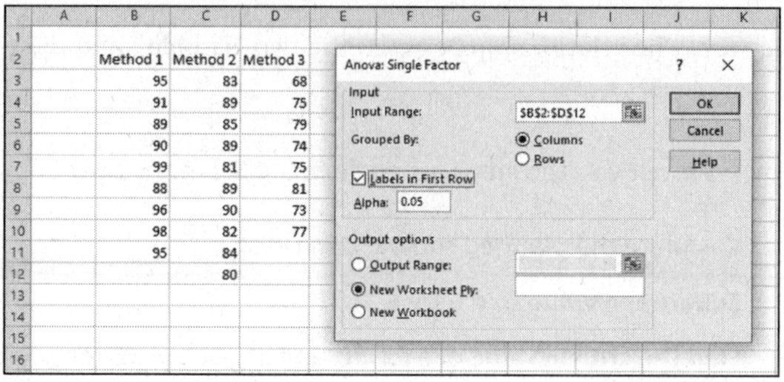

FIGURE 12-2:
The Anova: Single
Factor data
analysis tool
dialog box.

The steps for using this tool are:

1. **Enter the data for each sample into a separate data array.**

For this example, the data in the Method 1 sample are in column B, the data in the Method 2 sample are in column C, and the data for the Method 3 sample are in column D.

2. **Select Data | Data Analysis to open the Data Analysis dialog box.**

3. **In the Data Analysis dialog box, scroll down the Analysis Tools list and select Anova: Single Factor.**

4. **Click OK to open the Anova: Single Factor dialog box.**

This is the dialog box in Figure 12-2.

5. **In the Input Range box, enter the cell range that holds all the data.**

For the example, the data are in $B$2:$D$12. (Note the $ signs for absolute referencing.)

6. **If the cell ranges include column headings, select the Labels check box.**

I included the headings in the ranges, so I selected the box.

7. **The Alpha box has 0.05 as a default. Change that value if you're so inclined.**

8. **In the Output Options, select a radio button to indicate where you want the results.**

I selected New Worksheet Ply to put the results on a new page in the worksheet.

9. **Click OK.**

Because I selected New Worksheet Ply, a newly created page opens with the results.

Figure 12-3 shows the tool's output, after I expand the columns. The output features two tables: SUMMARY and ANOVA. The SUMMARY table provides summary statistics of the samples — the number in each group, the group sums, averages, and variances. The ANOVA table presents the Sums of Squares, df, Mean Squares, F, P-value, and critical F for the indicated df. The P-value is the proportion of area that the F cuts off in the upper tail of the F-distribution. If this value is less than .05, reject H_0.

	A	B	C	D	E	F	G	H
1	Anova: Single Factor							
2								
3	SUMMARY							
4	*Groups*	*Count*	*Sum*	*Average*	*Variance*			
5	Method 1	9	841	93.44444	16.27778			
6	Method 2	10	852	85.2	14.17778			
7	Method 3	8	602	75.25	15.64286			
8								
9								
10	ANOVA							
11	*Source of Variation*	*SS*	*df*	*MS*	*F*	*P-value*	*F crit*	
12	Between Groups	1402.678	2	701.3389	45.82389	6.38E-09	3.402826	
13	Within Groups	367.3222	24	15.30509				
14								
15	Total	1770	26					
16								

Comparing the means

Excel's ANOVA tool does not provide a built-in facility for carrying out planned (or unplanned) comparisons among the means. With a little ingenuity, however, you can use the Excel worksheet function SUMPRODUCT to do those comparisons.

The worksheet page with the ANOVA output is the launching pad for the planned comparisons. In this section, I take you through one planned comparison — the mean of Method 1 versus the mean of Method 2.

Begin by creating columns that hold important information for the comparisons. Figure 12-4 shows what I mean. I put the comparison coefficients in column J, the squares of those coefficients in column K, and the reciprocal of each sample size (1/n) in column L.

A few rows below those cells, I put t-test-related information — the t-test numerator, the denominator, and the value of t. I use separate cells for the numerator and denominator to simplify the formulas. You can put them together in one big formula and just have a cell for t, but it's hard to keep track of everything.

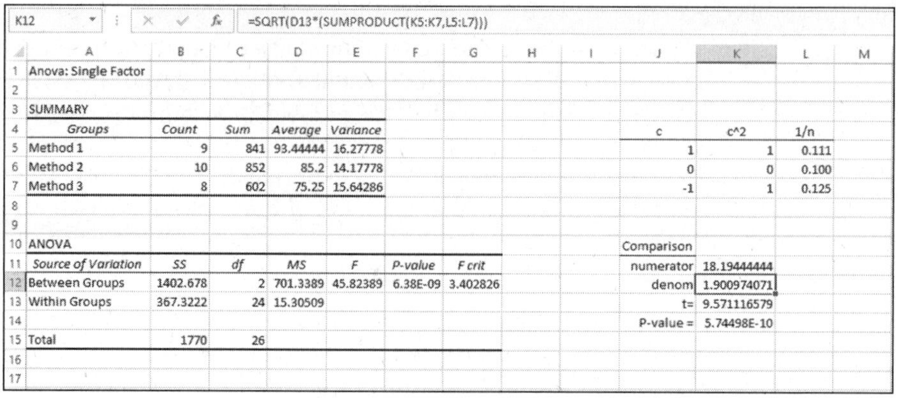

| K12 | ▼ | : | × | ✓ | fx | =SQRT(D13*(SUMPRODUCT(K5:K7,L5:L7))) |

FIGURE 12-4:
Carrying out a
planned
comparison.

SUMPRODUCT takes arrays of cells, multiplies the numbers in the corresponding cells, and sums the products. (This function is on the Math & Trig Functions menu, not the Statistical Functions menu.) I used SUMPRODUCT to multiply each coefficient by each sample mean and then add the products. I stored that result in K11. That's the numerator for the planned comparison t-test. The formula for K11 is

```
=SUMPRODUCT(J5:J7,D5:D7)
```

The array J5:J7 holds the comparison coefficients, and D5:D7 holds the sample means.

K12 holds the denominator. I selected K12 in Figure 12-4 so that you could see its formula in the Formula bar:

```
=SQRT(D13*(SUMPRODUCT(K5:K7,L5:L7)))
```

D13 has the MS_W. SUMPRODUCT multiplies the squared coefficients in K5:K7 by the reciprocals of the sample sizes in L5:L7 and sums the products. SQRT takes the square root of the whole thing.

K13 holds the value for t. That's just K11 divided by K12.

K14 presents the P-value for t — the proportion of area that t cuts off in the upper tail of the t-distribution with df = 24. The formula for that cell is

```
=T.DIST.RT(K13,C13)
```

The arguments are the calculated t (in K13) and the degrees of freedom for MS_W (in C13).

If you change the coefficients in J5:J7, you instantaneously create and complete another comparison.

In fact, I'll do that right now, and show you Scheffé's post hoc comparison. That one, in this example, compares the mean of Method 1 with the mean of Method 3. Figure 12-5 shows the extra information for this test, starting a couple of rows below the t-test.

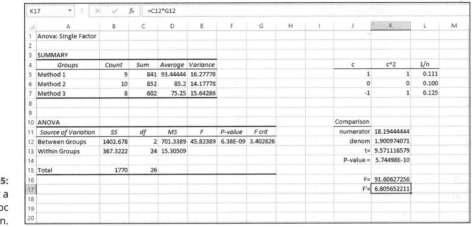

FIGURE 12-5:
Carrying out a
post hoc
comparison.

Cell K16 holds F, the square of the t value in K13. K17 has F', the product of C12 (df_B, which is the number of samples − 1) and G12 (the critical value of F for 2 and 24 degrees of freedom and $\alpha = .05$). K16 is greater than K17, so reject H_0 for this comparison.

Another Kind of Hypothesis, Another Kind of Test

The preceding ANOVA works with independent samples. As Chapter 11 explains, sometimes you work with matched samples. For example, sometimes a person provides data in a number of different conditions. In this section, I introduce the ANOVA you use when you have more than two matched samples.

This type of ANOVA is called *repeated measures*. You'll see it called other names, too, like *randomized blocks* or *within subjects*.

Working with repeated measures ANOVA

To show how this works, I extend the example from Chapter 11. In that example, ten people participate in a weight-loss program. Table 12-3 shows their data over a three-month period.

TABLE 12-3

Data for the Weight-Loss Example

Person	Before	One Month	Two Months	Three Months	Mean
1	198	194	191	188	192.75
2	201	203	200	196	200.00
3	210	200	192	188	197.50
4	185	183	180	178	181.50
5	204	200	195	191	197.50
6	156	153	150	145	151.00
7	167	166	167	166	166.50
8	197	197	195	192	195.25
9	220	215	209	205	212.25
10	186	184	179	175	181.00
Mean	192.4	189.5	185.8	182.4	187.525

Is the program effective? This question calls for a hypothesis test:

H_0: $\mu_{Before} = \mu_1 = \mu_2 = \mu_3$

H_1: Not H_0

Once again, I set $\alpha = .05$

As in the previous ANOVA, start with the variances in the data. The MS_T is the variance in all 40 scores from the grand mean, which is 187.525:

$$MS_T = \frac{(198 - 187.525)^2 + (201 - 187.525)^2 + \ldots + (175 - 187.525)^2}{(40 - 1)} = 318.20$$

The people participating in the weight-loss program also supply variance. Each one's overall mean (his or her average over the four measurements) varies from the grand mean. Because these data are in the rows, I call this MS_{Rows}:

$$MS_{Rows} = \frac{(192.75 - 187.525)^2 + (200 - 187.525)^2 + \ldots + (181 - 187.525)^2}{(10 - 1)} = 1292.41$$

The means of the columns also vary from the grand mean:

$$MS_{Columns} = \frac{(192.4 - 187.525)^2 + (189.5 - 187.525)^2 + (185.8 - 187.525)^2 + (182.4 - 187.525)^2}{(4 - 1)} = 189.69$$

One more source of variance is in the data. Think of it as the variance left over after you pull out the variance in the rows and the variance in the columns from the total variance. Actually, it's more correct to say that it's the Sum of Squares left over when you subtract the SS_{Rows} and the $SS_{Columns}$ from the SS_T.

This variance is called MS_{Error}. As I say earlier, in the ANOVA the denominator of an F is called an *error term.* So the word *error* here gives you a hint that this MS is a denominator for an F.

To calculate MS_{Error}, you use the relationships among the Sums of Squares and among the df.

$$MS_{Error} = \frac{SS_{Error}}{df_{Error}} = \frac{SS_T - SS_{Rows} - SS_{Columns}}{df_T - df_{Rows} - df_{Columns}} = \frac{209.175}{27} = 7.75$$

Here's another way to calculate the df_{Error}:

$$df_{Error} = (\text{number of rows - 1})(\text{number of columns - 1})$$

To perform the hypothesis test, you calculate the F:

$$F = \frac{MS_{Columns}}{MS_{Error}} = \frac{189.69}{7.75} = 24.49$$

With 3 and 27 degrees of freedom, the critical F for $\alpha = .05$ is 2.96. (Look it up or use the Excel worksheet function F.INV.RT.) The calculated F is larger than the critical F, so the decision is to reject H_0.

What about an F involving MS_{Rows}? That one doesn't figure into H_0 for this example. If you find a significant F, all it shows is that people are different from one another with respect to weight and that doesn't tell you very much.

As is the case with the ANOVA I showed you earlier, you plan comparisons to zero in on the differences. You can use the same formula, except you substitute MS_{Error} for MS_W:

$$t = \frac{c_1\bar{x}_1 + c_2\bar{x}_2 + c_3\bar{x}_3 + c_4\bar{x}_4}{\sqrt{MS_{Error}\left[\dfrac{c_1^2}{N_1} + \dfrac{c_2^2}{N_2} + \dfrac{c_3^2}{N_3} + \dfrac{c_4^2}{N_4}\right]}} = \frac{c_1\bar{x}_1 + c_2\bar{x}_2 + c_3\bar{x}_3 + c_4\bar{x}_4}{\sqrt{MS_{Error}\left[\dfrac{c_1^2 + c_2^2 + c_3^2 + c_4^2}{N}\right]}}$$

The formula works out to the expression on the right because in a repeated measures design all the Ns are the same.

The df for this test is df_{Error}.

For Scheffé's post hoc test, you also follow the same procedure as earlier and substitute MS_{Error} for MS_W. The only other change is to substitute $df_{Columns}$ for df_B and substitute df_{Error} for df_W when you find F'.

Getting trendy

In situations like the one in the weight-loss example, you have an independent variable that's quantitative — its levels are numbers (0 months, 1 month, 2 months, 3 months). Not only that, but in this case, the intervals are equal.

With that kind of an independent variable, it's often a good idea to look for trends in the data rather than just plan comparisons among means. If you graph the means in the weight-loss example, they seem to approximate a line, as Figure 12-6 shows. *Trend analysis* is the statistical procedure that examines that pattern. The objective is to see if the pattern contributes to the significant differences among the means.

A trend can be linear, as it apparently is in this example, or nonlinear (in which the means fall on a curve). In this example, I only deal with linear trend.

To analyze a trend, you use comparison coefficients — those numbers you use in planned comparisons. You just use them in a slightly different way than you did before.

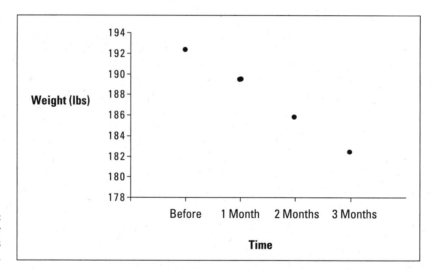

FIGURE 12-6:
The means for
the weight-loss
example.

Here, you use comparison coefficients to find a Sum of Squares for linear trend. I abbreviate that as SS_{Linear}. This is a portion of $SS_{Columns}$. In fact,

$$SS_{Linear} + SS_{Nonlinear} = SS_{Columns}$$

Also,

$$df_{Linear} + df_{Nonlinear} = df_{Columns}$$

After you calculate SS_{Linear}, you divide it by df_{Linear} to produce MS_{Linear}. This is extremely easy because $df_{Linear} = 1$. Divide MS_{Linear} by MS_{Error} and you have an F. If that F is higher than the critical value of F with df = 1 and df_{Error} at your α –level, then weight is decreasing in a linear way over the time period of the weight-loss program.

The comparison coefficients are different for different numbers of samples. For four samples, the coefficients are −3, −1, 1, and 3. To form the SS_{Linear}, the formula is

$$SS_{Linear} = \frac{N\left(\sum c\bar{x}\right)^2}{\sum c^2}$$

In this formula, N is the number of people and c represents the coefficients. Applying the formula to this example,

$$SS_{Linear} = \frac{N\left(\sum c\bar{x}\right)^2}{\sum c^2} = \frac{10\left[(-3)(192.4)+(-1)(189.5)+(1)(185.8)+(3)(182.4)\right]^2}{(-3)^2+(-1)^2+(3)^2+(1)^2} = 567.845$$

This is such a large proportion of $SS_{Columns}$ that $SS_{Nonlinear}$ is really small:

$$SS_{Nonlinear} = SS_{Columns} - SS_{Linear} = 569.075 - 567.845 = 1.23$$

As I point out earlier, df = 1, so MS_{Linear} is conveniently the same as SS_{Linear}.

Finally,

$$F = \frac{MS_{Linear}}{MS_{Error}} = \frac{567.85}{7.75} = 73.30$$

The critical value for F with 1 and 27 degrees of freedom and α = .05 is 4.21 (which I use F.INV.RT to calculate). Because the calculated value is larger than the critical value, statisticians would say the data shows a *significant linear component*. This, of course, verifies what you see shown earlier in Figure 12-6.

Data analysis tool: Anova: Two Factor Without Replication

Huh? Is that a misprint? *Two-Factor???* Without Replication?? What's that all about?

Here's the story: If you're looking through the data analysis tools for something like *Anova: Single Factor Repeated Measures*, you won't find it. The tool you're looking for is there, but it's hiding out under a different name.

A LITTLE MORE ON TREND

The coefficients I show you represent one possible component of what underlies the differences among the four means in the example — the linear component. With four means, it's also possible to have other components. I lump those other components together into a category I call *nonlinear*. Now I discuss them explicitly.

One possibility is that four means can differ from one another and form a trend that looks like a curve, as in the next figure.

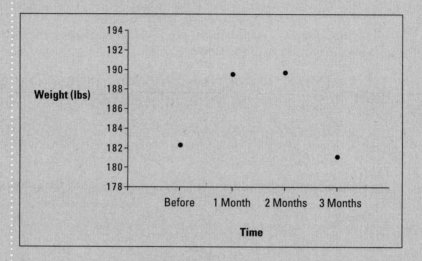

Four means can form still another kind of trend:

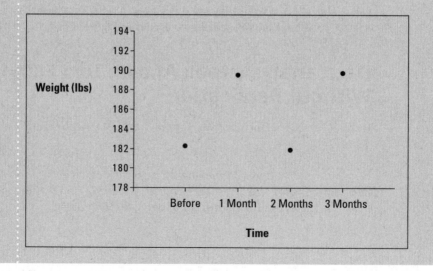

The first kind, where the trend changes direction once is called a *quadratic* component. In the first figure, it increases, and then it decreases. The second, where the trend changes direction twice, is called a *cubic* component. In the second figure, it increases, decreases, and then increases again. In Figure 12-6, the trend is linear and doesn't change direction (it just keeps decreasing).

Quadratic and cubic components have coefficients, too, and here they are:

Quadratic: 1, –1, –1, 1

Cubic: –1, 3, –3, 1

You test for these components the same way you test for the linear component. A trend can be a combination of components: If you have a significant F, one or more of these trend components might be significant.

Linear, quadratic, and cubic are as far as you can go with four means. With five means, you can look for those three plus a *quartic component* (three direction-changes), and with six you can try to scope out all of the preceding plus a *quintic component* (four direction-changes). What do the coefficients look like?

For five means, they're:

Linear: –2, –1, 0, 1, 2

Quadratic: 2, –1, –2, –1, 2

Cubic: -1, 2, 0, –2, 1

Quartic: 1, –4, 6, –4, 1

And for six means:

Linear: –5, –3, –1, 1, 3, 5

Quadratic: 5, –1, –4, –4, –1, 5

Cubic: –5, 7, 4, –4, –7, 5

Quartic: 1, –3, 2, 2, –3, 1

Quintic: –1, 5, –10, 10, –5, 1

I could go on with more means, coefficients, and exotic component names (hextic? septic?), but enough already. This should hold you for a while.

Figure 12-7 shows this tool's dialog box along with the data for the preceding weight-loss example.

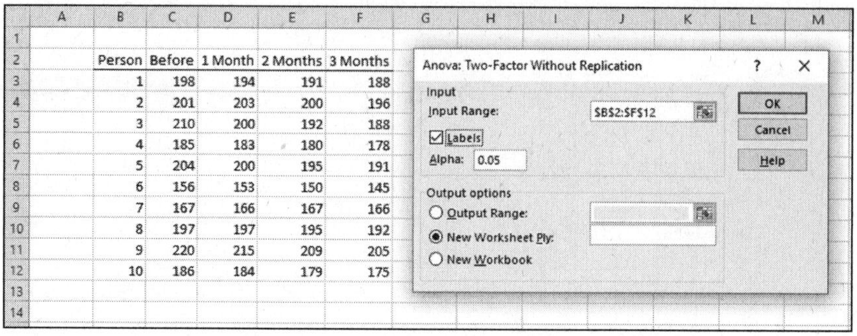

FIGURE 12-7:
The Anova: Two
Factor Without
Replication data
analysis tool
dialog box.

The steps for using this tool are:

1. **Type the data for each sample into a separate data array. Put the label for each person in a data array.**

   For this example, the labels for Person are in column B. The data in the Before sample are in column C, the data in the 1 Month sample are in column D, the data for the 2 Month sample are in column E, and the data for the 3 Month sample are in column F.

2. **Select DATA | Data Analysis to open the Data Analysis dialog box.**

3. **In the Data Analysis dialog box, scroll down the Analysis Tools list and select Anova: Two Factor Without Replication.**

4. **Click OK to open the select Anova: Two Factor Without Replication dialog box.**

   This is the dialog box shown in Figure 12-7.

5. **In the Input Range box, type the cell range that holds all the data.**

   For the example, the data are in $B$2:$F$12. Note the $ signs for absolute referencing. Note also — and this is important — the Person column is part of the data.

6. **If the cell ranges include column headings, select the Labels option.**

   I included the headings in the ranges, so I selected the box.

7. **The Alpha box has 0.05 as a default. Change that value if you want a different α.**

8. **In the Output Options, select a radio button to indicate where you want the results.**

   I selected New Worksheet Ply to put the results on a new page in the worksheet.

9. Click OK.

Because I selected New Worksheet Ply, a newly created page opens with the results.

Figure 12-8 shows the tool's output, after I expand the columns. The output features two tables: SUMMARY and ANOVA.

	A	B	C	D	E	F	G	H
3	SUMMARY	Count	Sum	Average	Variance			
4	1	4	771	192.75	18.25			
5	2	4	800	200	8.666667			
6	3	4	790	197.5	94.33333			
7	4	4	726	181.5	9.666667			
8	5	4	790	197.5	32.33333			
9	6	4	604	151	22			
10	7	4	666	166.5	0.333333			
11	8	4	781	195.25	5.583333			
12	9	4	849	212.25	43.58333			
13	10	4	724	181	24.66667			
14								
15	Before	10	1924	192.4	377.6			
16	1 Month	10	1895	189.5	342.9444			
17	2 Months	10	1858	185.8	298.8444			
18	3 Months	10	1824	182.4	296.2667			
19								
20								
21	ANOVA							
22	Source of Variation	SS	df	MS	F	P-value	F crit	
23	Rows	11631.73	9	1292.414	166.8229	2.7098E-21	2.250131	
24	Columns	569.075	3	189.6917	24.48512	7.3047E-08	2.960351	
25	Linear	567.845	1	567.845	73.29659	3.5565E-09	4.210008	
26	NonLinear	1.23	2	0.615	0.079383			
27	Error	209.175	27	7.747222				
28								
29	Total	12409.98	39					
30								

FIGURE 12-8: Output from the Anova: Two Factor Without Replication data analysis tool.

The SUMMARY table is in two parts. The first part provides summary statistics for the rows. The second part provides summary statistics for the columns. Summary statistics include the number of scores in each row and in each column along with the sums, means, and variances.

The ANOVA table presents the Sums of Squares, df, Mean Squares, F, P-values, and critical F-ratios for the indicated df. The table features two values for F. One F is for the rows, and the other is for the columns. The P-value is the proportion of area that the F cuts off in the upper tail of the F-distribution. If this value is less than .05, reject H_0.

Although the ANOVA table includes an F for the rows, this doesn't concern you in this case, because H_0 is only about the columns in the data. Each row represents the data for one person. A high F just implies that people are different from one another, and that's not news.

Analyzing trend

Excel's Anova: Two-Factor Without Replication tool does not provide a way for performing a trend analysis. As with the planned comparisons, a little ingenuity takes you a long way. The Excel worksheet functions SUMPRODUCT and SUMSQ help with the calculations.

The worksheet page with the ANOVA output gives the information you need to get started. In this section, I take you through the analysis of linear trend.

I start by putting the comparison coefficients for linear trend into J15 through J18, as shown in Figure 12-9.

In J22 through J24, I put information related to SS_{Linear} — the numerator, the denominator, and the value of the Sum of Squares. I use separate cells for the numerator and denominator to simplify the formulas.

As I point out earlier, SUMPRODUCT takes arrays of cells, multiplies the numbers in the corresponding cells, and sums the products. (This function is on the Math & Trig menu, not the Statistical Functions menu.) I used SUMPRODUCT to multiply each coefficient by each sample mean and then add the products. I stored that result in J22. That's the numerator for the SS_{Linear}. I selected J22 so that you could see its formula in the Formula bar:

```
=B15*SUMPRODUCT(J15:J18,D15:D18)^2
```

J22		× ✓ fx	=B15*SUMPRODUCT(J15:J18,D15:D18)^2							
	A	B	C	D	E	F	G	H	I	J
3	SUMMARY	Count	Sum	Average	Variance					
4	1	4	771	192.75	18.25					
5	2	4	800	200	8.666667					
6	3	4	790	197.5	94.33333					
7	4	4	726	181.5	9.666667					
8	5	4	790	197.5	32.33333					
9	6	4	604	151	22					
10	7	4	666	166.5	0.333333					
11	8	4	781	195.25	5.583333					
12	9	4	849	212.25	43.58333					
13	10	4	724	181	24.66667					
14										coefficients
15	Before	10	1924	192.4	377.6					-3
16	1 Month	10	1895	189.5	342.9444					-1
17	2 Months	10	1858	185.8	298.8444					1
18	3 Months	10	1824	182.4	296.2667					3
19										
20										
21	ANOVA									
22	Source of Variation	SS	df	MS	F	P-value	F crit		Numerator	11356.9
23	Rows	11631.73	9	1292.414	166.8229	2.7098E-21	2.250131		Denominator	20
24	Columns	569.075	3	189.6917	24.48512	7.3047E-08	2.960351		SS linear =	567.845
25	Linear	567.845	1	567.845	73.29659	3.5565E-09	4.210008			
26	NonLinear	1.23	2	0.615	0.079383					
27	Error	209.175	27	7.747222						
28										
29	Total	12409.98	39							
30										

FIGURE 12-9:
Carrying out a trend analysis.

The value in B15 is the number in each column. The array J15:J18 holds the comparison coefficients, and D15:D18 holds the column means.

J23 holds the denominator. Its formula is

```
=SUMSQ(J15:J18)
```

SUMSQ (another function on the Math & Trig Functions menu) squares the coefficients in J15:J18 and adds them.

J24 holds the value for SS_{Linear}. That's J22 divided by J23.

Figure 12-9 also shows that in the ANOVA table I've inserted two rows above the row for Error. One row holds the SS, df, MS, F, P-Value, and critical F for Linear, and the other holds these values for Nonlinear. $SS_{Nonlinear}$ in B26 is B24-B25.

The F for Linear is D25 divided by D27. The formula for the P-Value in F25 is

```
=F.DIST.RT(E25,C25,C27)
```

The first argument, E25, is the F. The second and third arguments are the df.

The formula for the critical F in F25 is

```
=F.INV.RT(0.05,C25,C27)
```

The first argument is α, and the second and third are the df.

Chapter 13

Slightly More Complicated Testing

n Chapter 11, I show you how to test hypotheses with two samples. In Chapter 12, I show you how to test hypotheses when you have more than two samples. The common thread through both chapters is that one independent variable (also called a *factor*) is involved.

Many times, you have to test the effects of more than one factor. In this chapter, I show how to analyze two factors within the same set of data. Several types of situations are possible, and I describe Excel data analysis tools that deal with each one.

Cracking the Combinations

FarKlempt Robotics, Inc., manufactures battery-powered robots. They want to test three rechargeable batteries for these robots on a set of three tasks: climbing, walking, and assembling. Which combination of battery and task results in the longest battery life?

They test a sample of nine robots. They randomly assign each robot one battery and one type of task. FarKlempt tracks the number of days each robot works before recharging. The data are in Table 13-1.

TABLE 13-1

Task	Battery 1	Battery 2	Battery 3	Average
Climbing	12	15	20	15.67
Walking	14	16	19	16.33
Assembling	11	14	18	14.33
Average	12.33	15.00	19.00	15.44

This calls for two hypothesis tests:

$H_0: \mu_{Battery1} = \mu_{Battery2} = \mu_{Battery3}$

$H_1:$ Not H_0

and

$H_0: \mu_{Climbing} = \mu_{Walking} = \mu_{Assembling}$

$H_1:$ Not H_0

In both tests, set $\alpha = .05$.

Breaking down the variances

The appropriate analysis for these tests is an analysis of variance (ANOVA). Each variable — Batteries and Tasks — is also called a *factor*. So this analysis is called a *two-factor ANOVA*.

To understand this ANOVA, consider the variances inside the data. First, focus on the variance in the whole set of nine numbers — MS_T. (T in the subscript stands for *Total.*) The mean of those numbers is 15.44. Because it's the mean of all the numbers, it goes by the name *grand mean*.

This variance is

$$MS_T = \frac{(12-15.44)^2 + (15-15.44)^2 + \ldots + (18-15.44)^2}{9-1} = \frac{76.22}{8} = 9.53$$

The means of the three batteries (the column means) also vary from 15.44. That variance is

$$MS_{Batteries} = \frac{(3)(12.33-15.44)^2 + (3)(15.00-15.44)^2 + (3)(19.00-15.44)^2}{3-1} = \frac{67.56}{2} = 33.78$$

Why does the 3 appear as a multiplier of each squared deviation? When you deal with means, you have to take into account the number of scores that produce each mean.

Similarly, the means of the tasks (the row means) vary from 15.44:

$$MS_{Tasks} = \frac{(3)(15.67-15.44)^2 + (3)(16.33-15.44)^2 + (3)(14.33-15.44)^2}{3-1} = \frac{6.22}{2} = 3.11$$

One variance is left. It's called MS_{Error}. This is what remains when you subtract the $SS_{Batteries}$ and the SS_{Tasks} from the SS_T, and divide that by the df that remains when you subtract $df_{Batteries}$ and df_{Tasks} from df_T:

$$MS_{Error} = \frac{SS_T - SS_{Batteries} - SS_{Tasks}}{df_T - df_{Batteries} - df_{Tasks}} = \frac{2.44}{4} = 0.61$$

To test the hypotheses, you calculate one F for the effects of the batteries and another for the effects of the tasks. For both, the denominator (the *error term*) is MS_{Error}:

$$F = \frac{MS_{Batteries}}{MS_{Error}} = \frac{33.77}{0.61} = 55.27$$

$$F = \frac{MS_{Tasks}}{MS_{Error}} = \frac{2.44}{0.61} = 5.09$$

Each F has 2 and 4 degrees of freedom. With $\alpha = .05$, the critical F in each case is 6.94. The decision is to reject H_0 for the batteries (they differ from one another to an extent greater than chance), but not for the tasks.

To zero in on the differences for the batteries, you carry out planned comparisons among the column means. (See Chapter 12 for the details.)

Data analysis tool: Anova: Two-Factor Without Replication

Excel's Anova: Two-Factor Without Replication tool carries out the analysis I just outlined. (I use this tool for another type of analysis in Chapter 12.) *Without Replication* means that only one robot is assigned to each battery-task combination. If you assign more than one to each combination, that's *replication*.

Figure 13-1 shows this tool's dialog box along with the data for the Batteries-Tasks example.

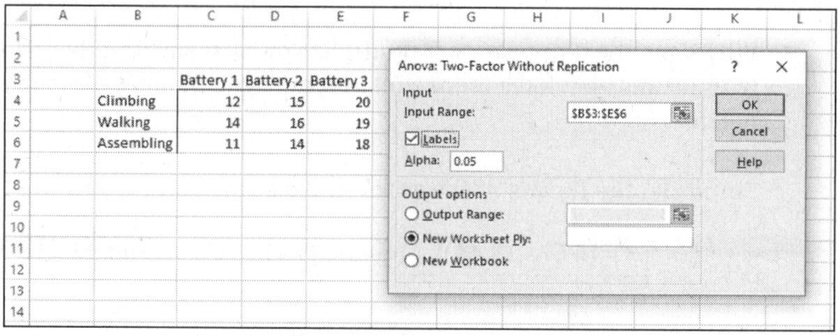

FIGURE 13-1:
The Anova:
Two-Factor
Without
Replication data
analysis tool
dialog box along
with the
Batteries-Tasks
data.

The steps for using this tool are:

1. **Enter the data into the worksheet, and include labels for the rows and columns.**

   For this example, the labels for the tasks are in cells B4, B5, and B6. The labels for the batteries are in cells C3, D3, and E3. The data are in cells C4 through E6.

2. **Select DATA | Data Analysis to open the Data Analysis dialog box.**

3. **In the Data Analysis dialog box, scroll down the Analysis Tools list and select Anova: Two-Factor Without Replication.**

4. **Click OK to open the Anova: Two-Factor Without Replication dialog box.**

   This is the dialog box in Figure 13-1.

5. **In the Input Range box, enter the cell range that holds all the data.**

   For the example, the data range is $B$3:$E$6. Note the $ signs for absolute referencing. Note also — and this is important — the row labels are part of the data range. The column labels are, too. The first cell in the data range, B2, is blank, but that's okay.

6. **If the cell ranges include column headings, select the Labels option.**

   I included the headings in the ranges, so I selected the box.

7. **The Alpha box has 0.05 as a default. Change that value if you want a different α.**

8. **In the Output Options, select a radio button to indicate where you want the results.**

   I selected New Worksheet Ply to put the results on a new page in the worksheet.

9. **Click OK.**

   Because I selected New Worksheet Ply, a newly created page opens with the results.

Figure 13-2 shows the tool's output, after I expanded the columns. The output features two tables: SUMMARY and ANOVA.

The SUMMARY table is in two parts. The first part provides summary statistics for the rows. The second part provides summary statistics for the columns. Summary statistics include the number of scores in each row and in each column along with the sums, means, and variances.

	A	B	C	D	E	F	G	H
1	Anova: Two-Factor Without Replication							
2								
3	SUMMARY	Count	Sum	Average	Variance			
4	Climbing	3	47	15.66667	16.33333			
5	Walking	3	49	16.33333	6.333333			
6	Assembling	3	43	14.33333	12.33333			
7								
8	Battery 1	3	37	12.33333	2.333333			
9	Battery 2	3	45	15	1			
10	Battery 3	3	57	19	1			
11								
12								
13	ANOVA							
14	Source of Variation	SS	df	MS	F	P-value	F crit	
15	Rows	6.222222	2	3.111111	5.090909	0.079553	6.944272	
16	Columns	67.55556	2	33.77778	55.27273	0.001219	6.944272	
17	Error	2.444444	4	0.611111				
18								
19	Total	76.22222	8					
20								
21								

The ANOVA table presents the Sums of Squares, df, Mean Squares, F, P-values, and critical F for the indicated df. The table features two values for F. One F is for the rows, and the other is for the columns. The P-value is the proportion of area that the F cuts off in the upper tail of the F-distribution. If this value is less than .05, reject H_0.

In this example, the decisions are to reject H_0 for the batteries (the columns) and to not reject H_0 for the tasks (the rows).

Cracking the Combinations Again

The preceding analysis involves one score for each combination of the two factors. Assigning one individual to each combination is appropriate for robots and other manufactured objects, where you can assume that one object is pretty much the same as another.

When people are involved, it's a different story. Individual variation among humans is something you can't overlook. For this reason, it's necessary to assign a sample of people to a combination of factors — not just one person.

Rows and columns

I illustrate with an example. Imagine that a company has two methods of presenting its training information. One is via a person who presents the information orally, and the other is via a text. Imagine also that the information is presented in either a humorous way or in a technical way. I refer to the first factor as Presentation Method and to the second as Presentation Style.

Combining the two levels of Presentation Method with the two levels of Presentation Style gives four combinations. The company randomly assigns 4 people to each combination, for a total of 16 people. After providing the training, they test the 16 people on their comprehension of the material.

Figure 13-3 shows the combinations, the four comprehension scores within each combination, and summary statistics for the combinations, rows, and columns.

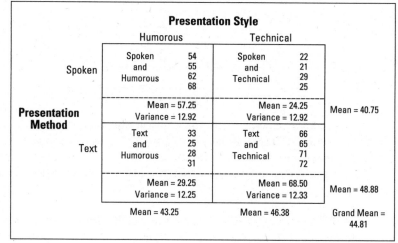

FIGURE 13-3: Combining the levels of Presentation Method with the levels of Presentation Style.

Here are the hypotheses:

$H_0: \mu_{Spoken} = \mu_{Text}$

$H_1:$ Not H_0

and

$H_0: \mu_{Humorous} = \mu_{Technical}$

$H_1:$ Not H_0

Because the two presentation methods (Spoken and Text) are in the rows, I refer to Presentation Type as the *row factor*. The two presentation styles (Humorous and Technical) are in the columns, so Presentation Style is the *column factor*.

Interactions

When you have rows and columns of data, and you're testing hypotheses about the row factor and the column factor, you have an additional consideration. Namely, you have to be concerned about the row–column combinations. Do the combinations result in peculiar effects?

For the example I present, it's possible that combining Spoken and Text with Humorous and Technical yields something unexpected. In fact, you can see that in the data in Figure 13-3: For Spoken presentation, the Humorous style produces a higher average than the Technical style. For Text presentation, the Humorous style produces a lower average than the Technical style.

A situation like that is called an *interaction*. In formal terms, an interaction occurs when the levels of one factor affect the levels of the other factor differently. The label for the interaction is row factor X column factor, so for this example, that's Method X Type.

The hypotheses for this are

H_0: Presentation Method does not interact with Presentation Style

H_1: Not H_0

The analysis

The statistical analysis, once again, is an analysis of variance (ANOVA). As is the case with the earlier ANOVAs I show you, it depends on the variances in the data.

The first variance is the total variance, labeled MS_T. That's the variance of all 16 scores around their mean (the "grand mean"), which is 44.81:

$$MS_T = \frac{(54 - 44.81)^2 + (55 - 44.81)^2 + ... + (72 - 44.81)^2}{16 - 1} = \frac{5674.44}{15} = 378.30$$

The denominator tells you that df = 15 for MS_T.

The next variance comes from the row factor. That's MS_{Method}, and it's the variance of the row means around the grand mean:

$$MS_{Method} = \frac{(8)(40.75 - 44.81)^2 + (8)(48.88 - 44.81)^2}{2 - 1} = \frac{264.06}{1} = 264.06$$

The 8 multiplies each squared deviation because you have to take into account the number of scores that produced each row mean. The df for MS_{Method} is the number of rows − 1, which is 1.

Similarly, the variance for the column factor is

$$MS_{Style} = \frac{(8)(43.25 - 44.81)^2 + (8)(46.38 - 44.81)^2}{2 - 1} = \frac{39.06}{1} = 39.06$$

The df for MS_{Style} is 1 (the number of columns − 1).

Another variance is the pooled estimate based on the variances within the four row-column combinations. It's called the MS_{Within}, or MS_W. (For details on MS_W and pooled estimates, see Chapter 12.). For this example,

$$MS_W = \frac{(4-1)(12.92) + (4-1)(12.92) + (4-1)(12.25) + (4-1)(12.33)}{(4-1) + (4-1) + (4-1) + (4-1)} = \frac{151.25}{12} = 12.60$$

This one is the error term (the denominator) for each F that you calculate. Its denominator tells you that df = 12 for this MS.

The last variance comes from the interaction between the row factor and the column factor. In this example, it's labeled $MS_{Method \times Type}$. You can calculate this in a couple of ways. The easiest way is to take advantage of this general relationship:

$$SS_{Row \times Column} = SS_T - SS_{Row\ Factor} - SS_{Column\ Factor} - SS_W$$

And this one:

$$df_{Row \times Column} = df_T - df_{Row\ Factor} - df_{Column\ Factor} - df_W$$

Another way to calculate this is

$$df_{Row \times Column} = (\text{number of rows - 1})(\text{number of columns - 1})$$

The MS is

$$MS_{Row \times Column} = \frac{SS_{Row \times Column}}{df_{Row \times Column}}$$

For this example,

$$MS_{Method \times Style} = \frac{SS_{Method \times Style}}{df_{Method \times Style}} = \frac{5764.44 - 264.06 - 39.06 - 151.25}{15 - 12 - 1 - 1} = \frac{5220.06}{1} = 5220.06$$

To test the hypotheses, you calculate three Fs:

$$F = \frac{MS_{Style}}{MS_W} = \frac{39.06}{12.60} = 3.10$$

$$F = \frac{MS_{Method}}{MS_W} = \frac{264.06}{12.60} = 20.95$$

$$F = \frac{MS_{Method \times Style}}{MS_W} = \frac{5220.06}{12.60} = 414.15$$

For df = 1 and 12, the critical F at α = .05 is 4.75. (You can use the Excel function FINV to verify.) The decision is to reject H_0 for the Presentation Method and for the Method X Style interaction, and to not reject H_0 for the Presentation Style.

Data analysis tool: Anova: Two-Factor With Replication

Excel provides a data analysis tool that handles everything I just spelled out in the previous section. This one is called Anova: Two-Factor With Replication. *Replication* means that you have more than one score in each row–column combination.

Figure 13-4 shows this tool's dialog box along with the data for the batteries-tasks example.

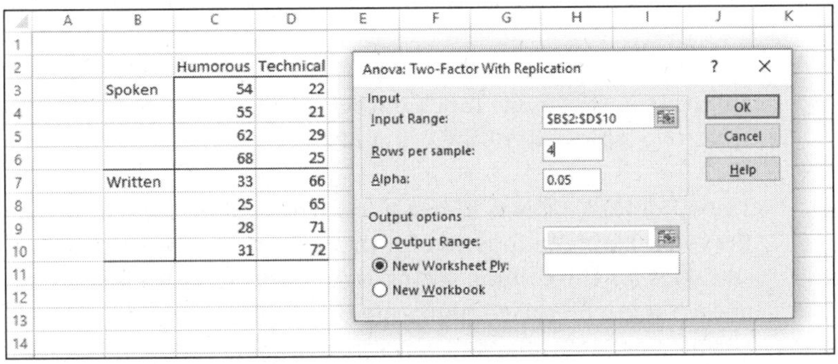

FIGURE 13-4:
The Anova: Two-Factor With Replication data analysis tool dialog box along with the type-method data.

The steps for using this tool are:

1. **Enter the data into the worksheet and include labels for the rows and columns.**

   For this example, the labels for the presentation methods are in cells B3 and B7. The presentation types are in cells C2 and D2. The data are in cells C3 through D10.

2. **Select Data | Data Analysis to open the Data Analysis dialog box.**

3. **In the Data Analysis dialog box, scroll down the Analysis Tools list and select Anova: Two-Factor With Replication.**

4. **Click OK to open the Anova: Two-Factor With Replication dialog box.**

This is the dialog box in Figure 13-4.

5. **In the Input Range box, type the cell range that holds all the data.**

For the example, the data are in $B$2:$D$10. Note the $ signs for absolute referencing. Note also — again, this is important — the labels for the row factor (presentation method) are part of the data range. The labels for the column factor are part of the range, too. The first cell in the range, B2, is blank, but that's okay.

6. **In the Rows per Sample box, type the number of scores in each combination of the two factors.**

I typed **4** into this box.

7. **The Alpha box has 0.05 as a default. Change that value if you want a different α.**

8. **In the Output Options, select a radio button to indicate where you want the results.**

I selected New Worksheet Ply to put the results on a new page in the worksheet.

9. **Click OK.**

Because I selected New Worksheet Ply, a newly created page opens with the results.

Figure 13-5 shows the tool's output, after I expand the columns. The output features two tables: SUMMARY and ANOVA.

The SUMMARY table is in two parts. The first part provides summary statistics for the factor combinations and for the row factor. The second part provides summary statistics for the column factor. Summary statistics include the number of scores in each row–column combination, in each row, and in each column along with the counts, sums, means, and variances.

The ANOVA table presents the Sums of Squares, df, Mean Squares, F, P-values, and critical F for the indicated df. The table features three values for F. One F is for the row factor, one for the column factor, and one for the interaction. In the table, the row factor is called Sample. The P-value is the proportion of area that the F cuts off in the upper tail of the F-distribution. If this value is less than .05, reject H_0.

▲	A	B	C	D	E	F	G
1	Anova: Two-Factor With Replication						
2							
3	SUMMARY	Humorous	Technical	Total			
4	Spoken						
5	Count	4	4	8			
6	Sum	239	97	336			
7	Average	59.75	24.25	42			
8	Variance	42.91666667	12.91666667	384			
9							
10	Written						
11	Count	4	4	8			
12	Sum	117	274	391			
13	Average	29.25	68.5	48.875			
14	Variance	12.25	12.33333333	450.6964			
15							
16	Total						
17	Count	8	8				
18	Sum	356	371				
19	Average	44.5	46.375				
20	Variance	289.4285714	570.2678571				
21							
22	ANOVA						
23	Source of Variation	SS	df	MS	F	P-value	F crit
24	Sample	189.0625	1	189.0625	9.404145	0.009778	4.747225
25	Columns	14.0625	1	14.0625	0.699482	0.419301	4.747225
26	Interaction	5587.5625	1	5587.563	277.9306	1.15E-09	4.747225
27	Within	241.25	12	20.10417			
28							
29	Total	6031.9375	15				

FIGURE 13-5: Output from the Anova: Two-Factor With Replication data analysis tool.

In this example, the decisions are to reject H_0 for the Presentation Method (the row factor, labeled Sample in the table), to not reject H_0 for the Presentation Style (the column factor), and to reject H_0 for the interaction.

Two Kinds of Variables . . . at Once

What happens when you have a Between Groups variable and a Within Groups variable . . . at the same time? (It's called a *Mixed* design.) How can that happen?

Very easily. Here's an example. Suppose you want to study the effects of presentation media on the reading speeds of fourth-graders. You randomly assign your fourth-graders (I'll call them *subjects*) to read either e-readers or books. That's the Between Groups variable.

Let's say you're also interested in the effects of font. So you assign each subject to read each of these fonts: Haettenschweiler, Arial, and Calibri. (I've never seen a document in Haettenschweiler, but it's my favorite font because "Haettenschweiler" is fun to say. Try it. Am I right?) Because each subject reads all the fonts, that's the Within Groups variable. For completeness, you have to randomly order the fonts for each subject.

What would the ANOVA table look like? Table **13-2** shows you in a generic way. It's categorized into a set of sources that make up Between Groups variability, and a set of sources that make up Within Groups variability.

In the Between category, A is the name of the Between Groups variable. Read "S/A" as "S within A." This just says that the people in one level of A are different from the people in the other levels of A.

In the Within category, B is the name of the Within Groups. A X B is the interaction of the two variables. B X S/A is something like the B variable interacting with subjects within A. As you can see, anything associated with B falls into the Within Groups category.

TABLE 13-2   **The ANOVA Table for the Mixed ANOVA (One Between Groups Variable and One Within Groups Variable)**

Source	SS	df	MS	F
Between	$SS_{Between}$	$df_{Between}$		
A	SS_A	df_A	SS_A/df_A	$MS_A/MS_{S/A}$
S/A	$SS_{S/A}$	$df_{S/A}$	$SS_{S/A}/df_{S/A}$	
Within	SS_{Within}	df_{Within}		
B	SS_B	df_B	SS_B/df_B	$MS_B/MS_{B \times S/A}$
A X B	$SS_{A \times B}$	$df_{A \times B}$	$SS_{A \times B}/df_{A \times B}$	$MS_{A \times B}/MS_{B \times S/A}$
B X S/A	$SS_{B \times S/A}$	$df_{B \times S/A}$	$SS_{B \times S/A}/df_{B \times S/A}$	
Total	SS_{Total}	df_{Total}		

The first thing to note is the three F-ratios. The first one tests for differences among the levels of A, the second for differences among the levels of B, and the third for the interaction of the two. Notice also that the denominator for the first F-ratio is different from the denominator for the other two. This happens more and more as ANOVAs increase in complexity.

Next, it's important to be aware of some relationships. At the top level:

$$SS_{Between} + SS_{Within} = SS_{Total}$$

$$df_{Between} + df_{Within} = df_{Total}$$

The Between component breaks down further:

$$SS_A + SS_{S/A} = SS_{Between}$$

$$df_A + df_{S/A} = df_{Between}$$

The Within component breaks down, too:

$$SS_B + SS_{A \times B} + SS_{B \times S/A} = SS_{Within}$$

$$df_B + df_{A \times B} + df_{B \times S/A} = df_{Within}$$

Knowing these relationships helps complete the ANOVA table after Excel has gone through its paces.

Using Excel with a Mixed Design

Someday, Excel's Analysis ToolPak might have a choice labeled ANOVA: Mixed Design. That day, unfortunately, is not today. Instead, I use two ToolPak tools and knowledge about this type of design to provide the analysis.

I begin with the data for the study I describe earlier. Figure 13-6 shows a worksheet with the data. The levels of the Between Group variable, Media (the A variable), are in the left column. The levels of the Within Group variable, Font (the B variable), are in the top row. Each cell entry is a reading speed in words per minute.

FIGURE 13-6:
Data for a study with a Between Group variable and a Within Group variable.

	A	B	C	D	E	F
1			Subject	Haettenschweiler	Arial	Callibri
2			1	48	40	38
3		Book	2	55	43	45
4			3	46	45	44
5			4	61	53	53
6			5	43	45	47
7		E-reader	6	50	52	54
8			7	56	57	57
9			8	53	53	55
10						

Next, Figure 13-7 shows the completed ANOVA table.

How do you get there? Surprisingly, it's pretty easy, although quite a few steps are involved. All you have to do is run two ANOVAs on the same data and combine the ANOVA tables. The relationships I show you in the preceding section complete the pieces in the puzzle.

FIGURE 13-7:
The completed
ANOVA table for
the analysis of
the data in
Figure 13-6.

	ANOVA						
2	ANOVA						
3	*Source of Variation*	SS	df	MS	F	P-value	F crit
4	Between Group	638.2917	7				
5	Media	108.375	1	108.375	1.22708	0.310396	5.987378
6	Subject/Media	529.9167	6	88.31944			
7							
8	Within Group	202.6667	16				
9	Font	40.08333	2	20.04167	5.681102	0.018366	3.885294
10	Media X Font	120.25	2	60.125	17.04331	0.000312	3.885294
11	Font X Subject/Media	42.33333	12	3.527778			
12							
13	Total	840.9583	23				

Follow these steps:

1. **With the data entered into a worksheet, select Data | Data Analysis.**

   This opens the Data Analysis dialog box.

2. **From the Data Analysis dialog box, select Anova: Two-Factor Without Replication.**

   This opens the Anova: Two-Factor Without Replication dialog box.

3. **In the Input Range box, enter the cell range that holds the data.**

   For this example, that's C1:F9. This range includes the column headers, so select the Labels check box.

4. **With the New Worksheet Ply radio button selected, click OK.**

   The result is the ANOVA table in Figure 13-8.

FIGURE 13-8:
The ANOVA table
for the first of
two ANOVAs.

	ANOVA						
18	ANOVA						
19	*Source of Variation*	SS	df	MS	F	P-value	F crit
20	Rows	638.2916667	7	91.18452381	7.851870835	0.000590448	2.764199257
21	Columns	40.08333333	2	20.04166667	1.72578165	0.213823725	3.738891832
22	Error	162.5833333	14	11.61309524			
23							
24	Total	840.9583333	23				

5. **Modify the ANOVA table: Insert rows for terms from the second ANOVA, change names of the Sources of Variance, and delete unnecessary values.**

   First, insert four rows between Rows and Columns (between Row 20 and the original Row 21).

   Next, change Rows to Between Group and Columns to Font (the name of the B variable).

   Then, delete all the information from the row that has *Error* in the Source column.

   Finally, delete the *F*-ratios, *P*-values, and *F*-crits. The ANOVA table now looks like Figure 13-9.

FIGURE 13-9:
The first ANOVA table after modifications.

	ANOVA						
18	ANOVA						
19	Source of Variation	SS	df	MS	F	P-value	F crit
20	Between Group	638.2916667	7	91.18452381			
21							
22							
23							
24							
25	Font	40.08333333	2	20.04166667			
26							
27							
28	Total	840.9583333	23				

6. **Once again, select Data | Data Analysis.**

7. **This time, from the Data Analysis dialog box choose ANOVA: Two-Factor With Replication.**

8. **In the Input Range box, enter the cell array that holds the data, including the column headers.**

   To do this, select C1:F9 in the worksheet.

9. **In the Rows Per Sample box, enter the number of subjects within each level of the Between Groups variable.**

   For this example, that's 4.

10. **With the New Worksheet Ply radio button selected, click OK.**

11. **Copy the resulting ANOVA table and paste it into the worksheet with the first ANOVA, just below the first ANOVA table.**

   The worksheet should look like Figure 13-10.

	ANOVA						
18	ANOVA						
19	Source of Variation	SS	df	MS	F	P-value	F crit
20	Between Group	638.2916667	7	91.18452381			
21							
22							
23							
24							
25	Font	40.08333333	2	20.04166667			
26							
27							
28	Total	840.9583333	23				
29							
30	ANOVA						
31	Source of Variation	SS	df	MS	F	P-value	F crit
32	Sample	108.375	1	108.375	3.408912189	0.081355668	4.413873419
33	Columns	40.08333333	2	20.04166667	0.630406291	0.543727248	3.554557146
34	Interaction	120.25	2	60.125	1.891218873	0.179677714	3.554557146
35	Within	572.25	18	31.79166667			
36							
37	Total	840.9583333	23				

12. **Add Within Group to the first ANOVA table, four rows under Between Group, and calculate values for SS and df.**

Type **Within Group** into row 24. The SS for Within Group is the SS Total – SS Between Group (B28-B20). The df for Within Group is the df Total – df Between Group (C28-C20).

13. **Copy the Sample row of data from the second ANOVA table and paste it into the first ANOVA table just below Between Group.**

Copy and paste just the Source name (Sample), its SS and its df.

14. **Change *Sample* to the name of the Between Group variable (the A variable).**

Change Sample to Media.

15. **In the next row, enter the name of the source for S/A, and calculate its SS, df, and MS.**

Enter Subject/Media. The SS is the SS Between Group – SS Media (B20:B21). The df is the df Between Group – df Media (C20:C21). The MS is the SS divided by the df (B22/C22).

16. **In the appropriate cell, calculate the *F* ratio for the A variable.**

That's MS Media divided by MS Subject/Media (D21/D22) calculated in E21. The ANOVA table now looks like Figure 13-11.

FIGURE 13-11:
The ANOVA table with the information for the Between Group variable and part of the information for the Within Group variable.

	Source of Variation	SS	df	MS	F	P-value	F crit
18	ANOVA						
19	Source of Variation	SS	df	MS	F	P-value	F crit
20	Between Group	638.2916667	7	91.18452381			
21	Media	108.375	1	108.375	1.22707973		
22	Subject/Media	529.9166667	6	88.31944444			
23							
24	Within Group	202.6666667	16				
25	Font	40.08333333	2	20.04166667			
26							
27							
28	Total	840.9583333	23				

17. **From the second ANOVA table, copy the Interaction, its SS, its df, and its MS, and paste into the first ANOVA table in the row just below the name of the B variable. Change Interaction to the name of the interaction between the A variable and the B variable.**

Copy the information from Row 34 into Row 26, just below Font. Change Interaction to Media X Font.

18. **In the next row, type the name of the source for B X S/A and calculate its SS, df, and MS.**

Type **Font X Subject/Media** into A27. The SS is the SS Within Group – SS Font – SS Media X Font (B24 – B25 – B26). The df is the df Within Group – df Font – df Media X Font (C24 – C25 – C26). The MS is the SS divided by the df (B27/C27).

19. In the appropriate cells, calculate the remaining *F*-ratios.

In E25, divide D25 by D27. In E26, divide D26 by D27. For clarity, insert a row just above Total. The table now looks like Figure 13-12.

To make the table look like Figure 13-7, shown earlier, use $\texttt{F.DIST.RT}$ to find the *P*-values, and $\texttt{F.INV.RT}$ to find the *F*-crits. (I discuss these functions in Chapter 11.) You can also delete the value for $MS_{\text{Between Group}}$, because it serves no purpose.

For some nice cosmetic effects, indent the sources under the main categories (Between Groups and Within Groups), and center the df for the main categories.

And what about the analysis? The completed ANOVA table shows no effect of Media, a significant effect of Font, and a Media X Font interaction.

	Source of Variation	SS	df	MS	F	P-value	F crit
18	ANOVA						
19	*Source of Variation*	SS	df	MS	F	P-value	F crit
20	Between Group	638.2916667	7	91.18452381			
21	Media	108.375	1	108.375	1.22707973		
22	Subject/Media	529.9166667	6	88.31944444			
23							
24	Within Group	202.6666667	16				
25	Font	40.08333333	2	20.04166667	5.681102362		
26	Media X Font	120.25	2	60.125	17.04330709		
27	Font X Subject/Media	42.33333333	12	3.527777778			
28							
29	Total	840.9583333	23				

FIGURE 13-12: The ANOVA table with all the SS, df, MS and *F*-ratios.

REMEMBER

This procedure uses Anova: Two-Factor With Replication, a tool that depends on an equal number of replications (rows) for each combination of factors. So for this procedure to work, you have to have an equal number of people in each level of the Between Groups variable.

Graphing the Results

Because this isn't a built-in tool, Excel doesn't produce the descriptive statistics for each combination of conditions. You have to have those statistics (means and standard errors) to create a chart of the results.

This, of course, isn't hard to do. Figure 13-13 shows the table of means and the table of standard errors along with the data. Each entry in the means table is just the AVERAGE function applied to the appropriate cell range. So the value in D13 is

```
=AVERAGE(D2:D5)
```

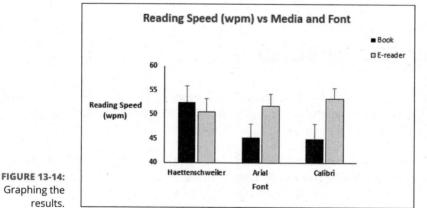

D18			f_x	=STDEV.S(D2:D5)/SQRT(COUNT(D2:D5))		
	A	B	C	D	E	F
1			Subject	Haettenschweiler	Arial	Calibri
2			1	48	40	38
3		Book	2	55	43	45
4			3	46	45	44
5			4	61	53	53
6			5	43	45	47
7		E-reader	6	50	52	54
8			7	56	57	57
9			8	53	53	55
10						
11						
12				Haettenschweiler	Arial	Calibri
13		Means	Book	52.5	45.25	45
14			E-reader	50.5	51.75	53.25
15						
16						
17				Haettenschweiler	Arial	Calibri
18		Standard Errors	Book	3.43	2.78	3.08
19			E-reader	2.78	2.50	2.17
20						

FIGURE 13-13: The data along with the Means table and the Standard Errors table.

Each entry in the Standard Errors table is the result of applying three functions to the appropriate cell range. To show you an example, I've selected D18 so that its value appears in the Formula bar in the figure:

```
=STDEV.S(D2:D5)/SQRT(COUNT(D2:D5))
```

Figure 13-14 shows the column chart for the results. To create it, I select the means table (C12:F14) and select Insert | Recommended Charts and then select the Clustered Column option. Then I added the error bars for the standard errors (see Chapter 22) and tweaked the chart. (Refer to Chapter 3.)

FIGURE 13-14: Graphing the results.

The chart clearly illustrates the Media X Font interaction. For Haettenschweiler, the reading speed is higher with the book. For each of the others, the reading speed is higher with the E-reader.

After the ANOVA

As I point out in Chapter 12, a significant result in an ANOVA tells you that an effect is lurking somewhere in the data. Post-analysis tests tell you where. Two types of tests are possible — either planned or unplanned. Chapter 12 provides the details.

In this example, the Between Groups variable has only two levels. For this reason, had a significant effect resulted, no further test would be necessary. The Within Groups variable, Font, is significant. Ordinarily, the test would proceed as in Chapter 12. In this case, however, the interaction between Media and Font necessitates a different path.

With the interaction, post-analysis tests can proceed in either (or both) of two ways. You can examine the effects of each level of the A variable on the levels of the B variable, or you can examine the effects of each level of the B variable on the levels of the A variable. Statisticians refer to these as *simple main effects.*

For this example, the first way examines the means for the three fonts in a book and the means for the three fonts in the E-reader. The second way examines the means for the book versus the mean for the E-reader with Haettenschweiler font, with Arial, and with Calibri.

Statistics texts provide complicated formulas for calculating these analyses. Excel makes them easy. To analyze the three fonts in the book, do a repeated measures ANOVA for Subjects 1 through 4. To analyze the three fonts in the E-reader, do a repeated measures ANOVA for Subjects 5 through 8.

For the analysis of the book versus the E-reader in the Haettenschweiler font, that's a single-factor ANOVA for the Haettenschweiler data. To do this, you'd have to rearrange the numbers into two columns. Of course, you'd go through a similar procedure for each of the other fonts.

Chapter 14

Regression: Linear and Multiple

O ne of the main things you do when you work with statistics is make predictions. The idea is to take data on one or more variables, and use these data to predict a value of another variable. To do this, you have to understand how to summarize relationships among variables, and to test hypotheses about those relationships.

In this chapter, I introduce *regression*, a statistical way to do just that. Regression also enables you to use the details of relationships to make predictions. First, I show you how to analyze the relationship between one variable and another. Then I show you how to analyze the relationship between a variable and two others. These analyses involve a good bit of calculation, and Excel is more than equal to the task.

The Plot of Scatter

Sahutsket University is an exciting, dynamic institution. Every year, the school receives thousands of applications. One challenge the Admissions Office faces is this: Applicants want the Office to predict what their GPAs (grade-point averages on a 4.0 scale) will be if they attend Sahutsket.

What's the best prediction? Without knowing anything about an applicant, and only knowing its own students' GPAs, the answer is clear: It's the average GPA at Sahutsket U. Regardless of who the applicant is, that's all the Admissions Office can say if its knowledge is limited.

With more knowledge about the students and about the applicants, a more accurate prediction becomes possible. For example, if Sahutsket keeps records on its students' total SAT scores, the Admissions Office can match up each student's GPA with his or her SAT score and see if the two pieces of data are somehow related. If they are, an applicant can supply his or her SAT score, and the Admissions Office can use that score to help make a prediction.

Figure 14-1 shows the GPA–SAT matchup in a graphic way. Because the points are scattered, it's called a *scatterplot.* By convention, the vertical axis (the *y-axis*) represents what you're trying to predict. That's also called the *dependent variable* or the *y-variable.* In this case, that's GPA. Also by convention, the horizontal axis (the *x-axis*) represents what you're using to make your prediction. That's also called the *independent variable* or the *x-variable.* Here, that's SAT.

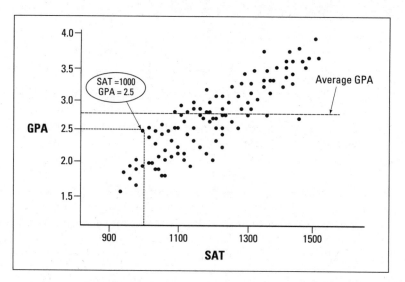

FIGURE 14-1:
SATs and GAPs in the Sahutsket University student body.

Each point in the graph represents an individual student's GPA and SAT. In a real scatterplot of a university student body, you'd see many more points than I show here. The general tendency of the set of points seems to be that high SAT scores are associated with high GPAs and low SAT scores are associated with low GPAs.

I singled out one of the points. It shows a Sahutsket student with an SAT score of 1,000 and a GPA of 2.5. I also show the average GPA to give you a sense that knowing the GPA–SAT relationship provides an advantage over knowing only the mean.

How do you make that advantage work for you? You start by summarizing the relationship between SAT and GPA. The summary is a line through the points. How and where do you draw the line?

I get to that in a minute. First, I have to tell you about lines in general.

Graphing Lines

In the world of mathematics, a *line* is a way to picture a relationship between an independent variable (x) and a dependent variable (y). In this relationship,

$$y = 4 + 2x$$

if I supply a value for x, I can figure out the corresponding value for y. The equation says to take the x-value, multiply by 2, and then add 4.

If $x = 1$, for example, $y = 6$. If $x = 2$, $y = 8$. Table 14-1 shows a number of x-y pairs in this relationship, including the pair in which $x = 0$.

TABLE 14-1

x-y Pairs in $y = 4 + 2x$

x	y
0	4
1	6
2	8
3	10
4	12
5	14
6	16

Figure 14-2 shows these pairs as points on a set of x-y axes, along with a line through the points. Each time I list an x-y pair in parentheses, the x-*value* is first.

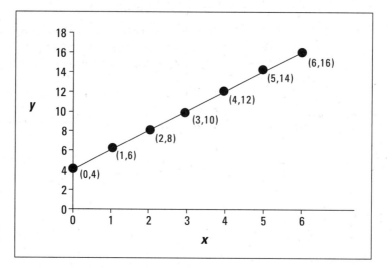

FIGURE 14-2:
The graph for
$y = 4 + 2x$.

As the figure shows, the points fall neatly onto the line. The line *graphs* the equation $y = 4 + 2x$. In fact, whenever you have an equation like this, where x isn't squared or cubed or raised to any power higher than 1, you have what mathematicians call a *linear* equation. (If x is raised to a higher power than 1, you connect the points with a curve, not a line.)

REMEMBER

A couple of things to keep in mind about a line: You can describe a line in terms of how slanted it is, and where it runs into the y-axis.

The how-slanted-it-is part is called the *slope.* The slope tells you how much y changes when x changes by one unit. In the line in Figure 14-2, when x changes by one (from 4 to 5, for example), y changes by two (from 12 to 14).

The where-it-runs-into-the-y-axis part is called the *y-intercept* (or sometimes just the *intercept*). That's the value of y when $x = 0$. In Figure 14-2, the y-intercept is 4.

You can see these numbers in the equation. The slope is the number that multiplies x and the intercept is the number you add to x. In general,

$$y = a + bx$$

where a represents the intercept and b represents the slope.

The slope can be a positive number, a negative number, or zero. In Figure 14-2, the slope is positive. If the slope is negative, the line is slanted in a direction opposite to what you see in Figure 14-2. A negative slope means that y *decreases* as x increases. If the slope is zero, the line is parallel to the horizontal axis. If the slope is zero, y doesn't change as x changes.

The same applies to the intercept — it can be a positive number, a negative number, or zero. If the intercept is positive, the line cuts off the y-axis *above* the x-axis. If the intercept is negative, the line cuts off the y-axis *below* the x-axis. If the intercept is zero, it intersects with the y-axis and the x-axis, at the point called the *origin*.

And now, back to what I was originally talking about.

Regression: What a Line!

I mention earlier that a line is the best way to summarize the relationship in the scatterplot in Figure 14-1. It's possible to draw an infinite amount of straight lines through the scatterplot. Which one best summarizes the relationship?

Intuitively, the "best fitting" line ought to be the one that goes through the maximum number of points and isn't too far away from the points it doesn't go through. For statisticians, that line has a special property: If you draw that line through the scatterplot, then draw distances (in the vertical direction) between the points and the line, and then square those distances and add them up, the sum of the squared distances is a minimum.

Statisticians call this line the *regression line*, and indicate it as

$$y' = a + bx$$

Each y' is a point on the line. It represents the best prediction of y for a given value of x.

To figure out exactly where this line is, you calculate its slope and its intercept. For a regression line, the slope and intercept are called *regression coefficients*.

The formulas for the regression coefficients are pretty straightforward. For the slope, the formula is

$$b = \frac{\sum(x - \bar{x})(y - \bar{y})}{\sum(x - \bar{x})^2}$$

The intercept formula is

$$a = \bar{y} - b\bar{x}$$

I illustrate with an example. To keep the numbers manageable and comprehensible, I use a small sample instead of the thousands of students you'd find in a scatterplot of an entire university student body. Table 14-2 shows a sample of data from 20 Sahutsket University students.

TABLE 14-2

SAT Scores and GPAs for 20 Sahutsket University Students

Student	SAT	GPA
1	990	2.2
2	1150	3.2
3	1080	2.6
4	1100	3.3
5	1280	3.8
6	990	2.2
7	1110	3.2
8	920	2.0
9	1000	2.2
10	1200	3.6
11	1000	2.1
12	1150	2.8
13	1070	2.2
14	1120	2.1
15	1250	2.4
16	1020	2.2
17	1060	2.3
18	1550	3.9
19	1480	3.8
20	1010	2.0
Mean	1126.5	2.705
Variance	26171.32	0.46
Standard Deviation	161.78	0.82

For this set of data, the slope of the regression line is

$$b = \frac{\begin{array}{c}(990-1126.5)(2.2-2.705)+(1150-1126.5)(3.2-2.705) \\ +...+(1010-1126.5)(2.0-2.705)\end{array}}{(2.2-2.705)^2+(3.2-2.705)^2+...+(2.0-2.705)^2} = 0.0034$$

The intercept is

$$a = \bar{y} - b\bar{x} = 2.705 - 0.0034(1126.5) = -1.1538$$

So the equation of the best-fitting line through these 20 points is

$$y' = -1.1538 + 0.0034x$$

or in terms of GPAs and SATs:

$$Predicted\ GPA = -1.1538 + 0.0034(SAT)$$

Using regression for forecasting

Based on this sample and this regression line, you can take an applicant's SAT score — say, 1230 — and predict the applicant's GPA:

$$Predicted\ GPA = -1.1538 + 0.0034(1230) = 3.028$$

Without this rule, the only prediction is the mean GPA, 2.705.

Variation around the regression line

In Chapter 5, I describe how the mean doesn't tell the whole story about a set of data. You have to show how the scores vary around the mean. For that reason, I introduce the variance and standard deviation.

You have a similar situation here. To get the full picture of the relationship in a scatterplot, you have to show how the scores vary around the regression line. Here, I introduce the *residual variance* and *standard error of estimate,* which are analogous to the variance and the standard deviation.

The residual variance is sort of an average of the squared deviations of the observed y-values around the predicted y-values. Each deviation of a data point from a predicted point $(y - y')$ is called a *residual,* hence the name. The formula is

$$s_{yx}^2 = \frac{\sum(y-y')^2}{N-2}$$

I say *sort of* because the denominator is $N-2$ rather than N. The reason for the -2 is beyond the scope of this discussion. As I discuss earlier, the denominator of a variance estimate is *degrees of freedom* (df), and that concept comes in handy in a little while.

The standard error of estimate is

$$s_{yx} = \sqrt{s_{yx}^2} = \sqrt{\frac{\sum (y - y')^2}{N - 2}}$$

To show you how the residual error and the standard error of estimate play out for the data in the example, here's Table 14-3. This table extends Table 14-2 by showing the predicted GPA for each SAT score.

TABLE 14-3   **SAT Scores, GPAs, and Predicted GPAs for 20 Sahutsket University Students**

Student	SAT	GPA	Predicted GPA
1	990	2.2	2.24
2	1150	3.2	2.79
3	1080	2.6	2.55
4	1100	3.3	2.61
5	1280	3.8	3.23
6	990	2.2	2.24
7	1110	3.2	2.65
8	920	2.0	2.00
9	1000	2.2	2.27
10	1200	3.6	2.96
11	1000	2.1	2.27
12	1150	2.8	2.79
13	1070	2.2	2.51
14	1120	2.1	2.68
15	1250	2.4	3.13
16	1020	2.2	2.34
17	1060	2.3	2.48
18	1550	3.9	4.16
19	1480	3.8	3.92

Student	SAT	GPA	Predicted GPA
20	1010	2.0	2.31
Mean	1126.5	2.705	
Variance	26171.32	0.46	
Standard Deviation	161.78	0.82	

As the table shows, sometimes the predicted GPA is pretty close, and sometimes it's not. One predicted value (4.16) is impossible.

For these data, the residual variance is

$$s_{yx}^2 = \frac{\sum(y-y')^2}{N-2} = \frac{(2.2-2.24)^2 + (3.2-2.79)^2 + \ldots + (2.0-2.31)^2}{20-2} = \frac{2.91}{18} = .16$$

The standard error of estimate is

$$s_{yx} = \sqrt{s_{yx}^2} = \sqrt{.16} = .40$$

If the residual variance and the standard error of estimate are small, the regression line is a good fit to the data in the scatterplot. If the residual variance and the standard error of estimate are large, the regression line is a poor fit.

What's "small"? What's "large"? What's a "good" fit?

Keep reading.

Testing hypotheses about regression

The regression equation you are working with,

$$y' = a + bx$$

summarizes a relationship in a scatterplot of a sample. The regression coefficients a and b are sample statistics. You can use these statistics to test hypotheses about population parameters, and that's what you do in this section.

The regression line through the population that produces the sample (like the entire Sahutsket University student body, past and present) is the graph of an equation that consists of parameters, rather than statistics. By convention, remember, Greek letters stand for parameters, so the regression equation for the population is

$$y' = \alpha + \beta x + \varepsilon$$

The first two Greek letters on the right are α (alpha) and β (beta), the equivalents of *a* and *b*. What about that last one? It looks something like the Greek equivalent of *e*. What's it doing there?

That last term is the Greek letter *epsilon*. It represents *error* in the population. In a way, *error* is an unfortunate term. It's a catchall for "things you don't know or things you have no control over." Error is reflected in the residuals — the deviations from the predictions. The more you understand about what you're measuring, the more you decrease the error.

You can't measure the error in the relationship between SAT and GPA, but it's lurking there. Someone might score low on the SAT, for example, and then go on to have a wonderful college career with a higher-than-predicted GPA. On a scatterplot, this person's SAT–GPA point looks like an error in prediction. As you find out more about that person, you might discover that he or she was sick on the day of the SAT, and that explains the "error."

You can test hypotheses about α, β, and ε, and that's what you do in the upcoming subsections.

Testing the fit

You begin with a test of how well the regression line fits the scatterplot. This is a test of ε, the error in the relationship.

The objective is to decide whether the line really does represent a relationship between the variables. It's possible that what looks like a relationship is just due to chance and the equation of the regression line doesn't mean anything (because the amount of error is overwhelming) — or it's possible that the variables are strongly related.

These possibilities are testable, and you set up hypotheses to test them:

H_0: No real relationship

H_1: Not H_0

Although those hypotheses make nice light reading, they don't set up a statistical test. To set up the test, you have to consider the variances. To consider the variances, you start with the deviations. Figure 14-3 focuses on one point in a scatterplot and its deviation from the regression line (the residual) and from the mean of the *y*-variable. It also shows the deviation between the regression line and the mean.

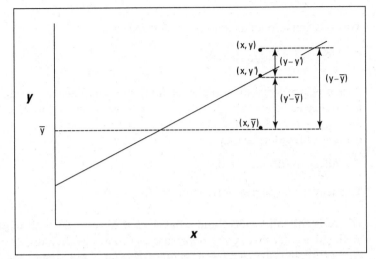

FIGURE 14-3:
The deviations in
a scatterplot.

As the figure shows, the distance between the point and the regression line and the distance between the regression line and the mean add up to the distance between the point and the mean:

$$(y - y') + (y' - \bar{y}) = (y - \bar{y})$$

This sets the stage for some other important relationships.

Start by squaring each deviation. That gives you $(y - y')^2$, $(y' - \bar{y})^2$, and $(y - \bar{y})^2$. If you add up each of the squared deviations, you have

$$\sum (y - y')^2$$

You just saw this one. That's the numerator for the residual variance. It represents the variability around the regression line— the "error" I mention earlier. In the terminology of Chapter 12, the numerator of a variance is called a Sum of Squares, or SS. So this is $SS_{Residual}$.

$$\sum (y' - \bar{y})^2$$

This one is new. The deviation $(y' - \bar{y})$ represents the gain in prediction due to using the regression line rather than the mean. The sum reflects this gain, and is called $SS_{Regression}$.

$$\sum (y - \bar{y})^2$$

I show you this one in Chapter 5 — although I use x rather than y. That's the numerator of the variance of y. In Chapter 12 terms, it's the numerator of *total variance*. This one is SS_{Total}.

This relationship holds among these three sums:

$$SS_{Residual} + SS_{Regression} = SS_{Total}$$

Each one is associated with a value for degrees of freedom — the denominator of a variance estimate. As I point out in the preceding section, the denominator for $SS_{Residual}$ is $N-2$. The df for SS_{Total} is $N-1$. (See Chapters 5 and 12.) As with the SS, the degrees of freedom add up:

$$df_{Residual} + df_{Regression} = df_{Total}$$

This leaves one degree of freedom for Regression.

Where is this all headed, and what does it have to do with hypothesis testing? Well, since you asked, you get variance estimates by dividing SS by df. Each variance estimate is called a *Mean Square*, abbreviated MS (again, see Chapter 12):

$$MS_{Regression} = \frac{SS_{Regression}}{df_{Regression}}$$

$$MS_{Residual} = \frac{SS_{Residual}}{df_{Residual}}$$

$$MS_{Total} = \frac{SS_{Total}}{df_{Total}}$$

Now for the hypothesis part. If H_0 is true and what looks like a relationship between x and y is really no big deal, the piece that represents the gain in prediction because of the regression line ($MS_{Regression}$) should be no greater than the variability around the regression line ($MS_{Residual}$). If H_0 is not true, and the gain in prediction is substantial, then $MS_{Regression}$ should be a lot bigger than $MS_{Residual}$.

So the hypotheses now set up as

$$H_0: \sigma^2_{Regression} \leq \sigma^2_{Residual}$$

$$H_1: \sigma^2_{Regression} > \sigma^2_{Residual}$$

These are hypotheses you can test. How? To test a hypothesis about two variances, you use an F test. (See Chapter 11.) The test statistic here is

$$F = \frac{MS_{Regression}}{MS_{Residual}}$$

To show you how it all works, I apply the formulas to the Sahutsket example. The $MS_{Residual}$ is the same as s_{yx}^2 from the preceding section, and that value is 0.16. The $MS_{Regression}$ is

$$MS_{Regression} = \frac{(2.24 - 2.705)^2 + (2.79 - 2.705)^2 + ... + (2.31 - 2.705)^2}{1} = 5.83$$

This sets up the F:

$$F = \frac{MS_{Regression}}{MS_{Residual}} = \frac{5.83}{0.16} = 36.03$$

With 1 and 18 df and α = .05, the critical value of F is 4.41. (You can use the worksheet function F.INV.RT to verify.) The calculated F is greater than the critical F, so the decision is to reject H_0. That means the regression line provides a good fit to the data in the sample.

Testing the slope

Another question that arises in linear regression is whether the slope of the regression line is significantly different from zero. If it's not, the mean is just as good a predictor as the regression line.

The hypotheses for this test are:

H_0: $\beta \leq 0$

H_1: $\beta > 0$

The statistical test is t, which I discuss in Chapters 9, 10, and 11 in connection with means. The t-test for the slope is

$$t = \frac{b - \beta}{s_b}$$

with df = N-2. The denominator estimates the standard error of the slope. This term sounds more complicated than it is. The formula is

$$s_b = \frac{s_{yx}}{s_x \sqrt{(N-1)}}$$

where s_x is the standard deviation of the x-variable. For the data in the example

$$s_b = \frac{s_{yx}}{s_x \sqrt{(N-1)}} = \frac{0.402}{(161.776)\sqrt{(20-1)}} = .00057$$

$$t = \frac{b - \beta}{s_b} = \frac{.0034 - 0}{.00057} = 5.96$$

The actual value is 6.00. If you round s_{yx} and s_b to a manageable number of decimal places before calculating, you end up with 5.96. Either way, this is larger than the critical value of t for 18 df and α = .05 (2.10), so the decision is to reject H_0. This example, by the way, shows why it's important to test hypotheses. The slope, 0.0034, looks like a very small number. (Possibly because it's a very small number.) Still, it's big enough to reject H_0 in this case.

Testing the intercept

For completeness, I include the hypothesis test for the intercept. I doubt you'll have much use for it, but it appears in the output of some of Excel's regression-related capabilities. I want you to understand all aspects of that output (which I tell you about in a little while), so here it is.

The hypotheses are

$H_0: \alpha = 0$

$H_1: \alpha \neq 0$

The test, once again, is a t-test. The formula is

$$t = \frac{a - \alpha}{s_a}$$

The denominator is the estimate of the standard error of the intercept. Without going into detail, the formula for s_a is

$$s_a = s_{yx} \sqrt{\frac{1}{N} + \frac{\bar{x}^2}{(N-1)s_x^2}}$$

where $\bar{x}^2$ is the squared mean of the x-variable and s_x^2 is the variance of the x-variable. Applying this formula to the data in the example,

$$s_a = s_{yx} \sqrt{\frac{1}{N} + \frac{\bar{x}^2}{(N-1)s_x^2}} = 0.649$$

The t-test is

$$t = \frac{a - \alpha}{s_a} = \frac{-1.15}{0.649} = -1.78$$

With 18 degrees of freedom, and the probability of a Type I error at .05, the critical t is 2.45 for a two-tailed test. It's a two-tailed test because H_1 is that the intercept doesn't equal zero — it doesn't specify whether the intercept is greater than zero or less than zero. Because the calculated value isn't more negative than the negative critical value, the decision is to not reject H_0.

Worksheet Functions for Regression

Excel is a big help for computation-intensive work like linear regression. An assortment of functions and data analysis tools makes life a lot easier.

In this section, I concentrate on the worksheet functions and on two array functions.

Figure 14-4 shows the data I use to illustrate each function. The data are GPA and SAT scores for 20 students in the example I show you earlier. As the figure shows, the SAT scores are in C3:C22 and the GPAs are in D3:D22. The SAT is the x-variable and GPA is the y-variable.

	A	B	C	D
1				
2		Student	SAT	GPA
3		1	990	2.2
4		2	1150	3.2
5		3	1080	2.6
6		4	1100	3.3
7		5	1280	3.8
8		6	990	2.2
9		7	1110	3.2
10		8	920	2.0
11		9	1000	2.2
12		10	1200	3.6
13		11	1000	2.1
14		12	1150	2.8
15		13	1070	2.2
16		14	1120	2.1
17		15	1250	2.4
18		16	1020	2.2
19		17	1060	2.3
20		18	1550	3.9
21		19	1480	3.8
22		20	1010	2.0
23				

FIGURE 14-4: Data for the regression-related worksheet functions.

To clarify what the functions do, I define names for the data arrays. I define SAT as the name for C3:C22 and I define GPA as the name for D3:D22. That way, I can use those names in the arguments for the functions. If you don't know how to define a name for an array, go to Chapter 2.

SLOPE, INTERCEPT, STEYX

These three functions work the same way, so I give a general description and provide details as necessary for each function. Follow these steps:

1. **With the data entered, select a cell.**

2. **From the Statistical Functions menu, select a regression function to open its Function Arguments dialog box.**

- To calculate the slope of a regression line through the data, select SLOPE.

- To calculate the intercept, select INTERCEPT.

- To calculate the standard error of estimate, select STEYX.

Figures 14-5, 14-6, and 14-7 show the Function Arguments dialog boxes for these three functions.

3. **In the Function Arguments dialog box, enter the appropriate values for the arguments.**

In the Known_y's box, I enter the name for the cell range that holds the scores for the *y*-variable. For this example, that's GPA (defined as the name for C3:C22).

In the Known_x's box, I enter the name for the cell range that holds the scores for the *x*-variable. For this example, it's SAT (defined as the name for D3:D22). After I enter this name, the answer appears in the dialog box.

- SLOPE's answer is .00342556. (See Figure 14-5.)

- INTERCEPT's answer is –1.153832541. (See Figure 14-6.)

- STEYX's answer is 0.402400043. (See Figure 14-7.)

4. **Click OK to put the answer into the selected cell.**

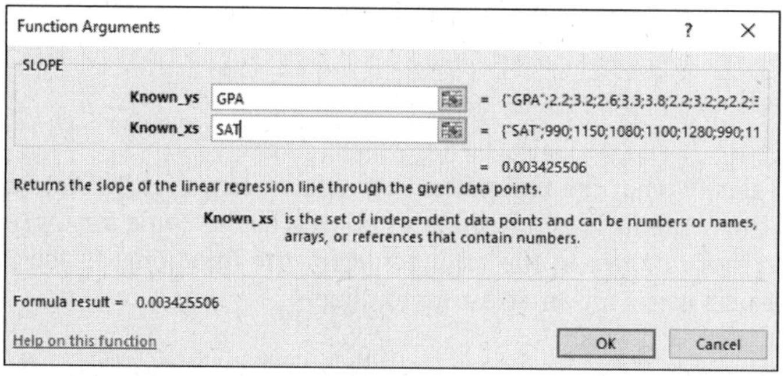

FIGURE 14-5:
The Function
Arguments dialog
box for SLOPE.

FORECAST.LINEAR

This one is a bit different from the preceding three. In addition to the columns for the *x* and *y* variables, for FORECAST.LINEAR (renamed from FORECAST in earlier Excels, but still called FORECAST in the Mac version), you supply a value for *x* and the answer is a prediction based on the linear regression relationship between the *x*-variable and the *y*-variable.

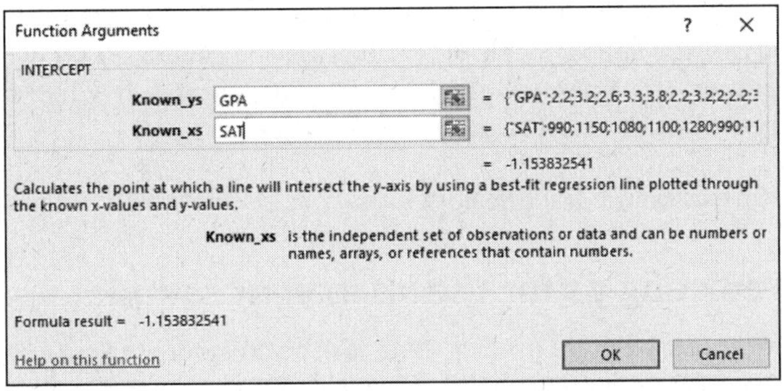

FIGURE 14-6:
The Function
Arguments dialog
box for
INTERCEPT.

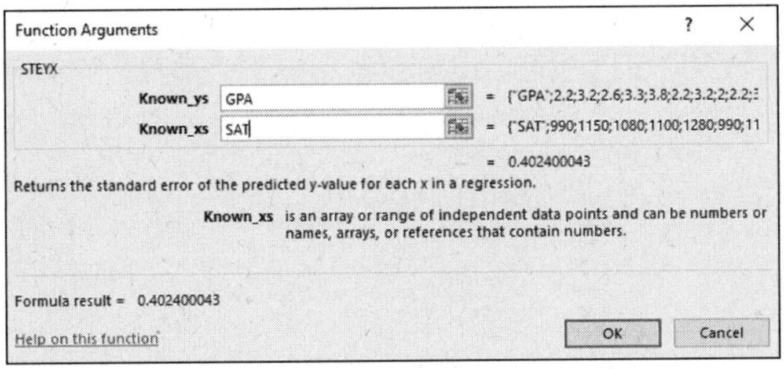

FIGURE 14-7:
The Function
Arguments dialog
box for STEYX.

Figure 14-8 shows the Function Arguments dialog box for FORECAST.LINEAR. In the X box, I entered 1290. For this SAT, the figure shows the predicted GPA is 3.265070236.

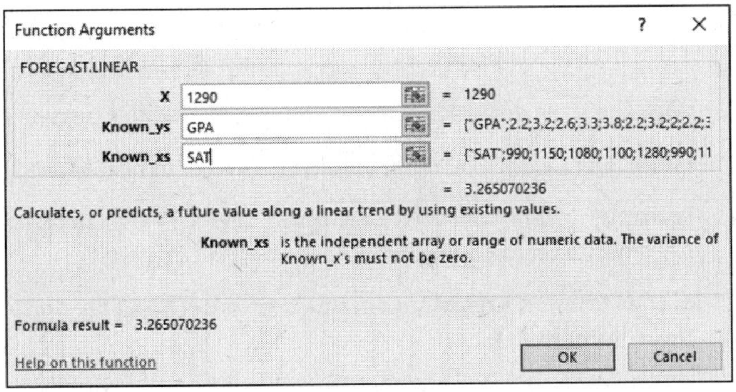

FIGURE 14-8:
The Function
Arguments
dialog box for
FORECAST.
LINEAR.

Array function: TREND

TREND is a versatile function. You can use TREND to generate a set of predicted *y*-values for the *x*-values in the sample.

You can also supply a new set of x-values and generate a set of predicted y-values, based on the linear relationship in your sample. It's like applying FORECAST repeatedly in one fell swoop.

In this section, I describe both uses.

Predicting y's for the x's in your sample

First, I use TREND to predict GPAs for the 20 students in the sample. Figure 14-9 shows TREND set up to do this. I include the Formula bar in this screen shot so that you can see what the formula looks like for this use of TREND.

| E3 | | ⁝ | × | ✓ | f_x | =TREND(D3:D22,C3:C22,,TRUE) |

▲	A	B	C	D	E	F	G	H	I	J	K
1											
2		Student	SAT	GPA	Predicted GPA		Function Arguments			?	×
3		1	990	2.2	:C22,,TRUE)						
4		2	1150	3.2			TREND				
5		3	1080	2.6			Known_ys	D3:D22	▦	= {2.2;3.2;2.6;3.3;3.8;2.2;3.2;2.2;2.2;3.6;2.1;	
6		4	1100	3.3			Known_xs	C3:C22	▦	= {990;1150;1080;1100;1280;990;1110;92	
7		5	1280	3.8			New_xs		▦	= reference	
8		6	990	2.2			Const	TRUE	▦	= TRUE	
9		7	1110	3.2						= {2.23741842716514;2.78549939166021	
10		8	920	2.0			Returns numbers in a linear trend matching known data points, using the least squares method.				
11		9	1000	2.2							
12		10	1200	3.6			Const is a logical value: the constant b is calculated normally if				
13		11	1000	2.1			Const = TRUE or omitted; b is set equal to 0 if Const = FALSE.				
14		12	1150	2.8							
15		13	1070	2.2			Formula result = 2.237418427				
16		14	1120	2.1							
17		15	1250	2.4			Help on this function			OK	Cancel
18		16	1020	2.2							
19		17	1060	2.3							
20		18	1550	3.9							
21		19	1480	3.8							
22		20	1010	2.0							
23											

FIGURE 14-9: The Function Arguments dialog box for TREND, along with data. TREND is set up to predict GPAs for the sample SATs.

1. **With the data entered, select a column for TREND's answers.**

   I select E3:E22. That puts the predicted GPAs right next to the sample GPAs.

2. **From the Statistical Functions menu, select TREND to open the Function Arguments dialog box for TREND.**

3. **In the Function Arguments dialog box, enter the appropriate values for the arguments.**

   In the Known_y's box, I enter the cell range that holds the scores for the y-variable. For this example, that's D3:D22.

   In the Known_x's box, enter the cell range that holds the scores for the x-variable. For this example, it's C3:C22.

Why didn't I just enter GPA and SAT as in the previous examples? When I do that, and complete the next step, Excel doesn't calculate the values. (This happened in Excel 2013 as well.)

I left the New_x's box blank.

In the Const box, I typed TRUE (or I could leave it blank) to calculate the y-intercept, or I would type FALSE to set the y-intercept to zero.

(I really don't know why you'd enter FALSE.) A note of caution: In the dialog box, the instruction for the Const box refers to b. That's the y-intercept. Earlier in the chapter, I use a to represent the y-intercept, and b to represent the slope. No usage is standard for this.

4. **IMPORTANT: Do *not* click OK. Because this is an array function, press Ctrl+Shift+Enter to put TREND's answers into the selected array.**

Figure 14-10 shows the answers in E3:E22. I include the Formula bar so you can see that Excel surrounds the completed array formula with curly brackets.

	A	B	C	D	E	F
E3				fx	{=TREND(D3:D22,C3:C22,,TRUE)}	
1						
2		Student	SAT	GPA	Predicted GPA	
3		1	990	2.2	2.237418427	
4		2	1150	3.2	2.785499392	
5		3	1080	2.6	2.54571397	
6		4	1100	3.3	2.61422409	
7		5	1280	3.8	3.230815175	
8		6	990	2.2	2.237418427	
9		7	1110	3.2	2.648479151	
10		8	920	2.0	1.997633005	
11		9	1000	2.2	2.271673487	
12		10	1200	3.6	2.956774693	
13		11	1000	2.1	2.271673487	
14		12	1150	2.8	2.785499392	
15		13	1070	2.2	2.511458909	
16		14	1120	2.1	2.682734211	
17		15	1250	2.4	3.128049994	
18		16	1020	2.2	2.340183608	
19		17	1060	2.3	2.477203849	
20		18	1550	3.9	4.155701803	
21		19	1480	3.8	3.915916381	
22		20	1010	2.0	2.305928548	
23						

FIGURE 14-10: The results of TREND: Predicted GPAs for the sample SATs.

Predicting a new set of y's for a new set of x's

Here, I use TREND to predict GPAs for four new SAT scores. Figure 14-11 shows TREND set up for this, with the name New_SAT defined for the cell range that holds the new scores. The figure also shows the selected cell range for the results. Once again, I include the Formula bar to show you the formula for this use of the function.

1. **With the data entered, select a cell range for `TREND`'s answers.**

   I selected G8:G11.

2. **From the Statistical Functions menu, select TREND to open the Function Arguments dialog box for TREND.**

3. **In the Function Arguments dialog box, enter the appropriate values for the arguments.**

   In the Known_y's box, enter the name of the cell range that holds the scores for the *y*-variable. For this example, that's D3:D22.

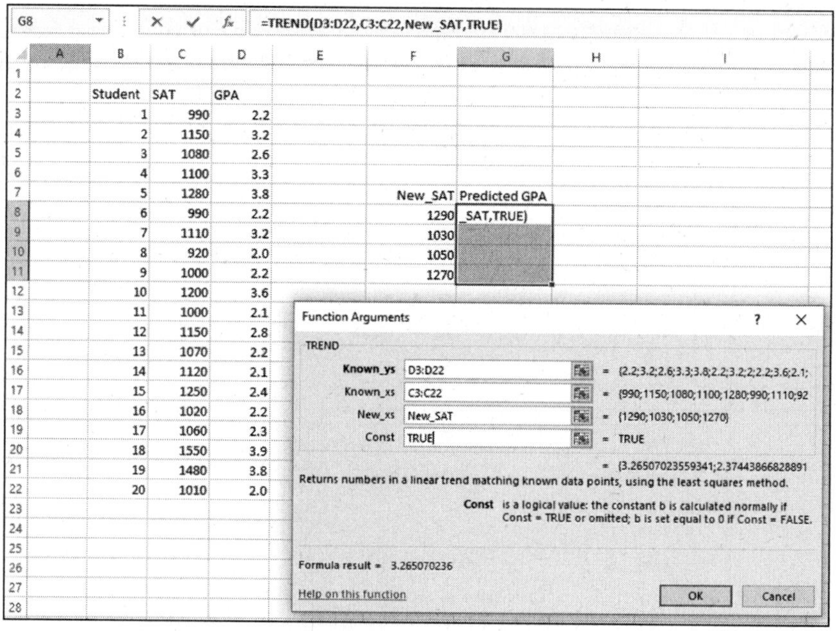

Student	SAT	GPA
1	990	2.2
2	1150	3.2
3	1080	2.6
4	1100	3.3
5	1280	3.8
6	990	2.2
7	1110	3.2
8	920	2.0
9	1000	2.2
10	1200	3.6
11	1000	2.1
12	1150	2.8
13	1070	2.2
14	1120	2.1
15	1250	2.4
16	1020	2.2
17	1060	2.3
18	1550	3.9
19	1480	3.8
20	1010	2.0

FIGURE 14-11: The Function Arguments dialog box for `TREND`, along with data. `TREND` is set up to predict GPAs for a new set of SATs.

In the Known_x's box, enter the name of the cell range that holds the scores for the *x*-variable. For this example, it's C3:C22.

In the New_x's box, enter the name of the cell range that holds the new scores for the *x*-variable. Here, that's New_SAT. (A named array works in this context.)

In the Const box, the choices are to enter `TRUE` (or leave it blank) to calculate the *y*-intercept, or `FALSE` to set the *y*-intercept to zero. I entered `TRUE`. (Again, I really don't know why you'd enter `FALSE`.)

4. IMPORTANT: Do *not* click OK. Because this is an array function, press Ctrl+Shift+Enter to put TREND's answers into the selected column.

Figure 14-12 shows the answers in G8:G11. Again, I include the Formula bar to show you that Excel surrounds the completed array formula with curly brackets.

| G8 | ▼ : | × ✓ | f_x | {=TREND(D3:D22,C3:C22,New_SAT,TRUE)} |

	A	B	C	D	E	F	G
1							
2		Student	SAT	GPA			
3		1	990	2.2			
4		2	1150	3.2			
5		3	1080	2.6			
6		4	1100	3.3			
7		5	1280	3.8		New_SAT	Predicted GPA
8		6	990	2.2		1290	3.265070236
9		7	1110	3.2		1030	2.374438668
10		8	920	2.0		1050	2.442948789
11		9	1000	2.2		1270	3.196560115
12		10	1200	3.6			
13		11	1000	2.1			
14		12	1150	2.8			
15		13	1070	2.2			
16		14	1120	2.1			
17		15	1250	2.4			
18		16	1020	2.2			
19		17	1060	2.3			
20		18	1550	3.9			
21		19	1480	3.8			
22		20	1010	2.0			

FIGURE 14-12: The results of TREND: Predicted GPAs for a new set of SATs.

Array function: LINEST

LINEST combines SLOPE, INTERCEPT, and STEYX, and throws in a few extras. Figure 14-13 shows the Function Arguments dialog box for LINEST, along with the data and the selected array for the answers. Notice that it's a five-row-by-two-column array. For linear regression, that's what the selected array has to be. How would you know the exact row-column dimensions of the array if I didn't tell you? Well . . . you wouldn't.

Here are the steps for using LINEST:

1. With the data entered, select a five-row-by-two-column array of cells for LINEST's results.

I selected G7:H11.

2. From the Statistical Functions menu, select LINEST to open the Function Arguments dialog box for LINEST.

3. In the Function Arguments dialog box, enter the appropriate values for the arguments.

In the Known_y's box, I entered the cell range that holds the scores for the *y*-variable. For this example, that's D3:D22.

In the Known_x's box, I entered the cell range that holds the scores for the *x*-variable. For this example, it's C3:C22. (Named arrays won't work here, either.)

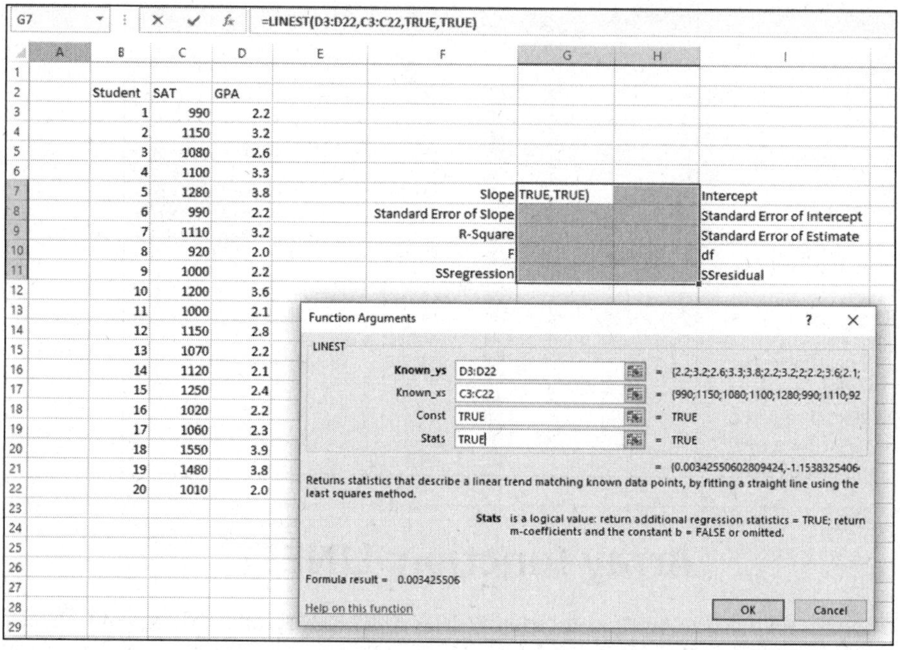

FIGURE 14-13:
The Function Arguments dialog box for LINEST, along with the data and the selected array for the results.

In the Const box, the choices are to enter TRUE (or leave it blank) to calculate the *y*-intercept, or FALSE to set the *y*-intercept to zero. I entered TRUE.

In the Stats box, the choices are to enter TRUE to return regression statistics in addition to the slope and the intercept, or FALSE (or leave it blank) to return just the slope and the intercept. I entered TRUE.

In the dialog box, *b* refers to intercept and *m-coefficient* refers to slope. As I mention earlier, no set of symbols is standard for this.

4. IMPORTANT: Do *not* click OK. Because this is an array function, press Ctrl+Shift+Enter to put LINEST's answers into the selected array.

Figure 14-14 shows LINEST's results. They're not labeled in any way, so I added the labels for you in the worksheet. The left column gives you the slope, standard error of the slope, something called "R Square," F, and the $SS_{Regression}$. What's R Square? That's another measure of the strength of the relationship between SAT and GPA in the sample. I discuss it in detail in Chapter 15.

The right column provides the intercept, standard error of the intercept, standard error of estimate, degrees of freedom, and $SS_{Residual}$.

G7		✕ ✓	f_x	{=LINEST(D3:D22,C3:C22,TRUE,TRUE)}				
	A	B	C	D	E	F	G	H	I

		B	C	D	E	F	G	H	I
1									
2		Student	SAT	GPA					
3		1	990	2.2					
4		2	1150	3.2					
5		3	1080	2.6					
6		4	1100	3.3					
7		5	1280	3.8		Slope	0.003425506	-1.15383254	Intercept
8		6	990	2.2		Standard Error of Slope	0.000570648	0.649101962	Standard Error of Intercept
9		7	1110	3.2		R-Square	0.666876472	0.402400043	Standard Error of Estimate
10		8	920	2.0		F	36.03400989	18	df
11		9	1000	2.2		SSregression	5.834835693	2.914664307	SSresidual
12		10	1200	3.6					
13		11	1000	2.1					
14		12	1150	2.8					
15		13	1070	2.2					
16		14	1120	2.1					
17		15	1250	2.4					
18		16	1020	2.2					
19		17	1060	2.3					
20		18	1550	3.9					
21		19	1480	3.8					
22		20	1010	2.0					

FIGURE 14-14: LINEST's results in the selected array.

Data Analysis Tool: Regression

Excel's Regression data analysis tool does everything LINEST does (and more) and labels the output for you, too. Figure 14-15 shows the Regression tool's dialog box, along with the data for the SAT–GPA example.

The steps for using this tool are:

1. **Type the data into the worksheet, and include labels for the columns.**

2. **Select Data| Data Analysis to open the Data Analysis dialog box.**

3. **In the Data Analysis dialog box, scroll down the Analysis Tools list and select Regression.**

4. **Click OK to open the Regression dialog box.**

   This is the dialog box shown in Figure 14-15.

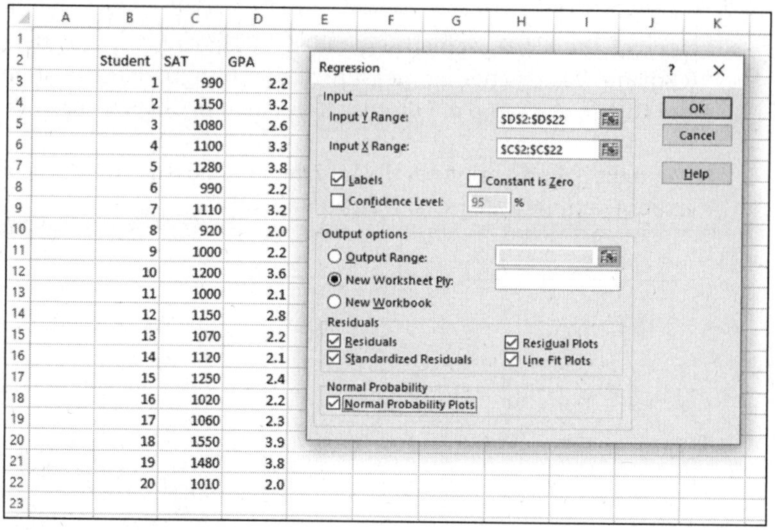

FIGURE 14-15:
The Regression
data analysis tool
dialog box,
along with the
SAT-GPA data.

5. **In the Input Y Range box, enter the cell range that holds the data for the y-variable.**

For the example, the GPAs (including the label) are in $D$2:$D$22.

Note the $ signs for absolute referencing. Excel adds these when you select the cells in the spreadsheet.

6. **In the Input X Range box, enter the cell range that holds the data for the x-variable.**

The SATs (including the label) are in $C$2:$C$22.

7. **If the cell ranges include column headings, select the Labels check box.**

I included the headings in the ranges, so I selected the box.

8. **The Alpha box has 0.05 as a default. Change that value if you want a different alpha.**

9. **In the Output Options, select a radio button to indicate where you want the results.**

I selected New Worksheet Ply to put the results on a new page in the worksheet.

10. **The Residuals area provides four capabilities for viewing the deviations between the data points and the predicted points. Check as many as you like.**

I selected all four. I explain them when I show you the output.

11. **Select the Normal Probability Plots option if you want to produce a graph of the percentiles of the *y*-variable.**

I selected this one so I could show it to you in the output.

12. **Click OK.**

Because I selected New Worksheet Ply, a newly created page opens with the results.

TIP

A word about Steps 4 and 5: Notice that I didn't enter the names for the cell ranges (GPA and SAT). Instead, I entered the ranges ($D$2:$D$22 and $C$2:$C$22). Why? When I define a name for a cell range, I don't include the cell that holds the name (for reasons I explain in Chapter 2). Following this practice, however, creates a small hurdle when you use a data analysis tool: You can't select the Labels check box if the defined names aren't in the named range. Selecting that check box makes the variable names show up in the output — which is a good thing. So . . . I just enter the cell range including the name cell and select the Labels check box.

Tabled output

Figure 14-16 shows the upper half of the tool's tabled output, after I expand the columns. The title is Summary Output. This part of the output features one table for the regression statistics, another for ANOVA, and one for the regression coefficients.

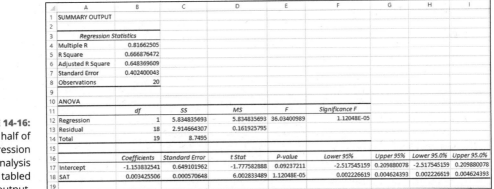

FIGURE 14-16: The upper half of the Regression data analysis tool's tabled output.

	A	B	C	D	E	F	G	H	I
1	SUMMARY OUTPUT								
2									
3	*Regression Statistics*								
4	Multiple R	0.81662505							
5	R Square	0.666876472							
6	Adjusted R Square	0.648369609							
7	Standard Error	0.402400043							
8	Observations	20							
9									
10	ANOVA								
11		*df*	*SS*	*MS*	*F*	*Significance F*			
12	Regression	1	5.834835693	5.834835693	36.03400989	1.12048E-05			
13	Residual	18	2.914664307	0.161925795					
14	Total	19	8.7495						
15									
16		*Coefficients*	*Standard Error*	*t Stat*	*P-value*	*Lower 95%*	*Upper 95%*	*Lower 95.0%*	*Upper 95.0%*
17	Intercept	-1.153832541	0.649101962	-1.777582888	0.09237211	-2.517545159	0.209880078	-2.517545159	0.209880078
18	SAT	0.003425506	0.000570648	6.002833489	1.12048E-05	0.002226619	0.004624393	0.002226619	0.004624393
19									

The first three rows of the Regression Statistics table present information related to R^2, a measure of the strength of the SAT–GPA relationship in the sample. The fourth row shows the standard error of estimate and the fifth gives the number of individuals in the sample.

The ANOVA table shows the results of testing

H_0: $\sigma_{\text{Regression}} \leq \sigma_{\text{Residual}}$

H_1: $\sigma_{\text{Regression}} > \sigma_{\text{Residual}}$

If the value in the F-significance column is less than .05 (or whatever alpha level you're using), reject H_0. In this example, it's less than .05.

Just below the ANOVA table is a table that gives the information on the regression coefficients. Excel doesn't name it, but I refer to it as the *coefficients table*. The Coefficients column provides the values for the intercept and the slope. The slope is labeled with the name of the x-variable. The Standard Error column presents the standard error of the intercept and the standard error of the slope.

The remaining columns provide the results for the t-tests of the intercept and the slope. The P-value column lets you know whether to reject H_0 for each test. If the value is less than your alpha, reject H_0. In this example, the decision is to reject H_0 for the slope, but not for the intercept.

Figure 14-17 shows the lower half of the Regression tool's tabled output.

RESIDUAL OUTPUT					PROBABILITY OUTPUT		
Observation	Predicted GPA	Residuals	Standard Residuals			Percentile	GPA
1	2.237418427	-0.037418427	-0.095536221			2.5	2
2	2.785499392	0.414500608	1.058297332			7.5	2
3	2.54571397	0.05428603	0.138602356			12.5	2.1
4	2.61422409	0.68577591	1.750913753			17.5	2.1
5	3.230815175	0.569184825	1.453234976			22.5	2.2
6	2.237418427	-0.037418427	-0.095536221			27.5	2.2
7	2.648479151	0.551520849	1.408135554			32.5	2.2
8	1.997633005	0.002366995	0.006043379			37.5	2.2
9	2.271673487	-0.071673487	-0.182995776			42.5	2.2
10	2.956774693	0.643225307	1.642274131			47.5	2.3
11	2.271673487	-0.171673487	-0.43831442			52.5	2.4
12	2.785499392	0.014500608	0.037022757			57.5	2.6
13	2.511458909	-0.311458909	-0.795212664			62.5	2.8
14	2.682734211	-0.582734211	-1.487829085			67.5	3.2
15	3.128049994	-0.728049994	-1.858847373			72.5	3.2
16	2.340183608	-0.140183608	-0.357914887			77.5	3.3
17	2.477203849	-0.177203849	-0.452434465			82.5	3.6
18	4.155701803	-0.255701803	-0.652854376			87.5	3.8
19	3.915916381	-0.115916381	-0.295956132			92.5	3.8
20	2.305928548	-0.305928548	-0.78109262			97.5	3.9

Here, you find the Residual Output and the Probability Output. The Residual Output is a table that shows the predicted value and the residual ($y-y'$) for each individual in the sample. It also shows the *standard residual* for each observation, which is

$$\text{standard residual} = \frac{\text{residual - average residual}}{s_{yx}}$$

The tabled data on residuals and standard residuals are useful for analyzing the variability around the regression line. You can scan these data for outliers, for example, and see if outliers are associated with particular values of the x-variable. (If they are, it might mean that something weird is going on in your sample.)

The Probability Output is a table of the percentiles in the y-variable data in the sample. (Yes, Percentile Output would be a better name.)

Graphic output

Figures 14-18, 14-19, and 14-20 show the Regression tool's graphic output. The Normal Probability Plot in Figure 14-18 is a graphic version of the Probability Output table. The SAT Residual Plot in Figure 14-19 shows the residuals graphed against the x-variable: For each SAT score in the sample, this plot shows the corresponding residual. Figure 14-20 shows the SAT Line Fit Plot — a look at the observed and the predicted y-values.

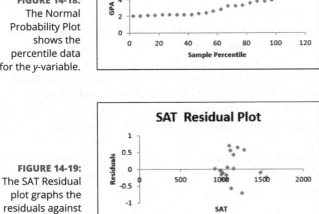

FIGURE 14-18:
The Normal Probability Plot shows the percentile data for the y-variable.

FIGURE 14-19:
The SAT Residual plot graphs the residuals against the x-variable.

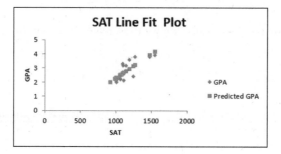

FIGURE 14-20:
The SAT Line Fit
Plot shows the
observed *y*-values
and the predicted
y-values.

If you've used the Regression tool in Excel 2007, you'll notice a change in the Normal Probability Plot and the Line Fit Plot. In Excel 2007, they appear as column charts. You can use Excel's graphics capabilities to easily change them to that format.

Juggling Many Relationships at Once: Multiple Regression

Linear regression is a great tool for making predictions. When you know the slope and the intercept of the line that relates two variables, you can take a new *x*-value and predict a new *y*-value. In the example you've been working through, you take a SAT score and predict a GPA for a Sahutsket University student.

What if you knew more than just the SAT score for each student? What if you had the student's high-school average (on a 100 scale), and you could use that information, too? If you could combine SAT score with HS average, you might have a more accurate predictor than SAT score alone.

When you work with more than one independent variable, you're in the realm of *multiple regression*. As in linear regression, you find regression coefficients for the best-fitting line through a scatterplot. Once again, *best-fitting* means that the sum of the squared distances from the data points to the line is a minimum.

With two independent variables, however, you can't show a scatterplot in two dimensions. You need three dimensions, and that becomes difficult to draw. Instead, I just show you the equation of the regression line:

$$y' = a + b_1 x_1 + b_2 x_2$$

For the SAT-GPA example, that translates to

$$Predicted\ GPA = a + b_1(SAT) + b_2(High\ School\ Average)$$

You can test hypotheses about the overall fit, and about all three of the regression coefficients.

I won't go through all the formulas for finding the coefficients, because that gets *really* complicated. Instead, I go right to the Excel capabilities.

A few things to bear in mind before I proceed:

>> You can have any number of *x*-variables. I just use two in the upcoming example.

>> Expect the coefficient for SAT to change from linear regression to multiple regression. Expect the intercept to change, too.

>> Expect the standard error of estimate to decrease from linear regression to multiple regression. Because multiple regression uses more information than linear regression, it reduces the error.

Excel Tools for Multiple Regression

The good news about Excel's multiple regression tools is that they're the same ones I just told you about for linear regression: You just use them in a slightly different way.

The bad news is . . . well . . . uh . . . I can't think of any bad news!

TREND revisited

I begin with TREND. Earlier, I show you how to use this function to predict values based on one *x*-variable. Change what you enter into the dialog box, and it predicts values based on more than one.

Figure 14-21 shows the TREND dialog box and data for 20 students. In the data, I add a column for each student's high-school average. I define HS_Average as the name for the data in this column. The figure also shows the selected column for TREND's predictions. I include the Formula bar in this screen shot so you can see what the formula looks like.

Follow these steps:

1. **With the data entered, select a column for** TREND**'s answers.**

I selected F3:F22. That puts the predicted GPAs right next to the sample GPAs.

2. **From the Statistical Functions menu, select TREND to open the Function Arguments dialog box for** TREND**.**

3. **In the Function Arguments dialog box, enter the appropriate values for the arguments.**

In the Known_y's box, I entered the cell range that holds the scores for the y-variable. For this example, that's E3:E22.

In the Known_x's box, I entered the cell range that holds the scores for the x-variables. This range is C3:D22, the cells that hold the SAT scores and the high-school averages.

I entered the ranges rather than defined names because names don't work with this function in my copy of Excel.

I left the New_x's box blank.

In the Const box, the choices are TRUE (or leave it blank) to calculate the y-intercept, or FALSE to set the y-intercept to zero. I entered TRUE. (I really don't know why you'd enter FALSE.) *A note of caution:* In the dialog box, the instruction for the Const box refers to *b*. That's the y-intercept. Earlier in the chapter, I use *a* to represent the y-intercept, and *b* to represent the slope. No particular usage is standard for this. Also, the dialog box makes it sound like this function works only for linear regression. As you're about to see, it works for multiple regression, too.

4. IMPORTANT: Do *not* click OK. Because this is an array function, press Ctrl+Shift+Enter to put TREND's answers into the selected column.

Figure 14-22 shows the answers in F3:F22. Note the difference between the Formula bar in Figure 14-21 and the one in Figure 14-22. After the function completes its work, Excel adds curly brackets to indicate an array formula.

So TREND predicts the values, and I haven't even shown you how to find the coefficients yet!

F3			$\times$ $\checkmark$ f_x	{=TREND(E3:E22,C3:D22,,TRUE)}		
	A	B	C	D	E	F
1						
2		Student	SAT	HS_Average	GPA	Predicted GPA
3		1	990	75	2.2	2.048403376
4		2	1150	87	3.2	2.967217927
5		3	1080	88	2.6	2.831485598
6		4	1100	79	3.3	2.499039035
7		5	1280	92	3.8	3.511405481
8		6	990	80	2.2	2.261402606
9		7	1110	85	3.2	2.780114135
10		8	920	80	2.0	2.083070431
11		9	1000	84	2.2	2.457278015
12		10	1200	91	3.6	3.264997435
13		11	1000	74	2.1	2.031279555
14		12	1150	75	2.8	2.456019776
15		13	1070	78	2.2	2.380011114
16		14	1120	72	2.1	2.251792163
17		15	1250	80	2.4	2.923779255
18		16	1020	78	2.2	2.252630989
19		17	1060	85	2.3	2.65273401
20		18	1550	89	3.9	4.071458617
21		19	1480	90	3.8	3.935726288
22		20	1010	83	2.0	2.440154194
23						

FIGURE 14-22: The results of TREND: Predicted GPAs for the sample SATs and high-school averages.

LINEST revisited

To find the multiple regression coefficients, I turn again to LINEST.

In Figure 14-23, you can see the data and the dialog box for LINEST, along with the data and the selected array for the answers. The selected array is five-rows-by-three-columns. It's always five rows. The number of columns is equal to the number of regression coefficients. For linear regression, it's two — the slope and the intercept. For this case of multiple regression, it's three.

Here are the steps for using LINEST for multiple regression with three coefficients:

1. **With the data entered, select a five-row-by-three-column array of cells for LINEST's results.**

   I selected H3:J7.

2. **From the Statistical Functions menu, select LINEST to open the Function Arguments dialog box for LINEST.**

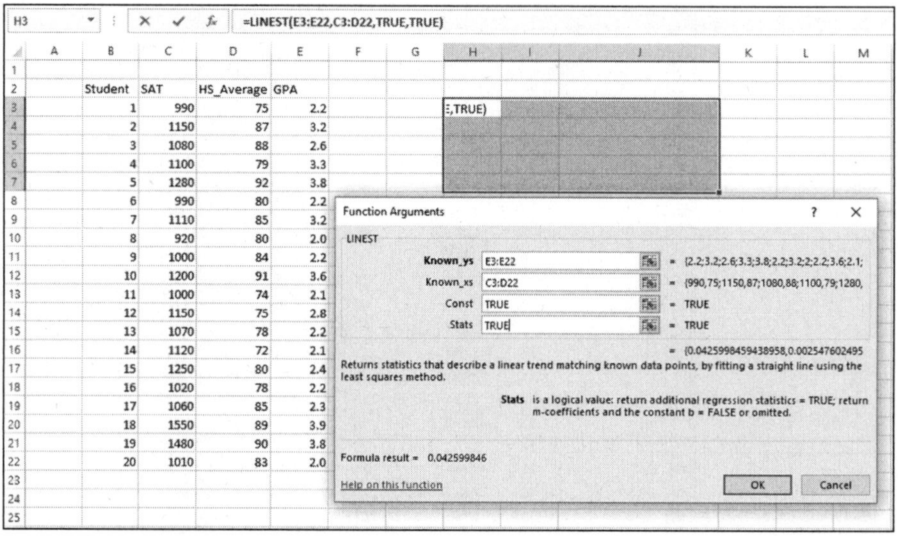

FIGURE 14-23: The Function Arguments dialog box for LINEST, along with the data and the selected array for the results of a multiple regression.

3. **In the Function Arguments dialog box, enter the appropriate values for the arguments.**

   In the Known_y's box, enter the column that holds the scores for the *y*-variable. For this example, that's E3:E22, the GPAs.

   In the Known_x's box, enter the cell range that holds the scores for the *x*-variables. For this example, it's C3:D22, the SAT scores and the high-school averages.

   In the Const box, enter **TRUE** (or leave it blank) to calculate the *y*-intercept. Enter **FALSE** to set the *y*-intercept to zero. I typed TRUE.

   In the Stats box, enter **TRUE** to return regression statistics in addition to the slope and the intercept, or **FALSE** (or leave it blank) to return just the slope and the intercept. I entered TRUE. The dialog box refers to the intercept as *b* and to the other coefficients as *m-coefficients*. I use *a* to represent the slope and *b* to refer to the other coefficients. No set of symbols is standard.

4. **IMPORTANT: Do *not* click OK. Because this is an array function, press Ctrl+Shift+Enter to put LINEST's answers into the selected array.**

Figure 14-24 shows LINEST's results. They're not labeled in any way, so I added the labels for you in the worksheet. I also drew a box around part of the results to clarify what goes with what.

	A	B	C	D	E	F	G	H	I	J	K
1											
2		Student	SAT	HS_Average	GPA			b2	b1	Intercept	
3		1	990	75	2.2		Coefficient	0.04259985	0.0025476	-3.6687115	
4		2	1150	87	3.2		Standard Error	0.01581193	0.00058975	1.08810549	
5		3	1080	88	2.6		R Square	0.76655182	0.34662701	#N/A	Standard Error of Estimate
6		4	1100	79	3.3		F	27.9106501	17	#N/A	df
7		5	1280	92	3.8		SSregression	6.70694515	2.04255485	#N/A	SSresidual
8		6	990	80	2.2						
9		7	1110	85	3.2						
10		8	920	80	2.0						
11		9	1000	84	2.2						
12		10	1200	91	3.6						
13		11	1000	74	2.1						
14		12	1150	75	2.8						
15		13	1070	78	2.2						
16		14	1120	72	2.1						
17		15	1250	80	2.4						
18		16	1020	78	2.2						
19		17	1060	85	2.3						
20		18	1550	89	3.9						
21		19	1480	90	3.8						
22		20	1010	83	2.0						
23											

FIGURE 14-24: LINEST's multiple results in the selected array.

The entries that stand out are the ugly #N/A symbols in the last three rows of the rightmost column. These indicate that LINEST doesn't put anything into these cells.

The top two rows of the array provide the values and standard errors for the coefficients. I drew the box around those rows to separate them from the three remaining rows, which present information in a different way. Before I get to those rows, I'll just tell you that the top row gives you the information for writing the regression equation:

$$y' = a + .0025x_1 + .043x_2$$

In terms of SAT, GPA, and high-school average, it's

$$Predicted\ GPA = -3.67 + .0025(SAT) + .043(High\ School\ Average)$$

The third row has R Square (a measure of the strength of the relationship between GPA and the other two variables, which I cover in Chapter 15) and the standard error of estimate. Compare the standard error of estimate for the multiple regression with the standard error for the linear regression, and you'll see that the multiple one is smaller. (Never mind. I'll do it for you. It's .40 for the linear and 0.35 for the multiple.)

The fourth row shows the F-ratio that tests the hypothesis about whether or not the line is a good fit to the scatterplot, and the df for the denominator of the F. The df for the numerator (not shown) is the number of coefficients minus 1. You can use F.INV.RT to verify that this F with df = 2 and 17 is significant.

The last row gives you $SS_{Regression}$ and $SS_{Residual}$.

Regression data analysis tool revisited

To use the Regression data analysis tool for multiple regression, you trot out the same technique you'd use with TREND and LINEST: Specify the appropriate array for the x-variables, and you're off and running.

Here are the steps:

1. **Type the data into the worksheet, and include labels for the columns.**

2. **Select Data | Data Analysis to open the Data Analysis dialog box.**

3. **In the Data Analysis dialog box, scroll down the Analysis Tools list and select Regression.**

4. **Click OK to open the Regression dialog box.**

   This is the dialog box shown back in Figure 14-15.

5. **In the Input Y Range box, enter the cell range that holds the data for the _y_-variable.**

   The GPAs (including the label) are in $E$2:$E$22. Note the $ signs for absolute referencing. Excel adds them when you select the cell range in the worksheet.

6. **In the Input X Range box, enter the cell range that holds the data for the _x_-variable.**

   The SATs and the high-school averages (including the labels) are in $C$2:$D$22.

7. **If the cell ranges include column headings, select the Labels check box.**

   I included the labels in the ranges, so I selected the box.

8. **The Alpha box has 0.05 as a default. Change that value if you want a different alpha.**

In the Output Options, select a radio button to indicate where you want the results.

9. **I selected New Worksheet Ply to put the results on a new page in the worksheet.**

10. **The Residuals area provides four capabilities for viewing the deviations between the data points and the predicted points. Select as many as you like.**

I selected all four.

11. **The option in the Normal Probability Plot area produces a graph of the percentiles of the *y*-variable.**

I selected this one.

12. **Click OK.**

Go back to the section "Data Analysis Tool: Regression" for the details of what's in the output. It's the same as earlier, with a couple of changes and additions because of the new variable. Figure 14-25 shows the Regression Statistics, the ANOVA table, and the Coefficients table.

FIGURE 14-25: Part of the output from the Regression data analysis tool: Regression Statistics, ANOVA table, and Coefficients table.

	A	B	C	D	E	F	G	H	I
1	SUMMARY OUTPUT								
2									
3	*Regression Statistics*								
4	Multiple R	0.875529451							
5	R Square	0.76655182							
6	Adjusted R Square	0.739087328							
7	Standard Error	0.346627012							
8	Observations	20							
9									
10	ANOVA								
11		*df*	*SS*	*MS*	*F*	*Significance F*			
12	Regression	2	6.706945148	3.353473	27.91065	4.26206E-06			
13	Residual	17	2.042554852	0.12015					
14	Total	19	8.7495						
15									
16		*Coefficients*	*Standard Error*	*t Stat*	*P-value*	*Lower 95%*	*Upper 95%*	*Lower 95.0%*	*Upper 95.0%*
17	Intercept	-3.66871154	1.088105488	-3.37165	0.003623	-5.964413448	-1.373009632	-5.964413448	-1.373009632
18	SAT	0.002547602	0.000589753	4.319781	0.000465	0.001303333	0.003791872	0.001303333	0.003791872
19	HS_Average	0.042599846	0.015811932	2.694158	0.015361	0.009239586	0.075960106	0.009239586	0.075960106
20									

The ANOVA table shows the new df (2, 17, and 19 for Regression, Residual, and Total, respectively). The coefficients table adds information for the HS Average. It shows the values of all the coefficients, as well as standard errors, and *t*-test information for hypothesis testing.

If you go through the example, you'll see the table of residuals in the output. Compare the absolute values of the residuals from the linear regression with the absolute values of the residuals from the multiple regression; you'll see the multiple ones are smaller, on average.

The graphic output has some additions, too: A scatterplot of HS Average and GPA that also shows predicted GPAs, and a plot of residuals and HS Average.

Chapter 15

Correlation: The Rise and Fall of Relationships

I n Chapter 14, I show you the ins and outs of regression, a tool for summarizing relationships between (and among) variables. In this chapter, I introduce you to the ups and downs of correlation, another tool for looking at relationships.

I use the example of SAT scores and GPA from Chapter 14, and show how to think about the data in a slightly different way. The new concepts connect to what I show you in the preceding chapter, and you'll see how that works. I also show you how to test hypotheses about relationships and how to use Excel functions and data analysis tools for correlation.

Scatterplots Again

A *scatterplot* is a graphical way of showing a relationship between two variables. Figure 15-1 is a scatterplot that represents the GPAs and SAT scores of 20 students at the fictional Sahutsket University. The GPAs are on a 4.0 scale and the SATs are total SAT scores.

Each point represents one student. A point's location in the horizontal direction represents the student's SAT. That same point's location in the vertical direction represents the student's GPA.

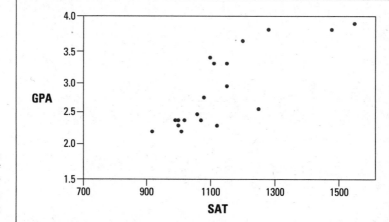

Understanding Correlation

In Chapter 14, I refer to the SAT as the *independent variable* and to the GPA as the *dependent variable.* The objective in Chapter 14 is to use SAT to predict GPA. Here's a very important point: Although I use scores on one variable to *predict* scores on the other, I do *not* mean that the score on one variable *causes* a score on the other. *Relationship* doesn't necessarily mean *causality.*

Correlation is a statistical way of looking at a relationship. When two things are correlated, it means that they vary together. *Positive* correlation means that high scores on one are associated with high scores on the other, and that low scores on one are associated with low scores on the other. The scatterplot in Figure 15-1 is an example of positive correlation.

Negative correlation, on the other hand, means that high scores on the first thing are associated with *low* scores on the second. Negative correlation also means that low scores on the first are associated with high scores on the second. An example is the correlation between body weight and the time spent on a weight-loss program. If the program is effective, the higher the amount of time spent on the program, the lower the body weight. Also, the lower the amount of time spent on the program, the higher the body weight.

Table 15-1, a repeat of Table 14-2, shows the data from the scatterplot.

TABLE 15-1

SAT Scores and GPAs for 20 Sahutsket University Students

Student	SAT	GPA
1	990	2.2
2	1150	3.2
3	1080	2.6
4	1100	3.3
5	1280	3.8
6	990	2.2
7	1110	3.2
8	920	2.0
9	1000	2.2
10	1200	3.6
11	1000	2.1
12	1150	2.8
13	1070	2.2
14	1120	2.1
15	1250	2.4
16	1020	2.2
17	1060	2.3
18	1550	3.9
19	1480	3.8
20	1010	2.0
Mean	1126.5	2.705
Variance	26171.32	0.46
Standard Deviation	161.78	0.82

In keeping with the way I use SAT and GPA in Chapter 14, SAT is the x-variable and GPA is the y-variable.

The formula for calculating the correlation between the two is

$$r = \frac{\left[\frac{1}{N-1}\right]\sum(x-\bar{x})(y-\bar{y})}{s_x s_y}$$

The term on the left, r, is called the *correlation coefficient.* It's also called *Pearson's product-moment correlation coefficient,* after its creator, Karl Pearson.

The two terms in the denominator on the right are the standard deviation of the x-variable and the standard deviation of the y-variable. The term in the numerator is called the *covariance.* So another way to write this formula is

$$r = \frac{\text{cov}(x,y)}{s_x s_y}$$

The covariance represents x and y varying together. Dividing the covariance by the product of the two standard deviations imposes some limits. The lower limit of the correlation coefficient is −1.00, and the upper limit is +1.00.

A correlation coefficient of −1.00 represents perfect negative correlation (low x-scores associated with high y-scores, and high x-scores associated with low y-scores). A correlation of +1.00 represents perfect positive correlation (low x-scores associated with low y-scores, and high x-scores associated with high y-scores). A correlation of 0.00 means that the two variables are not related.

Applying the formula to the data in Table 15-1,

$$r = \frac{\left[\frac{1}{N-1}\right]\sum(x-\bar{x})(y-\bar{y})}{s_x s_y}$$

$$= \frac{\left[\frac{1}{20-1}\right]\left[(990-1126.5)(2.2-2.705)+...+(1010-1126.5)(2.0-2.705)\right]}{(161.78)(0.82)} = .817$$

What, exactly, does this number mean? I'm about to tell you.

Correlation and Regression

Figure 15-2 shows the scatterplot with the line that "best fits" the points. It's possible to draw an infinite number of lines through these points. Which one is best?

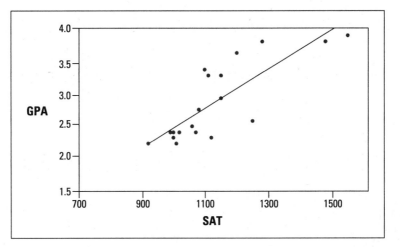

To be "best," a line has to meet a specific standard: If you draw the distances in the vertical direction between the points and the line, and you square those distances, and then you add those squared distances, the best-fitting line is the one that makes the sum of those squared distances as small as possible. This line is called the *regression line.*

The regression line's purpose in life is to enable you to make predictions. As I mention in Chapter 14, without a regression line, your best predicted value of the y-variable is the mean of the y's. A regression line takes the x-variable into account and delivers a more precise prediction. Each point on the regression line represents a predicted value for y. In the symbology of regression, each predicted value is a y'.

Why do I tell you all of this? Because correlation is closely related to regression. Figure 15-3 focuses on one point in the scatterplot, and its distance to the regression line and to the mean. (This is a repeat of Figure 14-3.)

Notice the three distances laid out in the figure. The distance labeled $(y-y')$ is the difference between the point and the regression line's prediction for where the point should be. (In Chapter 14, I call that a *residual.*) The distance labeled $(y - \bar{y})$ is the difference between the point and the mean of the y's. The distance labeled $(y' - \bar{y})$ is the gain in prediction capability that you get from using the regression line to predict the point instead of using the mean to predict the point.

Figure 15-3 shows the three distances are related like this:

$$(y - y') + (y' - \bar{y}) = (y - \bar{y})$$

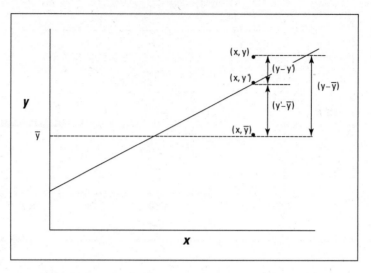

As I point out in Chapter 14, you can square all the residuals and add them, square all the deviations of the predicted points from the mean and add them, and square all the deviations of the actual points from the mean and add them, too.

It turns out that these sums of squares are related in the same way as the deviations I just showed you:

$$SS_{Residual} + SS_{Regression} = SS_{Total}$$

If $SS_{Regression}$ is large in comparison to $SS_{Residual}$, it indicates that the relationship between the x-variable and the y-variable is a strong one. It means that throughout the scatterplot, the variability around the regression line is small.

On the other hand, if $SS_{Regression}$ is small in comparison to $SS_{Residual}$, it means that the relationship between the x-variable and the y-variable is weak. In this case, the variability around the regression line is large throughout the scatterplot.

One way to test $SS_{Regression}$ against $SS_{Residual}$ is to divide each by its degrees of freedom (1 for $SS_{Regression}$ and $N-2$ for $SS_{Residual}$) to form variance estimates (also known as Mean Squares, or MS), and then divide one by the other to calculate an F. If $MS_{Regression}$ is significantly larger than $MS_{Residual}$, you have evidence that the x-y relationship is strong. (See Chapter 14 for details.)

Here's the clincher, as far as correlation is concerned: Another way to assess the size of $SS_{Regression}$ is to compare it with SS_{Total}. Divide the first by the second. If the ratio is large, this tells you the x-y relationship is strong. This ratio has a name. It's called the *coefficient of determination*. Its symbol is r^2. Take the square root of this coefficient, and you have . . . the correlation coefficient!

$$r = r^2 = \pm\sqrt{\frac{SS_{Regression}}{SS_{Total}}}$$

The plus-or-minus sign ($\pm$) means that r is either the positive or negative square root, depending on whether the slope of the regression line is positive or negative.

So, if you calculate a correlation coefficient and you quickly want to know what its value signifies, just square it. The answer — the coefficient of determination — lets you know the proportion of the SS_{Total} that's tied up in the relationship between the x-variable and the y-variable. If it's a large proportion, the correlation coefficient signifies a strong relationship. If it's a small proportion, the correlation coefficient signifies a weak relationship.

In the GPA–SAT example, the correlation coefficient is .817. The coefficient of determination is

$$r^2 = (.817)^2 = .667$$

In this sample of 20 students, the $SS_{Regression}$ is 66.7 percent of the SS_{Total}. Sounds like a large proportion, but what's large? What's small? These questions scream out for hypothesis tests.

Testing Hypotheses About Correlation

In this section, I show you how to answer important questions about correlation. Like any other kind of hypothesis testing, the idea is to use sample statistics to make inferences about population parameters. Here, the sample statistic is r, the correlation coefficient. By convention, the population parameter is ρ (rho), the Greek equivalent of r. (Yes, it does look like the letter p, but it really is the Greek equivalent of r.)

Two kinds of questions are important in connection with correlation: (1) Is a correlation coefficient greater than zero? (2) Are two correlation coefficients different from one another?

Is a correlation coefficient greater than zero?

Returning once again to the Sahutsket SAT–GPA example. You can use the sample r to test hypotheses about the population ρ — the correlation coefficient for all students at Sahutsket University.

Assuming you know in advance (before you gather any sample data) that any correlation between SAT and GPA should be positive, the hypotheses are

$H_0: \rho \le 0$

$H_1: \rho > 0$

I set $\alpha = .05$

The appropriate statistical test is a t-test. The formula is

$$t = \frac{r - \rho}{s_r}$$

This test has $N-2$ df.

For the example, the values in the numerator are set: r is .817 and ρ (in H_0) is zero. What about the denominator? I won't burden you with the details. I'll just tell you that it's

$$\sqrt{\frac{1-r^2}{N-2}}$$

With a little algebra, the formula for the t-test simplifies to

$$t = \frac{r\sqrt{N-2}}{\sqrt{1-r^2}}$$

For the example,

$$t = \frac{r\sqrt{N-2}}{\sqrt{1-r^2}} = \frac{.817\sqrt{20-2}}{\sqrt{1-.817^2}} = 6.011$$

With df = 18 and $\alpha = .05$ (one-tailed), the critical value of t is 2.10 (use the worksheet function TINV to check). Because the calculated value is greater than the critical value, the decision is to reject H_0.

Do two correlation coefficients differ?

In a sample of 24 students at Farshimmelt College, the correlation between SAT and GPA is .752. Is this different from the correlation (.817) at Sahutsket University? If you have no way of assuming that one correlation should be higher than the other, the hypotheses are

$H_0: \rho_{Sahusket} = \rho_{Farshimmelt}$

$H_1: \rho_{Sahusket} \ne \rho_{Farshimmelt}$

Again, α = .05.

For highly technical reasons, you can't set up a *t*-test for this one. In fact, you can't even work with .817 and .752, the two correlation coefficients.

Instead, what you do is *transform* each correlation coefficient into something else and then work with the two "something elses" in a formula that gives you — believe it or not — a z-test.

TECHNICAL STUFF

The transformation is called *Fisher's r to z transformation.* Fisher is the statistician who's remembered as the *F* in the *F*-test. He transforms the *r* into a *z* by doing this:

$$z_r = \frac{1}{2}\left[\log_e(1+r) - \log_e(1-r)\right]$$

If you know what $\log_e$ means, fine. If not, don't worry about it. (I explain it in Chapter 22.) Excel takes care of all of this for you, as you see in a moment.

Anyway, for this example

$$z_{.817} = \frac{1}{2}\left[\log_e(1+.817) - \log_e(1-.817)\right] = 1.1477$$

$$z_{.752} = \frac{1}{2}\left[\log_e(1+.752) - \log_e(1-.752)\right] = 0.9775$$

After you transform *r* to *z*, the formula is

$$Z = \frac{z_1 - z_2}{\sigma_{z_1-z_2}}$$

The denominator turns out to be easier than you might think. It is

$$\sigma_{z_1-z_2} = \sqrt{\frac{1}{N_1-3} + \frac{1}{N_2-3}}$$

For this example:

$$\sigma_{z_1-z_2} = \sqrt{\frac{1}{N_1-3} + \frac{1}{N_2-3}} = \sqrt{\frac{1}{20-3} + \frac{1}{20-3}} = .326$$

The whole formula is

$$Z = \frac{z_1 - z_2}{\sigma_{z_1-z_2}} = \frac{1.1477 - 0.9775}{.326} = .522$$

The next step is to compare the calculated value to a standard normal distribution. For a two-tailed test with α = .05, the critical values in a standard normal distribution are 1.96 in the upper tail and -1.96 in the lower tail. The calculated value falls between those two, so the decision is to not reject H_0.

Worksheet Functions for Correlation

Excel provides two worksheet functions for calculating correlation — and, they do exactly the same thing in exactly the same way! Why Excel offers both CORREL and PEARSON I do not know, but there you have it. Those are the two main correlation functions.

The others are RSQ, COVARIANCE.P, and COVARIANCE.S. RSQ calculates the coefficient of determination (the square of the correlation coefficient). COVARIANCE.P determines covariance the way I show you in the earlier section "Understanding Correlation." It uses *N*-1. COVARIANCE.S uses *N*.

CORREL and PEARSON

Figure 15-4 shows the data for the Sahutsket SAT–GPA example, along with the Function Arguments dialog box for CORREL.

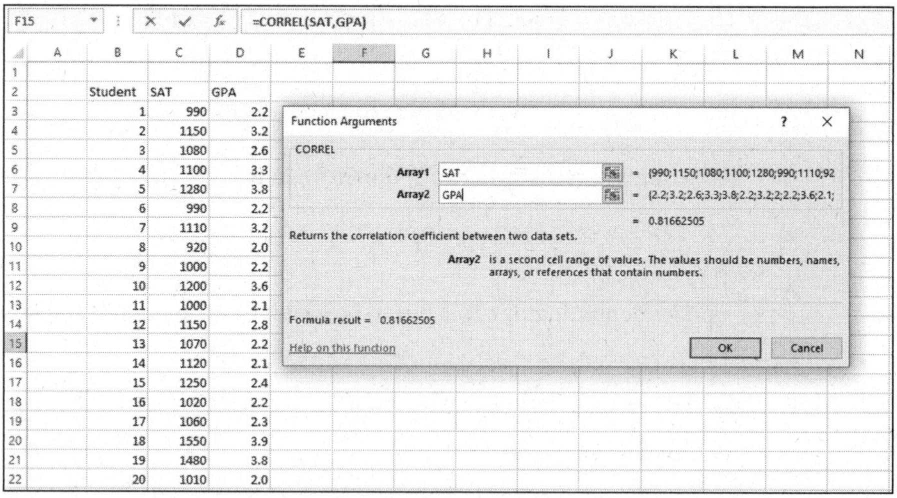

FIGURE 15-4:
The Function Arguments dialog box for CORREL, along with data.

To use this function, follow these steps:

1. Type the data into cell arrays and select a cell for CORREL's answer.

I've entered the SAT data into C3:C22 and the GPA data into D3:D22, and selected F15. I've defined SAT as the name of C3:C22 and GPA as the name of D3:D22. (Read Chapter 2 to see how to do this.)

2. **From the Statistical Functions menu, select CORREL to open its Function Arguments dialog box.**

3. **In the Function Arguments dialog box, enter the appropriate values for the arguments.**

   In the Array1 box, I entered SAT — the name I assigned to the cell range (C3:C22) that holds the scores for one of the variables.

   In the Array2 box, I entered GPA — the name I assigned to the cell range (D3:D22) that holds the scores for the other variable.

   With values entered for each argument, the answer, 0.81662505, appears in the dialog box.

4. **Click OK to put the answer into the selected cell.**

   Selecting PEARSON instead of CORREL gives you exactly the same answer, and you use it exactly the same way.

ITEM ANALYSIS: A USEFUL APPLICATION OF CORRELATION

Instructors often want to know how performance on a particular exam question is related to overall performance on the exam. Ideally, someone who knows the material answers the question correctly; someone who doesn't answers it incorrectly. If everyone answers it correctly — or if no one does — it's a useless question. This evaluation is called *item analysis.*

Suppose it's possible to answer the exam question either correctly or incorrectly, and it's possible to score from 0 to 100 on the exam. Arbitrarily, you can assign a score of 0 for an incorrect answer to the question, and 1 for a correct answer, and then calculate a correlation coefficient where each pair of scores is either 0 or 1 for the question and a number from 0 to 100 for the exam. The score on the exam question is called a *dichotomous variable,* and this type of correlation is called *point biserial correlation.*

If the point biserial correlation is high for an exam question, it's a good idea to retain that question. If the correlation is low, the question probably serves no purpose.

Because one of the variables can only be 0 or 1, the formula for the biserial correlation coefficient is a bit different from the formula for the regular correlation coefficient. If you use Excel for the calculations, however, that doesn't matter. Just use CORREL (or PEARSON) in the way I outline.

RSQ

If you have to quickly calculate the coefficient of determination (r^2), RSQ is the function for you. I see no particular need for this function because it's easy enough to use CORREL and then square the answer.

Here's what the Excel Formula bar looks like after you fill in the RSQ Function Arguments dialog box for this example:

```
=RSQ(GPA,SAT)
```

In terms of the dialog box, the only difference between this one and CORREL (and PEARSON) is that the boxes you fill in are called Known_y's and Known_x's rather than Array1 and Array2.

COVARIANCE.P and COVARIANCE.S

As far as calculating correlations go, I see no need for these formulas. Just for completeness, I'll tell you that COVARIANCE.P calculates covariance like this:

$$\text{covariance} = \left[\frac{1}{N}\right]\sum(x-\bar{x})(y-\bar{y})$$

and COVARIANCE.S calculates covariance like this:

$$\text{covariance} = \left[\frac{1}{N-1}\right]\sum(x-\bar{x})(y-\bar{y})$$

The P in the first function tells you that it's calculating the covariance for a population and the S in the second tells you it's calculating the covariance for a sample (or more correctly, for estimating covariance in a population).

You use these functions the same way you use CORREL. After you fill in the Function Arguments dialog box for COVARIANCE.P for this example, the formula in the Formula bar is

```
=COVARIANCE.P(SAT,GPA)
```

If you want to use this function to calculate *r*, you divide the answer by the product of STDEV.P(SAT) and STDEV.P(GPA). I leave it to you to figure out how you'd use COVARIANCE.S to calculate *r*. I don't know why you'd bother with all of this when you can just use CORREL.

Data Analysis Tool: Correlation

If you have to calculate a single correlation coefficient, you'll find that Excel's Correlation data analysis tool does the same thing CORREL does, although the output is in tabular form. This tool becomes useful when you have to calculate multiple correlations on a set of data.

For example, Figure 15-5 shows SAT, high school average, and GPA for 20 Sahutsket University students, along with the dialog box for the Correlation data analysis tool.

The steps for using this tool are:

1. **Type the data into the worksheet and include labels for the columns.**

   In this example, the data (including labels) are in C2:E22.

2. **Select Data | Data Analysis to open the Data Analysis dialog box.**
3. **In the Data Analysis dialog box, scroll down the Analysis Tools list and select Correlation.**
4. **Click OK to open the Correlation dialog box.**

   This dialog box is shown in Figure 15-5.

5. **In the Input Range box, enter the cell range that holds all the data.**

   I entered \$C\$2:\$E\$22. Note the \$ signs for absolute referencing. Excel adds them when you select the cell range in the spreadsheet.

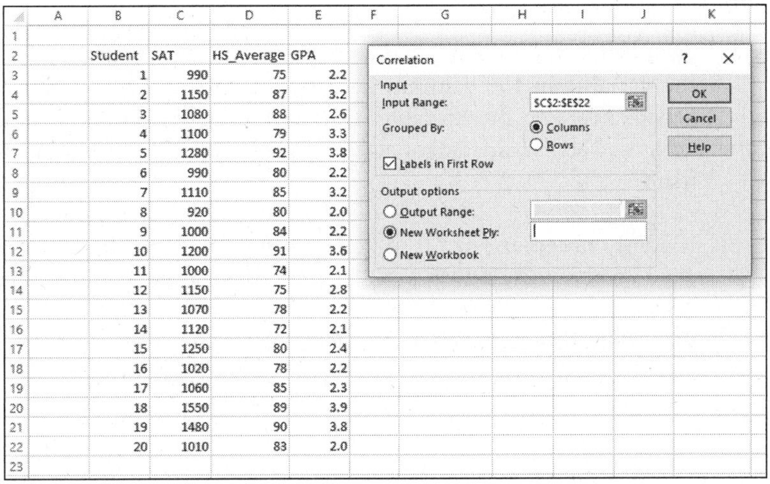

Student	SAT	HS_Average	GPA
1	990	75	2.2
2	1150	87	3.2
3	1080	88	2.6
4	1100	79	3.3
5	1280	92	3.8
6	990	80	2.2
7	1110	85	3.2
8	920	80	2.0
9	1000	84	2.2
10	1200	91	3.6
11	1000	74	2.1
12	1150	75	2.8
13	1070	78	2.2
14	1120	72	2.1
15	1250	80	2.4
16	1020	78	2.2
17	1060	85	2.3
18	1550	89	3.9
19	1480	90	3.8
20	1010	83	2.0

FIGURE 15-5: The Correlation data analysis tool dialog box, along with data for SAT, High School Average, and GPA.

6. **To the right of Grouped By, select a radio button to indicate if the data are organized in columns or rows.**

I chose the Columns radio button.

7. **If the cell ranges include column headings, select the Labels check box.**

I included the headings in the ranges, so I selected the box.

8. **In the Output Options, select a radio button to indicate where you want the results.**

I selected New Worksheet Ply to put the results on a new page in the worksheet.

9. **Click OK.**

Because I selected New Worksheet Ply, a newly created page opens with the results.

Tabled output

Figure 15-6 shows the tool's tabled output, after I expand the columns. The table is a *correlation matrix.*

FIGURE 15-6:
The Correlation
data analysis
tool's tabled
output.

	A	B	C	D	E
1		SAT	HS_Average	GPA	
2	SAT	1			
3	HS_Average	0.552527329	1		
4	GPA	0.81662505	0.714353653	1	
5					

Each cell in the matrix represents the correlation of the variable in the row with the variable in the column. Cell B3 presents the correlation of SAT with High School Average, for example. Each cell in the main diagonal contains 1. This is because each main diagonal cell represents the correlation of a variable with itself.

It's only necessary to fill in half the matrix. The cells above the main diagonal would contain the same values as the cells below the main diagonal.

What does this table tell you, exactly? Read on. . . .

Multiple correlation

The correlation coefficients in this matrix combine to produce a *multiple correlation coefficient*. This is a number that summarizes the relationship between the dependent variable — GPA, in this example — and the two independent variables (SAT and High School Average).

To show you how these correlation coefficients combine, I abbreviate GPA as G, SAT as S, and High School Average as H. So r_{GS} is the correlation coefficient for GPA and SAT, r_{GH} is the correlation coefficient for GPA and High School Average, and r_{SH} is the correlation coefficient for SAT and High School Average.

Here's the formula that puts them all together:

$$R_{G.SH} = \sqrt{\frac{r_{GS}^2 + r_{GH}^2 - 2r_{GS}r_{GH}r_{SH}}{1 - r_{GS}^2}}$$

The uppercase R on the left indicates that this is a multiple correlation coefficient, as opposed to the lowercase r that indicates a correlation between two variables. The subscript $G.SH$ means that the multiple correlation is between GPA and the combination of SAT and High School Average.

This is the calculation that produces Multiple R in the Regression Statistics section of the Regression data analysis tool's results. (See Chapter 14.)

For this example,

$$R_{G.SH} = \sqrt{\frac{(.816625)^2 + (.714354)^2 - 2(.816625)(.714354)(.552527)}{1 - (.816625)^2}} = .875529$$

Because I use the same data to show you multiple regression in Chapter 14, this value (with some additional decimal places) is in Figure 14-25, in cell B4.

If you square this number, you get the *multiple coefficient of determination*. In Chapter 14, I tell you about R Square, and that's what this is. It's another item in the Regression Statistics that the Regression data analysis tool calculates. You also find it in LINEST's results, although it's not labeled.

For this example, that result is

$$R_{G.SH}^2 = (.875529)^2 = .766552$$

You can see this number in Figure 14-3 in cell H5 (the LINEST results). You can also see it in Figure 14-25, cell B5 (the Regression data analysis tool report).

Here's some more information about R^2 as it relates to Excel. In addition to R^2 — or, as Excel likes to write it, R Square — the Regression data analysis tool calculates *Adjusted R Square*. In Figure 14-25, it's in cell B6. Why is it necessary to adjust R Square?

In multiple regression, adding independent variables (like High School Average) sometimes makes the regression equation less accurate. The multiple coefficient of determination, R Square, doesn't reflect this. Its denominator is SS_{Total} (for the dependent variable), and that never changes. The numerator can only increase or stay the same. So any decline in accuracy doesn't result in a lower R Square.

Taking degrees of freedom into account fixes the flaw. Every time you add an independent variable, you change the degrees of freedom and that makes all the difference. Just so you know, here's the adjustment:

$$Adjusted\ R^2 = 1 - \left(1 - R^2\right)\left[\frac{(N-1)}{(N-k-1)}\right]$$

The k in the denominator is the number of independent variables.

Partial correlation

GPA and SAT are associated with High School Average (in the example). Each one's association with High School Average might somehow hide the true correlation between them.

What would their correlation be if you could remove that association? Another way to say it is this: What would be the GPA–SAT correlation if you could hold High School Average constant?

One way to hold High School Average constant is to find the GPA–SAT correlation for a sample of students who have one High School Average — 87, for example. In a sample like that, the correlation of each variable with High School Average is zero. This usually isn't feasible in the real world, however.

Another way is to find the *partial correlation* between GPA and SAT. This is a statistical way of removing each variable's association with High School Average in your sample. You use the correlation coefficients in the correlation matrix to do this:

$$r_{GS.H} = \frac{r_{GS} - r_{GH}r_{SH}}{\sqrt{1 - r_{GH}^2}\ \sqrt{1 - r_{SH}^2}}$$

Once again, *G* stands for GPA, *S* for SAT, and *H* for High School Average. The subscript *GS.H* means that the correlation is between GPA and SAT with High School Average "partialled out."

For this example,

$$r_{GS.H} = \frac{.816625 - (.714353)(.552527)}{\sqrt{1-(.714353)^2}\sqrt{1-(.552527)^2}} = .547005$$

Semipartial correlation

It's also possible to remove the correlation with High School Average from just SAT without removing it from GPA. This is called *semipartial correlation*. The formula for this one also uses the correlation coefficients from the correlation matrix:

$$r_{G(S.H)} = \frac{r_{GS} - r_{GH}r_{SH}}{\sqrt{1-r_{SH}^2}}$$

The subscript *G(S.H)* means the correlation is between GPA and SAT with High School Average partialled out of SAT only.

Applying this formula to the example,

$$r_{G(S.H)} = \frac{.816625 - (.714353)(.552527)}{\sqrt{1-(.552527)^2}} = .315714$$

Some statistics textbooks refer to semipartial correlation as *part correlation*.

Data Analysis Tool: Covariance

You use the Covariance data analysis tool the same way you use the Correlation data analysis tool. I won't go through the steps again. Instead, I just show you the tabled output in Figure 15-7. The data are from Figure 15-5.

FIGURE 15-7:
The Covariance data analysis tool's tabled output for SAT, High School Average, and GPA.

	A	B	C	D	E
1		SAT	HS_Average	GPA	
2	SAT	24862.75			
3	HS_Average	512.375	34.5875		
4	GPA	85.1675	2.77875	0.437475	
5					

The table is a *covariance matrix.* Each cell in the matrix shows the covariance of the variable in the row with the variable in the column (calculated the way COVARIANCE.P would do it, by using N in the formula). Cell C4 shows the covariance of GPA with High School Average. The main diagonal in this matrix presents the variance of each variable (which is equivalent to the covariance of a variable with itself). In this case, the variance is what you compute if you use VARP.

Again, it's only necessary to fill half the matrix. Cells above the main diagonal would hold the same values as the cells below the main diagonal.

As is the case with COVAR, I don't see why you'd use this tool. I just include it for completeness.

Testing Hypotheses About Correlation

Excel has no worksheet function for testing hypotheses about r. As I point out earlier, you perform a t-test whose formula is

$$t = \frac{r\sqrt{N-2}}{\sqrt{1-r^2}}$$

With 0.817 stored in cell H12, I used this formula to calculate t:

```
=H12*SQRT(20-2)/SQRT(1-H12^2)
```

I then used the answer (6.011 and some additional decimal places) as input to TDIST (along with 18 df and 1 tail) to find that the one-tailed probability of the result is way less than .05.

Worksheet functions: FISHER, FISHERINV

Excel handles the rather complex transformations that enable you to test hypotheses about the difference between two correlation coefficients. FISHER transforms r to z. FISHERINV does the reverse. Just to refresh your memory, you use the transformed values in the formula

$$Z = \frac{z_1 - z_2}{\sigma_{z_1 - z_2}}$$

in which the denominator is

$$\sigma_{z_1 - z_2} = \sqrt{\frac{1}{N_1 - 3} + \frac{1}{N_2 - 3}}$$

In the example I discuss earlier (Sahutsket versus Farshimmelt), the correlation coefficients were .817 and .752, and I did a two-tailed test. The first step is to transform each correlation. I'll walk you through the steps for using FISHER to transform .817:

1. **Select a cell for FISHER's answer.**

   I selected B3 for the transformed value.

2. **From the Statistical Functions menu, select FISHER to open its Function Arguments dialog box.**

   The FISHER Function Arguments dialog box appears, as shown in Figure 15-8.

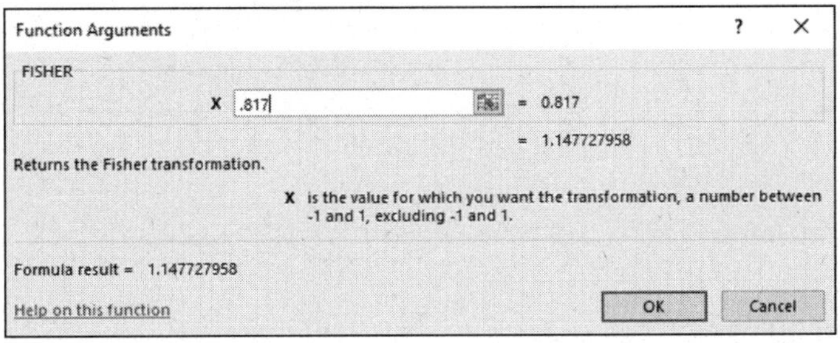

FIGURE 15-8:
The FISHER
Function
Arguments
dialog box.

3. **In the Function Arguments dialog box, type the appropriate value for the argument.**

   In the x box, I typed .817, the correlation coefficient. The answer, 1.147728, appears in the dialog box.

4. **Click OK to put the answer into the selected cell.**

I selected B4 to store the transformation of .752. Next, I used this formula to calculate Z

```
=(B3–B4)/SQRT((1/(20–3))+(1/(24–3)))
```

Finally, I used NORM.S.INV to find the critical value of z for rejecting H_0 with a two-tailed α of .05. Because the result of the formula (0.521633) is less than that critical value (1.96), the decision is to not reject H_0.

Chapter 16

It's About Time

In many fields (science, medicine, business), it's often necessary to take measurements over successive intervals of time. When you have this kind of data, you have yourself a *time series*. This chapter tells you about time series and how to use Excel to understand them and use them to make forecasts.

A Series and Its Components

Managers often have to base their decisions on time series — like sales figures — and the numbers in a time series typically show numerous ups and downs.

Here's an example. The (totally fictional) FarDrate Timepiece Corporation markets the beautifully designed MeesKyte watch, and they gather the quarterly national sales figures. Figure 16-1 shows a spreadsheet and a graph of these sales figures from 2011–2015.

Take a look at the graph. The peaks and valleys seem pretty regular. Sales peak in the last quarter of every year — perhaps people buy these watches as holiday gifts. Sales also peak somewhat (but not as much) in the middle of each year — maybe parents are buying MeesKyte watches as graduation presents. This pattern repeats from year to year, and it's called the *seasonal component* of the time series.

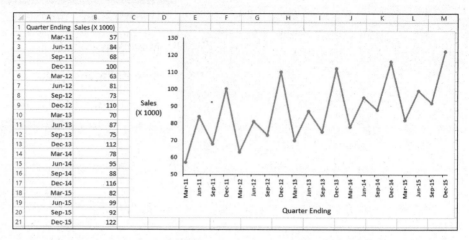

	A	B
1	Quarter Ending	Sales (X 1000)
2	Mar-11	57
3	Jun-11	84
4	Sep-11	68
5	Dec-11	100
6	Mar-12	63
7	Jun-12	81
8	Sep-12	73
9	Dec-12	110
10	Mar-13	70
11	Jun-13	87
12	Sep-13	75
13	Dec-13	112
14	Mar-14	78
15	Jun-14	95
16	Sep-14	88
17	Dec-14	116
18	Mar-15	82
19	Jun-15	99
20	Sep-15	92
21	Dec-15	122

FIGURE 16-1: Quarterly sales figures for the FarDrate MeesKyte watch.

We also see sales moving generally in an upward direction. That might result from an expanding economy, or perhaps increasing awareness of the brand (or both). This is called the *trend component* of the time series. In this example, the trend is linear, but that's not always the case in a time series.

And we see the peaks and valleys varying around the upward trend. This is called the *cyclic component* of the time series.

Finally, sporadic nonrecurring influences can affect a time series. This is known as the *irregular component* of a time series.

A Moving Experience

A mean that takes all the peaks and valleys into account might obscure the big picture of the overall trend.

One way to smooth out the bumps and still see the big picture is to calculate a *moving average.* This is an average calculated from the most recent scores in the time series. It moves because you keep calculating it over the time series. As you add a score to the front end, you delete one from the back end.

So we have the MeesKyte sales figures for 20 quarters, and we decide to keep a moving average for the most recent five quarters. Start with the average from quarters 1–5 of those 20 quarters (Mar 11 through Mar 12). Then average the prices from quarters 2–6 (Apr 11 through Apr 12). Next, average quarters 3–7, and so on, until you average the final 5 quarters of the time series.

REMEMBER

A moving average is a *forecast*. It's a best guess based on averaging the sales figures of the most recent five quarters.

Excel provides two ways of calculating the moving average. One is quick and dirty, (it's a trendline option on the chart), and the other is a data analysis tool.

Lining up the trend

Here's how to use the trendline option:

1. **Enter your data into a spreadsheet.**

   I entered the data into Columns A and B, rows 1-21. Row 1 contains headings.

2. **Select the data and insert a line chart.**

   On the Insert tab, in the Charts area, select Line Chart with Markers.

3. **Move the cursor into the chart to make the Chart Elements tool (the plus sign) visible.**

4. **Click the Chart Elements tool.**

5. **In the pop-up menu, select Trendline | More Options.**

6. **In the Format Trendline panel, select Moving Average and change the period.**

   I changed it to 5 for this example.

Figure 16-2 shows the Format Trendline panel and the moving average line in the chart. The beauty of this technique is that it enables you to experiment with different periods (also known as *intervals*) for the moving average and immediately see how each one looks on the chart. Unfortunately, this technique does not show you the numerical values of the moving averages. To calculate those values, you use . . .

Data Analysis tool: Moving Average

The Moving Average tool charts the moving average and presents the numerical values, too. Unlike with the trendline technique, however, you can't experiment with different periods on the fly.

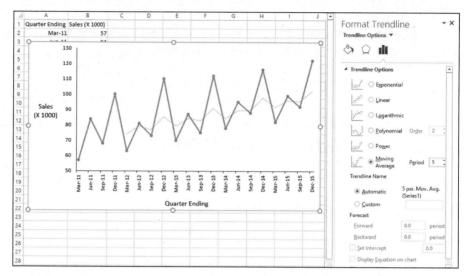

FIGURE 16-2:
Formatting the
trendline to
produce a moving
average.

The steps are:

1. **With the data entered into the spreadsheet, select Data | Data Analysis and select Moving Average from Analysis Tools.**

This opens the Moving Average dialog box.

2. **In the Input Range box, enter the data array.**

For this example, that's B1 through B21. I don't include the column with the dates.

3. **Fill in the remaining boxes.**

I select the Labels in First Row check box, and I enter 5 in the Interval box. (The word *Interval* corresponds to the word *Period* in the trendline technique.) Then I enter cells C2:C22 in the Output Range box and click the Chart Output check box and the Standard Errors check box. Figure 16-3 shows the Moving Average dialog box after all these entries.

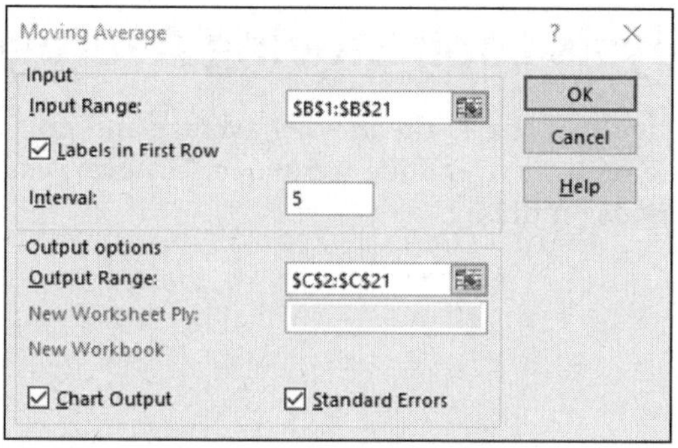

FIGURE 16-3:
The completed
Moving Average
dialog box.

4. Click OK.

This puts the moving averages in Column C and the standard errors in Column D, and then creates a chart of the data and the moving averages. Figure 16-4 shows all this.

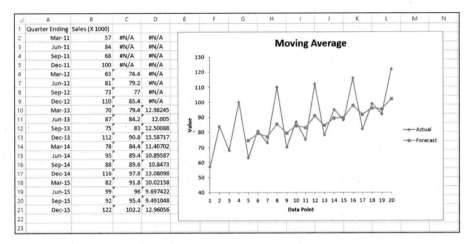

FIGURE 16-4:
The results:
Moving averages,
standard errors,
and a chart.

Ignore the ugly-looking #N/A symbols. Each number in Column C is a moving average — which, as I mention earlier, is a forecast of the number of sales on the basis of the preceding five quarters.

Each number in Column D is a standard error. In this context, a *standard* error is the square root of the average of the squared differences between the sales and the forecast for the previous five quarters. So the first standard error in cell D10 is

$$\sqrt{\frac{(63-74.4)^2+(81-79.2)^2+(73-77)^2+(110-85.4)^2+(70-79.4)^2}{5}}=12.98245$$

The graph (stretched out from its original appearance and with a reformatted vertical axis) shows the moving average in the series labeled Forecast. Sometimes the forecast matches up with the data, sometimes it doesn't. As the figure shows, the moving average smoothes out the peaks and the valleys in the sales data.

In general, how many scores should you include in the interval? That's up to you. Include too many and you risk obsolete data influencing your results. Include too few and you risk missing something important.

TIP

The Moving Average tool doesn't put the dates on the x-axis, but you can put them in the chart after it's created. Right-click in the chart, choose Select Data from the contextual menu that appears, and then choose Edit the Horizontal (Category) Axis Labels.

How To Be a Smoothie, Exponentially

Exponential smoothing is similar to a moving average. It's a technique for forecasting based on prior data. In contrast with the moving average, which works just with a sequence of actual values, exponential smoothing takes its previous prediction into account.

Exponential smoothing operates according to a *damping factor* — a number between zero and one. With α representing the damping factor, the formula is

$$y'_t = (1 - \alpha) y_{t-1} + \alpha y'_{t-1}$$

In terms of sales figures from the preceding example, y'_t represents the predicted sales at a time: *t*. If *t* is the current quarter, *t-1* is the immediately preceding quarter. So y_{t-1} is the preceding quarter's actual sales and y'_{t-1} is the preceding quarter's predicted sales. The sequence of predictions begins with the first predicted value as the observed value from the immediately preceding quarter.

A larger damping factor gives more weight to the preceding quarter's prediction. A smaller damping factor gives greater weight to the preceding quarter's actual value. A damping factor of 0.5 weighs each one equally.

Figure 16-5 shows the dialog box for the Exponential Smoothing data analysis tool. It's similar to the Moving Average tool, except for the Damping Factor box.

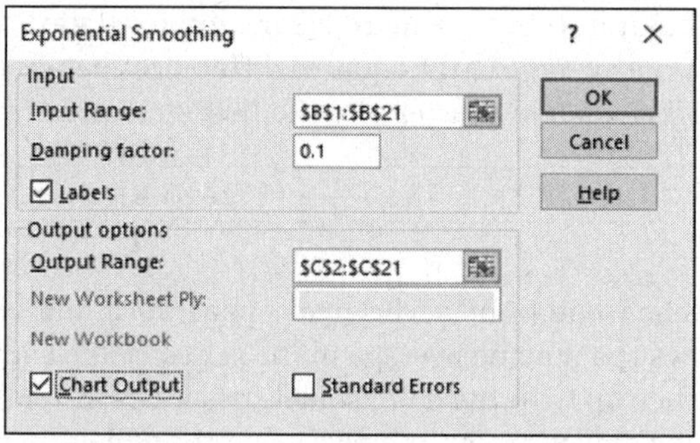

FIGURE 16-5: The Exponential Smoothing data analysis tool dialog box.

I applied exponential smoothing to the data from the preceding example. I did this three times with 0.1, 0.5, and 0.9 as the damping factors. Figure 16-6 shows the graphic output for each result.

The highest damping factor, 0.9, results in the flattest sequence of forecasts. The lowest, 0.1, forecasts the most pronounced set of peaks and valleys. How should you set the damping factor? Like the interval in the moving average, that's up to you. Your experience and the specific area of application are the determining factors.

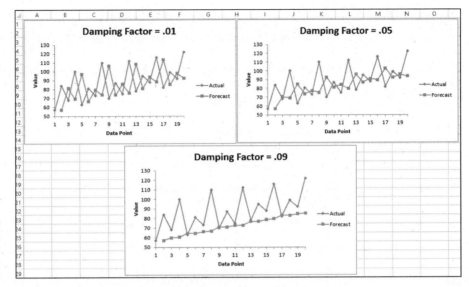

FIGURE 16-6:
Exponential
smoothing with
three damping
factors.

You might have noticed from Figure 16-6, however, that the predictions of exponential smoothing don't appear to be all that accurate for this example.

What to do? Read on. . . .

One-Click Forecasting!

New to Excel 2016 (Windows only) is a capability that enables you to select a time series and with a mouse-click (several, actually) receive a set of extrapolated forecasts along with confidence intervals for each forecast.

The new forecasting capability uses Excel's new (Windows only) FORECAST functions:

>> FORECAST.ETS creates a forecast based on triple exponential smoothing. (See the earlier sidebar "Tripling the fun — exponentially.")

>> FORECAST.ETS.CONFINT returns a confidence interval for a forecast value.

>> FORECAST.ETS.STAT returns values of statistics associated with the ETS forecast.

>> FORECAST.ETS.SEASONALITY determines the length of the seasonal pattern within the data.

I could tell you about each one, but I don't think you'll ever use any of them individually.

TRIPLING THE FUN — EXPONENTIALLY

The basis of Excel's new forecasting tool is a more complex form of exponential smoothing than you've seen so far. Think of the concept I tell you about in the previous section as *single exponential smoothing*.

When you have a trend component (like the overall upward linear trend in the example), single exponential smoothing loses accuracy. Figure 16-6 might have suggested that to you.

With trend in the data, you have to add a little something extra:

$$y'_t = (1-\alpha)y_{t-1} + \alpha(y'_{t-1} + b_{t-1})$$

and

$$b_t = \gamma(y'_t - y'_{t-1}) + (1-\gamma)b_{t-1}$$

In that last equation, the letter in front of the first parentheses that looks like a *y* is actually the Greek letter *gamma*. These equations add trend to the mix. This is called *double exponential smoothing*.

When the data show seasonality as well as trend (as in the FarDrate example), *triple exponential smoothing* (abbreviated as ETS) saves the day. The three equations for triple exponential smoothing are the brainchildren of statisticians Charles Holt and Peter Winters, and so this is called the Holt-Winters method.

The first is an overhaul of single exponential smoothing:

$$y'_t = (1-\alpha)\left(\frac{y_{t-1}}{I_{t-L}}\right) + \alpha(y'_{t-1} + b_{t-1})$$

The second is one you just saw:

$$b_t = \gamma(y'_t - y'_{t-1}) + (1-\gamma)b_{t-1}$$

The third is:

$$I_t = \beta\left(\frac{y_t}{y'_t}\right) + (1-\beta)I_{t-L}$$

The first equation is the overall smoothing, the second is the trend smoothing, and the third is the seasonal smoothing.

I is called the seasonal index, and *L* is the number of periods per season.

Each of the three coefficients — α, β, and γ — is a number between zero and one.

The mathematics behind fitting these coefficients to the data is pretty intense, but Excel's Forecast Sheet (that one-click forecasting tool) makes them easy to work with.

Let's forecast!

Here are the steps:

1. **Enter the data, with dates in one column.**

   As per our example, the data are in Columns A and B.

2. **Select the data.**

3. **On the Data tab, in the Forecast area, select Forecast Sheet.**

   This opens the Create Forecast Worksheet dialog box shown in Figure 16-7. As you can see, Excel is already hard at work figuring things out for you. The blue line is the data, the bold orange line is the forecasts, and the lighter orange lines are the 95% confidence limits for the forecasts.

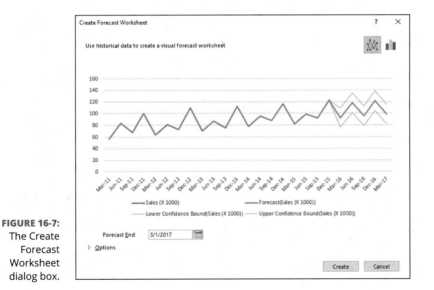

FIGURE 16-7: The Create Forecast Worksheet dialog box.

4. **In the Create Forecast Worksheet dialog box, click the Options arrow in the bottom left corner.**

This expands the dialog box, as Figure 16-8 shows.

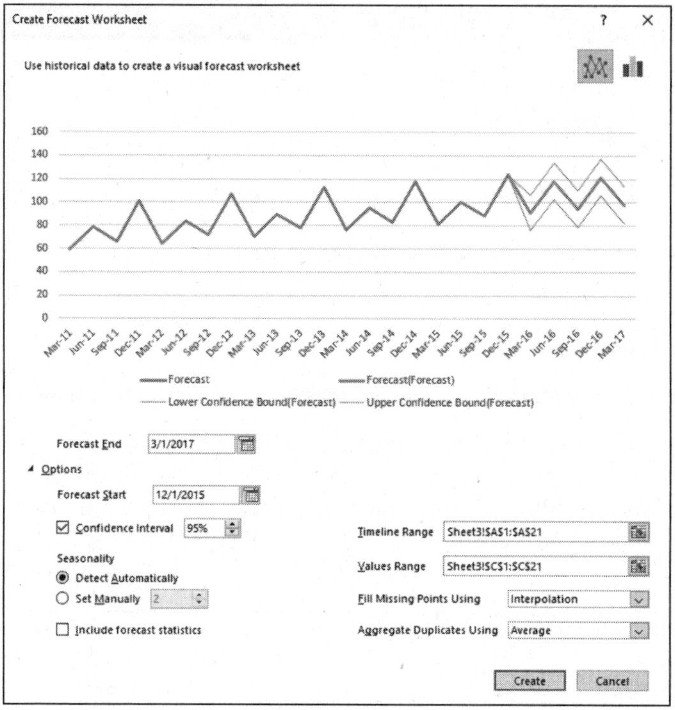

FIGURE 16-8:
The expanded
Create Forecast
Worksheet
dialog box.

5. **Make necessary modifications in the expanded dialog box.**

To get an idea about forecast accuracy, I move the date in the Forecast Start box back to March 31, 2015. This way, I can match some of the forecasts with data.

The Seasonality area shows 2 in the grayed-out box next to Set Manually. This means that FORECAST.ETS.SEASONALITY has detected a pattern that repeats every two quarters. As the FarDrate CEO, though, I believe that the pattern repeats every four quarters, so I select the Set Manually radio button and change the 2 to 4. The chart in the dialog box changes immediately to show way more accurate forecasts and narrower 95% confidence limits.

I select the check box next to Include Forecast Statistics. I have the option of changing confidence intervals and some other things, but what I've done is sufficient.

6. **Click Create.**

This opens the created Forecast Worksheet, shown in Figure 16-9.

Quarter Ending	Sales (X 1000)	Forecast(Sales (X 1000))	Lower Confidence Bound(Sales (X 1000))	Upper Confidence Bound(Sales (X 1000))
Mar-11	57			
Jun-11	84			
Sep-11	68			
Dec-11	100			
Mar-12	63			
Jun-12	81			
Sep-12	73			
Dec-12	110			
Mar-13	70			
Jun-13	87			
Sep-13	75			
Dec-13	112			
Mar-14	78			
Jun-14	95			
Sep-14	88			
Dec-14	116			
Mar-15	82	82	82.00	82.00
Jun-15	99	100.7574952	95.35	106.17
Sep-15	92	89.72409623	84.27	95.18
Dec-15	122	124.5590706	119.06	130.06
Mar-16		86.09650995	80.55	91.64
Jun-16		106.3702619	100.78	111.96
Sep-16		95.33686292	89.71	100.97
Dec-16		130.1718373	124.50	135.85
Mar-17		91.70927663	85.99	97.43

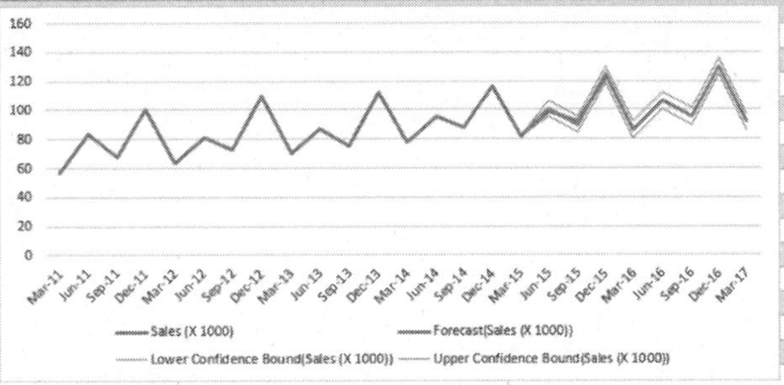

FIGURE 16-9: The created Forecast Worksheet.

Along with the chart, the Forecast Worksheet shows the forecast values in Column C (calculated by `FORECAST.ETS`), and the confidence limits in Columns D and E (calculated by `FORECAST.ETS.CONFINT`).

The Forecast Worksheet also provides the Forecast Statistics in Columns G and H (courtesy of `FORECAST.ETS.STAT`), rows 1-8, as Figure 16-10 shows.

Statistic	Value
Alpha	0.126
Beta	0.001
Gamma	0.001
MASE	0.095
SMAPE	0.026
MAE	2.317
RMSE	2.812

FIGURE 16-10: The Forecast Statistics.

Alpha, Beta, and Gamma are the values I refer to in the sidebar. The other four are measures of how well the forecasts fit the data. The first two are a bit involved, so I'll let them slide.

The third one, MAE, is the *mean absolute error* — the average of the absolute value of the differences between data and forecasts. The last one, RMSE, is *root mean squared error*, which is the average of the squared deviations of the data from the forecasts. You can think of the standard error of estimate in regression (refer to Chapter 14) as a root mean square error adjusted for degrees of freedom.

Chapter 17

Non-Parametric Statistics

The statistical methods I cover in earlier chapters have a couple of things in common. First, we assume ratio (or at least interval) data. (If you don't know what that means, reread the section entitled "Types of data" in Chapter 1.) Second, we can use sample statistics to estimate parameters of the sampling distribution, and we use the central limit theorem to characterize the nature of the distribution so that we can test hypotheses.

Sometimes we have to analyze nominal data or ordinal data (again, Chapter 1). And sometimes we can't specify the distribution of the variable we're working with.

To deal with these cases, statisticians have developed *non-parametric* statistical tests. The list of these tests is long, and growing all the time. Many of them require special lookup tables for hypothesis tests.

I want to avoid those special tables. So, to make the cut for this chapter, a test had to either (a) test hypotheses via a well-known distribution built into Excel or (b) work with a well-known distribution when samples are large. Of the non-parametric tests that fit the bill, I chose six classical ones.

Because Excel has no special data analysis tools or built-in functions for these tests, the general plan is to translate the test formulas into Excel formulas and then use an Excel statistical function (NORM.DIST or CHISQ.DIST.RT) to perform the hypothesis test.

The easiest way to tell you about each test is to show you the finished spreadsheet and describe the steps it takes to get there.

Independent Samples

The non-parametric tests I show you in this section are analogous to the independent groups t-test and to the one-factor analysis of variance.

Two samples: Mann-Whitney U test

The Mann-Whitney U test is one of the best-known non-parametric tests. You use it to test whether two independent samples come from the same population in situations where you don't have interval or ratio data (and thus can't use the t-test).

When the data are ordinal, statisticians work with the ranks of the data rather than with the original data points, and that's what this test does.

Imagine a study in which 40 people are randomly assigned to watch either a stressful movie or a cartoon. Then they have to rate how stressed they feel on a scale of 1 (least stressed) to 100 (most stressed).

Figure 17-1 shows a spreadsheet with the data in columns A and B. The null hypothesis is that the two groups came out of the same population. The alternative hypothesis is that the stress would be higher after the stressful movie, so this can be a one-tailed test at $\alpha = .05$.

The first order of business is to rank each score (in ascending order) in the context of all scores. If the null hypothesis is true, the high ranks and the low ranks (and all those in between) should be distributed about equally through the two groups.

I can base the formula for the Mann-Whitney U test on either the ranks in column A or the ranks in column B.

If I choose A, the formula is

$$U = N_A N_B + \frac{N_A(N_A + 1)}{2} - R_A$$

▲	A	B	C	D	E	F	G	H
1	Stressful Movie	Cartoon		Rank Movie	Rank Cartoon		NA	NB
2	87	32		39	9		20	20
3	55	15		25	2			
4	31	18		8	3		U =	271
5	45	20		19	4		Mean =	200
6	67	43		31	18		St dev =	36.96845502
7	68	23		32	6			
8	22	76		5	36		p =	0.972606167
9	71	56		33	26			
10	46	49		20	22			
11	37	34		13	11			
12	39	53		15	24			
13	41	14		16	1			
14	74	47		35	21			
15	58	77		27	37			
16	60	35		28	12			
17	83	62		38	29			
18	33	38		10	14			
19	73	89		34	40			
20	52	29		23	7			
21	64	42		30	17			
22				481	339			
23								

FIGURE 17-1:
The Mann-
Whitney U test.

If I choose B, it's

$$U = N_A N_B + \frac{N_B(N_B + 1)}{2} - R_B$$

R_A is the sum of the ranks in column A, R_B is the sum of the ranks in column B, N_A is the number of scores in column A, and N_B is the number of scores in column B.

With large samples, the sampling distribution of U is approximately a normal distribution with

$$\mu_U = \frac{N_A N_B}{2}$$

and

$$\sigma_U = \sqrt{\frac{(N_A)(N_B)(N_A + N_B + 1)}{12}}$$

Back to Figure 17-1. The ranks for the scores in columns A and B appear in columns D and E. How did I get them? Easy. In cell D2, I type

```
=RANK.AVG(A2,$A$2:$B$21,1)
```

Then I autofill columns D and E.

Now it's a matter of translating either U-formula into an Excel formula. For clarity, I define NA as the name of the value in cell G2 — the number of scores in column A, and NB for the value in H2 — the number of scores in column B.

I choose to base the U-formula on column A, so in cell H4 I type

```
=NA*NB +((NA*(NA+1))/2)-E22
```

I press Enter, and the result, 271, appears.

Now for the test. For the mean of the sampling distribution, I type

```
=(NA*NB)/2
```

into cell H5 and

```
=SQRT((NA*NB*(NA+NB+1))/12)
```

into H6. To calculate the probability associated with U, I type

```
=NORM.DIST(H4,H5,H6,TRUE)
```

into H8. The result, 0.97, means that the probability of U being less than the calculated value is greater than 0.95. So the probability of a result more extreme is less than .05, and I can reject the null hypothesis.

More than two samples: Kruskal-Wallis one-way ANOVA

FarKlempt Robotics, Inc., surveys its employees about their level of satisfaction with their jobs. They ask developers, managers, maintenance workers, and tech writers to rate job satisfaction on a scale of 1 (least satisfied) to 100 (most satisfied). Six employees are in each category. Figure 17-2 shows a spreadsheet with the data in columns A through D, rows 1–7. The null hypothesis is that the samples all come from the same population. The alternative hypothesis is that they do not.

The appropriate non-parametric test is the Kruskal–Wallis One-Way Analysis of Variance. As with the Mann–Whitney, I start by ranking all 24 scores in ascending order. Again, if the null hypothesis true, the ranks should be distributed about equally throughout the groups.

The formula for this statistic is

$$H = \left[\frac{12}{N(N+1)} \sum \frac{R^2}{n} \right] - 3(N+1)$$

FIGURE 17-2:
The Kruskal–Wallis One-Way Analysis of Variance.

	A	B	C	D	E	F	G
1	Developer	Manager	Maintenance	Tech Writer		N_Total	n_group
2	25	63	54	79		24	6
3	58	70	61	50			
4	57	52	95	77			
5	51	56	80	64			
6	42	62	78	55		H =	7.98
7	59	76	81	53		p =	0.0464269
8							
9	Rdeveloper	Rmanager	Rmaint	Rtechwriter			
10	1	15	7	21			
11	11	17	13	3			
12	10	5	24	19			
13	4	9	22	16			
14	2	14	20	8			
15	12	18	23	6			
16	40	78	109	73			
17							

N is the total number of scores, and n is the number of scores in each group. To keep things easy, I specified the same number of scores in each group, but that's not necessary for this test. R is the sum of the ranks in a group. H is distributed approximately as chi-square with df = number of groups — 1, when each n is greater than 5.

Looking back at Figure 17-2, the ranks for the data are in rows 9–15 of columns A through D. Row 16 holds the sums of the ranks in each group. I defined N_Total as the name for the value in cell F2, the total number of scores. I defined n_group as the name for the value in G2, the number of scores in each group.

To calculate H, I type

```
=(12/(N_Total*(N_Total+1)))*(SUMSQ(A16:D16)/n_group)-3*
    (N_Total+1)
```

into cell G6.

For the hypothesis test, I type

```
=CHISQ.DIST.RT(G6,3)
```

into G7. The result is less than .05, so I reject the null hypothesis.

Matched Samples

The non-parametric tests I show you in this main section are analogous to the matched groups t-test and to the Repeated Measures Analysis of Variance.

Two samples: Wilcoxon matched-pairs signed ranks

This test works with the differences between matched pairs. It goes a bit further than that, though. In addition to the direction of the differences, the Wilcoxon test considers the sizes of the differences. So this test is useful when you have ordinal data and enough precision that you can rank the differences between pairs.

Here's an example. A social worker studies 26 pairs of identical twins. Each child in a twin-pair either attends a public school or is home-schooled. At the end of a school year, the social worker rates all the children on sociability on a scale of 1 (least sociable) to 100 (most sociable). The null hypothesis is that the two groups don't differ. The alternative hypothesis is that they do.

Figure 17-3 shows the data in columns A and B, rows 1-27. The interpair differences are in column C, and the ranks of the differences are in column D.

	A	B	C	D	E	F	G
1	Public School Twin	Home School Twin	Difference	Rank of Difference		N	
2	64	54	10	14		26	
3	44	51	-7	6			
4	51	48	3	11		# of positive differences =	18
5	34	39	-5	8		# of negative differences =	8
6	84	25	59	26			
7	66	46	20	19		Sum of less frequent ranks =	36
8	61	78	-17	3			
9	22	58	-36	1		Mean =	175.5
10	39	30	9	13		Standard Deviation =	39.37321425
11	78	38	40	25			
12	40	51	-11	4		p =	0.000197788
13	51	47	4	12			
14	54	39	15	16			
15	71	43	28	21			
16	70	43	27	20			
17	86	48	38	23			
18	74	72	2	10			
19	69	53	16	17			
20	63	30	33	22			
21	43	53	-10	5			
22	50	49	1	9			
23	50	56	-6	7			
24	33	51	-18	2			
25	52	39	13	15			
26	45	26	19	18			
27	56	17	39	24			
28							

FIGURE 17-3: The Wilcoxon matched-pairs signed ranks test.

Now things get interesting. The next step is to see how many pairs have a negative difference, and how many have a positive difference. If the null hypothesis is true, the sum of the ranks for the positive differences should be about the same as the sum of the ranks for the negative differences.

You work with the less frequent category and add up its ranks. I refer to that sum as T. If the number of pairs, N, is larger than 25, then T is normally distributed with

$$\mu_T = \frac{N(N+1)}{4}$$

and

$$\sigma_T = \sqrt{\frac{N(N+1)(2N+1)}{24}}$$

On the spreadsheet, I calculate the number of positive differences by typing

```
=COUNTIF(C2:C27,">0")
```

in cell G4 and the number of negative differences by typing

```
=COUNTIF(C2:C27,"<0")
```

in G5.

The results show 8 negative differences and 18 positive differences, so the next step is to add up the ranks of the negative differences. To do that, I type

```
=SUMIF(C2:C27,"<0",D2:D27)
```

in cell G7.

To test the hypotheses, I have to calculate the mean and the standard deviation of the sampling distribution. I define N as the label for cell F2, which holds the number of twin-pairs.

So I type

```
=(N*(N+1))/4
```

into cell G9 for the mean and type

```
=SQRT((N*(N+1)*(2*N +1))/24)
```

into cell G10 for the standard deviation.

And finally, to test the hypotheses, I type

```
=NORMDIST(G7,G9,G10,TRUE)
```

into G12. The very low value (way less than .05) indicates that I can reject the null hypothesis.

More than two samples: Friedman two-way ANOVA

With ordinal data and more than two matched samples, the Friedman two-way ANOVA is the appropriate non-parametric test. In this test, we rank the data within each sample.

Figure 17-4 shows an example. Twenty people rate their knowledge of economics, geography, and history on a scale of 1 (least knowledge) to 10 (most knowledge). The data are in columns A through D and rows 1–21. Think of economics, geography, and history as three matched samples. They're "matched" because the three numbers in each row represent the data for the same person. The ranks within each sample are in columns F through H.

	A	B	C	D	E	F	G	H	I	J	K
1	Person	Economics	Geography	History		Reconomics	Rgeography	Rhistory		Total_N	groups
2	1	9	5	7		3	1	2		20	3
3	2	8	7	9		2	1	3			
4	3	2	7	8		1	2	3			
5	4	4	5	9		1	2	3			
6	5	8	2	7		3	1	2			
7	6	5	4	6		2	1	3		χ^2 =	10.9
8	7	1	10	9		1	3	2		p =	0.004296
9	8	5	1	10		2	1	3			
10	9	9	4	10		2	1	3			
11	10	7	3	8		2	1	3			
12	11	4	7	9		1	2	3			
13	12	6	8	10		1	2	3			
14	13	9	5	10		2	1	3			
15	14	3	6	9		1	2	3			
16	15	5	7	3		2	3	1			
17	16	4	2	3		3	1	2			
18	17	7	8	10		1	2	3			
19	18	3	7	8		1	2	3			
20	19	9	5	7		3	1	2			
21	20	7	9	8		1	3	2			
22						35	33	52			
23											

FIGURE 17-4: The Friedman two-way analysis of variance.

The null hypothesis is that the three different areas of knowledge yield no differences, and the alternative hypothesis is that they do. If the null hypothesis is true, the sums of the ranks for each area should be about the same.

Friedman referred to the test statistic as χ_r^2, so I will too. The formula is

$$\chi_r^2 = \left[\frac{12}{Nk(k+1)} \sum R^2 \right] - 3N(k+1)$$

N is the number of individuals, and k is the number of groups (economics, geography, and history). With a large enough sample (more than 9), χ_r^2 is distributed as chi-square with k-1 degrees of freedom.

To determine the ranks in columns F through H, I type

```
=RANK.AVG(B2,$B2:$D2,1)
```

into F2. Note the dollar sign ($) to the left of each column, but not to the left of each row number. This allows me to autofill all the cells from F2 to H21. Then I sum the ranks in row 22.

For clarity in the Excel formula, I define Total_N as the label for J2 (the number of people in the study) and group as the label for K2 (the number of areas of knowledge).

To calculate χ_r^2, I type

```
=(12/(Total_N*groups*(groups+1))*SUMSQ(F22:H22))-
   3*Total_N*(groups+1)
```

into cell K7.

To test the hypotheses, I type

```
=CHISQ.DIST.RT(K7,groups-1)
```

into K8. The value is lower than .05, so I reject the null hypothesis.

More than two samples: Cochran's Q

Wait. What? Another test for more than two samples? This one's a different animal. The other tests in this chapter work with ordinal data. This one works with nominal data.

The spreadsheet in Figure 17-5 holds the data for a study of 20 people solving anagram problems. The anagrams are either easy (column B), of medium difficulty (column C), or difficult (column D). If a person solves an anagram within one minute, that's a "Success" denoted by 1. If not, it's a "Failure", denoted by 0.

	A	B	C	D	E	F	G	H
1	Person	Easy	Medium	Difficult	L		k	
2	1	1	0	0	1		3	
3	2	1	1	0	2			
4	3	0	1	1	2			
5	4	0	0	0	0		Q =	10.125
6	5	1	0	0	1		p =	0.006329715
7	6	1	1	0	2			
8	7	1	1	0	2			
9	8	0	1	0	1			
10	9	1	0	0	1			
11	10	0	0	0	0			
12	11	1	1	0	2			
13	12	0	1	0	1			
14	13	1	1	0	2			
15	14	1	1	1	3			
16	15	1	1	0	2			
17	16	1	1	1	3			
18	17	1	1	0	2			
19	18	1	1	0	2			
20	19	1	0	1	2			
21	20	0	1	1	2			
22	G	14	14	5				
23								

FIGURE 17-5:
Cochran's Q test.

The null hypothesis is that the three difficulty levels yield no differences. The alternative hypothesis is that they differ. If the null hypothesis is true, the sums for the three conditions (cells B22, C22, and D22) will be about equal.

The formula for this test is

$$Q = \frac{k(k-1)\sum\left(G-\bar{G}\right)^2}{k\sum L - \sum L^2}$$

According to longstanding usage for this test, G represents a column sum, L represents a row sum, and k is the number of conditions (three, in this example). The sampling distribution of Q approximates chi-square with $k-1$ degrees of freedom.

For clarity in the upcoming Excel formula, I define L as the name for the row sums in column E, G as the name for the column sums in row 22, and k as the name for the value in cell G2 (the number of conditions).

The formula for Q in cell H5 is thus:

```
=(k*(k-1)*DEVSQ(G))/(k*SUM(L)-SUMSQ(L))
```

TIP

Need a refresher on DEVSQ? Go to Chapter 5.

To test the hypotheses, I type

```
=CHISQ.DIST.RT(H5,k-1)
```

into cell H6. The value is lower than .05, which indicates that I should reject the null hypothesis.

Correlation: Spearman's r$_s$

Spearman's correlation coefficient, r$_s$, was the earliest non-parametric test based on ranks. For a sample of individuals each measured on two variables, the idea is to rank each score within its own variable. Then, for each individual subtract one rank from the other. If correlation is perfect (in the positive direction), all the differences are zero.

Figure 17-6 shows an example of what I mean. An industrial psychologist rated the sociability of 20 employees of the FarDrate Timepiece Corporation. The scale ranged from 1 (least sociable) to 100 (most sociable). Each FarDrate employee also rated his or her job satisfaction on a scale of 1 (least satisfaction) to 80 (most satisfaction). The null hypothesis is that sociability is not correlated with job satisfaction. The alternative hypothesis is that these two variables are correlated.

The data are in columns B and C, and the ranks are in columns E and F. The differences between each pair of ranks are in column G.

	A	B	C	D	E	F	G	H	I	J
1	Person	Sociability (1 - 100)	Job Satisfaction (1 - 80)		Rsoc	Rjobsat	Difference		Number_of_Pairs	
2	1	84	78		16	20	-4		20	
3	2	45	52		5	9	-4			
4	3	91	70		18	15	3		r$_s$ =	0.571429
5	4	34	38		3	4	-1			
6	5	67	55		11	11	0		t =	2.954196
7	6	74	57		14	13	1		p =	0.008489
8	7	51	77		6	19	-13			
9	8	32	56		1	12	-11			
10	9	59	32		9	2	7			
11	10	71	75		13	17	-4			
12	11	42	42		4	6	-2			
13	12	53	46		8	7	1			
14	13	64	49		10	8	2			
15	14	99	72		20	16	4			
16	15	92	68		19	14	5			
17	16	81	39		15	5	10			
18	17	33	22		2	1	1			
19	18	68	54		12	10	2			
20	19	52	36		7	3	4			
21	20	90	76		17	18	-1			
22										

FIGURE 17-6:
Spearman's r$_s$.

The formula is

$$r_S = 1 - \frac{6\sum d^2}{N^3 - N}$$

where d is an interpair difference. As is the case with the regular correlation coefficient (see Chapter 15), if the null hypothesis is true, the value of r_S should be around zero.

To calculate the ranks in column E, I type

```
=RANK.AVG(B2,$B$2:$B$21,1)
```

into E2 and autofilled. For the ranks in column E, I type

```
=RANK.AVG(C2,$C$2:$C$21,1)
```

into F2 and autofilled.

I don't have to type a complicated Excel formula into cell J4 to calculate the correlation coefficient. Why? Because Excel and mathematical statistics team up for a swell surprise: All I have to do is type

```
=CORREL(E2:E21,F2:F21)
```

into J4. That's all there is to it. Using CORREL on the ranks gives the same answer as the formula I just showed you. (So it isn't really necessary to calculate the interpair rank differences in column G.)

The hypothesis test is also familiar if you've read Chapter 15. Calculate

$$t = \frac{r_S\sqrt{N-2}}{\sqrt{1-r_S^2}}$$

N is the number of pairs, and the test has $N-2$ degrees of freedom.

I define Number_of_pairs as the name for the value in cell I2. So I type

```
=J4*SQRT(Number_of_Pairs-2)/SQRT(1-J4^2)
```

into J6 and

```
=T.DIST.2T(J6,Number_of_Pairs-2)
```

into J7. I use the two-tailed t distribution function because I didn't know the correlation's direction in advance. And once again, the low p-value tells me to reject the null hypothesis.

A Heads-Up

A couple of things I'd like you to be aware of. First, I didn't put any tied ranks in these examples. As it turns out, ties present a few wrinkles for the rank-based statistics (except for the Friedman two-way ANOVA), and I wanted to avoid all that.

Second, be aware that additional non-parametric tests are lurking in the remainder of the book. In Chapter 18, you find hypothesis testing based on the binomial distribution. In Chapter 22, I tell you about a way to test the independence of two nominal variables.

4

Probability

Chapter 18

Introducing Probability

Throughout this book, I toss around the concept of probability because it's the basis of hypothesis testing and inferential statistics. Most of the time, I represent probability as the proportion of area under part of a distribution. For example, the probability of a Type I error (a.k.a. α) is the area in a tail of the standard normal distribution or the t distribution.

In this chapter, I explore probability in greater detail, including random variables, permutations, and combinations. I examine probability's fundamentals and applications and then zero in on a couple of specific probability distributions. Then, after telling you about probability concepts, I discuss probability-related Excel worksheet functions.

What Is Probability?

Most of us have an intuitive idea about what probability is all about. Toss a fair coin and you have a 50-50 chance it comes up "heads." Toss a fair die (one of a pair of dice) and you have a one-in-six chance it comes up "2."

If you wanted to be more formal in your definition, you'd most likely say something about all the possible things that could happen, and the proportion of those things you care about. Two things can happen when you toss a coin, and if you only care about one of them (heads), the probability of that event happening is one out of two. Six things can happen when you toss a die, and if you only care about one of them (2), the probability of that event happening is one out of six.

Experiments, trials, events, and sample spaces

Statisticians and others who work with probability refer to a process like tossing a coin or throwing a die as an *experiment*. Each time you go through the process, that's a *trial*.

This might not fit your personal definition of an experiment (or of a trial, for that matter), but for a statistician, an *experiment* is any process that produces one of at least two distinct results (like heads or tails).

Another piece of the definition of an experiment: You can't predict the result with certainty. Each distinct result is called an *elementary outcome*. Put a bunch of elementary outcomes together and you have an *event*. For example, with a die, the elementary outcomes 2, 4, and 6 make up the event "even number."

Put all the possible elementary outcomes together and you've got yourself a *sample space*. The numbers 1, 2, 3, 4, 5, and 6 make up the sample space for a die. "Heads" and "tails" make up the sample space for a coin.

Sample spaces and probability

How does all this play into probability? If each elementary outcome in a sample space is equally likely, the probability of an event is

$$\text{pr}\left(\text{Event}\right) = \frac{\text{Number of Elementary Outcomes in the Event}}{\text{Number of Elementary Outcomes in the Sample Space}}$$

So the probability of tossing a die and getting an even number is

$$\text{pr}\left(\text{Even Number}\right) = \frac{\text{Number of Even-Numbered Elementary Outcomes}}{\text{Number of Possible Outcomes of a Die}} = \frac{3}{6} = .5$$

If the elementary outcomes are not equally likely, you find the probability of an event in a different way. First, you have to have some way of assigning a probability to each one. Then you add up the probabilities of the elementary outcomes that make up the event.

A couple of things to bear in mind about outcome probabilities: Each probability has to be between zero and one. All the probabilities of elementary outcomes in a sample space have to add up to 1.00.

How do you assign those probabilities? Sometimes you have advance information — such as knowing that a coin is biased toward coming up heads 60 percent of the time. Sometimes you just have to think through the situation to figure out the probability of an outcome.

Here's a quick example of "thinking through." Suppose a die is biased so that the probability of an outcome is proportional to the numerical label of the outcome: A 6 comes up six times as often as a 1, a 5 comes up five times as often as a 1, and so on. What is the probability of each outcome? All the probabilities have to add up to 1.00, and all the numbers on a die add up to 21 (1+2+3+4+5+6 = 21), so the probabilities are: pr(1) = 1/21, pr(2) = 2/21, . . . , pr(6) = 6/21.

Compound Events

Some rules for dealing with compound events help you "think through." A *compound* event consists of more than one event. It's possible to combine events by either union or intersection (or both).

Union and intersection

On a toss of a fair die, what's the probability of rolling a 1 or a 4? Mathematicians have a symbol for *or*. It's called *union*, and it looks like this: $\cup$. Using this symbol, the probability of a 1 or a 4 is $pr(1 \cup 4)$.

In approaching this kind of probability, it's helpful to keep track of the elementary outcomes. One elementary outcome is in each event, so the event "1 or 4" has two elementary outcomes. With a sample space of six outcomes, the probability is 2/6 or 1/3. Another way to calculate this is

$$pr(1 \cup 4) = pr(1) + pr(4) = \frac{1}{6} + \frac{1}{6} = \frac{2}{6} = \frac{1}{3}$$

Here's a slightly more involved one: What's the probability of rolling a number between 1 and 3 or a number between 2 and 4?

Just adding the elementary outcomes in each event won't get it done this time. Three outcomes are in the event "between 1 and 3," and three are in the event "between 2 and 4." The probability can't be 3 + 3 divided by the six outcomes in the sample space, because that's 1.00, leaving nothing for $pr(5)$ and $pr(6)$. For the same reason, you can't just add the probabilities.

The challenge arises in the overlap of the two events. The elementary outcomes in "between 1 and 3" are 1, 2, and 3. The elementary outcomes in "between 2 and 4" are 2, 3, and 4. Two outcomes overlap: 2 and 3. In order to not count them twice, the trick is to subtract them from the total.

A couple of things will make life easier as I proceed. I abbreviate "between 1 and 3" as A and "between 2 and 4" as B. Also, I use the mathematical symbol for "overlap." The symbol is $\cap$ and it's called *intersection*.

Using the symbols, the probability of "between 1 and 3" or "between 2 and 4" is

$$pr(A \cup B) =$$

$$\frac{\text{Number of Outcomes in A} + \text{Number of Outcomes in B} - \text{Number of Outcomes in } (A \cap B)}{\text{Number of Outcomes in the Sample Space}}$$

$$pr(A \cup B) = \frac{3+3-2}{6} = \frac{4}{6} = \frac{2}{3}$$

You can also work with the probabilities:

$$pr(A \cup B) = \frac{3}{6} + \frac{3}{6} - \frac{2}{6} = \frac{4}{6} = \frac{2}{3}$$

The general formula is

$$pr(A \cup B) = pr(A) + pr(B) - pr(A \cap B)$$

Why was it okay to just add the probabilities together in the earlier example? Because $pr(1 \cap 4)$ is zero: It's impossible to roll a 1 and a 4 in the same toss of a die. Whenever $pr(A \cap B) = 0$, A and B are said to be *mutually exclusive*.

Intersection again

Imagine throwing a coin and rolling a die at the same time. These two experiments are *independent* because the result of one has no influence on the result of the other.

What's the probability of getting Heads and a 4? You use the intersection symbol and write this as $pr(\text{Heads} \cap 4)$

$$pr(\text{Heads} \cap 4) = \frac{\text{Number of Elementary Outcomes in Heads} \cap 4}{\text{Number of Elementary Outcomes in the Sample Space}}$$

Start with the sample space. Table 18-1 lists all elementary outcomes.

TABLE 18-1 **The Elementary Outcomes in the Sample Space for Throwing a Coin and Rolling a Die**

Heads, 1	Tails, 1
Heads, 2	Tails, 2
Heads, 3	Tails, 3
Heads, 4	Tails, 4
Heads, 5	Tails, 5
Heads, 6	Tails, 6

As the table shows, 12 outcomes are possible. How many outcomes are in the event "Heads and 4"? Just one. So

$$pr\left(\text{Heads} \cap 4\right) = \frac{\text{Number of Elementary Outcomes in Heads} \cap 4}{\text{Number of Elementary Outcomes in the Sample Space}} = \frac{1}{12}$$

You can also work with the probabilities:

$$pr\left(\text{Heads} \cap 4\right) = pr\left(\text{Heads}\right) \times pr\left(4\right) = \frac{1}{12}$$

In general, if A and B are independent,

$$pr\left(A \cap B\right) = pr\left(A\right) \times pr\left(B\right)$$

Conditional Probability

In some circumstances, you narrow the sample space. For example, suppose I toss a die and I tell you the result is greater than 2. What's the probability that it's a 5?

Ordinarily, the probability of a 5 would be 1/6. In this case, however, the sample space isn't 1, 2, 3, 4, 5, and 6. When you know the result is greater than 2, the sample space becomes 3, 4, 5, and 6. The probability of a 5 is now 1/4.

This is an example of *conditional probability*. It's "conditional" because I've given a "condition" — the toss resulted in a number greater than 2. The notation for this is

$$pr\left(5 \mid \text{Greater than 2}\right)$$

The vertical line is shorthand for the word *given*, and you read that notation as "the probability of a 5 given Greater than 2."

Working with the probabilities

In general, if you have two events A and B,

$$pr(A \mid B) = \frac{pr(A \cap B)}{pr(B)}$$

as long as $pr(B)$ isn't zero.

For the intersection in the numerator on the right, this is *not* a case where you just multiply probabilities together. In fact, if you could do that, you wouldn't have a conditional probability, because that would mean A and B are independent. If they're independent, one event can't be conditional on the other.

You have to think through the probability of the intersection. In a die, how many outcomes are in the event "5 ∩ Greater than 2"? Just one, so $pr(5 \cap \text{Greater than 2})$ is 1/6, and

$$pr(5 \mid \text{Greater than 2}) = \frac{pr(5 \cap \text{Greater than 2})}{pr(\text{Greater than 2})} = \frac{1/6}{4/6} = \frac{1}{4}$$

The foundation of hypothesis testing

All the hypothesis testing I show you in previous chapters involves conditional probability. When you calculate a sample statistic, compute a statistical test, and then compare the test statistic against a critical value, you're looking for a conditional probability. Specifically, you're trying to find

$$pr(\text{obtained test statistic or a more extreme value} \mid H_0 \text{ is true})$$

If that conditional probability is low (less than .05 in all the examples I show you in hypothesis-testing chapters), you reject H_0.

Large Sample Spaces

When dealing with probability, it's important to understand the sample space. In the examples I show you, the sample spaces are small. With a coin or a die, it's easy to list all the elementary outcomes.

The world, of course, isn't that simple. In fact, probability problems that live in statistics textbooks aren't even that simple. Most of the time, sample spaces are large and it's not convenient to list every elementary outcome.

Take, for example, rolling a die twice. How many elementary outcomes are in the sample space consisting of both tosses? You can sit down and list them, but it's better to reason it out: Six possibilities for the first toss, and each of those six can pair up with six possibilities on the second. So the sample space has $6 \times 6 = 36$ possible elementary outcomes. (This is similar to the coin-and-die sample space in Table 18-1, where the sample space consists of $2 \times 6 = 12$ elementary outcomes. With 12 outcomes, it is easy to list them all in a table. With 36 outcomes, it starts to get . . . well . . . dicey.)

Events often require some thought, too. What's the probability of rolling a die twice and totaling 5? You have to count the number of ways the two tosses can total 5, and then divide by the number of elementary outcomes in the sample space (36). You total a 5 by getting any of these pairs of tosses: 1 and 4, 2 and 3, 3 and 2, or 4 and 1. That totals four ways, and they don't overlap (excuse me — intersect), so

$$\text{pr}(5) = \frac{\text{Number of Ways of Rolling a 5}}{\text{Number of Possible Outcomes of Two Tosses}} = \frac{4}{36} = .11$$

Listing all the elementary outcomes for the sample space is often a nightmare. Fortunately, shortcuts are available, as I show in the upcoming subsections. Because each shortcut quickly helps you count a number of items, another name for a shortcut is a *counting rule*.

Believe it or not, I just slipped one counting rule past you. A couple of paragraphs ago, I say that in two tosses of a die you have a sample space of $6 \times 6 = 36$ possible outcomes. This is the *product rule:* If N_1 outcomes are possible on the first trial of an experiment, and N_2 outcomes on the second trial, the number of possible outcomes is $N_1 N_2$. Each possible outcome on the first trial can associate with all possible outcomes on the second. What about three trials? That's $N_1 N_2 N_3$.

Now for a couple more counting rules.

Permutations

Suppose you have to arrange five objects into a sequence. How many ways can you do that? For the first position in the sequence, you have five choices. After you make that choice, you have four choices for the second position. Then you have three choices for the third, two for the fourth, and one for the fifth. The number of ways is $(5)(4)(3)(2)(1) = 120$.

In general, the number of sequences of N objects is $N(N-1)(N-2) \ldots (2)(1)$. This kind of computation occurs fairly frequently in probability world, and it has its own notation, $N!$ You don't read this by screaming out "N" in a loud voice. Instead, it's "N factorial." By definition, $1! = 1$, and $0! = 1$.

Now for the good stuff. If you have to order the 26 letters of the alphabet, the number of possible sequences is 26!, a huge number. But suppose the task is to create 5-letter sequences so that no letter repeats in the sequence. How many ways can you do that? You have 26 choices for the first letter, 25 for the second, 24 for the third, 23 for the fourth, 22 for the fifth, and that's it. So that's (26)(25) (24)(23)(22). Here's how that product is related to 26!:

$$\frac{26!}{21!}$$

Each sequence is called a *permutation*. In general, if you take permutations of N things r at a time, the notation is $_NP_r$ (the P stands for *permutation*). The formula is

$$_NP_r = \frac{N!}{(N-r)!}$$

Just for completeness, here's another wrinkle. Suppose that I allow repetitions in these sequences of 5. That is, aabbc is a permissible sequence. In that case, the number of sequences is $26 \times 26 \times 26 \times 26 \times 26$, or as mathematicians would say, "26 raised to the fifth power." Or as mathematicians would write, "26^5."

Combinations

In the preceding example, these sequences are different from one another: *abcde, adbce, dbcae,* and on and on and on. In fact, you could come up with 5! = 120 of these different sequences just for the letters a, b, c, d, and e.

Suppose that I add the restriction that one of these sequences is no different from another, and all I'm concerned about is having sets of five nonrepeating letters in no particular order. Each set is called a *combination*. For this example, the number of combinations is the number of permutations divided by 5!:

$$\frac{26!}{5!(21!)}$$

In general, the notation for combinations of N things taken r at a time is $_NC_r$ (the C stands for *combination*). The formula is

$$_NC_r = \frac{N!}{r!(N-r)!}$$

Now for that completeness wrinkle again. Suppose that I allow repetitions in these sequences. How many sequences would I have? It turns out to be equivalent to $N+r-1$ things taken $N-1$ at a time, or $_{N+r+1}C_{N-1}$. For this example, that would be $_{30}C_{25}$.

Worksheet Functions

Excel provides functions that help you with factorials, permutations, and combinations.

FACT

FACT, which computes factorials, is surprisingly not categorized as Statistical. Instead, you'll find it on the Math & Trig Functions menu. It's easy to use. Supply it with a number, and it returns the factorial. Here are the steps:

1. Select a cell for FACT's answer.

2. From the Math & Trig Functions menu, select FACT to open its Function Arguments dialog box.

3. In the Function Arguments dialog box, enter the appropriate value for the argument.

In the Number box, I typed the number whose factorial I want to compute.

The answer appears in the dialog box. If I enter 5, for example, 120 appears.

4. Click OK to put the answer into the selected cell.

PERMUT and PERMUTIONA

You find these two on the Statistical Functions menu. As its name suggests, PERMUT enables you to calculate $_NP_r$. Here's how to use it to find $_{26}P_5$, the number of 5-letter sequences (no repeating letters) that you can create from the 26 letters of the alphabet. In a permutation, remember, *abcde* is considered different from *bcdae*. Follow these steps:

1. Select a cell for PERMUT's answer.

2. From the Statistical Functions menu, select PERMUT to open its Function Arguments dialog box. (See Figure 18-1.)

3. In the Function Arguments dialog box, type the appropriate values for the arguments.

In the Number box, I entered the N in $_NP_r$. For this example, N is 26.

In the Number_chosen box, I entered the r in $_NP_r$. That would be 5.

With values entered for both arguments, the answer appears in the dialog box. For this example, the answer is 7893600.

4. Click OK to put the answer into the selected cell.

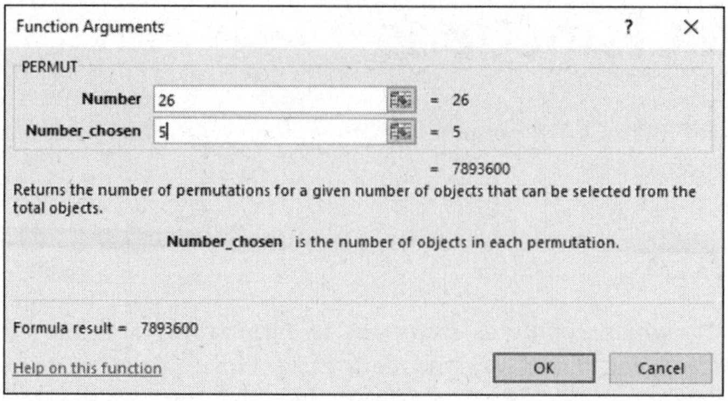

FIGURE 18-1:
The Function
Arguments
dialog box for
PERMUT.

PERMUTIONA does the same thing, but with repetitions allowed. Its Function Arguments dialog box looks exactly like the one for PERMUT. Its answer is equivalent to N^r. For this example, by the way, that answer is 1181376.

COMBIN and COMBINA

COMBIN works pretty much the same way as PERMUT. Excel categorizes COMBIN and COMBINA as Math & Trig functions.

Here's how you use them to find $_{26}C_5$, the number of ways to construct a 5-letter sequence (no repeating letters) from the 26 letters of the alphabet. In a combination, *abcde* is considered equivalent to *bcdae*.

1. **Select a cell for COMBIN's answer.**

2. **From the Math & Trig Functions menu, select COMBIN to open its Function Arguments dialog box.**

3. **In the Function Arguments dialog box, type the appropriate values for the arguments.**

   In the Number box, I entered the *N* in $_NC_r$. Once again, *N* is 26.

   In the Number_chosen box, I entered the *r* in $_NC_r$. And again, *r* is 5.

   With values entered for both arguments, the answer appears in the dialog box. For this example, the answer is 65870.

4. **Click OK to put the answer into the selected cell.**

If you allow repetitions, use COMBINA. Its Function Arguments dialog box looks just like COMBIN's. For this example, its answer is equivalent to $_{30}C_{25}$ (142506).

Random Variables: Discrete and Continuous

Return to tosses of a fair die, where six elementary outcomes are possible. If I use *x* to refer to the result of a toss, *x* can be any whole number from 1 to 6. Because *x* can take on a set of values, it's a variable. Because *x*'s possible values correspond to the elementary outcomes of an experiment (meaning you can't predict its values with absolute certainty), *x* is called a *random variable.*

Random variables come in two varieties. One variety is *discrete,* of which die-tossing is a good example. A discrete random variable can take on only what mathematicians like to call a *countable* number of values — like the numbers 1 through 6. Values between the whole numbers 1 through 6 (like 1.25 or 3.1416) are impossible for a random variable that corresponds to the outcomes of die-tosses.

The other kind of random variable is *continuous.* A continuous random variable can take on an infinite number of values. Temperature is an example. Depending on the precision of a thermometer, having temperatures like 34.516 degrees is possible.

Probability Distributions and Density Functions

Back to die-tossing again. Each value of the random variable *x* (1–6, remember) has a probability. If the die is fair, each probability is 1/6. Pair each value of a discrete random variable like *x* with its probability, and you have a *probability distribution.*

Probability distributions are easy enough to represent in graphs. Figure 18-2 shows the probability distribution for *x.*

A random variable has a mean, a variance, and a standard deviation. Calculating these parameters is pretty straightforward. In the random-variable world, the mean is called the *expected value,* and the expected value of random variable *x* is abbreviated as *E(x).* Here's how you calculate it:

$$E(x) = \sum x(pr(x))$$

For the probability distribution in Figure 18-2, that's

$$E(x) = \sum x(pr(x)) = (1)\left(\frac{1}{6}\right) + (2)\left(\frac{1}{6}\right) + (3)\left(\frac{1}{6}\right) + (4)\left(\frac{1}{6}\right) + (5)\left(\frac{1}{6}\right) + (6)\left(\frac{1}{6}\right) = 3.5$$

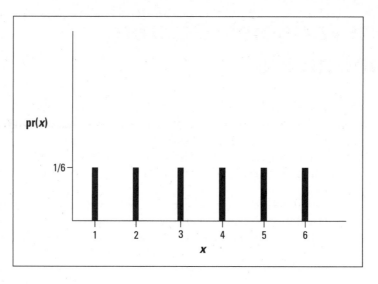

FIGURE 18-2:
The probability
distribution
for x, a random
variable based on
the tosses of
a fair die.

The variance of a random variable is often abbreviated as $V(x)$, and the formula is

$$V(x) = \sum x^2 \left(pr(x) \right) - \left[E(x) \right]^2$$

Working with the probability distribution in Figure 18-2 once again,

$$V(x) = \left(1^2\right)\left(\frac{1}{6}\right) + \left(2^2\right)\left(\frac{1}{6}\right) + \left(3^2\right)\left(\frac{1}{6}\right) + \left(4^2\right)\left(\frac{1}{6}\right) + \left(5^2\right)\left(\frac{1}{6}\right) + \left(6^2\right)\left(\frac{1}{6}\right) - \left[3.5\right]^2 = 2.917$$

The standard deviation is the square root of the variance, which in this case is 1.708.

For continuous random variables, things get a little trickier. You can't pair a value with a probability, because you can't really pin down a value. Instead, you associate a continuous random variable with a mathematical rule (an equation) that generates *probability density,* and the distribution is called a *probability density function.* To calculate the mean and variance of a continuous random variable, you need calculus.

In Chapter 8, I show you a probability density function — the standard normal distribution. I reproduce it here as Figure 18-3.

In the figure, $f(x)$ represents the probability density. Because probability density can involve some heavyweight mathematical concepts, I won't go into it. As I mention in Chapter 8, think of probability density as something that turns the area under the curve into probability.

Although you can't speak of the probability of a specific value of a continuous random variable, you can work with the probability of an interval. To find the probability that the random variable takes on a value within an interval, you find the proportion of the total area under the curve that's inside that interval. Figure 18-3 shows this. The probability that x is between 0 and 1σ is .3413.

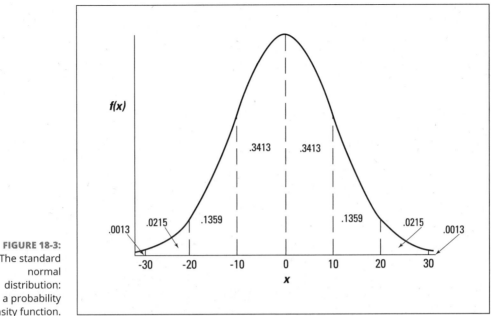

FIGURE 18-3:
The standard
normal
distribution:
a probability
density function.

For the rest of this chapter, I deal only with discrete random variables. A specific one is up next.

The Binomial Distribution

Imagine an experiment that has these six characteristics:

>> The experiment consists of *N* identical trials.

A trial could be a toss of a die or a toss of a coin.

>> Each trial results in one of two elementary outcomes.

>> It's standard to call one outcome a *success* and the other a *failure.* For die-tossing, a success might be a toss that comes up 3, in which case a failure is any other outcome.

>> The probability of a success remains the same from trial to trial.

Again, it's pretty standard to use *p* to represent the probability of a success, and *1-p* (or *q*) to represent the probability of a failure.

>> The trials are independent.

>> The discrete random variable *x* is the number of successes in the *N* trials.

This type of experiment is called a *binomial experiment*. The probability distribution for x follows this rule:

$$pr(x) = \frac{N!}{x!(n-x)!}p^x(1-p)^{N-x}$$

On the extreme right, $p^x(1-p)^{N-x}$ is the probability of one combination of x successes in N trials. The term to its immediate left is $_NC_x$, the number of possible combinations of x successes in N trials.

This is called the *binomial distribution*. You use it to find probabilities like the probability you'll get four 3's in ten tosses of a die:

$$pr(4) = \frac{10!}{4!(6!)}\left(\frac{1}{6}\right)^4\left(\frac{5}{6}\right)^6 = .054$$

The *negative binomial distribution* is closely related. In this distribution, the random variable is the number of trials before the xth success. For example, you use the negative binomial to find the probability of five tosses that result in anything but a 3 before the fourth time you roll a 3.

For this to happen, in the eight tosses before the fourth 3, you have to get five non-3's and three successes (tosses when a 3 comes up). Then the next toss results in a 3. The probability of a combination of four successes and five failures is $p^4(1-p)^5$. The number of ways you can have a combination of five failures and four-to-one successes is $_{5+4-1}C_{4-1}$. So the probability is

$$pr(5 \text{ failures before the 4th success}) = \frac{(5+4-1)!}{(4-1)!(5!)}\left(\frac{1}{6}\right)^4\left(\frac{5}{6}\right)^5 = .017$$

In general, the negative binomial distribution (sometimes called the *Pascal distribution*) is

$$pr(f \text{ failures before the xth success}) = \frac{(f+x-1)!}{(x-1)!(f!)}p^x(1-p)^f$$

Worksheet Functions

These distributions are computation intensive, so I get to the worksheet functions right away.

BINOM.DIST and BINOM.DIST.RANGE

These are Excel's worksheet functions for the binomial distribution. Use `BINOM.DIST` to calculate the probability of getting four 3's in ten tosses of a fair die:

1. Select a cell for `BINOM.DIST`'s answer.

2. From the Statistical Functions menu, select BINOM.DIST to open its Function Arguments dialog box. (See Figure 18-4.)

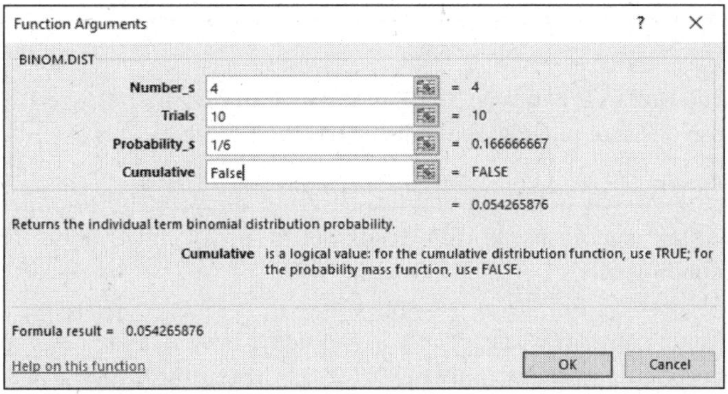

FIGURE 18-4:
The BINOM.DIST Function Arguments dialog box.

3. In the Function Arguments dialog box, type the appropriate values for the arguments.

In the Number_s box, I entered the number of successes. For this example, the number of successes is 4.

In the Trials box, I entered the number of trials. The number of trials is 10.

In the Probability_s box, I entered the probability of a success. I entered 1/6, the probability of a 3 on a toss of a fair die.

In the Cumulative box, one possibility is FALSE for the probability of exactly the number of successes entered in the Number_s box. The other is TRUE for the probability of getting that number of successes or fewer. I entered FALSE.

With values entered for all the arguments, the answer appears in the dialog box.

4. Click OK to put the answer into the selected cell.

To give you a better idea of what the binomial distribution looks like, I use `BINOM.DIST` (with `FALSE` entered in the Cumulative box) to find $pr(0)$ through $pr(10)$, and then I use Excel's graphics capabilities (refer to Chapter 3) to graph the results. Figure 18-5 shows the data and the graph.

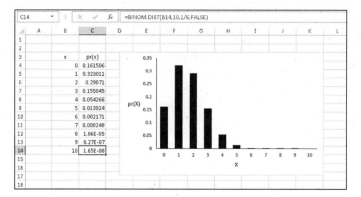

FIGURE 18-5:
The binomial distribution for *x* successes in ten tosses of a die, with *p* = 1/6.

Incidentally, if you type **TRUE** in the Cumulative box, the result is .984 (and some more decimal places), which is $pr(0) + pr(1) + pr(2) + pr(3) + pr(4)$.

Figure 18-5 is helpful if you want to find the probability of getting between four and six successes in ten trials. Find $pr(4)$, $pr(5)$, and $pr(6)$ and add the probabilities.

A much easier way, especially if you don't have a chart like Figure 18-5 handy or if you don't want to apply BINOM.DIST three times, is to use BINOM.DIST.RANGE. Figure 18-6 shows the dialog box for this function, supplied with values for the arguments. After all the arguments are entered, the answer (0.069460321) appears in the dialog box.

FIGURE 18-6:
The Function Arguments dialog box for BINOM. DIST.RANGE.

Function Arguments	? ✕
BINOM.DIST.RANGE	

Trials	10		= 10
Probability_s	1/6		= 0.166666667
Number_s	4		= 4
Number_s2	6		= 6

= 0.069460321

Returns the probability of a trial result using a binomial distribution.

Number_s2 if provided this function returns the probability that the number of successful trials shall lie between number_s and number_s2.

Formula result = 0.069460321

Help on this function   OK   Cancel

TIP

If you don't put a value in the Number_s2 box, BINOM.DIST.RANGE returns the probability of whatever you entered into the Number_s box. If you don't put a value in the Number_s box, the function returns the probability of, at most, the number of successes in the Number_s2 box (for example, the cumulative probability).

NEGBINOM.DIST

As its name suggests, NEGBINOM.DIST handles the negative binomial distribution. I use it here to work out the earlier example — the probability of getting five failures (tosses that result in anything but a 3) before the fourth success (the fourth 3). Here are the steps:

1. Select a cell for NEGBINOM.DIST's answer.

2. From the Statistical Functions menu, select NEGBINOM.DIST to open its Function Arguments dialog box. (See Figure 18-7.)

3. In the Function Arguments dialog box, type the appropriate values for the arguments.

In the Number_f box, I entered the number of failures. The number of failures is 5 for this example.

In the Number_s box, I entered the number of successes. For this example, that's 4.

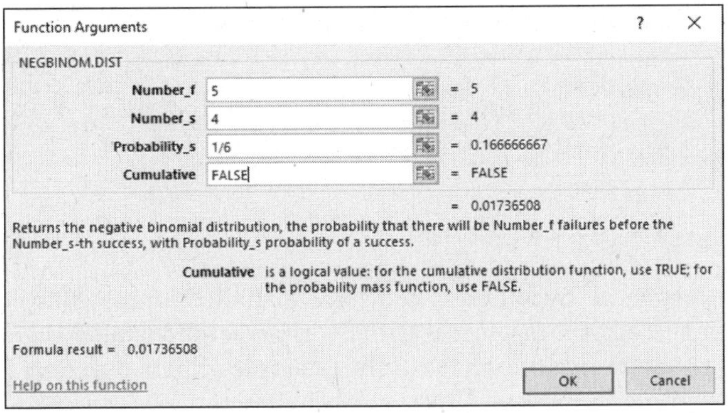

FIGURE 18-7:
The NEGBINOM.
DIST Function
Arguments
dialog box.

In the Probability_s box, I entered 1/6, the probability of a success.

In the Cumulative box, I entered FALSE. This gives the probability of the number of successes. If I enter TRUE, the result is the probability of at most that number of successes.

With values entered for all the arguments, the answer appears in the dialog box. The answer is 0.017 and some additional decimal places.

4. Click OK to put the answer into the selected cell.

Hypothesis Testing with the Binomial Distribution

Hypothesis tests sometimes involve the binomial distribution. Typically, you have some idea about the probability of a success, and you put that idea into a null hypothesis. Then you perform N trials and record the number of successes. Finally, you compute the probability of getting that many successes or a more extreme amount if your H_0 is true. If the probability is low, reject H_0.

When you test in this way, you're using sample statistics to make an inference about a population parameter. Here, that parameter is the probability of a success in the population of trials. By convention, Greek letters represent parameters. Statisticians use π (pi), the Greek equivalent of p, to stand for the probability of a success in the population.

Continuing with the die-tossing example, suppose you have a die and you want to test whether or not it's fair. You suspect that if it's not, it's biased toward 3. Define a toss that results in 3 as a success. You toss it ten times. Four tosses are successes. Casting all this into hypothesis-testing terms:

H_0: $\pi \leq 1/6$

$H_{1:}$ $\pi > 1/6$

As I usually do, I set $\alpha = .05$.

To test these hypotheses, you have to find the probability of getting at least four successes in ten tosses with $p = 1/6$. That probability is $pr(4) + pr(5) + pr(6) + pr(7) + pr(8) + pr(9) + pr(10)$. If the total is less than .05, reject H_0.

That's a lot of calculating. You can use `BINOM.DIST` to take care of it all (as I did when I set up the worksheet shown earlier in Figure 18-5), or you can take a different route. You can find a critical value for the number of successes, and if the number of successes is greater than the critical value, reject H_0.

How do you find the critical value? You can use a convenient worksheet function that I'm about to show you.

BINOM.INV

This function is tailor-made for binomial-based hypothesis testing. Give `BINOM.INV` the number of trials, the probability of a success, and a criterion cumulative probability. `BINOM.INV` returns the smallest value of *x* (the number of successes) for which the cumulative probability is greater than or equal to the criterion.

Here are the steps for the hypothesis testing example I just showed you:

1. **Select a cell for BINOM.INV's answer.**

2. **From the Statistical Functions menu, select BINOM.INV and click OK to open its Function Arguments dialog box. (See Figure 18-8.)**

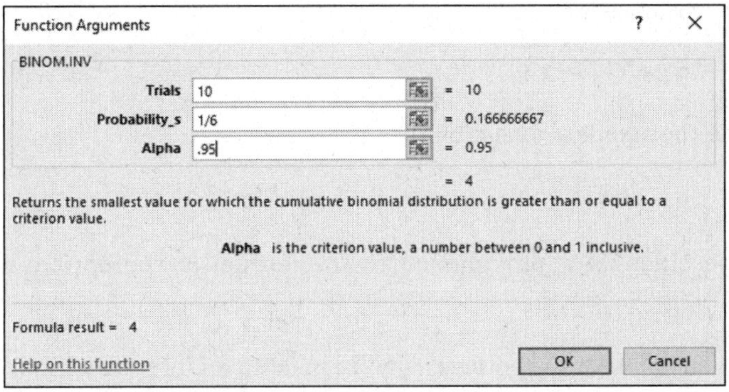

FIGURE 18-8:
The BINOM.INV
Function
Arguments
dialog box.

3. **In the Function Arguments dialog box, enter the appropriate values for the arguments.**

In the Trials box, I entered 10, the number of trials.

In the Probability_s box, I entered the probability of a success. In this example it's 1/6, the value of π according to H_0.

In the Alpha box, I entered the cumulative probability to exceed. I entered .95 because I want to find the critical value that cuts off the upper 5 percent of the binomial distribution.

With values entered for the arguments, the critical value, 4, appears in the dialog box.

4. **Click OK to put the answer into the selected cell.**

As it happens, the critical value is the number of successes in the sample. The decision is to reject H_0.

More on hypothesis testing

In some situations, the binomial distribution approximates the standard normal distribution. When this happens, you use the statistics of the normal distribution to answer questions about the binomial distribution.

Those statistics involve z-scores, which means that you have to know the mean and the standard deviation of the binomial. Fortunately, they're easy to compute. If N is the number of trials and π is the probability of a success, the mean is

$$\mu = N\pi$$

the variance is

$$\sigma^2 = N\pi(1-\pi)$$

and the standard deviation is

$$\sigma = \sqrt{N\pi(1-\pi)}$$

The binomial approximation to the normal is appropriate when $N\pi \geq 5$ and $N(1-\pi) \geq 5$.

When you test a hypothesis, you're making an inference about π, and you have to start with an estimate. You run N trials and get x successes. The estimate is

$$P = \frac{x}{N}$$

To create a z-score, you need one more piece of information — the standard error of P. This sounds harder than it is, because this standard error is just

$$\sigma_P = \sqrt{\frac{\pi(1-\pi)}{N}}$$

Now you're ready for a hypothesis test.

Here's an example. The CEO of FarKlempt Robotics, Inc., believes that 50 percent of FarKlempt robots are purchased for home use. A sample of 1,000 FarKlempt customers indicates that 550 of them use their robots at home. Is this significantly different from what the CEO believes? The hypotheses:

$H_0: \pi = .50$

$H_1: \pi \neq .50$

I set $\alpha = .05$

$N\pi = 500$, and $N(1-\pi) = 500$, so the normal approximation is appropriate.

First, calculate P:

$$P = \frac{x}{N} = \frac{550}{1000} = .55$$

Now create a z-score:

$$z = \frac{P-\pi}{\sqrt{\dfrac{\pi(1-\pi)}{N}}} = \frac{.55-.50}{\sqrt{\dfrac{(.50)(1-.50)}{1000}}} = \frac{.05}{\sqrt{\dfrac{.25}{1000}}} = 3.162$$

With $\alpha = .05$, is 3.162 a large enough z-score to reject H_0? An easy way to find out is to use the worksheet function NORM.S.DIST. (See Chapter 8.) If you do, you'll find that this z-score cuts off less than .01 of the area in the upper tail of the standard normal distribution. The decision is to reject H_0.

The Hypergeometric Distribution

Here's another distribution that deals with successes and failures.

I start with an example. In a set of 16 light bulbs, 9 are good and 7 are defective. If you randomly select 6 light bulbs out of these 16, what's the probability that 3 of the 6 are good? Consider selecting a good light bulb as a "success."

When you finish selecting, your set of selections is a combination of three of the nine good light bulbs together with a combination of three of the seven defective light bulbs. The probability of getting three good bulbs is a . . . well . . . combination of counting rules:

$$pr(3) = \frac{\left({}_9C_3\right)\left({}_7C_3\right)}{{}_{16}C_6} = \frac{(84)(35)}{8008} = .37$$

Each outcome of the selection of the good light bulbs can associate with all outcomes of the selection of the defective light bulbs, so the product rule is appropriate for the numerator. The denominator (the sample space) is the number of possible combinations of 6 items in a group of 16.

This is an example of the *hypergeometric distribution.* In general, with a small population that consists of N_1 successes and N_2 failures, the probability of x successes in a sample of m items is

$$pr(x) = \frac{\left({}_{N_1}C_x\right)\left({}_{N_2}C_{m-x}\right)}{{}_{N_1+N_2}C_m}$$

The random variable x is said to be a *hypergeometrically distributed random variable.*

HYPGEOM.DIST

This function calculates everything for you when you deal with the hypergeometric distribution. Here's how to use it to work through the preceding example:

1. **Select a cell for** `HYPGEOM.DIST`**'s answer.**

2. **From the Statistical Functions menu, select HYPGEOM.DIST to open its Function Arguments dialog box. (See Figure 18-9.)**

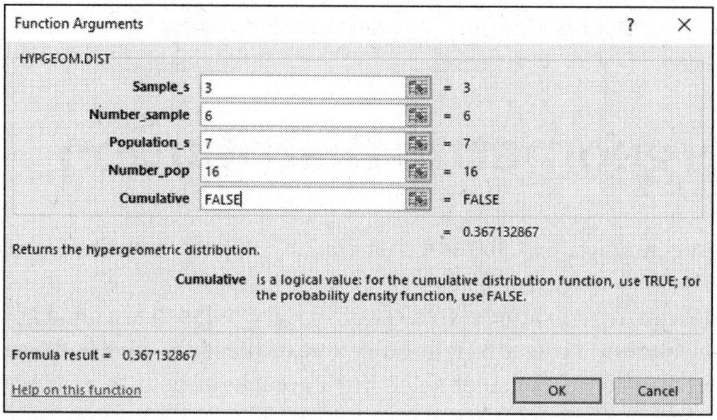

FIGURE 18-9:
The HYPGEOM.
DIST Function
Arguments
dialog box.

3. **In the Function Arguments dialog box, enter the appropriate values for the arguments.**

    In the Sample_s box, I entered the number of successes in the sample. That number is 3 for this example.

    In the Number_sample box, I entered the number of items in the sample. The sample size for this example is 6.

    In the Population_s box, I entered the number of successes in the population. In this example that's 7, the number of good light bulbs.

    In the Number_pop box, I entered the number of items in the population. The total number of light bulbs is 16, and that's the population size.

    In the Cumulative box, I entered FALSE. This gives the probability of the number of successes I entered in the Sample_s box. If I enter TRUE, the function returns the probability of, at most, that number of successes (for example, the cumulative probability).

With values entered for all the arguments, the answer appears in the dialog box. The answer is 0.367 and some additional decimal places.

4. **Click OK to put the answer into the selected cell.**

As I do with the binomial, I use HYP.GEOM.DIST to calculate $pr(0)$ through $pr(6)$ for this example. Then I use Excel's graphics capabilities (refer to Chapter 3) to graph the results. Figure 18-10 shows the data and the chart. My objective is to help you visualize and understand the hypergeometric distribution.

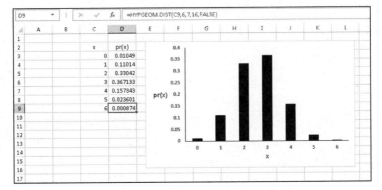

FIGURE 18-10: The hypergeometric distribution for x successes in a six-item sample from a population that consists of seven successes and nine failures.

Chapter 19
More on Probability

I n Chapter 18, I delve into probability in a semiformal way, and introduce distributions of random variables. The binomial distribution is the starting point. In this chapter, I examine additional distributions.

One of the symbols on the pages of this book (and other books in the *For Dummies* series) lets you know that "technical stuff" follows. It might have been a good idea to hang that symbol above this chapter's title. So here's a small note of caution: Some mathematics follows. I put the math in to help you understand what you're doing when you work with the dialog boxes of the Excel functions I describe.

Are these functions on the esoteric side? Well . . . yes. Will you ever have occasion to use them? Well . . . you just might.

Discovering Beta

The beta distribution (not to be confused with *beta*, the probability of a Type 2 error) is a sort of chameleon in the world of distributions. It takes on a wide variety of appearances, depending on the circumstances. I won't give you all the mathematics behind the beta distribution, because the full treatment involves calculus.

The beta distribution connects with the binomial distribution, which I discuss in Chapter 18. The connection is this: In the binomial, the random variable x is the number of successes in N trials with p as the probability of a success. N and p are constants. In the beta distribution, the random variable x is the probability of a success, with N and the number of successes as constants.

Why is this useful? In the real world, you usually don't know the value of p, and you're trying to find it. Typically, you conduct a study, find the number of successes in a set of trials, and then you have to estimate p. Beta shows you the likelihood of possible values of p for the number of trials and successes in your study.

Some of the math is complicated, but I can at least show you the rule that generates the density function for N trials with r successes, when N and r are whole numbers:

$$f(x\,|\,r,N) = \frac{(N-1)!}{(r-1)!(N-r-1)!}x^{r-1}(1-x)^{N-r-1}$$

The vertical bar in the parentheses on the left means "given." So this density function is for specific values of N and r. Calculus enters the picture when N and r aren't whole numbers. (Density function? "Given"? Refer to Chapter 18.)

To give you an idea of what this function looks like, I used Excel to generate and graph the density function for four successes in ten trials. Figure 19-1 shows the data and the graph. Each value on the x-axis is a possible value for the probability of a success. The curve shows probability density. As I point out in Chapter 18, probability density is what makes the area under the curve correspond to probability. The curve's maximum point is at $x = .4$, which is what you would expect for four successes in ten trials. I selected cell C3 so that the Formula bar shows how I used BETA.DIST to calculate the probabilities.

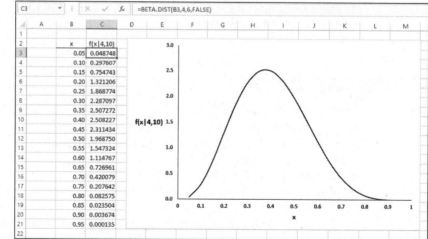

FIGURE 19-1:
The Beta Density function for four successes in ten trials.

Suppose I toss a die (one of a pair of dice) and I define a success as any toss that results in a 3. I assume I'm tossing a fair die, so I assume that $p = pr(3) = 1/6$. Suppose I toss a die ten times and get four 3's. How good does that fair-die assumption look?

The graph in Figure 19-1 gives you a hint: The area to the left of .16667 (the decimal equivalent of 1/6) is a pretty small proportion of the total area, meaning that the probability that p is 1/6 or less is pretty low.

Now, if you have to go to all the trouble of creating a graph and then guesstimate proportions of area to come up with an answer like "pretty low," you're doing a whole lot of work for very little return. Fortunately, Excel has a better way.

BETA.DIST

BETA.DIST eliminates the need for all the graphing and guesstimating. This function enables you to work with the cumulative beta distribution to determine the probability that p is less than or equal to some value. Considering the complexity of beta, BETA.DIST is surprisingly easy to work with.

TIP

In the BETA.DIST Function Arguments dialog box, and in the BETA.DIST Help file, you see *Alpha* and *Beta.* The dialog box tells you each one is a "parameter *to* the distribution," and the Help file tells you that each is "a parameter *of* the distribution." Aside from altering the preposition, neither one is much help — at least, not in any way that helps you apply Alpha and Beta.

So here are the nuts and bolts: For the example you're working through, Alpha is the number of successes, and Beta is the number of failures.

When you put the density function in terms of Alpha (α) and Beta (β), it's

$$f(x) = \frac{(\alpha + \beta - 1)!}{(\alpha - 1)!(\beta - 1)!} x^{\alpha-1} (1-x)^{\beta-1}$$

Again, this applies only when α and β are both whole numbers. If that's not the case, you need calculus to compute $f(x)$.

The steps are:

1. **Select a cell for BETA.DIST's answer.**

2. **From the Statistical Functions menu, select BETA.DIST to open its Function Arguments dialog box. (See Figure 19-2.)**

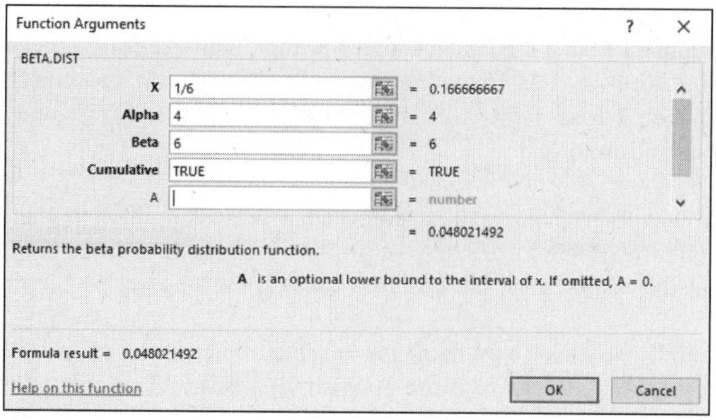

FIGURE 19-2:
The BETA.DIST
Function
Arguments
dialog box.

3. **In the Function Arguments dialog box, type the appropriate values for the arguments.**

The X box holds the probability of a success. For this example, the probability of a success is ⅙.

Excel refers to Alpha and Beta (coming up next) as *parameters to the distribution.* I treat them as "number of successes" and "number of failures." So I enter 4 in the Alpha box and 6 in the Beta box.

In the Cumulative box, I typed TRUE. This gives the area under the Beta function curve between 0 and 1/6. If I type FALSE, it gives the height of the Beta function at the value of X. As the Formula bar in Figure 19-1 shows, I typed FALSE to create the chart.

The A box is an evaluation limit for the value in the X box. In English, that means a lower bound for the value. It isn't relevant for this type of example. I left this box blank, which by default sets A = 0. Incidentally, the Help file refers to an optional B box that sets an upper bound on X. As you can see, no B box is here. The Help file is referring to something in an earlier version of this function.

After all the entries, the answer appears in the dialog box.

The answer for this example is .048021492. "Pretty low" indeed. With four successes in ten tosses, you'd intuitively expect that *p* is greater than 1/6.

4. **Click OK to put the answer into the selected cell.**

The beta distribution has wider applicability than I show you here. Consequently, you can put all kinds of numbers (within certain restrictions) into the boxes. For example, the value you put into the X box can be greater than 1.00, and you can enter values that aren't whole numbers into the Alpha box and the Beta box.

BETA.INV

This one is the inverse of BETA.DIST. If you enter a probability and values for successes and failures, it returns a value for p. For example, if you supply it with .048021492, four successes, and six failures, it returns 0.1666667 — the decimal equivalent of 1/6.

TIP

BETA.INV has a more helpful application. You can use it to find the confidence limits for the probability of a success.

Suppose you've found r successes in N trials and you're interested in the 95 percent confidence limits for the probability of a success. The lower limit is

$$\text{BETA.INV}(.025, r, N - r)$$

The upper limit is

$$\text{BETA.INV}(.975, r, N - r)$$

1. Select a cell for BETA.INV's answer.

2. From the Statistical Functions menu, select BETA.INV to open its Function Arguments dialog box. (See Figure 19-3.)

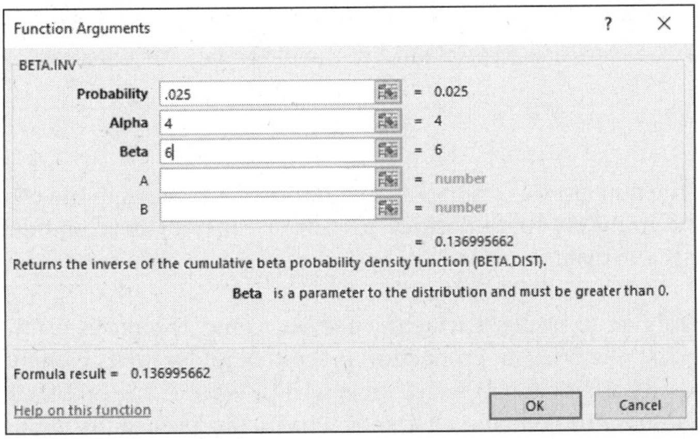

Function Arguments dialog box:

Function Arguments	? ✕
BETA.INV	
Probability	.025 ▮ = 0.025
Alpha	4 ▮ = 4
Beta	6| ▮ = 6
A	▮ = number
B	▮ = number
	= 0.136995662

Returns the inverse of the cumulative beta probability density function (BETA.DIST).

                    Beta is a parameter to the distribution and must be greater than 0.

Formula result = 0.136995662

Help on this function   OK   Cancel

FIGURE 19-3:
The BETA.INV Function Arguments dialog box.

3. In the Function Arguments dialog box, enter the appropriate values for the arguments.

The X box holds a cumulative probability. For the lower bound of the 95 percent confidence limits, the probability is .025.

In the Alpha box, I entered the number of successes. For this example, that's 4.

In the Beta box, I entered the number of failures (*not* the number of trials). The number of failures is 6.

The A box and the B box are evaluation limits for the value in the X box. These aren't relevant for this type of example. I left them blank, which by default sets A = 0 and B=1.

With the entries for X, Alpha, and Beta, the answer appears in the dialog box. The answer for this example is .13699536.

4. **Click OK to put the answer into the selected cell.**

Entering .975 in the X box gives .700704575 as the result. So the 95 percent confidence limits for the probability of a success are .137 and .701 (rounded off) if you have four successes in ten trials.

With more trials, of course, the confidence limit narrows. For 40 successes in 100 trials, the confidence limits are .307 and .497.

Poisson

If you have the kind of process that produces a binomial distribution and you have an extremely large number of trials and a very small number of successes, the *Poisson distribution* approximates the binomial. The equation of the Poisson is

$$pr(x) = \frac{\mu^x e^{-\mu}}{x!}$$

In the numerator, μ is the mean number of successes in the trials, and *e* is 2.71828 (and infinitely more decimal places), a constant near and dear to the hearts of mathematicians.

Here's an example. FarKlempt Robotics, Inc., produces a universal joint for its robots' elbows. The production process is under strict computer control, so that the probability a joint is defective is .001. What is the probability that in a sample of 1,000, one joint is defective? What's the probability that two are defective? Three?

Named after 19th century mathematician Siméon–Denis Poisson, this distribution is computationally easier than the binomial — or at least it was when mathematicians had no computational aids. With Excel, you can easily use `BINOM.DIST` to do the binomial calculations.

First, I apply the Poisson distribution to the FarKlempt example. If π = .001 and N = 1000, the mean is

$$\mu = N\pi = (1000)(.001) = 1$$

(Refer to Chapter 18 for an explanation of $\mu = N\pi$.)

Now for the Poisson. The probability that one joint in a sample of 1,000 is defective is

$$pr(1) = \frac{\mu^x e^{-\mu}}{x!} = \frac{1^1 (2.71828)^{-1}}{1!} = .368$$

For two defective joints in 1000, it's

$$pr(2) = \frac{\mu^x e^{-\mu}}{x!} = \frac{1^2 (2.71828)^{-2}}{2!} = .184$$

And for three defective joints in 1,000:

$$pr(3) = \frac{\mu^x e^{-\mu}}{x!} = \frac{1^3 (2.71828)^{-3}}{3!} = .061$$

REMEMBER

It may seem odd that I refer to a defective item as a "success." It's just a way of labeling a specific event.

POISSON.DIST

Here are the steps for using Excel's POISSON.DIST for the preceding example:

1. **Select a cell for POISSON.DIST's answer.**

2. **From the Statistical Functions menu, select POISSON.DIST to open its Function Arguments dialog box. (See Figure 19-4.)**

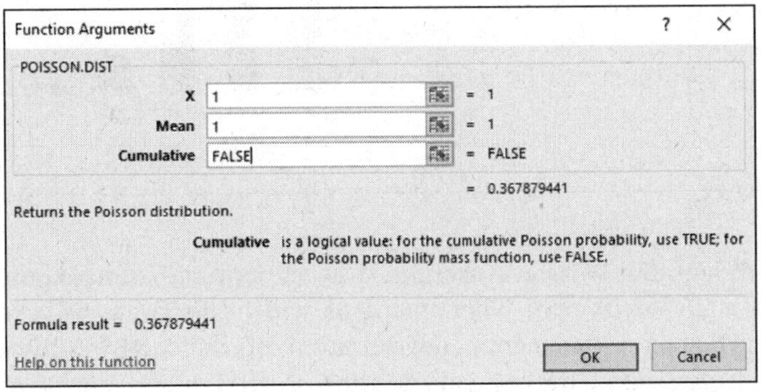

FIGURE 19-4:
The POISSON.
DIST Function
Arguments
dialog box.

3. In the Function Arguments dialog box, enter the appropriate values for the arguments.

In the X box, I entered the number of events for which I'm determining the probability. I'm looking for $pr(1)$, so I entered 1.

In the Mean box, I entered the mean of the process. That's $N\pi$, which for this example is 1.

In the Cumulative box, it's either TRUE for the cumulative probability or FALSE for just the probability of the number of events. I entered FALSE.

With the entries for X, Mean, and Cumulative, the answer appears in the dialog box. The answer for this example is .367879441.

4. Click OK to put the answer into the selected cell.

In the example, I show you the probability for two defective joints in 1,000 and the probability for three. To follow through with the calculations, I'd type **2** into the X box to calculate $pr(2)$, and **3** to find $pr(3)$.

As I mention earlier, in the 21st century it's pretty easy to calculate the binomial probabilities directly. Figure 19-5 shows you the Poisson and the binomial probabilities for the numbers in column B and the conditions of the example. I graphed the probabilities so you can see how close the two really are. I selected cell D3, so the Formula bar shows you how I used BINOM.DIST to calculate the binomial probabilities.

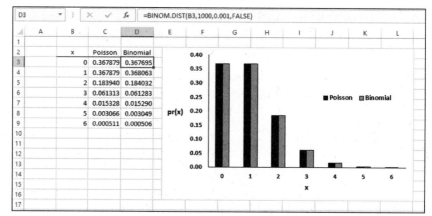

FIGURE 19-5: Poisson probabilities and binomial probabilities.

Although the Poisson's usefulness as an approximation is outdated, it has taken on a life of its own. Phenomena as widely disparate as reaction time data in psychology experiments, degeneration of radioactive substances, and scores in professional hockey games seem to fit Poisson distributions. This is why business analysts and scientific researchers like to base models on this distribution. ("Base models on"? What does *that* mean? I tell you all about it in Chapter 20.)

Working with Gamma

You may recall from Chapter 18 that the number of ways of arranging N objects in a sequence is $N!$ ("N factorial"). You might also recall that $N! = N(N-1)(N-2)...(2)(1)$. Obviously, the factorial only works for whole numbers, right?

The gamma function and GAMMA

Not so fast. Mathematicians (some pretty famous ones) have extended the factorial concept to include non-integers and even negative numbers (which gets very hairy). This extension is called the *gamma function*. When gamma's argument is a positive whole number — let's call it N — the result is $(N-1)!$. Otherwise, gamma returns the result of a calculus-based equation.

Rather than go into all the calculus, I'll just give you an example: $4! = 24$ and $5! = 120$. So the factorial of 4.3 (whatever that would mean) should be somewhere between 24 and 120. Because of the $N-1$ I just mentioned, you'd find this factorial by letting gamma loose on 5.3 (rather than 4.3). And gamma(5.3) = 38.08.

GAMMA is the worksheet function for gamma. GAMMA takes a single argument. Feed it a number and you get back its gamma-function value. For example,

```
=GAMMA(5.3)
```

returns 38.08.

The gamma distribution and GAMMA.DIST

All the preceding is mostly within the realm of theoretical mathematics. Things get more interesting (and more useful) when you tie gamma to a probability distribution. This marriage is called the *gamma distribution*.

The gamma distribution is related to the Poisson distribution in the same way the negative binomial distribution is related to the binomial. The negative binomial tells you the number of trials until a specified number of successes in a binomial distribution. The gamma distribution tells you how many samples you go through to find a specified number of successes in a Poisson distribution. Each sample can be a set of objects (as in the FarKlempt Robotics universal joint example), a physical area, or a time interval.

The probability density function for the gamma distribution is

$$f(x) = \frac{1}{\beta^{\alpha}(\alpha-1)!} x^{\alpha-1} e^{-x/\beta}$$

Again, this works when α is a whole number. If it's not, you guessed it — calculus. (By the way, when this function has only whole-number values of α, it's called the *Erlang distribution,* just in case anybody ever asks you.) The letter *e*, once again, is the constant 2.7818 I mention earlier.

Don't worry about the exotic-looking math. As long as you understand what each symbol means, you're in business. Excel does the heavy lifting for you.

So here's what the symbols mean. For the FarKlempt Robotics example, α is the number of successes and β corresponds to μ the Poisson distribution. The variable *x* tracks the number of samples. So, if *x* is 3, α is 2, and β is 1, you're talking about the probability density associated with finding the second success in the third sample, if the average number of successes per sample (of 1,000) is 1. (Where does 1 come from, again? That's 1,000 universal joints per sample multiplied by .001, the probability of producing a defective one.)

To determine probability, you have to work with area under the density function. This brings me to the Excel worksheet function designed for the gamma distribution.

GAMMA.DIST gives you a couple of options. You can use it to calculate the probability density, and you can use it to calculate probability. Figure 19-6 shows how I used the first option to create a graph of the probability density so you can see what the function looks like. Working within the context of the preceding example, I set Alpha to 2 and Beta to 1, and calculated the density for the values of *x* in column D.

The values in column E show the probability densities associated with finding the second defective universal joint in the indicated number of samples of 1,000. For example, cell E5 holds the probability density for finding the second defective joint in the third sample.

In real life, you work with probabilities rather than densities. Next, I show you how to use GAMMA.DIST to determine the probability of finding the second defective joint in the third sample.

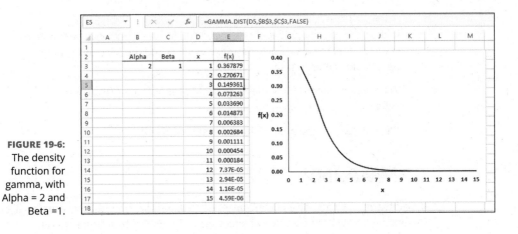

FIGURE 19-6:
The density
function for
gamma, with
Alpha = 2 and
Beta =1.

Here are the steps:

1. **Select a cell for GAMMA.DIST's answer.**

2. **From the Statistical Functions menu, select GAMMA.DIST to open its Function Arguments dialog box. (See Figure 19-7.)**

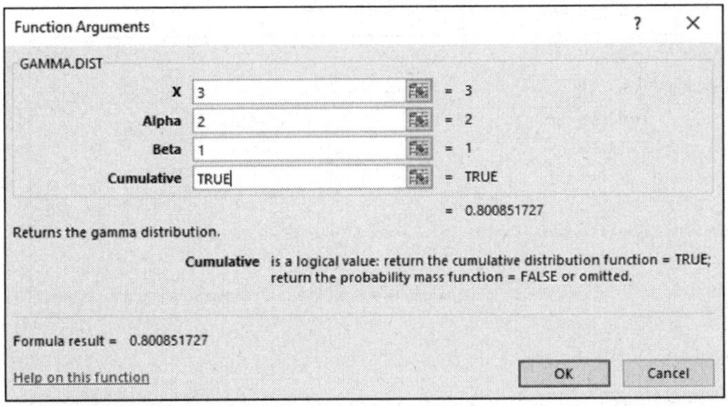

FIGURE 19-7:
The GAMMA.DIST
Function
Arguments
dialog box.

3. **In the Function Arguments dialog box, enter the appropriate values for the arguments.**

    The X box holds the number of samples for which I'm determining the probability. I'm looking for $pr(3)$, so I entered 3.

    In the Alpha box, I entered the number of successes. I want to find the second success in the third sample, so I entered 2.

    In the Beta box, I entered the average number of successes that occur within a sample. For this example, that's 1.

In the Cumulative box, the choices are TRUE for the cumulative distribution or FALSE to find the probability density. I want to find the probability, not the density, so I entered TRUE.

With values entered for X, Alpha, Beta, and Cumulative, the answer — .800851727 — appears in the dialog box.

4. **Click OK to put the answer into the selected cell.**

GAMMA.INV

If you want to know, at a certain level of probability, how many samples it takes to observe a specified number of successes, this is the function for you.

GAMMA.INV is the inverse of GAMMA.DIST. Enter a probability along with Alpha and Beta and it returns the number of samples. Its Function Arguments dialog box has a Probability box, an Alpha box, and a Beta box. Figure 19-8 shows what happens if you enter the cell that holds the answer for the preceding section (I stored it in cell A1) into the Probability box and the same numbers used earlier to get that answer for Alpha and Beta: The answer is 3.

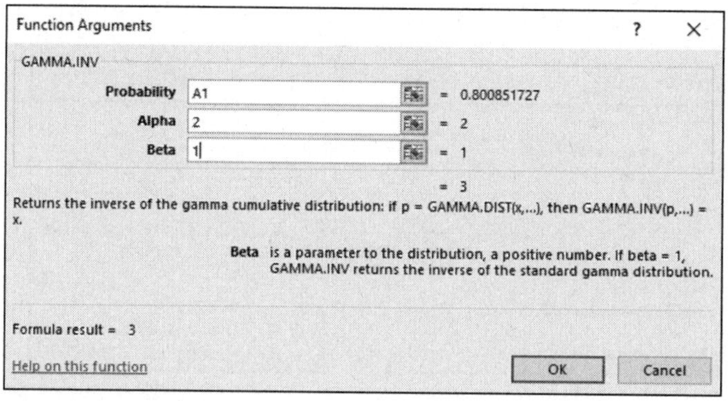

FIGURE 19-8: The GAMMA.INV Function Arguments dialog box.

Exponential

If you're dealing with the gamma distribution and you have Alpha = 1, you have the exponential distribution. This gives the probability that it takes a specified number of samples to get to the first success.

What does the density function look like? Excuse me . . . I'm about to go mathematical on you for a moment. Here, once again, is the density function for gamma:

$$f(x) = \frac{1}{\beta^{\alpha}(\alpha-1)!} x^{\alpha-1} e^{-x/\beta}$$

If $\alpha = 1$, it looks like this:

$$f(x) = \frac{1}{\beta} e^{-x/\beta}$$

Statisticians like substituting λ (the Greek letter *lambda*) for $\frac{1}{\beta}$, so here's the final version:

$$f(x) = \lambda e^{-\lambda x}$$

I bring this up because Excel's EXPON.DIST Function Arguments dialog box has a box for LAMBDA, and I want you to know what it means.

EXPON.DIST

Use EXPON.DIST to determine the probability that it takes a specified number of samples to get to the first success in a Poisson distribution. Here, I work once again with the universal joint example. I show you how to find the probability that you'll see the first success in the third sample. Here are the steps:

1. **Select a cell for EXPON.DIST's answer.**

2. **From the Statistical Functions menu, select EXPON.DIST to open its Function Arguments dialog box. (See Figure 19-9.)**

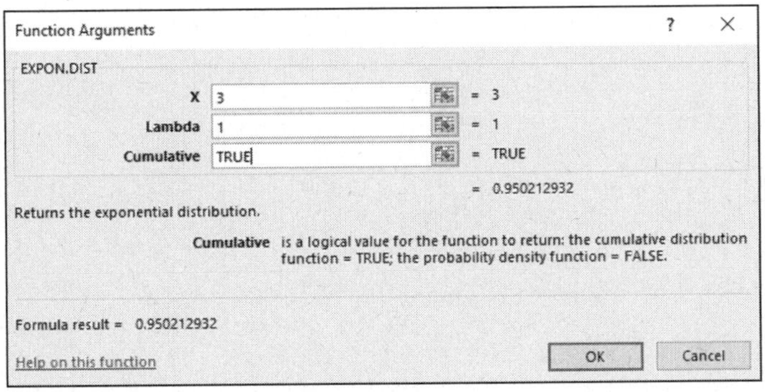

FIGURE 19-9:
The EXPON.DIST
Function
Arguments
dialog box.

3. **In the Function Arguments dialog box, enter the appropriate values for the arguments.**

In the X box, I entered the number of samples for which I'm determining the probability. I'm looking for $pr(3)$, so I typed 3.

In the Lambda box, I entered the average number of successes per sample. This goes back to the numbers I give you in the example — the probability of a success (.001) times the number of universal joints in each sample (1,000). That product is 1, so I entered 1 in this box.

In the Cumulative box, the choices are TRUE for the cumulative distribution or FALSE to find the probability density. I want to find the probability, not the density, so I entered TRUE.

With values entered for X, Lambda, and Cumulative, the answer appears in the dialog box. The answer for this example is .950212932.

4. **Click OK to put the answer into the selected cell.**

Chapter 20
A Career in Modeling

"Model" is a term that gets thrown around a lot these days. Simply put, a *model* is something you know and can work with that helps you understand something you know little about. A model is supposed to mimic, in some way, the thing it's modeling. A globe, for example, is a model of the earth. A street map is a model of a neighborhood. A blueprint is a model of a building.

Researchers use models to help them understand natural processes and phenomena. Business analysts use models to help them understand business processes. The models these people use might include concepts from mathematics and statistics — concepts that are so well known they can shed light on the unknown. The idea is to create a model that consists of concepts you understand, put the model through its paces, and see if the results look like real-world results.

In this chapter, I discuss modeling. My goal is to show how you can harness Excel's statistical capabilities to help you understand processes in your world.

Modeling a Distribution

In one approach to modeling, you gather data and group them into a distribution. Next, you try to figure out a process that results in that kind of a distribution. Restate that process in statistical terms so that it can generate a distribution, and then see how well the generated distribution matches up to the real one. This "process you figure out and restate in statistical terms" is the model.

If the distribution you generate matches up well with the real data, does this mean your model is "right"? Does it mean the process you guessed is the process that produces the data?

Unfortunately, no. The logic doesn't work that way. You can show that a model is wrong, but you can't prove that it's right.

Plunging into the Poisson distribution

In this section, I walk you through an example of modeling with the Poisson distribution. I introduce this distribution in Chapter 19, where I tell you it seems to characterize an array of processes in the real world. By "characterize a process," I mean that a distribution of real-world data looks a lot like a Poisson distribution. When this happens, it's possible that the kind of process that produces a Poisson distribution is also responsible for producing the data.

What is that process? Start with a random variable x that tracks the number of occurrences of a specific event in an interval. In Chapter 19, the "interval" is a sample of 1,000 universal joints, and the specific event is "defective joint." Poisson distributions are also appropriate for events occurring in intervals of time, and the event can be something like "arrival at a toll booth." Next, I outline the conditions for a *Poisson process*, and use both defective joints and toll booth arrivals to illustrate:

» The number of occurrences of the event in two non-overlapping intervals are independent.

The number of defective joints in one sample is independent of the number of defective joints in another. The number of arrivals at a toll booth during one hour is independent of the number of arrivals during another.

» The probability of an occurrence of the event is proportional to the size of the interval.

The chance that you'll find a defective joint is larger in a sample of 10,000 than it is in a sample of 1,000. The chance of an arrival at a toll booth is greater for one hour than it is for a half-hour.

» The probability of more than one occurrence of the event in a small interval is 0 or close to 0.

In a sample of 1,000 universal joints, you have an extremely low probability of finding two defective ones right next to one another. At any time, two vehicles don't arrive at a toll booth simultaneously.

As I show you in Chapter 19, the formula for the Poisson distribution is

$$pr(x) = \frac{\mu^x e^{-\mu}}{x!}$$

In this equation, μ represents the average number of occurrences of the event in the interval you're looking at, and e is the constant 2.781828 (followed by infinitely many more decimal places).

Visualizing the Poisson distribution

To gain a deeper understanding of the Poisson distribution, here's a way to visualize and experiment with it. Figure 20-1 shows a spreadsheet with a chart of the Poisson and the values I based it on.

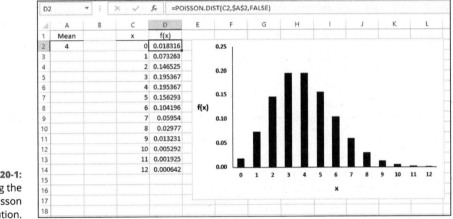

FIGURE 20-1:
Visualizing the Poisson distribution.

Cell A2 holds the value for the mean of the Poisson. I calculate the values for f(x) in column D by typing

```
=POISSON.DIST(C2,$A$2,FALSE)
```

into cell D2 and then autofilling. Using FALSE as the third argument causes the function to return the probability associated with the first argument. (TRUE returns the cumulative probability. For more on POISSON.DIST, see Chapter 19.)

Then I inserted a column chart and modified it somewhat. You'll learn this distribution when you try different values in A2 and note the effect on the chart.

Working with the Poisson distribution

Time to use the Poisson in a model. At the FarBlonJet Corporation, web designers track the number of hits per hour on the intranet home page. They monitor the page for 200 consecutive hours and group the data, as shown in Table 20-1.

TABLE 20-1 Hits Per Hour on the FarBlonJet Intranet Home Page

Hits/Hour	Observed Hours	Hits/Hour X Observed Hours
0	10	0
1	30	30
2	44	88
3	44	132
4	36	144
5	18	90
6	10	60
7	8	56
Total	200	600

The first column shows the variable Hits/Hour. The second column, Observed Hours, shows the number of hours in which each value of Hits/Hour occurred. In the 200 hours observed, 10 of those hours went by with no hits, 30 hours had one hit, 44 had two hits, and so on. These data lead the web designers to use a Poisson distribution to model Hits/Hour. Another way to say this: They believe a Poisson process produces the number of hits per hour on the web page.

Multiplying the first column by the second column results in the third column. Summing the third column shows that in the 200 observed hours, the intranet page received 600 hits. So the average number of hits/hour is 3.00.

Applying the Poisson distribution to this example,

$$pr(x) = \frac{\mu^x e^{-\mu}}{x!} = \frac{3^x e^{-3}}{x!}$$

From here on, I pick it up in Excel.

Using POISSON.DIST again

Figure 20-2 shows each value of x (hits/hour), the probability of each x if the average number of hits per hour is three, the predicted number of hours, and the observed number of hours (taken from the second column in Table 20-1). I selected cell B3 so that the Formula bar shows how I used the POISSON.DIST worksheet function. I autofilled column B down to cell B10. (For the details on using POISSON.DIST, see Chapter 19.)

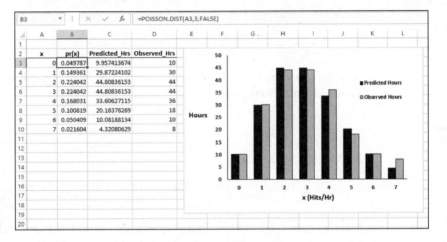

FIGURE 20-2:
Web page
hits/hour —
Poisson-predicted
(μ=3) and
observed.

To get the predicted number of hours, I multiplied each probability in column B by 200 (the total number of observed hours). I used Excel's graphics capabilities (see Chapter 3) to show you how close the predicted hours are to the observed hours. They look pretty close, don't they?

Testing the model's fit

Well, "looking pretty close" isn't enough for a statistician. A statistical test is a necessity. As is the case with all statistical tests, this one starts with a null hypothesis and an alternative hypothesis. Here they are:

H_0: The distribution of observed hits/hour follows a Poisson distribution.

H_1: Not H_0

The appropriate statistical test involves an extension of the binomial distribution. It's called the *multinomial distribution* — *multi* because it encompasses more categories than just "success" and "failure." It's difficult to work with, and Excel has no worksheet function to handle the computations.

Fortunately, pioneering statistician Karl Pearson (inventor of the correlation coefficient) noticed that χ^2 ("chi-square"), a distribution I show you in Chapter 10, approximates the multinomial. Originally intended for one-sample hypothesis tests about variances, χ^2 has become much better known for applications like the one I'm about to show you.

Pearson's big idea was this: If you want to know how well a hypothesized distribution (like the Poisson) fits a sample (like the observed hours), use the distribution to generate a hypothesized sample (your predicted hours, for instance), and work with this formula:

$$\chi^2 = \sum \frac{(\text{Observed} - \text{Predicted})^2}{\text{Predicted}}$$

Usually, this is written with *Expected* rather than *Predicted*, and both Observed and Expected are abbreviated. The usual form of this formula is

$$\chi^2 = \sum \frac{(O - E)^2}{E}$$

For this example,

$$\chi^2 = \sum \frac{(O - E)^2}{E} = \frac{(10 - 9.9574)^2}{9.9574} + \frac{(30 - 29.8722)^2}{29.8722} + \dots + \frac{(8 - 4.3208)^2}{4.3208}$$

What is that total? Excel figures it out for you. Figure 20-3 shows the same columns as earlier, with column F holding the values for $(O - E)^2/E$. I could have used this formula

```
=((D3–C3)^2)/C3
```

to calculate the value in F3 and then to autofill up to F10.

I chose a different route. First, I assigned the name Predicted_Hrs to C3:C10 and the name Observed_Hrs to D3:D10. Then I used an array formula (see Chapter 2). I selected F3:F10 and created this formula:

```
=(Observed_Hrs–Predicted_Hrs)^2/Predicted_Hrs
```

Pressing Ctrl+Shift+Enter puts the values into F3:F10. That key combination also puts the curly brackets into the formula in the Formula bar.

The sum of the values in column F is in cell F11, and that's χ^2. If you're trying to show that the Poisson distribution is a good fit to the data, you're looking for a low value of χ^2.

FIGURE 20-3:
Web page
hits/hour —
Poisson-predicted
(μ=3) and
observed, along
with the
calculations
needed to
compute χ².

The spreadsheet shows:

	A	B	C	D	E	F	G	H
F3		fx	{=(Observed_Hrs-Predicted_Hrs)^2/Predicted_Hrs}					
1								
2	x	pr(x)	Predicted_Hrs	Observed_Hrs		(O-E)²/E		
3	0	0.049787	9.957413674	10		0.000182		
4	1	0.149361	29.87224102	30		0.000546		
5	2	0.224042	44.80836153	44		0.014583		
6	3	0.224042	44.80836153	44		0.014583		
7	4	0.168031	33.60627115	36		0.170502		
8	5	0.100819	20.16376269	18		0.232192		
9	6	0.050409	10.08188134	10		0.000665		
10	7	0.021604	4.32080629	8		3.132857		
11					Sum =	3.566111		
12								

Okay. Now what? Is 3.5661 high or is it low?

To find out, you evaluate the calculated value of χ^2 against the χ^2 distribution. The goal is to find the probability of getting a value at least as high as the calculated value, 3.5661. The trick is to know how many degrees of freedom (df) you have. For a goodness-of-fit application like this one

$$df = k - m - 1$$

where k = the number of categories and m = the number of parameters estimated from the data. The number of categories is 8 (0 hits/hour through 7 hits/hour). The number of parameters? I used the observed hours to estimate the parameter μ, so m in this example is 1. That means df = 8 − 1 − 1 = 6.

Use the worksheet function CHISQ.DIST.RT on the value in F11, with 6 df. CHISQ.DIST.RT returns .73515, the probability of getting a χ^2 of at least 3.5661 if H_0 is true. (Refer to Chapter 10 for more on CHISQ.DIST.RT.) Figure 20-4 shows the χ^2 distribution with 6 df and the darkened area to the right of 3.5661.

If α = .05, the decision is to not reject H_0 — meaning you can't reject the hypothesis that the observed data come from a Poisson distribution.

This is one of those infrequent times when it's beneficial to not reject H_0 — if you want to make the case that a Poisson process is producing the data. If the probability had been just a little greater than .05, not rejecting H_0 would look suspicious. The large probability, however, makes nonrejection of H_0 — and an underlying Poisson process — seem more reasonable. (For more on this, see the sidebar "A point to ponder," in Chapter 10.)

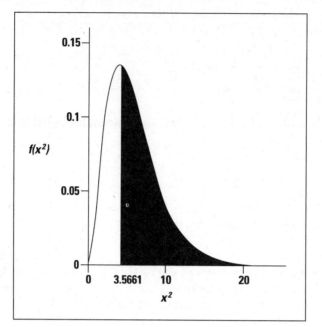

FIGURE 20-4:
The χ^2 distribution, df = 6. The shaded area is the probability of getting a χ^2 of at least 3.5661 if H_0 is true.

A word about CHISQ.TEST

Excel provides CHISQ.TEST, a worksheet function that on first look appears to carry out the test I show you with about one-tenth the work I did on the worksheet. Its Function Arguments dialog box provides one box for the observed values and another for the expected values.

One problem is that CHISQ.TEST does not return a value for χ^2. It skips that step and returns the probability that you'll get a χ^2 at least as high as the one you calculate from the observed values and the predicted values.

Another problem is that CHISQ.TEST's degrees of freedom are wrong for this case. CHISQ.TEST goes ahead and assumes that df = k-1 (7) rather than k-m-1 (6). You lose a degree of freedom because you estimate μ from the data. In other kinds of modeling, you lose more than one degree of freedom. Suppose, for example, you believe that a normal distribution characterizes the underlying process. In that case, you estimate μ and σ from the data, and you lose two degrees of freedom.

By basing its answer on less than the correct df, CHISQ.TEST gives you an inappropriately large (and misleading) value for the probability.

CHISQ.TEST would be perfect if it had an option for entering df, or if it returned a value for χ^2 (which you could then evaluate via CHI.DIST and the correct df).

When you don't lose any degrees of freedom, CHISQ.TEST works as advertised. Does that ever happen? In the next section, it does.

Playing ball with a model

Baseball is a game that generates huge amounts of statistics — and many study these statistics closely. SABR, the Society for American Baseball Research, has sprung from the efforts of a band of dedicated fan-statisticians (fantasticians?) who delve into the statistical nooks and crannies of the Great American Pastime. They call their work *sabermetrics*. (I made up *fantasticians*. They call themselves *sabermetricians*.)

The reason I mention this is that sabermetrics supplies a nice example of modeling. It's based on the obvious idea that during a game, a baseball team's objective is to score runs and to keep its opponent from scoring runs. The better a team does at both, the more games it wins. Bill James, who gave sabermetrics its name and is its leading exponent, discovered a neat relationship between the amount of runs a team scores, the amount of runs the team allows, and its winning percentage. He calls it the *Pythagorean percentage*:

$$\text{Pythagorean Percentage} = \frac{\left(\text{Runs Scored}\right)^2}{\left(\text{Runs Scored}\right)^2 + \left(\text{Runs Allowed}\right)^2}$$

Think of it as a model for predicting games won. (This is James' original formula, and I use it throughout. Over the years, sabermetricians have found that 1.83 is a more accurate exponent than 2.) Calculate this percentage and multiply it by the number of games a team plays. Then compare the answer to the team's wins. How well does the model predict the number of games each team won during the 2011 season?

To find out, I found all the relevant data for every Major League Baeball team for 2011. (Thank you, www.baseball-reference.com.) I put the data into the worksheet in Figure 20-5.

As Figure 20-5 shows, I used an array formula to calculate the Pythagorean percentage in column D. First, I assigned the name Runs_Scored to the data in column B, and the name Runs_Allowed to the data in column C. Then I selected D2:D31 and created the formula

```
=Runs_Scored^2/(Runs_Scored^2 + Runs_Allowed^2)
```

Next, I pressed Ctrl+Shift+Enter to put the values into D2:D31 and the curly brackets into the formula in the Formula bar.

D2				fx	{=Runs_Scored^2/(Runs_Scored^2 + Runs_Allowed^2)}	

	A	B	C	D	E	F	G
1	Team	Runs_Scored	Runs_Allowed	Pythagorean	Games_Played	Predicted_Wins	Wins
2	Arizona	719	713	0.504	162	82	79
3	Atlanta	573	760	0.362	162	59	67
4	Baltimore	713	693	0.514	162	83	81
5	Boston	748	753	0.497	162	80	78
6	Chicago Cubs	689	608	0.562	162	91	97
7	Chicago White Sox	622	701	0.440	162	71	76
8	Cincinatti	640	753	0.419	162	68	64
9	Cleveland	670	641	0.522	161	84	81
10	Colorado	737	844	0.433	162	70	68
11	Detroit	689	803	0.424	161	68	74
12	Houston	729	617	0.583	162	94	86
13	Kansas City	724	642	0.560	162	91	95
14	Los Angeles Angels	661	676	0.489	162	79	85
15	Los Angeles Dodgers	667	595	0.557	162	90	92
16	Miami	612	679	0.448	162	73	71
17	Milwaukee	654	737	0.441	162	71	68
18	Minnesota	697	700	0.498	162	81	83
19	New York Mets	684	612	0.555	162	90	90
20	New York Yankees	765	698	0.546	162	88	87
21	Oakland	693	729	0.475	162	77	68
22	Philadelphia	625	808	0.374	162	61	63
23	Pittsburgh	697	596	0.578	162	94	98
24	San Diego	650	731	0.442	162	72	74
25	Seattle	656	726	0.449	162	73	76
26	San Francisco	697	627	0.553	162	90	84
27	St. Louis	646	525	0.602	162	98	100
28	Tampa Bay	645	642	0.502	162	81	80
29	Texas	752	732	0.513	162	83	88
30	Toronto	891	671	0.638	162	103	93
31	Washington	703	635	0.551	162	89	83

FIGURE 20-5: Runs scored, runs allowed, predicted wins, and wins for each Major League baseball team in 2011.

Had I wanted to do it another way, I'd have put this formula in cell D2:

```
=B2^2/((B2^2)+(C2^2))
```

Then I would have autofilled the remaining cells in column D.

Finally, I multiplied each Pythagorean percentage in column D by the number of games each team played (28 teams played 162 games, 2 played 161) to get the predicted wins in column F. Because the number of wins can only be a whole number, I used the ROUND function to round off the predicted wins. For example, the formula that supplies the value in E3 is

```
=ROUND(D3*162,0)
```

The zero in the parentheses indicates that I wanted no decimal places.

Before proceeding, I assigned the name Predicted_Wins to the data in column F, and the name Wins to the data in column G.

How well does the model fit with reality? This time, CHISQ.TEST can supply the answer. I don't lose any degrees of freedom here: I didn't use the Wins data in column G to estimate any parameters, like a mean or a variance, and then apply those parameters to calculate Predicted Wins. Instead, the predictions came from other data — the runs scored and the runs allowed. For this reason, df = k − m − 1 = 30 − 0 − 1 = 29.

Here's how to use `CHISQ.TEST` (when it's appropriate!):

1. **With the data entered, select a cell for `CHISQ.TEST`'s answer.**

2. **From the Statistical Functions menu, select CHISQ.TEST and click OK to open the Function Arguments dialog box for `CHISQ.TEST`. (See Figure 20-6.)**

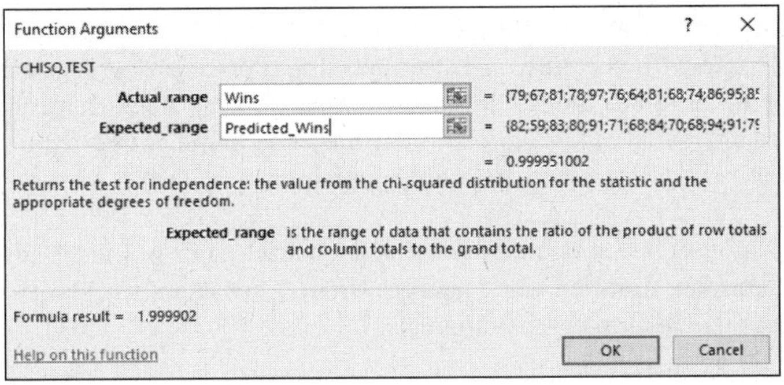

FIGURE 20-6:
The CHISQ.TEST
Function
Arguments
dialog box.

3. **In the Function Arguments dialog box, type the appropriate values for the arguments.**

In the Actual_range box, type the cell range that holds the scores for the observed values. For this example, that's Wins (the name for F2:F32).

In the Expected_range box, type the cell range that holds the predicted values. For this example, it's Predicted_Wins (the name for E2:E32).

With the cursor in the Expected_range box, the dialog box mentions a product of row totals and column totals. Don't let that confuse you. It has to do with a slightly different application of this function (which I cover in Chapter 22).

With values entered for Actual_range and for Expected_range, the answer appears in the dialog box. The answer here is .999951, which means that with 29 degrees of freedom, you have a huge chance of finding a value of χ^2 at least as high as the one you'd calculate from these observed values and these predicted values. Another way to say this: The calculated value of χ^2 is very low, meaning that the predicted wins are very close to the actual wins. Bottom line: The model fits the data extremely well.

4. **Click OK to put the answer into the selected cell.**

A Simulating Discussion

Another approach to modeling is to simulate a process. The idea is to define, as much as you can, what a process does and then somehow use numbers to represent that process and carry it out. It's a great way to find out what a process does in case other methods of analysis are very complex.

Taking a chance: The Monte Carlo method

Many processes contain an element of randomness. You just can't predict the outcome with certainty. To simulate this type of process, you have to have some way to simulate the randomness. Simulation methods that incorporate randomness are called *Monte Carlo* simulations. The name comes from the city in Monaco whose main attraction is gambling casinos.

In the next few sections, I show you a couple of examples. These examples aren't so complex that you can't analyze them. I use them for just that reason: You can check the results against analysis.

Loading the dice

In Chapter 18, I talk about a *die* (one member of a pair of dice) that's biased to come up according to the numbers on its faces: A 6 is six times as likely as a 1, a 5 is five times as likely, and so on. On any toss, the probability of getting a number n is $n/21$.

Suppose you have a pair of dice loaded this way. What would the outcomes of 200 tosses of these dice look like? What would be the average of those 200 tosses? What would be the variance and the standard deviation? You can use Excel to set up Monte Carlo simulations and answer these questions.

To start, I use Excel to calculate the probability of each outcome. Figure 20-7 shows how I did it. Column A holds all the possible outcomes of tossing a pair of dice (2–12). Columns C through N hold the possible ways of getting each outcome. Columns C, E, G, I, K, and M show the possible outcomes on the first die. Columns D, F, H, J, L, and N show the possible outcomes on the second die. Column B gives the probability of each outcome, based on the numbers in columns C–M. I highlighted B7, so the Formula bar shows I used this formula to have Excel calculate the probability of a 7:

```
=((C7*D7)+(E7*F7)+(G7*H7)+(I7*J7)+(K7*L7)+(M7*N7))/21^2
```

I autofilled the remaining cells in column B.

The sum in B14 confirms that I considered every possibility.

| B7 | | | f_x | =((C7*D7)+(E7*F7)+(G7*H7)+(I7*J7)+(K7*L7)+(M7*N7))/21^2 | | | | | | | | | |

	A	B	C	D	E	F	G	H	I	J	K	L	M	N
1	x	pr(x)	1st	2nd	1st	2nd	1st	2nd	1st	2nd	1st	2nd	1st	2nd
2	2	0.00227	1	1										
3	3	0.00907	2	1	1	2								
4	4	0.02268	3	1	2	2	1	3						
5	5	0.04535	4	1	3	2	2	3	1	4				
6	6	0.07937	5	1	4	2	3	3	2	4	1	5		
7	7	0.12698	6	1	5	2	4	3	3	4	2	5	1	6
8	8	0.15873	6	2	5	3	4	4	3	5	2	6		
9	9	0.17234	6	3	5	4	4	5	3	6				
10	10	0.16553	6	4	5	5	4	6						
11	11	0.13605	6	5	5	6								
12	12	0.08163	6	6										
13														
14	Sum =	1.00000												

FIGURE 20-7: Outcomes and probabilities for a pair of loaded dice.

Next, it's time to simulate the process of tossing the dice. Each toss, in effect, generates a value of the random variable *x* according to the probability distribution defined by column A and column B. How do you simulate these tosses?

Data analysis tool: Random Number Generation

Excel's Random Number Generation tool is tailor-made for this kind of simulation. Tell it how many values you want to generate, give it a probability distribution to work with, and it randomly generates numbers according to the parameters of the distribution. Each randomly generated number corresponds to a toss of the dice.

Here's how to use the Random Number Generation tool:

1. **Select Data | Data Analysis to open the Data Analysis dialog box.**

2. **In the Data Analysis dialog box, scroll down the Analysis Tools list and select Random Number Generation.**

3. **Click OK to open the Random Number Generation dialog box.**

    Figure 20-8 shows the Random Number Generation dialog box.

4. **In the Number of Variables box, type the number of variables you want to create random numbers for.**

    I know, I know . . . don't end a sentence with a preposition. As Winston Churchill said: "That's the kind of nonsense up with which I will not put." Hey, but seriously, I entered 1 for this example. I'm only interested in the outcomes of tossing a pair of dice.

5. **In the Number of Random Numbers box, type the number of numbers to generate.**

   I entered 200 to simulate 200 tosses of the loaded dice.

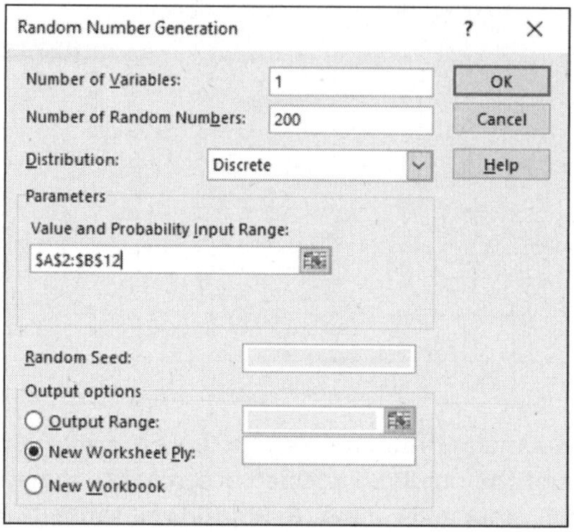

FIGURE 20-8:
The Random
Number
Generation
dialog box.

6. **In the Distribution box, click the down arrow to select the type of distribution.**

   You have seven options here. The choice you make determines what appears in the Parameters area of the dialog box, because different types of distributions have different types (and numbers) of parameters. You're dealing with a discrete random variable here, so the appropriate choice is Discrete.

7. **Choosing Discrete causes the Value and Probability Input Range box to appear under Parameters. Enter the array of cells that holds the values of the variable and the associated probabilities.**

   The possible outcomes of the tosses of the die are in A2:A12, and the probabilities are in B2:B12, so the range is A2:B12. Excel fills in the dollar signs ($) for absolute referencing.

8. **In the Output Options, select a radio button to indicate where you want the results.**

   I selected New Worksheet Ply to put the results on a new page in the worksheet.

9. **Click OK.**

Because I selected New Worksheet Ply, a newly created page opens with the results. Figure 20-9 shows the new page. The randomly generated numbers are in column A. The 200 rows of random numbers are too long to show you. I could have cut and pasted them into ten columns of 20 cells, but then you'd just be looking at 200 random numbers.

Instead, I used FREQUENCY to group the numbers into frequencies in columns C and D and then used Excel's graphics capabilities to create a graph of the results. I selected D2, so the formula box shows how I used FREQUENCY for that cell. As you can see, I defined Tosses as the name for A2:A201 and x as the name for C2:C12.

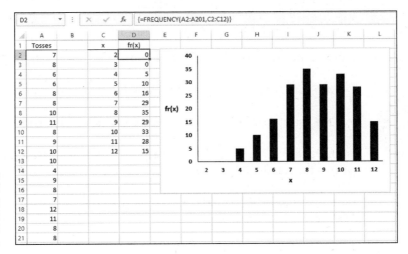

FIGURE 20-9: The results of simulating 200 tosses of a pair of loaded dice.

What about the statistics for these simulated tosses?

```
=AVERAGE(Tosses)
```

tells you the mean is 8.640.

```
=VAR.S(Tosses)
```

returns 4.191 as the estimate of the variance, and SQRT applied to the variance returns 2.047 as the estimate of the standard deviation.

How do these values match up with the parameters of the random variable? This is what I mean earlier by "checking against analysis." In Chapter 18, I show how to calculate the expected value (the mean), the variance, and the standard deviation for a discrete random variable.

The expected value is

$$E(x) = \sum x\big(pr(x)\big)$$

In the worksheet in Figure 20-7, shown earlier, I used the SUMPRODUCT worksheet function to calculate $E(x)$. The formula is

```
=SUMPRODUCT(A2:A12,B2:B12)
```

The expected value is 8.667.

The variance is

$$V(x) = \sum x^2\big(pr(x)\big) - \big[E(x)\big]^2$$

With $E(x)$ stored in B16, I used this formula:

```
=SUMPRODUCT(A2:A12,A2:A12,B2:B12)-B16^2
```

TIP

Note the use of A2:A12 twice in SUMPRODUCT. That gives you the sum of x^2.

The formula returns 4.444 as the variance. SQRT applied to that number gives 2.108 as the standard deviation.

Table 20-2 shows how closely the results from the simulation match up with the parameters of the random variable.

TABLE 20-2   **Statistics from the Loaded Dice-Tossing Simulation and the Parameters of the Discrete Distribution**

	Simulation Statistic	Distribution Parameter
Mean	8.640	8.667
Variance	4.191	4.444
Standard Deviation	2.047	2.108

Simulating the Central Limit Theorem

This might surprise you, but statisticians often use simulations to make determinations about some of their statistics. They do this when mathematical analysis becomes very difficult.

For example, some statistical tests depend on normally distributed populations. If the populations aren't normal, what happens to those tests? Do they still do what they're supposed to? To answer that question, statisticians might create non-normally distributed populations of numbers, simulate experiments with them, and apply the statistical tests to the simulated results.

In this section, I use simulation to examine an important statistical item — the Central Limit Theorem. In Chapter 9, I introduce the Central Limit Theorem in connection with the sampling distribution of the mean. In fact, I simulate sampling from a population with only three possible values to show you that even with a small sample size, the sampling distribution starts to look normally distributed.

Here, I use the Random Number Generation tool to set up a normally distributed population and draw 40 samples of 16 scores each. I calculate the mean of each sample and then set up a distribution of those means. The idea is to see how that distribution matches up with the Central Limit Theorem.

The distribution for this example has the parameters of the population of scores on the IQ test, a distribution I use for examples in several chapters. It's a normal distribution with μ = 100 and σ = 16. According to the Central Limit Theorem, the mean of the distribution of means should be 100, and the standard deviation (the standard error of the mean) should be 4.

For a normal distribution, the Random Number Generation dialog box looks like Figure 20-10. The first two entries cause Excel to generate 16 random numbers for a single variable. Choosing Normal in the Distribution box causes the Mean box and the Standard Deviation box to appear under Parameters. As the figure shows, I entered **100** for the Mean and **16** for the Standard Deviation. Under Output Options, I selected Output Range and entered a column of 16 cells. This puts the randomly generated numbers into the indicated column on the current page, and (because I specified 40 samples) into 39 adjoining columns. Then I used AVERAGE to calculate the mean for each column (each sample, in other words), and then ROUND to round off each mean.

Next, I copied the 40 rounded sample means to another worksheet so I could show you how they're distributed.

I calculated their mean and the standard deviation. I used FREQUENCY to group the means into a frequency distribution, and used Excel's graphics capabilities to graph the distribution. Does the Central Limit Theorem accurately predict the results? Figure 20-11 shows what I found.

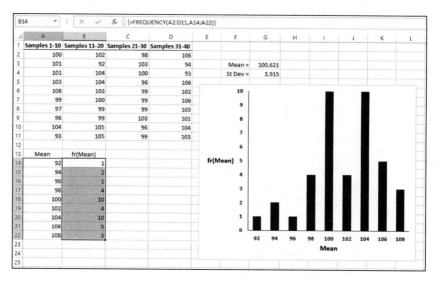

FIGURE 20-10:
The Random Number Generation dialog box for a normal distribution.

FIGURE 20-11:
The results of the Central Limit Theorem simulation.

The mean of the means, 100.621, is close to the Central Limit Theorem's predicted value of 100. The standard deviation of the means, 3.915, is close to the Central Limit's predicted value of 4 for the standard error of the mean. The graph shows the makings of a normal distribution, although it's slightly skewed. In general, the simulation matches up well with the Central Limit Theorem. If you try this, you'll get different numbers than mine, but your overall results should be in the same ballpark.

TIP

A couple of paragraphs ago, I said, "I copied the 40 rounded sample means to another worksheet." That's not quite a slam-dunk. When you try to paste a cell into another worksheet and that cell holds a formula, Excel usually balks and gives you an ugly-looking error message when you paste. This happens when the formula refers to cell locations that don't hold any values in the new worksheet.

To work around that, you have to do a little trick on the cell you want to copy. You have to convert its contents from a formula into the value that the formula calculates. The steps are:

1. **Select the cell or cell array you want to copy.**

2. **Right-click and select Copy from the contextual menu that appears (or just press Ctrl+C without right-clicking).**

3. **Right-click the cell where you want the copy to go.**

   This opens the contextual menu shown in Figure 20-12.

4. **From the contextual menu, under Paste Options, select Paste Values.**

   It's the second icon from the left — a clipboard labeled 123.

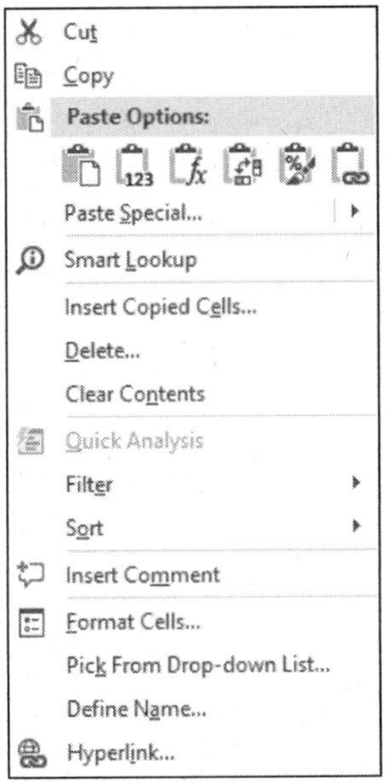

FIGURE 20-12:
When you copy a cell array and then right-click another cell, this menu pops up.

TIP
The contextual menu offers another helpful capability. Every so often in statistical work, you have to take a row of values and relocate them into a column, or vice versa. (I did that in this example.) Excel calls this *transposition*. To transpose, follow the same four steps, but in Step 4, select Transpose. This one is the fourth icon from the left — a clipboard with a two-headed arrow.

5

The Part of Tens

Chapter 21

Ten Statistical and Graphical Tips and Traps

The world of statistics is full of pitfalls, but it's also full of opportunities. Whether you're a user of statistics or someone who has to interpret them, it's possible to fall into the pitfalls. It's also possible to walk around them. Here are ten tips and traps from the areas of hypothesis testing, regression, correlation, and graphs.

Significant Doesn't Always Mean Important

As I say earlier in the book, *significance* is, in many ways, a poorly chosen term. When a statistical test yields a significant result, and the decision is to reject H_0, that doesn't guarantee that the study behind the data is an important one. Statistics can only help decision making about numbers and inferences about the processes that produced them. They can't make those processes important or earth shattering. Importance is something you have to judge for yourself — and no statistical test can do that for you.

Trying to Not Reject a Null Hypothesis Has a Number of Implications

Let me tell you a story: Some years ago, an industrial firm was trying to show that it was finally in compliance with environmental clean-up laws. The company took numerous measurements of the pollution in the body of water surrounding its factory, compared the measurements with a null hypothesis-generated set of expectations, and found that it couldn't reject H_0 with $\alpha = .05$. The measurements didn't differ significantly (there's that word again) from "clean" water.

This, the company claimed, was evidence that it had cleaned up its act. Closer inspection revealed that the data approached significance, but the pollution wasn't quite of a high enough magnitude to reject H_0. Does this mean the company is not polluting?

Not at all. In striving to "prove" a null hypothesis, the company had stacked the deck in favor of itself. It set a high barrier to get over, didn't clear it, and then patted itself on the back.

Every so often, it's appropriate to try and not reject H_0. When you set out on that path, be sure to set a high value of α (about .20–.30), so that small divergences from H_0 cause rejection of H_0. (I discuss this topic in Chapter 10, and I mention it in other parts of the book. I think it's important enough to mention again here.)

Regression Isn't Always Linear

When trying to fit a regression model to a scatterplot, the temptation is to immediately use a line. This is the best-understood regression model, and when you get the hang of it, slopes and intercepts aren't all that daunting.

But linear regression isn't the only kind of regression. It's possible to fit a curve through a scatterplot. I won't kid you: The statistical concepts behind curvilinear regression are more difficult to understand than the concepts behind linear regression.

It's worth taking the time to master those concepts, however. Sometimes, a curve is a much better fit than a line. (This is partly a plug for Chapter 22, where I take you through curvilinear regression — and some of the concepts behind it.)

Extrapolating Beyond a Sample Scatterplot Is a Bad Idea

Whether you're working with linear regression or curvilinear regression, keep in mind that it's inappropriate to generalize beyond the boundaries of the scatterplot.

Suppose you've established a solid predictive relationship between a test of mathematics aptitude and performance in mathematics courses, and your scatterplot covers only a narrow range of mathematics aptitude. You have no way of knowing whether the relationship holds up beyond that range. Predictions outside that range aren't valid.

Your best bet is to expand the scatterplot by testing more people. You might find that the original relationship tells only part of the story.

Examine the Variability Around a Regression Line

Careful analysis of residuals (the differences between observed and predicted values) can tell you a lot about how well the line fits the data. A foundational assumption is that variability around a regression line is the same up and down the line. If it isn't, the model might not be as predictive as you think. If the variability is systematic (greater variability at one end than at the other), curvilinear regression might be more appropriate than linear. The standard error of estimate won't always be the indicator.

A Sample Can Be Too Large

Believe it or not, this sometimes happens with correlation coefficients. A very large sample can make a small correlation coefficient statistically significant. For example, with 100 degrees of freedom and $\alpha = .05$, a correlation coefficient of .195

is cause for rejecting the null hypothesis that the population correlation coefficient is equal to zero.

But what does that correlation coefficient really mean? The coefficient of determination —r^2— is just .038, meaning that the $SS_{Regression}$ is less than 4 percent of the SS_{Total}. (See Chapter 15.) That's a very small association.

Bottom line: When looking at a correlation coefficient, be aware of the sample size. If it's large enough, it can make a trivial association turn out statistically significant. (Hmmm . . . *significance* — there it is again!)

Consumers: Know Your Axes

When you look at a graph, make sure you know what's on each axis. Make sure you understand the units of measure. Do you understand the independent variable? Do you understand the dependent variable? Can you describe each one in your own words? If the answer to any of these questions is "No," you don't understand the graph you're looking at.

When looking at a graph in a TV ad, be very wary if it disappears too quickly, before you can see what's on the axes. The advertiser may be trying to create a lingering false impression about a bogus relationship inside the graph. The graphed relationship might be as valid as that other staple of TV advertising — scientific proof via animated cartoon: Tiny animated scrub brushes cleaning cartoon teeth might not necessarily guarantee whiter teeth for you if you buy the product. (I know that's off-topic, but I had to get it in.)

Graphing a Categorical Variable as Though It's a Quantitative Variable Is Just Wrong

So you're just about ready to compete in the Rock-Paper-Scissors World Series. In preparation for this international tournament, you've tallied all your matches from the past ten years, listing the percentage of times you won when you played each role.

To summarize all the outcomes, you're about to use Excel's graphics capabilities to create a graph. One thing's sure: Whatever your preference rock-paper-scissors-wise, the graph absolutely, positively had better *not* look like Figure 21-1.

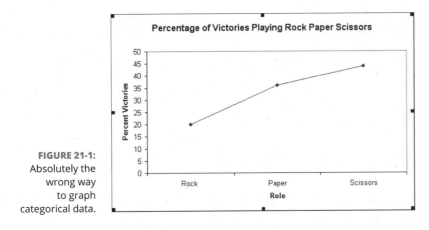

FIGURE 21-1: Absolutely the wrong way to graph categorical data.

So many people create these kinds of graphs — people who should know better. The line in the graph implies continuity from one point to another. With these data, of course, that's impossible. What's between rock and paper? Why are they equal units apart? Why are the three categories in that order? (Can you tell this is my pet peeve?)

Simply put, a line graph is not the proper graph when at least one of your variables is a set of categories. Instead, create a column graph. A pie chart works here, too, because the data are percentages and you have just a few slices. (See Chapter 3 for Yogi Berra's pie-slice guidelines.)

When I wrote the first edition of this book, I whimsically came up with the idea of a Rock-Paper-Scissors World Series for this example. Between then and now, I found out . . . there really is one! (The World RPS Society puts it on.)

Whenever Appropriate, Include Variability in Your Graph

When the points in your graph represent means, make sure that the graph includes the standard error of each mean. This gives the viewer an idea of the variability in the data — which is an important aspect of the data. Here's another plug: In Chapter 22, I show you how to do that in Excel.

Means by themselves don't always tell you the whole story. Take every opportunity to examine variances and standard deviations. You may find some hidden nuggets. Systematic variation — high values of variance associated with large means, for example — might be a clue about a relationship you didn't see before.

Be Careful When Relating Statistics Textbook Concepts to Excel

If you're serious about doing statistical work, you'll probably have occasion to look into a statistics text or two. Bear in mind that the symbols in some areas of statistics aren't standard: For example, some texts use M rather than $\bar{x}$ to represent the sample mean, and some represent a deviation from the mean with just x.

Connecting textbook concepts to Excel's statistical functions can be a challenge because of the texts and because of Excel. Messages in dialog boxes and in Help files might contain symbols other than the ones you read about, or they might use the same symbols but in a different way. This discrepancy might lead you to make an incorrect entry into a parameter in a dialog box, resulting in an error that's hard to trace.

Chapter 22

Ten Things (Twelve, Actually) That Just Didn't Fit in Any Other Chapter

wrote this book to show you all of Excel's statistical capabilities. My intent was to tell you about them in the context of the world of statistics, and I had a definite path in mind.

Some of the capabilities don't neatly fit along that path. I still want you to be aware of them, however, so here they are.

Graphing the Standard Error of the Mean

When you create a graph and your data are means, it's a good idea to include the standard error of each mean in your graph. This gives the viewer an idea of the spread of scores around each mean.

Figure 22-1 gives an example of a situation where this arises. The data are (fictional) test scores for four groups of people. Each column header indicates the amount of preparation time for the eight people within the group. I used Excel's graphics capabilities (refer to Chapter 3) to draw the graph. Because the independent variable is quantitative, a line graph is appropriate. (refer to Chapter 21 for a rant on my biggest peeve.)

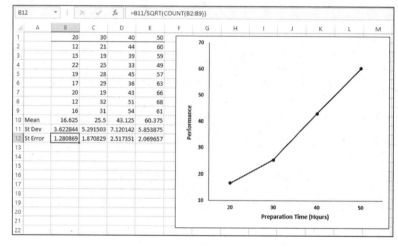

FIGURE 22-1:
Four groups, their means, standard deviations, and standard errors. The graph shows the group means.

For each group, I used AVERAGE to calculate the mean and STDEV.S to calculate the standard deviation. I also calculated the standard error of each mean. I selected cell B12, so the formula box shows you that I calculated the standard error for Column B via this formula:

```
=B11/SQRT(COUNT(B2:B9))
```

The trick is to get each standard error into the graph. In Excel 2013 this is easy to do, and it's different from earlier versions of Excel. Begin by selecting the graph. This causes the Design and Format tabs to appear. Select

Design | Add Chart Element | Error Bars | More Error Bars Options

Figure 22-2 shows what I mean.

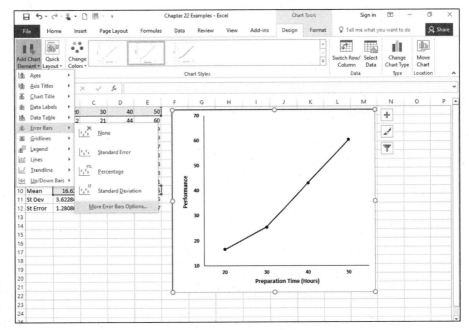

FIGURE 22-2:
The menu path
for inserting
error bars.

WARNING

In the Error Bars menu, you have to be careful. One selection is Standard Error. Avoid it. If you think this selection tells Excel to put the standard error of each mean on the graph, rest assured that Excel has absolutely no idea of what you're talking about. For this selection, Excel calculates the standard error of the set of four means — not the standard error within each group.

More Error Bar Options is the appropriate choice. This opens the Format Error Bars panel. (See Figure 22-3.)

In the Direction area of the panel, select the radio button next to Both, and in the End Style area, select the radio button next to Cap. (You can't see the Direction area in the figure, because I scrolled down to set up the screen shot.)

WARNING

Remember the cautionary note I gave you a moment ago? I have a similar one here. One selection in the Error Amount area is Standard Error. Avoid this one, too. It does not tell Excel to put the standard error of each mean on the graph.

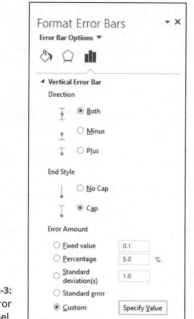

FIGURE 22-3:
The Format Error
Bars panel.

Scroll down to the Error Amount area and select the radio button next to Custom.
This activates the Specify Value button. Click that button to open the Custom Error
Bars dialog box, shown in Figure 22-4. With the cursor in the Positive Error Value
box, select the cell range that holds the standard errors ($B$12:$E$12). Tab to the
Negative Error Value box and do the same.

FIGURE 22-4:
The Custom Error
Bars dialog box.

That Negative Error Value box might give you a little trouble. Make sure that it's
cleared of any default values before you enter the cell range.

TIP

Click OK in the Custom Error Bars dialog box and close the Format Error Bars
dialog box, and the graph looks like Figure 22-5.

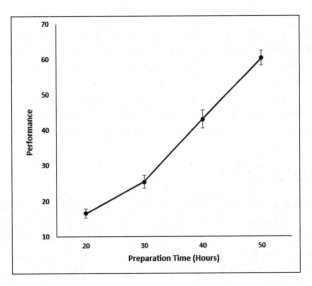

FIGURE 22-5:
The graph of the group means, including the standard error of each mean.

Probabilities and Distributions

Here are some probability-related worksheet functions. Although they're a little on the esoteric side, you might find some use for them.

PROB

If you have a probability distribution of a discrete random variable and you want to find the probability that the variable takes on a particular value, PROB is for you. Figure 22-6 shows the PROB Argument Functions dialog box along with a distribution.

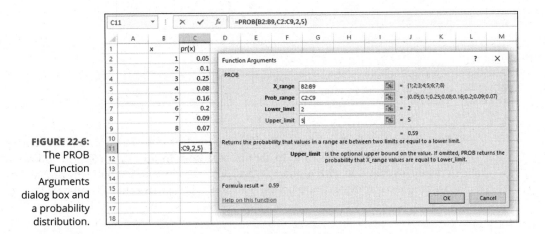

FIGURE 22-6:
The PROB Function Arguments dialog box and a probability distribution.

You supply the random variable (X_range), the probabilities (Prob_range), a lower limit, and an upper limit. PROB returns the probability that the random variable takes on a value between those limits (inclusive).

TIP

If you leave Upper Limit blank, PROB returns the probability of the value you gave for the lower limit. If you leave Lower Limit blank, PROB returns the probability of obtaining, at most, the upper limit (for example, the cumulative probability).

WEIBULL.DIST

This is a probability density function that's mostly applicable to engineering. It serves as a model for the time until a physical system fails. As engineers know, in some systems, the number of failures stays the same over time because shocks to the system cause failure. In others, like some microelectronic components, the number of failures decreases with time. In still others, wear-and-tear increases failures with time.

The Weibull distribution's two parameters allow it to reflect all these possibilities. One parameter, Alpha, determines how wide or narrow the distribution is. The other, Beta, determines where it's centered on the x-axis.

The Weibull probability density function is a rather complicated equation. Thanks to Excel, you don't have to worry about it. Figure 22-7 shows WEIBULL.DIST's Function Arguments dialog box.

Function Arguments		?	×
WEIBULL.DIST			
X	4000	=	4000
Alpha	.75	=	0.75
Beta	2000	=	2000
Cumulative	TRUE	=	TRUE
		=	0.813959862

Returns the Weibull distribution.

Cumulative is a logical value: for the cumulative distribution function, use TRUE; for the probability mass function, use FALSE.

Formula result = 0.813959862

Help on this function | OK | Cancel

FIGURE 22-7: The WEIBULL. DIST Function Arguments dialog box.

The dialog box in the figure answers the kind of question a product engineer would ask: Assume the time to failure of a bulb in an LCD projector follows a Weibull distribution with Alpha = .75 and Beta = 2,000 hours. What's the probability the bulb lasts at most 4,000 hours? The dialog box shows that the answer is .814.

Drawing Samples

Excel's Sampling data analysis tool is helpful for creating samples. You can tailor it in a couple of ways. If you're trying to put a focus group together and you have to select the participants from a pool of people, you could assign each one a number and have the Sampling tool select your group.

One way to select is *periodically.* You supply n, and Excel samples every nth number. The other way to select is *randomly.* You supply the number of individuals you want randomly selected and Excel does the rest.

Figure 22-8 presents the Sampling dialog box, three groups I had it sample from, and two columns of output.

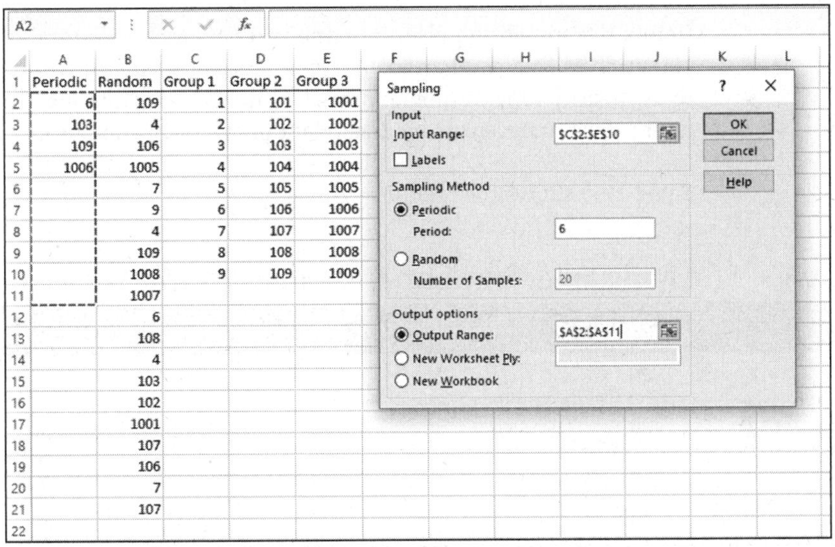

FIGURE 22-8:
The Sampling
data-analysis tool
dialog box,
sampled groups,
and results.

The first output column, Column A, shows the results of periodic sampling with a period of 6. Sampling begins with the sixth score in Group 1. Excel then counts out scores and delivers the sixth, and goes through that process again until it finishes in the last group. The periodic sampling process, as you can see, doesn't recycle. I supplied an output range up to cell A11, but Excel stopped after four numbers.

The second output column, Column B, shows the results of random sampling. I asked for 20 and that's what I got. If you closely examine the numbers in Column B, you'll see that the random sampling process can select a number more than once.

WARNING

Beware of a little quirk: The Labels check box seems to have no effect. When I specified an input range that includes C1, D1, and E1 and selected the Labels check box, I received this error message: `Sampling - Input range contains non-numeric data`. Not a showstopper, but a little annoying.

Testing Independence: The True Use of CHISQ.TEST

In Chapter 20, I show you how to use `CHISQ.TEST` to test the goodness of fit of a model to a set of data. In that chapter, I also warn you about the pitfalls of using this function in that context, and I mention that it's really intended for something else.

Here's the something else. Imagine you've surveyed a total of 200 people. Each person lives in a rural area, an urban area, or a suburb. Your survey asked them their favorite type of movie: drama, comedy, or animation. You want to know if their movie preference is independent of the environment in which they live.

Table 22-1 shows the results.

TABLE 22-1   **Living Environment and Movie Preference**

	Drama	Comedy	Animation	Total
Rural	40	30	10	80
Urban	20	30	20	70
Suburban	10	20	20	50
Total	70	80	50	200

The number in each cell represents the number of people in the environment, indicated in the row, who prefer the type of movie indicated in the column.

Do the data show that preference is independent of environment? This calls for a hypothesis test:

H_0: Movie preference is independent of environment

H_1: Not H_0

$\alpha = .05$

To get this done, you have to know what to expect if the two are independent. Then you can compare the data with the expected numbers and see whether they match. If they do, you can't reject H_0. If they don't, you reject H_0.

Concepts from probability help determine the expected data. In Chapter 18, I tell you that if two events are independent, you multiply their probabilities to find the probability that they occur together. Here, you can treat the tabled numbers as proportions, and the proportions as probabilities.

For example, in your sample, the probability is 80/200 that a person is from a rural environment. The probability is 70/200 that a person prefers drama. What's the probability that a person is in the category "rural and likes drama"? If the environment and preference are independent, that's (80/200) × (70/200). To turn that probability into an expected number of people, you multiply it by the total number of people in the sample: 200. So the expected number of people is (80 × 70)/200, which is 28. In general,

$$\text{Expected Number in a Cell} = \frac{\text{RowTotal} \times \text{ColumnTotal}}{\text{Total}}$$

After you have the expected numbers, you compare them to the observed numbers (the data) via this formula:

$$\chi^2 = \sum \left[\frac{\left(\text{Observed-Expected}\right)^2}{\text{Expected}} \right]$$

You test the result against a χ^2 (chi-square) distribution with df = (Number of Rows − 1) × (Number of Columns − 1), which in this case comes out to 4.

The `CHISQ.TEST` worksheet function performs the test. You supply the observed numbers and the expected numbers, and `CHISQ.TEST` returns the probability that a χ^2 at least as high as the result from the preceding formula could have resulted if the two types of categories are independent. If the probability is small (less than .05), reject H_0. If not, don't reject. `CHISQ.TEST` doesn't return a value of χ^2; it just returns the probability (under a χ^2 distribution with the correct df).

Figure 22-9 shows a worksheet with both the observed data and the expected numbers, along with CHISQ.TEST's Function Arguments dialog box. Before I ran `CHISQ.TEST`, I attached the name Observed to C3:E5, and the name Expected to C10:E12. (If you don't know how to do this, read Chapter 2.)

The figure shows that I've entered Observed into the Actual_range box, and Expected into the Expected_range box. The dialog box shows a very small probability, .00068, so the decision is to reject H_0. The data are consistent with the idea that movie preference is not independent of environment.

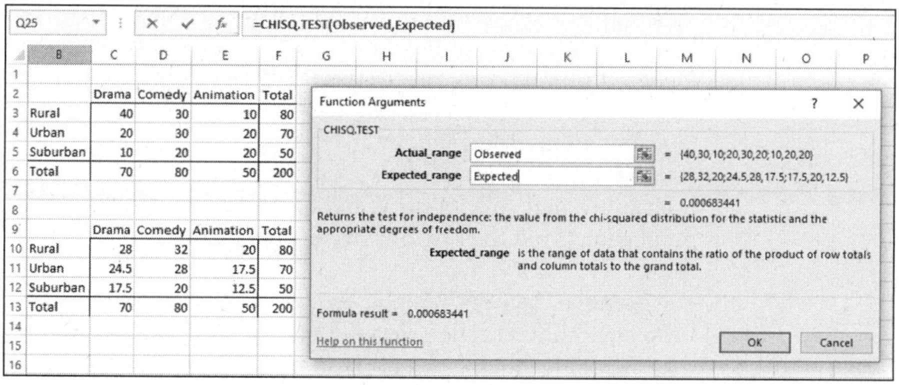

=CHISQ.TEST(Observed,Expected)

	Drama	Comedy	Animation	Total
Rural	40	30	10	80
Urban	20	30	20	70
Suburban	10	20	20	50
Total	70	80	50	200

	Drama	Comedy	Animation	Total
Rural	28	32	20	80
Urban	24.5	28	17.5	70
Suburban	17.5	20	12.5	50
Total	70	80	50	200

Function Arguments

CHISQ.TEST

Actual_range Observed = {40,30,10;20,30,20;10,20,20}

Expected_range Expected = {28,32,20;24.5,28,17.5;17.5,20,12.5}

= 0.000683441

Returns the test for independence: the value from the chi-squared distribution for the statistic and the appropriate degrees of freedom.

Expected_range is the range of data that contains the ratio of the product of row totals and column totals to the grand total.

Formula result = 0.000683441

Help on this function   OK   Cancel

FIGURE 22-9:
The CHISQ.TEST Function Arguments dialog box, with observed data and expected numbers.

Logarithmica Esoterica

TECHNICAL STUFF

The functions in this section are *really* out there. Unless you're a tech-head, you'll probably never use them. I present them for completeness. You might run into them while you're wandering through Excel's statistical functions, and wonder what they are.

They're based on what mathematicians call *natural logarithms,* which in turn are based on *e,* that constant I use at various points throughout this book. I begin with a brief discussion of logarithms, and then I turn to *e.*

What is a logarithm?

Plain and simple, a logarithm is an *exponent* — a power to which you raise a number. In the equation

$$10^2 = 100$$

2 is an exponent. Does that mean that 2 is also a logarithm? Well . . . yes. In terms of logarithms,

$$\log_{10} 100 = 2$$

That's really just another way of saying $10^2 = 100$. Mathematicians read it as "the logarithm of 100 to the base 10 equals 2." It means that if you want to raise 10 to some power to get 100, that power is 2.

How about 1,000? As you know

$$10^3 = 1000$$

so

$$\log_{10} 1000 = 3$$

How about 453? Uh . . . Hmmm . . . That's like trying to solve

$$10^x = 453$$

What could that answer possibly be? 10^2 means 10×10, and that gives you 100. 10^3 means $10 \times 10 \times 10$ and that's 1,000. But 453?

Here's where you have to think outside the dialog box. You have to imagine exponents that aren't whole numbers. I know, I know . . . How can you multiply a number by itself a fraction at a time? If you could, somehow, the number in that 453 equation would have to be between 2 (which gets you to 100) and 3 (which gets you to 1,000).

In the 16th century, mathematician John Napier showed how to do it, and logarithms were born. Why did Napier bother with this? One reason is that it was a great help to astronomers. Astronomers have to deal with numbers that are, well, astronomical. Logarithms ease computational strain in a couple of ways. One way is to substitute small numbers for large ones: The logarithm of 1,000,000 is 6 and the logarithm of 100,000,000 is 8. Also, working with logarithms opens up a helpful set of computational shortcuts. Before calculators and computers appeared on the scene, this was a very big deal.

Incidentally,

$$10^{2.6560982} = 453$$

meaning that

$$\log_{10} 453 = 2.6560982$$

You can use Excel to check that out if you don't believe me. Select a cell and type

```
=LOG(453,10)
```

Press Enter and watch what happens. Then just to close the loop, reverse the process. If your selected cell is — let's say — D3, select another cell and type

```
=POWER(10,D3)
```

or

```
=10^D3
```

Either way, the result is 453.

Ten, the number that's raised to the exponent, is called the *base*. Because it's also the base of our number system and we're all familiar with it, logarithms of base 10 are called *common logarithms*.

Does that mean you can have other bases? Absolutely. *Any* number (except 0 or 1 or a negative number) can be a base. For example,

$$6.4^2 = 40.96$$

So

$$\log_{6.4} 40.96 = 2$$

If you ever see log without a base, base 10 is understood, so

$$\log 100 = 2$$

In terms of bases, one number is special. . . .

What is *e*?

Which brings me to *e*, a constant that's all about growth. Before I get back to logarithms, I'll tell you about *e*.

Imagine the princely sum of $1 deposited in a bank account. Suppose the interest rate is 2 percent a year. (Good luck with *that*.) If it's simple interest, the bank adds $.02 every year, and in 50 years you have $2.

If it's compound interest, at the end of 50 years you have $(1 + .02)^{50}$ — which is just a bit more than $2.68, assuming the bank compounds the interest once a year.

Of course, if the bank compounds it twice a year, each payment is $.01, and after 50 years the bank has compounded it 100 times. That gives you $(1 + .01)^{100}$, or just over $2.70. What about compounding it four times a year? After 50 years — 200 compoundings — you have $(1 + .005)^{200}$, which results in the don't-spend-it-all-in-one-place amount of $2.71 and a tiny bit more.

Focusing on "just a bit more" and a "tiny bit more," and taking it to extremes, after one hundred thousand compoundings you have $2.718268. After one hundred million, you have $2.718282.

If you could get the bank to compound many more times in those 50 years, your sum of money approaches a *limit* — an amount it gets ever so close to, but never quite reaches. That limit is *e*.

The way I set up the example, the rule for calculating the amount is

$$\left(1+\left(1/n\right)\right)^n$$

where n represents the number of payments. Two cents is 1/50th of a dollar and I specified 50 years — 50 payments. Then I specified two payments a year (and each year's payments have to add up to 2 percent) so that in 50 years you have 100 payments of 1/100th of a dollar, and so on.

To see this in action, enter numbers into a column of a spreadsheet as I have in Figure 22-10. In cells C2 through C20, I have the numbers 1 through 10 and then selected steps through one hundred million. In D2, I put this formula

```
=(1+(1/C2))^C2
```

and then autofilled to D20. The entry in D20 is very close to *e*.

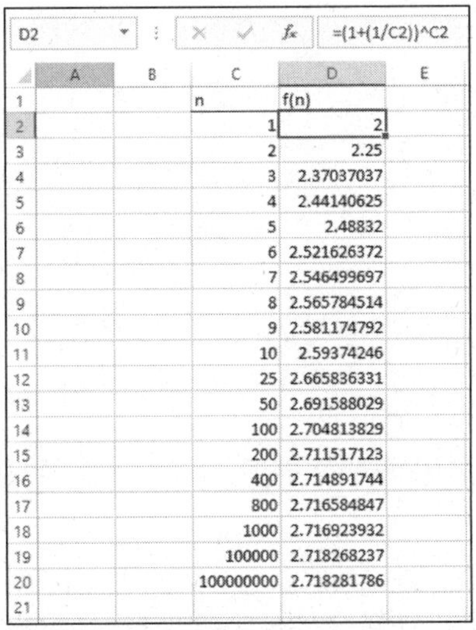
D2 =(1+(1/C2))^C2

	A	B	C	D	E
1			n	f(n)	
2			1	2	
3			2	2.25	
4			3	2.37037037	
5			4	2.44140625	
6			5	2.48832	
7			6	2.521626372	
8			7	2.546499697	
9			8	2.565784514	
10			9	2.581174792	
11			10	2.59374246	
12			25	2.665836331	
13			50	2.691588029	
14			100	2.704813829	
15			200	2.711517123	
16			400	2.714891744	
17			800	2.716584847	
18			1000	2.716923932	
19			100000	2.718268237	
20			100000000	2.718281786	
21					

FIGURE 22-10: Getting to *e*.

Mathematicians can tell you another way to get to *e:*

$$e = 1 + \frac{1}{1!} + \frac{1}{2!} + \frac{1}{3!} + \frac{1}{4!} + \ldots$$

Those exclamation points signify *factorial*. 1! = 1, 2! = 2 X 1, 3! = 3 X 2 X 1. (For more on factorials, refer to Chapter 16.)

Excel helps visualize this one, too. Figure 22-11 lays out a spreadsheet with selected numbers up to 170 in Column C. In D2, I put this formula:

```
=1+ 1/FACT(C2)
```

and, as the Formula bar in the figure shows, in D3 I put this one:

```
=D2 +1/ FACT(C3)
```

Then I autofilled up to D17. The entry in D17 is very close to e. In fact, from D11 on, you see no change, even if you increase the number of decimal places.

Why did I stop at 170? Because that takes Excel to the max. At 171, you get an error message.

So *e* is associated with growth. Its value is 2.781828 . . . The three dots mean you never quite get to the exact value (like π, the constant that enables you to find the area of a circle).

This number pops up in all kinds of places. It's in the formula for the normal distribution (see Chapter 8), and it's in distributions I discuss in Chapter 17. Many natural phenomena are related to *e*.

It's so important that scientists, mathematicians, and business analysts use it as the base for logarithms. Logarithms to the base *e* are called *natural logarithms*. A natural logarithm is abbreviated as *ln*.

Table 22-2 presents some comparisons (rounded to three decimal places) between common logarithms and natural logarithms:

TABLE 22-2

Some Common Logarithms (Log) and Natural Logarithms (Ln)

Number	Log	Ln
e	0.434	1.000
10	1.000	2.303
50	1.699	3.912
100	2.000	4.605
453	2.656	6.116
1000	3.000	6.908

One more thing. In many formulas and equations, it's often necessary to raise *e* to a power. Sometimes the power is a fairly complicated mathematical expression. Because superscripts are usually printed in small font, it can be a strain to have to constantly read them. To ease the eyestrain, mathematicians have invented a special notation: *exp*. Whenever you see *exp* followed by something in parentheses, it means to raise *e* to the power of whatever's in the parentheses. For example,

$$\exp(1.6) = e^{1.6} = 4.953$$

Excel's EXP function does that calculation for you.

Speaking of raising *e*, when Google, Inc., filed its IPO, it said it wanted to raise $2,718,281,828, which is *e* times a billion dollars rounded to the nearest dollar.

On to the Excel functions.

LOGNORM.DIST

A random variable is said to be *lognormally* distributed if its natural logarithm is normally distributed. Maybe the name is a little misleading, because I just said *log* means "common logarithm" and *ln* means "natural logarithm."

Unlike the normal distribution, the lognormal can't have a negative number as a possible value for the variable. Also unlike the normal, the lognormal is not symmetric — it's skewed to the right.

Like the Weibull distribution I describe earlier, engineers use it to model the breakdown of physical systems — particularly of the wear-and-tear variety. Here's where the large-numbers-to-small numbers property of logarithms comes into play. When huge numbers of hours figure into a system's life cycle, it's easier to think about the distribution of logarithms than the distribution of the hours.

Excel's LOGNORM.DIST works with the lognormal distribution. You specify a value, a mean, and a standard deviation for the lognormal. LOGNORM.DIST returns the probability that the variable is, at most, that value.

For example, FarKlempt Robotics, Inc., has gathered extensive hours-to-failure data on a universal joint component that goes into its robots. The company finds that hours-to-failure is lognormally distributed with a mean of 10 and a standard deviation of 2.5. What is the probability that this component fails in, at most, 10,000 hours?

Figure 22-12 shows the LOGNORM.DIST Function Arguments dialog box for this example. In the X box, I entered ln(10000). I entered 10 into the Mean box, 2.5 into the Standard_dev box, and TRUE into the Cumulative box. The dialog box shows the answer, .000929 (and some more decimals). If I enter FALSE into the Cumulative box, the function returns the probability density (the height of the function) at the value in the X box.

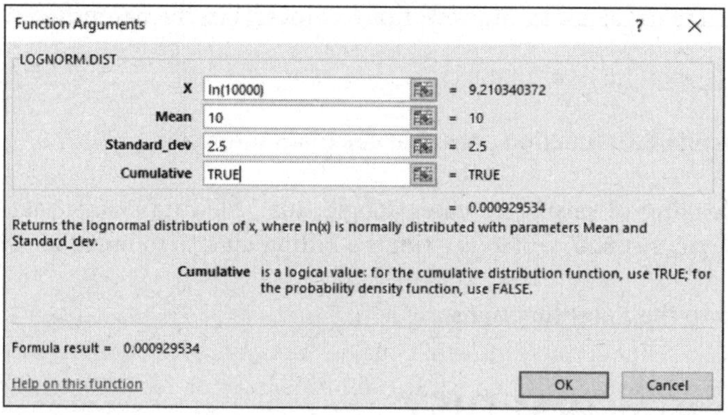

FIGURE 22-12:
The LOGNORM.
DIST Function
Arguments
dialog box.

LOGNORM.INV

LOGNORM.INV turns LOGNORM.DIST around. You supply a probability, a mean, and a standard deviation for a lognormal distribution. LOGNORM.INV gives you the value of the random variable that cuts off that probability.

To find the value that cuts off .001 in the preceding example's distribution, I used the LOGNORM.INV Function Arguments dialog box shown in Figure 22-13. With the indicated entries, the dialog box shows that the value is 9.722 (and more decimals).

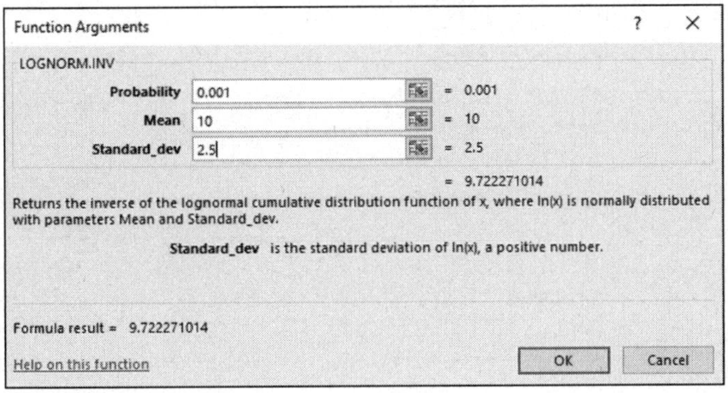

LOGNORM.INV

Probability	0.001	= 0.001
Mean	10	= 10
Standard_dev	2.5	= 2.5

= 9.722271014

Returns the inverse of the lognormal cumulative distribution function of x, where ln(x) is normally distributed with parameters Mean and Standard_dev.

Standard_dev is the standard deviation of ln(x), a positive number.

Formula result = 9.722271014

Help on this function   OK   Cancel

FIGURE 22-13:
The LOGNORM.
INV Function
Arguments
dialog box.

By the way, in terms of hours, that's 16,685 — just for .001.

Array Function: LOGEST

In Chapter 14, I tell you all about linear regression. It's also possible to have a relationship between two variables that's curvilinear rather than linear.

The equation for a line that fits a scatterplot is

$$y' = a + bx$$

One way to fit a curve through a scatterplot is with this equation:

$$y' = ae^{bx}$$

LOGEST estimates a and b for this curvilinear equation. Figure 22-14 shows the LOGEST Function Arguments dialog box and the data for this example. It also shows an array for the results. Before using this function, I attached the name x to B2:B12 and y to C2:C12.

Here are the steps for this function:

1. **With the data entered, select a five-row-by-two-column array of cells for LOGEST's results.**

    I selected F4:G8.

2. **From the Statistical Functions menu, select LOGEST to open the Function Arguments dialog box for LOGEST.**

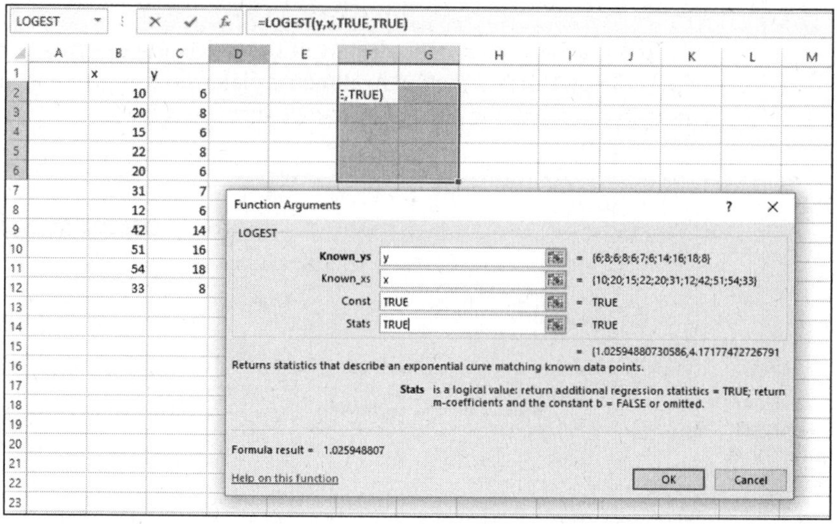

FIGURE 22-14:
The Function
Arguments
dialog box for
LOGEST, along
with the data and
the selected array
for the results.

3. **In the Function Arguments dialog box, type the appropriate values for the arguments.**

   In the Known_y's box, type the cell range that holds the scores for the *y*-variable. For this example, that's *y* (the name I gave to C2:C12).

   In the Known_x's box, type the cell range that holds the scores for the *x*-variable. For this example, it's *x* (the name I gave to B2:B12).

   In the Const box, the choices are TRUE (or leave it blank) to calculate the value of *a* in the curvilinear equation I showed you or FALSE to set *a* to 1. I typed TRUE.

   The dialog box uses *b* where I use *a*. No set of symbols is standard.

   In the Stats box, the choices are TRUE to return the regression statistics in addition to *a* and *b*, FALSE (or leave it blank) to return just *a* and *b*. I typed TRUE.

   Again, the dialog box uses *b* where I use *a* and *m-coefficient* where I use *b*.

4. ***Important:* Do *not* click OK. Because this is an array function, press Ctrl+Shift+Enter to put LOGEST's answers into the selected array.**

Figure 22-15 shows LOGEST's results. They're not labeled in any way, so I added the labels for you in the worksheet. The left column gives you the exp(*b*) (more on that in a moment), standard error of *b*, R Square, F, and the SS$_{regression}$. The right column provides *a*, standard error of *a*, standard error of estimate, degrees of freedom, and SS$_{residual}$. For more on these statistics, refer to Chapters 14 and 15.

⊿	A	B	C	D	E	F	G	H
1		x	y					
2		10	6		exp(slope)	1.025948807	4.1717747	intercept
3		20	8		st error of slope	0.00310866	0.0986791	st error of intercept
4		15	6		R Square	0.882981321	0.1506221	st error of estimate
5		22	8		F	67.91079792	9	df
6		20	6		SSregression	1.540693278	0.2041831	SSresidual
7		31	7					
8		12	6					
9		42	14					
10		51	16					
11		54	18					
12		33	8					
13								

FIGURE 22-15:
LOGEST's results in the selected array.

TIP

About exp(b). LOGEST, unfortunately, doesn't return the value of b — the exponent for the curvilinear equation. To find the exponent, you have to calculate the natural logarithm of what it does return. Applying Excel's LN worksheet function here gives 0.0256 as the value of the exponent.

So the curvilinear regression equation for the sample data is

$$y' = 4.1718e^{0.0256x}$$

or in that exp notation I told you about:

$$y' = 4.1718\exp(0.0256x)$$

TIP

A good way to help yourself understand all of this is to use Excel's graphics capabilities to create a scatterplot. (See Chapter 3.) Then right-click on a data point in the plot and select Add Trendline from the pop-up menu. This adds a linear trendline to the scatterplot and, more importantly, opens the Format Trendline panel (see Figure 22-16). Select the radio button next to Exponential, as I've done in the figure. Also, as I've done in the figure, toward the bottom of the panel, select the check box next to Display Equation on Chart.

Click Close, and you have a scatterplot complete with curve and equation. I reformatted mine in several ways to make it look clearer on the printed page. Figure 22-17 shows the result.

Array Function: GROWTH

GROWTH is curvilinear regression's answer to TREND. (See Chapter 14.) You can use this function in two ways: to predict a set of y-values for the x-values in your sample or to predict a set of y-values for a new set of x-values.

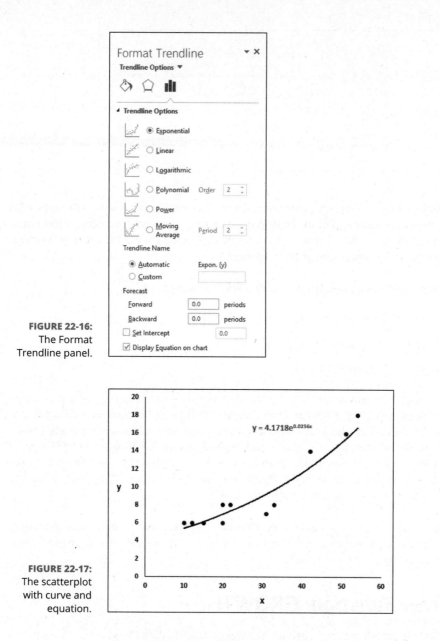

FIGURE 22-16:
The Format
Trendline panel.

FIGURE 22-17:
The scatterplot
with curve and
equation.

Predicting y's for the x's in your sample

Figure 22-18 shows GROWTH set up to calculate y's for the x's I already have. I included the Formula bar in this screen shot so that you can see what the formula looks like for this use of GROWTH.

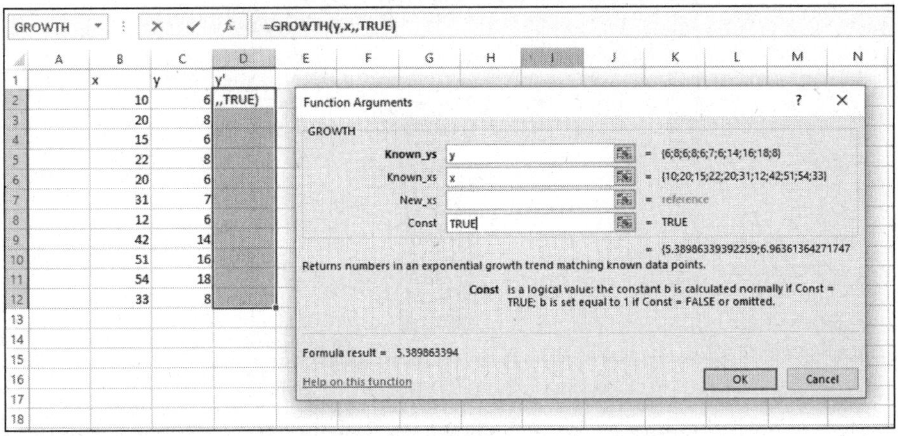

FIGURE 22-18:
The Function Arguments dialog box for GROWTH, along with the sample data. GROWTH is set up to predict x's for the sample y's.

Here are the steps:

1. **With the data entered, select a cell range for GROWTH's answers.**

   I selected D2:D12 to put the predicted y's right next to the sample y's.

2. **From the Statistical Functions menu, select GROWTH to open the Function Arguments dialog box for GROWTH.**

3. **In the Function Arguments dialog box, type the appropriate values for the arguments.**

   In the Known_y's box, type the cell range that holds the scores for the y-variable. For this example, that's y (the name I gave to C2:C12).

   In the Known_x's box, type the cell range that holds the scores for the x-variable. For this example, it's x (the name I gave to B2:B12).

   I'm not calculating values for new x's here, so I leave the New_x's box blank.

   In the Const box, the choices are TRUE (or leave it blank) to calculate a, or FALSE to set a to 1. I entered TRUE. (I really don't know why you'd enter FALSE.) Once again, the dialog box uses b where I use a.

4. *Important:* **Do *not* click OK. Because this is an array function, press Ctrl+Shift+Enter to put GROWTH's answers into the selected column.**

   Figure 22-19 shows the answers in D2:D12.

Predicting a new set of y's for a new set of x's

Here, I use GROWTH to predict y's for a new set of x's. Figure 22-20 shows GROWTH set up for this. In addition to the array named x and the array named y, I defined New_x as the name for B15:B22, the cell range that holds the new set of x's.

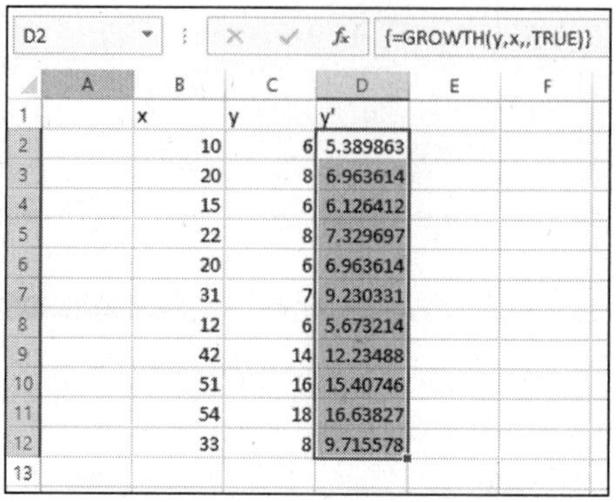

FIGURE 22-19:
The results
of GROWTH:
Predicted y's for
the sample x's.

Figure 22-20 also shows the selected array of cells for the results. Once again, I included the Formula bar to show you the formula for this use of the function.

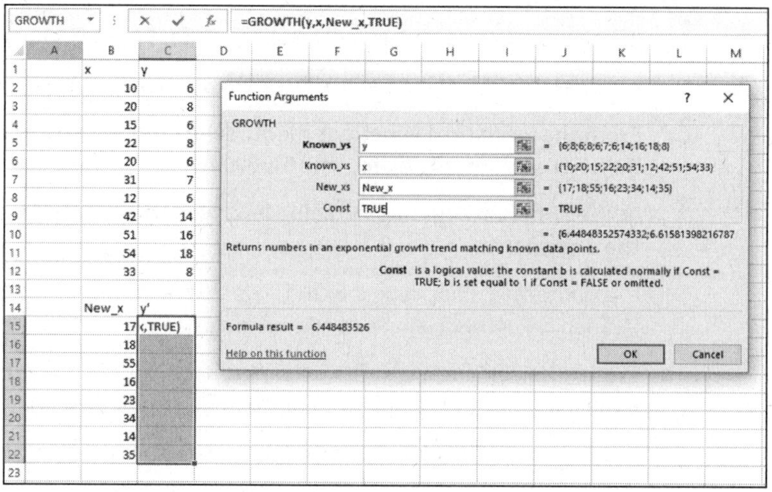

FIGURE 22-20:
The Function
Arguments dialog
box for GROWTH,
along with data.
GROWTH is set up
to predict y's for a
new set of x's.

To do this, follow these steps:

1. **With the data entered, select a cell range for GROWTH's answers.**

   I selected C15:C22.

2. **From the Statistical Functions menu, select GROWTH to open the Function Arguments dialog box for GROWTH.**

3. **In the Function Arguments dialog box, type the appropriate values for the arguments.**

   In the Known_y's box, enter the cell range that holds the scores for the *y*-variable. For this example, that's *y* (the name I gave to C2:C12).

   In the Known_x's box, enter the cell range that holds the scores for the *x*-variable. For this example, it's *x* (the name I gave to B2:B12).

   In the New_x's box, enter the cell range that holds the new scores for the *x*-variable. That's New_*x* (the name I gave to B15:B22).

   In the Const box, the choices are TRUE (or leave it blank) to calculate *a*, or FALSE to set *a* to 1. I typed TRUE. (Again, I really don't know why you'd enter FALSE.)

4. *Important:* **Do *not* click OK. Because this is an array function, press Ctrl+Shift+ Enter to put GROWTH's answers into the selected column.**

   Figure 22-21 shows the answers in C15:C22.

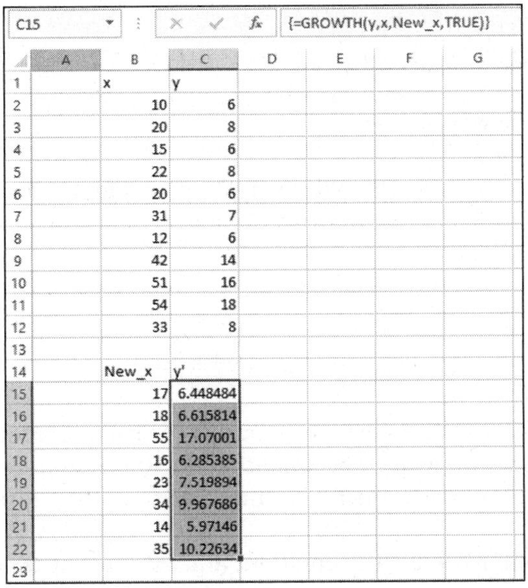

FIGURE 22-21:
The results
of GROWTH:
Predicted *y*'s for a
new set of *x*'s.

	A	B	C	D	E	F	G
		x	y				
1							
2		10	6				
3		20	8				
4		15	6				
5		22	8				
6		20	6				
7		31	7				
8		12	6				
9		42	14				
10		51	16				
11		54	18				
12		33	8				
13							
14		New_x	y'				
15		17	6.448484				
16		18	6.615814				
17		55	17.07001				
18		16	6.285385				
19		23	7.519894				
20		34	9.967686				
21		14	5.97146				
22		35	10.22634				
23							

C15 f_x {=GROWTH(y,x,New_x,TRUE)}

The logs of Gamma

Sounds like a science fiction thriller, doesn't it?

The GAMMA function I discuss in Chapter 19 extends factorials to the realm of non-whole numbers. Because factorials are involved, the numbers can get very large, very quickly. Logarithms are an antidote.

In an earlier version, Excel provided GAMMALN for finding the natural log of the gamma function value of the argument x. (Even before it provided GAMMA.)

In Excel 2013, GAMMALN receives a facelift and (presumably) greater precision. The new worksheet function is GAMMALN.PRECISE.

So the new function looks like this:

```
=GAMMALN.PRECISE(5.3)
```

It's equivalent to

```
=LN(GAMMA(5.3))
```

The answer, by the way, is 3.64.

Just so you know, I expanded to 14 decimal places and found no difference between GAMMALN and GAMMALN.PRECISE for this example.

Sorting Data

In behavioral science experiments, researchers typically present a variety of tasks for participants to complete. The conditions of the tasks are the independent variables. Measures of performance on these tasks are the dependent variables.

For methodological reasons, the conditions and order of the tasks are randomized so that different people complete the tasks in different orders. The data reflect these orders. To analyze the data, it becomes necessary to sort everyone's data into the same order.

The worksheet in Figure 22-22 shows data for one participant in one experiment. Width and Distance are independent variables; Moves and Errors are dependent variables. The objective is to sort the rows in increasing order of width and then in increasing order of distance.

	A	B	C	D	E	F
1		Width	Distance	Moves	Errors	
2		60	500	18	0	
3		30	1000	13	0	
4		240	500	23	1	
5		60	1000	15	1	
6		120	500	20	1	
7		240	1000	18	1	
8		30	500	12	2	
9		120	1000	16	1	
10						

FIGURE 22-22: Unsorted data.

Here's how to do it:

1. **Select the cell range that holds the data.**

   For this example, that's B2:E9.

2. **Select Data | Sort.**

   This opens the Sort dialog box, shown in Figure 22-23. When the dialog box opens, it shows just one row under Column. The row is labeled Sort By. Because I have headers in my data, I checked the box next to My Data Has Headers.

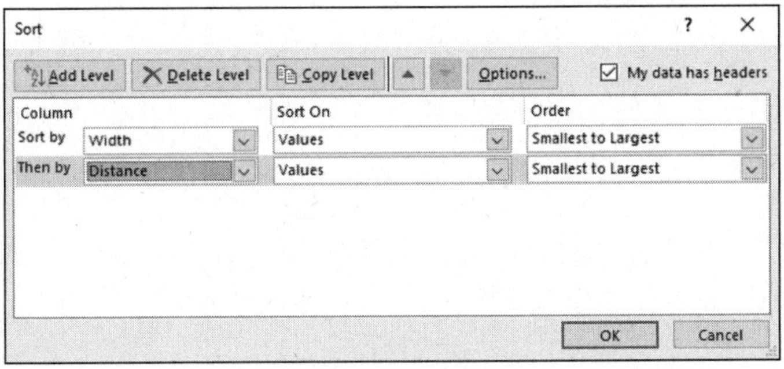

FIGURE 22-23: The Sort dialog box.

3. **From the drop-down menu in the box next to Sort By, select the first variable to sort by. Adjust Sort On and Order.**

   I selected Width and kept the default conditions for Sort On (Values) and Order (Smallest to Largest).

4. **Click the Add Level button.**

   This opens another row labeled Then By.

5. **In the drop-down menu in the box next to Then By, select the next variable to sort by, then adjust Sort On and Order.**

   I selected Distance and kept the default conditions.

6. **After the last variable, click OK.**

   The sorted data appear in Figure 22-24.

	A	B	C	D	E	F
1		Width	Distance	Moves	Errors	
2		30	500	12	2	
3		30	1000	13	0	
4		60	500	18	0	
5		60	1000	15	1	
6		120	500	20	1	
7		120	1000	16	1	
8		240	500	23	1	
9		240	1000	18	1	
10						

FIGURE 22-24: The data sorted by width and distance.

Appendix A

When Your Worksheet Is a Database

Excel's main function in life is to perform calculations. As the chapters in this book show, many of those calculations revolve around built-in statistical capabilities.

You can also set up a worksheet to store information in something like a database, although Excel is not as sophisticated as a dedicated database package. Excel offers database functions that are much like its statistical functions, so I thought I'd familiarize you with them.

Introducing Excel Databases

Strictly speaking, Excel provides a *data list*. This is an array of worksheet cells into which you enter related data in a uniform format. You organize the data in columns, and you put a name at the top of each column. In database terminology, each named column is a *field*. Each row is a separate *record*.

This type of structure is useful for keeping inventories, as long as they're not overly huge. You wouldn't use an Excel database for recordkeeping in a warehouse or a large corporation. For a small business, however, it might fit the bill.

The Satellites database

Figure A-1 shows an example. This is an inventory of the classic satellites in our solar system. By *classic*, I mean that astronomers discovered most of them before the 20th century, via conventional telescopes. The three 20th century entries are so dim that astronomers discovered them by examining photographic plates. Today's supertelescopes and space probes have revealed many more satellites that I didn't include.

	A	B	C	D	E	F	G	H
1		Name	Planet	Orbital_Period_Days	Average_Distance_X_1000_km	Year_Discovered	Discoverer	
2		*io	Saturn	1.26	>150	>1877	Galileo	
3				>20			Cassini	
4								
5								
6								
7								
8								
9								
10		Name	Planet	Orbital_Period_Days	Average_Distance_X_1000_km	Year_Discovered	Discoverer	
11		Amalthea	Jupiter	0.50	181.30	1892	Barnard	
12		Ariel	Uranus	2.52	191.24	1851	Lassell	
13		Callisto	Jupiter	16.69	1883.00	1610	Galileo	
14		Charon	Pluto	6.39	19.64	1978	Christy	
15		Deimos	Mars	1.26	23.46	1877	Hall	
16		Dione	Saturn	2.74	377.40	1684	Cassini	
17		Enceladus	Saturn	1.37	238.02	1789	Herschel	
18		Europa	Jupiter	3.55	670.90	1610	Galileo	
19		Ganymede	Jupiter	7.15	1070.00	1610	Galileo	
20		Hyperion	Saturn	21.28	1481.00	1848	Bond	
21		Iapetus	Saturn	79.33	3561.30	1671	Cassini	
22		Io	Jupiter	1.77	421.60	1610	Galileo	
23		Mimas	Saturn	9.42	185.52	1789	Herschel	
24		Miranda	Uranus	1.41	129.78	1948	Kuiper	
25		Moon	Earth	27.32	384.40	N/A	N/A	
26		Nereid	Neptune	360.14	5513.40	1949	Kuiper	
27		Oberon	Uranus	13.46	582.50	1787	Herschel	
28		Phobos	Mars	0.32	9.38	1877	Hall	
29		Phoebe	Saturn	-550.48	12952.00	1898	Pickering	
30		Rhea	Saturn	4.52	527.04	1672	Cassini	
31		Tethys	Saturn	1.89	294.66	1684	Cassini	
32		Titan	Saturn	15.94	1221.85	1655	Huygens	
33		Titania	Uranus	8.71	435.84	1787	Herschel	
34		Triton	Neptune	-5.88	354.80	1846	Lassell	
35		Umbriel	Uranus	4.14	265.97	1851	Lassell	

FIGURE A-1:
The Satellites database.

The database is in cells B10:G35. I defined Satellites as the name of this cell range. Notice that I included the field names in the range. (Reread Chapter 2 if you don't remember how to name a cell range.)

The Name field provides the name of the satellite; the Planet field indicates the planet around which the satellite revolves.

Orbital_Period_Days shows how long it takes for a satellite to make a complete revolution around its planet. Our moon, for example, takes a little over 27 days. A couple of records have negative values in this field. That means they revolve around the planet in a direction opposite to the planet's rotation.

Average Distance_X_1000_km is the average distance from the planet to the satellite in thousands of kilometers. The last two fields provide the year of discovery and the astronomer who discovered the satellite. For our moon, of course, those two are unknown.

REMEMBER

After you label each field, you attach a name to each cell that holds a field name. *Important point:* The range for each name is just the cell that holds the field name, *not* the whole column of data. So here, I define Name as the name of the cell labeled Name.

Okay, I worked really hard to set up the premise for the preceding sentence. Here are two examples that are easier to follow: I define Planet as the name of cell C10, and Orbital_Period_Days as the name of D10, and so on. Now I can use these field names in Excel's database formulas.

The criteria range

I copied the column headers — excuse me, field names — into the top row. I also put some information into nearby cells. This area is for the *criteria range*. This range enables you to use Excel's database functions to ask (and answer) questions about the data. Database honchos call this *querying*. Criteria are a part and parcel of each database function. (*Criteria* is plural. The singular form is *criterion*.)

It's not necessary to have this range at the top of the worksheet. You can designate any range in the worksheet as the criteria range.

When you use an Excel database function, it's in this format:

```
=FUNCTION(Database, Field, Criteria)
```

The function operates on the specified database, in the designated field, according to the indicated criteria.

For example, if you want to know how many satellites revolve around Saturn, you select a cell and enter

```
=DCOUNT(Satellites,Average_Distance_X_1000_km,C1:C2)
```

Here's what this formula means: In the database (B10:G35), DCOUNT tallies the amount of number-containing cells in the Average_Distance_X_1000_km field, constrained by the criterion specified in the cell range C1:C2. That criterion is equivalent to Planet = Saturn. Note that a criterion has to include at least one column header . . . uh . . . field name from the criteria range, and at least one row. Bear in mind that you can't use the actual field name in the criteria. You use the cell ID (like C1).

When you include more than one row, you're saying "or." For example, if your criterion happens to be G1:G3, you're specifying satellites discovered by Galileo or Cassini.

When you include more than one column in a criterion, you're saying "and." If your criterion is E1:F2, you're specifying satellites farther than 150,000 km from their planets and discovered after 1877.

The format of a database function

The formula I just showed you

```
=DCOUNT(Satellites,Average_Distance__X_1000_km,C1:C2)
```

is accessible via a Function Arguments dialog box, as is the case for all other worksheet functions in Excel. Figure A-2 shows the equivalent dialog box for the preceding formula, set against the backdrop of the database and the criteria range.

How do you open this dialog box? Unlike the Statistical Functions or the Math & Trig Functions, Database Functions do not reside on their own menu. Instead, you click the Insert Function button (it's in the Function Library area of the Formulas tab) to open the Insert Function dialog box. Then in that dialog box, select Database in the box labeled "or Select a Category", and then in the list of functions find the database function you're looking for.

Here's an example:

1. **Select a worksheet cell.**

   As Figure A-2 shows, I selected H6.

2. **Click the Insert Function button (it's labeled f_x) to open the Insert Function dialog box.**

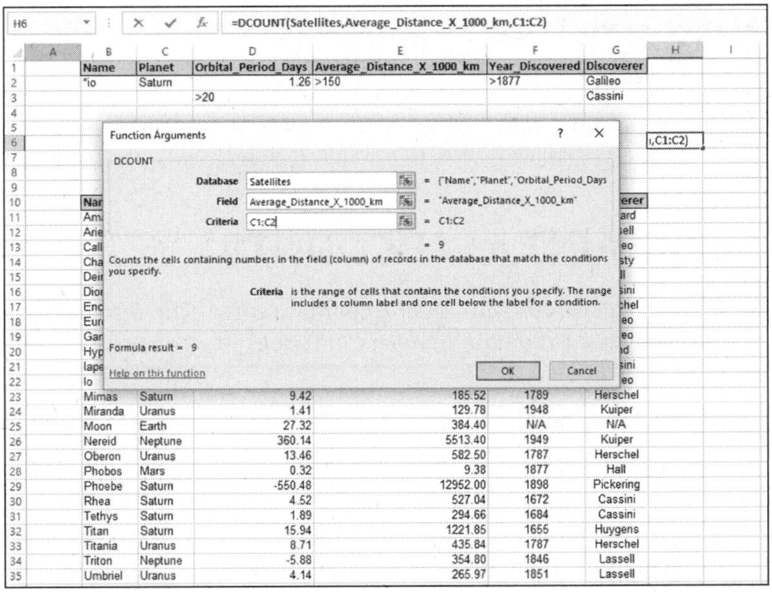

FIGURE A-2:
The DCOUNT
Function
Arguments
dialog box.

3. **In the Insert Function dialog box, select a function to open its Function Arguments dialog box.**

   From the Database category, I selected DCOUNT and that's the dialog box in Figure A-2.

4. **In the Function Arguments dialog box, enter the appropriate values for the arguments.**

   For the Database, I entered Satellites in the Database box. For the field, I entered Average_Distance_X_1000_km in the Field box. This isn't as keyboard intensive as it sounds. You can just select the appropriate cell range or cell from the spreadsheet. I selected the cell range for Satellites for the Database box, and I selected cell E10 for the Field box. Then I selected C1:C2 for the Criterion box.

   The answer, 9, appears in the dialog box.

5. **Click OK to put the answer into the selected cell.**

All the database functions follow the same format, you access them all the same way, and you fill in the same type of information in their dialog boxes. So I skip over that sequence of steps as I describe each function, and discuss only the equivalent worksheet formula.

Counting and Retrieving

One essential database capability is to let you know how many records meet a particular criterion. Another is to retrieve records. Here are the Excel versions.

DCOUNT *and* DCOUNTA

As I just showed you, DCOUNT counts records. The restriction is that the field you specify has to contain numbers. If it doesn't, the answer is zero, as in

```
=DCOUNT(Satellites,Name,C1:C2)
```

because no records in the Name field contain numbers.

DCOUNTA counts records in a different way. This one works with any field. It counts the number of nonblank records in the field that satisfy the criterion. So this formula returns 9:

```
=DCOUNTA(Satellites,Name,C1:C2)
```

Getting to "or"

Here's a tally that involves "or":

```
=DCOUNTA(Satellites,Name,D1:D3)
```

The criterion D1:D3 specifies satellites whose orbital period is 1.26 days or greater than 20 days — as I mention earlier, multiple rows mean "or." Five satellites meet that criterion: Deimos, Hyperion, Iapetus, our Moon, and Nereid.

Wildcards

Look closely at Figure A-1 and you see the cryptic entry *io in Cell B2. I did that so you'd know that Excel database functions can deal with wildcard characters. The formula

```
=DCOUNTA(Satellites,Name,B1:B2)
```

returns 3, the number of satellites with the letter-string io anywhere in their names (Dione, Io, and Hyperion).

DGET

DGET retrieves exactly one record. If the criteria you specify result in more than one record (or in no records), DGET returns an error message.

This formula

```
=DGET(Satellites,Name,D1:D2)
```

retrieves Deimos, the name of the satellite whose orbital period is 1.26 days.

This one

```
=DGET(Satellites,Name,E1:E2)
```

results in an error message because the criterion specifies more than one record.

Arithmetic

Excel wouldn't be Excel without calculation capabilities. Here are the ones it offers for its databases.

DMAX *and* DMIN

As their names suggest, DMAX and DMIN provide the maximum value and the minimum value according to your specifications. The formula

```
=DMAX(Satellites,Orbital_Period__Days,E1:E2)
```

returns 360.14. This is the maximum orbital period for any satellite that's farther than 150,000 km from its planet.

For the minimum value that meets this criterion,

```
=DMIN(Satellites,Orbital_Period__Days,E1:E2)
```

gives you −550.48. That's Phoebe, a satellite that revolves in the opposite direction to its planet's rotation.

DSUM

DSUM adds up the values in a field. To add all orbital periods in the satellites discovered by Galileo or Cassini, use this formula:

```
=DSUM(Satellites,Orbital_Period__Days,G1:G3)
```

That sum is 117.64.

TIP

Want to total up all the orbital periods? (I know, I know: =SUM(B11:B35). Just work with me here.)

This formula gets it done:

```
=DSUM(Satellites,Orbital_Period__Days,C1:C3)
```

Why? It's all in the criterion. C1:C3 means that Planet = Saturn or . . . anything else, because C3 is empty. The sum, by the way, is 35.457. Bottom line: Be careful whenever you include an empty cell in your criteria.

DPRODUCT

Here's a function that's probably here only because Excel's designers could create it. You specify the data values, and DPRODUCT multiplies them.

The formula

```
=DPRODUCT(Satellites,Orbital_Period__Days,G1:G2)
```

returns the product (749.832) of the orbital periods of the satellites Galileo discovered — a calculation I'm pretty sure Galileo never thought about.

Statistics

Which brings me to the statistical database functions. These work just like the similarly named worksheet functions.

DAVERAGE

Here's the formula for the average of the orbital periods of satellites discovered after 1887:

```
=DAVERAGE(Satellites,Orbital_Period__Days,F1:F2)
```

The average is negative (−36.4086) because the specification includes those two satellites with the negative orbital periods.

DVAR *and* DVARP

DVAR is the database counterpart of VAR, which divides the sum of N squared deviations by $N-1$. This is called *sample variance*.

DVARP is the database counterpart of VAR.P, which divides the sum of N squared deviations by N. This is the *population variance*. (For details on VAR.S and VAR.P, sample variance and population variance, and the implications of $N-1$ and N, see Chapter 5.)

Here's the sample variance for the orbital period of satellites farther than 150,000 kilometers from their planets and discovered after 1877:

```
=DVAR(Satellites,Orbital_Period__Days,E1:F2)
```

That turns out to be 210,358.1.

The population variance for that same subset of satellites is

```
=DVARP(Satellites,Orbital_Period__Days,E1:F2)
```

which is 140,238.7.

Once again, if you have multiple columns in the criteria, you're dealing with "and."

DSTDEV *and* DSTDEVP

These two return standard deviations. The standard deviation is the square root of the variance. (See Chapter 5.) DSTDEV returns the sample standard deviation, which is the square root of DVAR's returned value. DSTDEVP returns the population standard deviation, the square root of DVARP's returned value.

For the specifications in the preceding example, the sample standard deviation is

```
=DSTDEV(Satellites,Orbital_Period__Days,E1:F2)
```

which is 458.6481.

The population standard deviation is

```
=DSTDEVP(Satellites,Orbital_Period__Days,E1:F2)
```

This result is 374.4846.

According to form

Excel provides a data form to help you work with databases. Unfortunately, Excel 2016 didn't put a button for this form on the Ribbon. To access this button, you have to put it on the Quick Access toolbar.

Here's how to do it:

1. **Click the down arrow on the right of the Quick Access toolbar to open the Customize Quick Access Toolbar menu.**

2. **From this menu, select More Commands to open the Excel Options dialog box.**

3. **In the Choose Commands From drop-down menu, select Commands Not in the Ribbon.**

4. **In the list box on the left, scroll down and select Form.**

5. **Click the Add button to put *Form* into the list box on the right.**

6. **Click OK to close the Excel Options dialog box.**

   The Data Form button is now on the Quick Access toolbar.

To use the data form, highlight the entire cell range of the database, including the column headers. Then click the Data Form button.

Figure A-3 shows the appearance of the data form when you open it with the whole database selected. Excel fills in the field names automatically, and the fields populate with the values from the first record. You can use the form to navigate through the database, and to add a record. You can start with one record and use the New button to enter all the rest. (For me, it's easier to type each record.)

FIGURE A-3:
The data form for
working with
Excel databases.

Satellites		? ×
Na_me:	Amalthea	1 of 25
Plan_et:	Jupiter	New
_Orbital Period Days:	0.5	_Delete
A_verage Distance X 1000 km:	181.3	Resto_re
_Year Discovered:	1892	
D_iscoverer:	Barnard	Find _Prev
		Find _Next
		_Criteria
		C_lose

REMEMBER

Whenever you add records (and whichever way you add them), click Formulas |
Manage Names and increase the cell range attached to the database name.

The title on the data form is the same as the name on the bottom tab of the worksheet, so it's a good idea to put the name of the database on the tab. It's clearer what
the Form shows when something like Satellites is in its title rather than Sheet 1.

TIP

Pivot Tables

A *pivot table* is a cross-tabulation — another way of looking at the data. You can
reorganize the database and turn it (literally) on its side and inside out. And you
can do it in any number of ways.

For example, you can set up a pivot table that has the satellites in the rows and a
planet in each column, and has the data for the orbital period inside the cells.
Figure A-4 shows what I mean.

Figure A-5 shows a pivot table that presents another view of the data. This one
takes the spotlight off the individual satellites and puts it on the planets. Each
planet's row is divided into two rows — one for the orbital period and one for the
average distance. The numbers are the sums across each planet's satellites. Adding
up the orbital period for all of Jupiter's satellites gives you 29.66, for instance.

This example focuses on creating the pivot table shown in Figure A-4. Here's
what you do:

1. **Open the worksheet that holds the database.**

   In this case, it's Satellites.

2. **Select any cell in the range of the database.**

FIGURE A-4:
A pivot table of the satellites data showing satellites, planets, and orbital period.

	A	B	C	D	E	F	G	H	I	J
3	Sum of Orbital_Period_Days	Column Labels								
4	Row Labels	Earth	Jupiter	Mars	Neptune	Pluto	Saturn	Uranus	Grand Total	
5	Amalthea		0.5						0.5	
6	Ariel							2.52	2.52	
7	Callisto		16.69						16.69	
8	Charon					6.387			6.387	
9	Deimos			1.26					1.26	
10	Dione						2.74		2.74	
11	Enceladus						1.37		1.37	
12	Europa		3.55						3.55	
13	Ganymede		7.15						7.15	
14	Hyperion						21.28		21.28	
15	Iapetus						79.33		79.33	
16	Io		1.77						1.77	
17	Mimas						9.42		9.42	
18	Miranda							1.41	1.41	
19	Moon	27.32							27.32	
20	Nereid				360.14				360.14	
21	Oberon							13.46	13.46	
22	Phobos			0.32					0.32	
23	Phoebe						-550.48		-550.48	
24	Rhea						4.52		4.52	
25	Tethys						1.89		1.89	
26	Titan						15.94		15.94	
27	Titania							8.71	8.71	
28	Triton				-5.88				-5.88	
29	Umbriel							4.14	4.14	
30	Grand Total	27.32	29.66	1.58	354.26	6.387	-413.99	30.24	35.457	
31										

FIGURE A-5:
Another pivot table of the satellites data, showing planets, orbital period, and average distance.

	A	B	C	D
1				
2				
3		Values		
4	Row Labels	Sum of Orbital_Period_Days	Sum of Average_Distance_X_1000_km	
5	Earth	27.32	384.4	
6	Jupiter	29.66	4226.8	
7	Mars	1.58	32.84	
8	Neptune	354.26	5868.2	
9	Pluto	6.387	19.64	
10	Saturn	-413.99	20838.79	
11	Uranus	30.24	1605.33	
12	Grand Total	35.457	32976	

3. **Select Insert | PivotTable to open the Create PivotTable dialog box. (See Figure 1-6.)**

4. **Make your entries within this dialog box.**

Because I selected a cell within the database before I opened this dialog box, the first radio button is selected and the Table/Range box is filled in.

I selected the New Worksheet radio button to put the pivot table on a new worksheet.

5. **Click OK.**

The result is the PivotTable layout with the PivotTable Fields pane on a new worksheet. (See Figure A-7.)

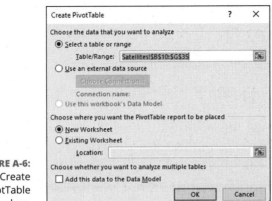

FIGURE A-6:
The Create
PivotTable
dialog box.

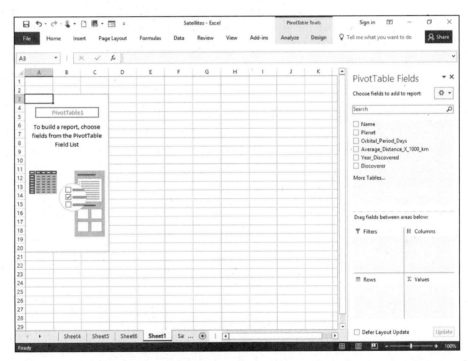

FIGURE A-7:
A new worksheet
containing the
PivotTable layout.

6. **Populate the PivotTable layout.**

To populate the PivotTable layout, you work with the PivotTable Fields pane.
Select a field, drag it into the appropriate box below, and drop it.

I begin with the rows. To make the names of the satellites appear in the rows, I
selected Name and dropped it into the Rows box. Figure A-8 shows the result.
In addition to the satellite names in the rows, the check box next to Name is

bold and selected, to indicate that it's in the table. Deselecting the check box removes Name from the table.

Next, I dropped Planet into the Columns box. (See Figure A-9.)

Dragging Orbital Period (Days) and dropping it into the Σ Values box results in the table shown earlier, in Figure A-4.

Dropping a field into the Report Filter box creates a sort of multipage version of the table. For example, putting Discoverer in the Report Filter box creates a drop-down menu that allows you to see only the data for each Discoverer.

The down arrow next to a field opens a menu of options for sorting and filtering that field.

The importance of pivot tables is that they allow you to get your hands dirty with the data. By dropping fields into and out of the table, you might see relationships and carry out analyses that might not occur to you if you look only at the original database.

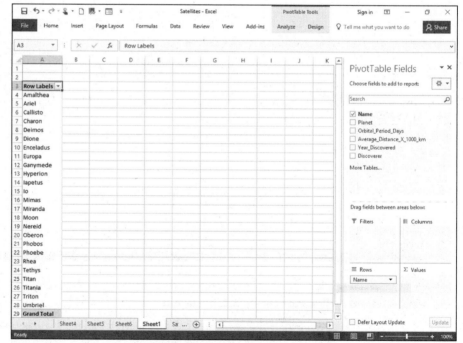

FIGURE A-8:
The PivotTable layout after dropping the Name field into the Row Labels box.

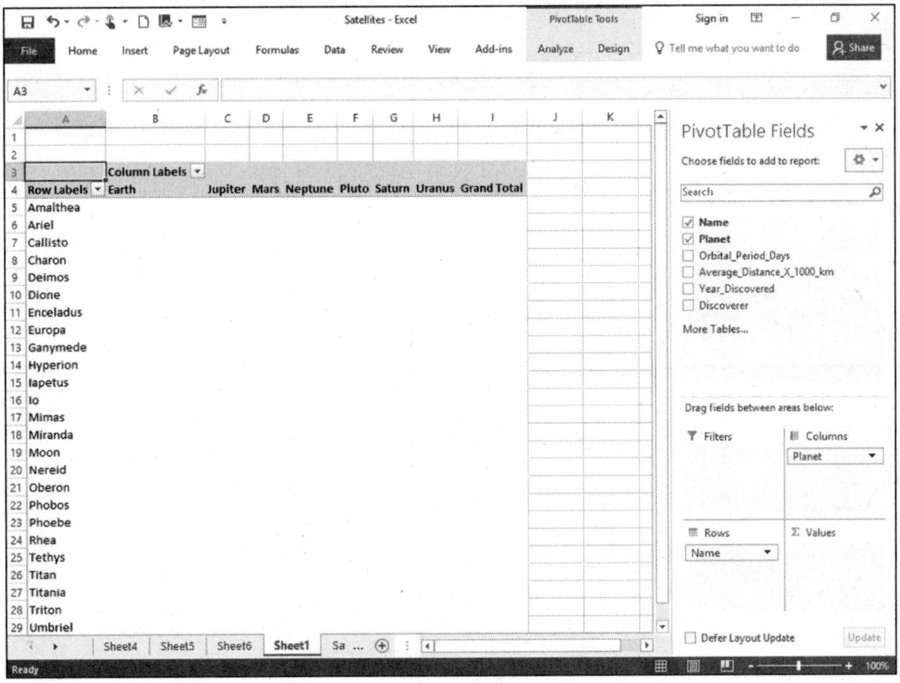

FIGURE A-9:
The PivotTable layout after dropping the Planet field into the Column Labels box.

Appendix B
The Analysis of Covariance

One of the major points of this book is that Excel comes with a surprising number of analytical tools and formulas. The toolset isn't as extensive as you'd find in a dedicated statistics package, but it's still impressive.

Some analyses, unfortunately, aren't part of Excel. And some of those might turn out to be important for you. In many cases, with a little ingenuity you can use the existing parts of Excel to perform those analyses anyway. In this appendix, I focus on one of those analyses.

Covariance: A Closer Look

In Chapter 15, I mention covariance in connection with correlation. I go over it briefly as the numerator of the correlation coefficient. I also mention that covariance represents two variables changing together.

What does that mean, exactly?

Imagine a group of people on whom you measure mathematical ability and sociability. (Just assume you have valid, reliable ways of measuring both.) If you find that the people with high mathematical ability are the most sociable, and the people with low mathematical ability are the least sociable, this thing called covariance is numerically high and positive. This type of positive relationship is called a *direct* relationship.

A different result is possible: The people with high mathematical ability might turn out to be the least sociable, and the people with low mathematical ability the most sociable. If that happens, covariance is numerically high and negative. This type of negative relationship is called an *inverse* relationship.

Still another result is possible. You might find no connection whatsoever between mathematical ability and sociability. In this case, the two variables are *independent,* and the numerical value of covariance is close to zero. It could be slightly positive, or it could be slightly negative, but it's close to zero.

Sounds a lot like correlation? It should. As I mention earlier, covariance is the numerator of the correlation coefficient. One way to look at it is that the correlation coefficient puts an upper and lower bound on covariance. With a little experience, you can understand what a correlation coefficient of .98 means, or a correlation coefficient of .62. Without a lot of context, it's hard to know what a covariance of 473.5 means.

Why You Analyze Covariance

So you've had a refresher on what covariance is. Why do you want to . . . uh . . . *analyze* it?

Let's begin with a typical study: You randomly assign people to different conditions and you assess their performance under those conditions. For example, you might randomly assign 15 children to one of three groups that differ on how to prepare for a math exam. One group prepares by listening to a human instructor. Another prepares by completing an interactive program on a computer. The third prepares by reading a textbook. Then they take the exam.

The children's performance on the test is the *dependent variable.* The three preparation conditions make up the *independent variable.* The goal is usually to find out whether the different conditions of the independent variable affect the dependent variable. Chapter 12 explains that this involves a hypothesis test that looks like this:

$H_0: \mu_{Instructor} = \mu_{Computer} = \mu_{Text}$

$H_1:$ Not H_0

In Chapter 12, I also point out that the appropriate statistical technique is the analysis of variance (ANOVA).

So far, so good. What about covariance?

In addition to the dependent variable and the independent variable, a third kind of variable can come into play. Here's how. Suppose you have another relevant measure for each of the 15 children: mathematics aptitude. In addition to preparation type, this could also affect each child's exam performance. This third variable is called the *covariate.* The relationship between the dependent variable and the covariate is covariance.

Big shots in the field of research design and analysis have a name for randomly assigning individuals to different conditions of the independent variable and keeping everything else the same (like the time of day you give the test, the amount of time each child prepares, and the amount of time each child has to take the test). They call this *experimental control.*

They also have a name for assessing the effects of a covariate — that is, its covariance with the dependent variable. They refer to that as *statistical control.* Both are valuable tools in the analyst's arsenal.

Bottom-line question: Why do you need statistical control? Suppose you carry out the study and find no significant differences among preparation groups. This could mean that experimental control wasn't powerful enough to discern an effect of preparation type. That's when statistical control can come to the rescue. Suppose mathematics aptitude affected performance in ways that masked the effects of preparation type. That is, does the possible correlation of performance with aptitude affect the results?

By combining experimental control with statistical control, analysis of covariance (ANCOVA) answers that question.

How You Analyze Covariance

How do you combine the two types of control?

In Chapter 12, I point out that ANOVA separates SS_{Total} into $SS_{Between}$ and SS_{Within}. Divide each SS by its degrees of freedom and you have three MS (variances). The $MS_{Between}$ reflects differences among group means. The MS_{Within} estimates the population variance. It's based on pooling the variances within the groups. If the

$MS_{Between}$ is significantly greater than the MS_{Within}, you can reject the null hypothesis. If not, you can't. (Read Chapter 12 if this all sounds strange to you.)

In ANCOVA, you use the relationship between the dependent variable and the covariate to *adjust* $SS_{Between}$ and SS_{Within}. If the relationship is strong, it's likely that the adjustment increases $SS_{Between}$ and reduces SS_{Within}. Statistics, like most other aspects of our world, feature no free lunches: The adjustment lowers the df_{Within} by 1. It might help to think of it this way:

ANOVA:

$$F = \frac{SS_{Between} / df_{Between}}{SS_{Within} / df_{Within}}$$

ANCOVA:

$$F = \frac{\left(SS_{Between} + \text{something based on relationship with covariate}\right) / df_{Between}}{\left(SS_{Within} + \text{something based on relationship with covariate}\right) / df_{Within-1}}$$

A possible outcome of the adjustment (if the relationship is strong) is that the F ratio is higher for ANCOVA than for ANOVA. In practical terms, this means that adding statistical control can result in a more powerful study (that is, greater capability to find an effect) than experimental control alone.

Here's a way to understand ANOVA versus ANCOVA: ANOVA helps you find a needle in a haystack. ANCOVA also does this, but it removes some of the hay from the haystack — and it makes the needle a little bigger, too.

ANCOVA in Excel

Although Excel has no built-in tools for ANCOVA, you can use what Excel does provide to make ANCOVA way easier than it looks in statistics books.

What does Excel provide? When it comes to covariance, recall that the COVARIANCE.P and COVARIANCE.S worksheet functions do all the calculations for you, as does the Covariance analysis tool.

It sounds like the Covariance analysis tool is ideal for something called analysis of covariance (ANCOVA). Oddly, it's not. You also have no use for worksheet functions as you proceed.

Instead, I show you two approaches that use other Excel features to carry out an ANCOVA. One approach uses the Anova: Single Factor analysis tool along with some worksheet functions. The other uses the Regression analysis tool along with some worksheet functions.

Both approaches tackle the data in Table B-1. In both methods, I use regression slopes to express the relationship between the dependent variable and the covariate.

TABLE B-1: **Data for Exam Performance with Three Preparation Methods and for Mathematics Aptitude**

Human		Computer		Text	
Math Aptitude	Exam	Math Aptitude	Exam	Math Aptitude	Exam
10	6	7	9	7	9
9	9	7	5	9	12
8	7	8	14	4	9
6	2	11	10	11	18
9	10	11	15	7	11

These methods are for the kind of research design I discuss in Chapter 12 (single-factor ANOVA). You can use ANCOVA for any kind of research design that involves ANOVA, but these two particular methods won't work for more complicated designs (as in Chapter 13, for example).

Method 1: ANOVA

When most statistics textbooks cover analysis of covariance, they show you a lot of arcane-looking computation formulas designed to avoid even more complex-looking regression-related calculations. The result is that they often obscure what ANCOVA is supposed to do.

With this method, and the next one, I show you how to harness Excel's power to work around all of that. My goal is to make ANCOVA a lot easier than it looks in stat books.

Figure B-1 shows the ANCOVA worksheet for this method. I also take you through the steps.

The data from Table B-1 are in cells B1:D13, separated into one table for the dependent variable data and another for the covariate data. I structure the data this way because I have to use the Anova: Single Factor tool on the dependent variable and again on the covariate. The input to the Anova tool is a contiguous range of cells, so the layout in Table B-1 doesn't work.

The first thing I do is set up to calculate b_{within}, a quantity I use to adjust the SS and to adjust group means for post-analysis testing.

What is b_{within}? Imagine a scatterplot for each of the three groups, and a regression line through each scatterplot. Each regression line has a slope. The value of b_{within} is the average of the group slopes, with each slope weighted by the variance of the covariate within the group.

	A	B	C	D	E	F	G	H	I	J	K	L	M
1		Human	Computer	Textbook				Anova: Dep Variable					
2		6	9	9				SUMMARY					
3		9	5	12				Groups	Count	Sum	Average	Variance	
4		7	14	9				Human	5	34	6.8	9.7	
5		2	10	18				Computer	5	53	10.6	16.3	
6		10	15	11				Textbook	5	59	11.8	13.7	
7													
8		X1	X2	X3				ANOVA					
9		10	7	7				Source	SS	df	MS	F	P-value
10		9	7	9				Between Groups	68.13333	2	34.06667	2.574307	0.117412
11		8	8	4				Within Groups	158.8	12	13.23333		
12		6	11	11									
13		9	10	7				Total	226.9333	14			
14	VarianceX	2.3	3.3	6.8	12.4								
15	SlopeXY	1.4565	1.0757576	1.235294				Anova: Covariate					
16	VarX*SlopeXY	3.35	3.55	8.4	15.3			SUMMARY					
17								Groups	Count	Sum	Average	Variance	
18	bwithin	1.2339						X1	5	42	8.4	2.3	
19	btotal	1.0267						X2	5	43	8.6	3.3	
20								X3	5	38	7.6	6.8	
21	Ancova												
22	Source of Variation	SS	df	MS	F	P-value		ANOVA					
23	Adjusted Between	88.409	2	44.20442	5.838222	0.018707		Source of Variation	SS	df	MS	F	P-value
24	Adjusted Within	83.287	11	7.571554				Between Groups	2.8	2	1.4	0.33871	0.719287
25	Adjusted Total	171.696	13					Within Groups	49.6	12	4.133333		
26													
27		Human	Computer	Textbook				Total	52.4	14			
28	Adjusted Means	6.5532	10.106452	12.54032									
29													

FIGURE B-1: The Method 1 ANCOVA worksheet for the data in Table B-1.

This might be a rare case where the formula is clearer than the words. Here it is:

$$b_{within} = \frac{\sum s_{xi}^2 b_i}{\sum s_{xi}^2}$$

So I used VAR.S to calculate the variance of each group within the covariate. Those variances are in row 14, labeled VarianceX. I could have run the Anova tool to get these variances. I did it this way for clarity. The sum of these variances, 12.4, is in cell E14.

Then I used SLOPE to calculate the slope within each group. Those are in row 15, labeled SlopeXY.

Row 16, labeled VarX*SlopeXY, contains the product of each group slope multiplied by the variance in that group. Cell E16 holds the sum of these products.

The value of b_{within} is in cell B18. The formula for that cell is

```
=E16/E14
```

Cell B19 holds another slope I use for SS adjustment. It's called b_{total}, and it represents the slope of the regression line drawn through a scatterplot of all the scores regardless of the group they're in. The formula for B19 is

```
=SLOPE(B2:D6,B9:D13)
```

Next, I constructed the spiffy-looking ANCOVA table in cells A21:F25. The objective of this whole process is to fill in this table. I formatted all the labels and borders to make the table look something like the results of an Anova:Single Factor analysis. Then I filled in the sources of variation in A23:A25, and the df in C23:C25. The df are the same as for ANOVA, except that you lose a df from the df_{Within}, and that, of course, is reflected in the df_{Total}.

The next order of business is to run the Anova:Single Factor analysis tool. I ran it once for the dependent variable and once for the covariate. Why for the covariate? After all, I'm not testing any hypotheses about math aptitude. The reason for an ANOVA on the covariate is that the ANOVA output provides SS values I need to complete the ANCOVA.

In Chapter 12, I explain how to use this tool. The only difference is that in this case, I direct the output to this worksheet rather than to separate worksheets.

I removed some rows from the Anova tool's outputs so that everything would fit into one screen shot, and I modified them a bit for clarity.

The values in the ANOVA tables enable me to fill in the ANCOVA table. The Adjusted SS_{Total} is

$$Adjusted\ SS_{TotalY} = SS_{TotalY} - b_{Total}^{2} SS_{TotalX}$$

$$Adjusted\ SS_{TotalY} = 226.93 - (1.03)^{2}(52.4) = 171.70$$

This means that

```
=I13-B19^2*I27
```

goes into cell B25 in the ANCOVA table. By the way, I rounded off to two decimal places to make everything look nicer on this page. The worksheet has way more decimal places.

Next up: Adjusted SS_{Within}. The formula for the adjustment is

$$Adjusted\ SS_{WithinY} = SS_{WithinY} - b^2_{Within}SS_{WithinX}$$

Numerically, that's

$$Adjusted\ SS_{WithinY} = 158.8 - (1.23)^2(49.6) = 83.29$$

So in cell B24, I put this formula:

```
=I11-B18^2*I25
```

Adjusted $SS_{Between}$? That's just

```
=B25-B24
```

in cell B23.

I complete the ANCOVA table by dividing each Adjusted SS by its df and then dividing the Adjusted $MS_{Between}$ by the Adjusted MS_{Within} to compute F.

That last column in the ANCOVA table, P-value, is a little trick courtesy of F.DIST.RT. The formula in cell F23 is

```
=F.DIST.RT(E23,C23,C24)
```

Just below the ANCOVA table, I put the adjusted means for the dependent variable. These enter into post-analysis testing, which I cover in a later section. For now, I just tell you that each adjusted mean is

$$Adjusted\ \bar{y}_i = \bar{y}_i - b_{within}(\bar{x}_i - \bar{X})$$

where that uppercase X with a bar over it represents the average of all 15 scores in the covariate.

For this example, the adjusted means are

$$Adjusted\ \bar{y}_{Human} = 6.8 - 1.23(8.4 - 8.2) = 6.55$$

$$Adjusted\ \bar{y}_{Computer} = 10.6 - 1.23(8.6 - 8.2) = 10.11$$

$$Adjusted\ \bar{y}_{Textbook} = 11.8 - 1.23(7.6 - 8.2) = 12.54$$

The adjustments increase the spread among the means.

In this worksheet, the group means are in the ANOVA outputs. Specifically, they're in K4:K6 for the dependent variable and in K18:K20 for the covariate. So the formula for the adjusted Human mean (in cell B28) is

```
=K4-B18*(K18-AVERAGE(B9:D13))
```

For the adjusted Computer mean (cell C28), it's

```
=K5-B18*(K19-AVERAGE(B9:D13))
```

and for the adjusted Textbook mean (cell D28), it's

```
=K6-B18*(K20-AVERAGE(B9:D13))
```

What's the benefit of ANCOVA? Take another look at Figure B-1. Compare the result of the dependent-variable ANOVA ($F_{2,12}$ = 2.57) with the result of the ANCOVA ($F_{2,11}$ = 5.84). Although you sacrificed a df, the P-value shows that the ANCOVA result is significant. The ANOVA result is not. The ANCOVA adjusted the $SS_{Between}$ upward, and it adjusted the SS_{Within} downward.

Bottom line: The relationship between the dependent variable and the covariate enables you to uncover a significant effect you might otherwise miss. In this example, ANCOVA avoids a Type II error.

Method 2: Regression

If the preceding method works, why am I bothering to show you yet another method? Even more important, why should you take the trouble to master it?

The reason I'd like you to read on is this: The method I'm about to show you asks you to change your mindset about the data. If you can do that, you'll find yourself open to another way of looking at statistical analysis and to mastering some new statistical concepts.

Here's what I mean. The worksheet in Figure B-2 shows the data from Table B-1 in a different type of layout. The figure also shows the work for the completed ANCOVA.

Column A has the math exam data, and column B has the math aptitude data, but they're not separated into three groups. What's going on here?

My plan is to treat this as a multiple regression. Exam is the dependent variable, and Math Aptitude is an independent variable. But it's not the only independent variable.

	Exam	Math Aptitude	Tag 1	Tag 2						
	A	B	C	D	E	F	G	H	I	J	K
1	Exam	Math Aptitude	Tag 1	Tag 2							
2	6	10	1	0							
3	9	9	1	0		*Regression Statistics*					
4	7	8	1	0		Multiple R	0.795605872				
5	2	6	1	0		R Square	0.632988704				
6	10	9	1	0		Adjusted R Square	0.532894714				
7	9	7	0	1		Standard Error	2.751645735				
8	5	7	0	1		Observations	15				
9	14	8	0	1							
10	10	11	0	1		ANOVA					
11	15	10	0	1			*df*	*SS*	*MS*	*F*	*Significance F*
12	9	7	0	0		Regression	3	143.6462366	47.88208	6.323943	0.00944713
13	12	9	0	0		Residual	11	83.28709677	7.571554		
14	9	4	0	0		Total	14	226.9333333			
15	18	11	0	0							
16	11	7	0	0			*Coefficients*	*Standard Error*	*t Stat*	*P-value*	*Lower 95%*
17						Intercept	2.422580645	3.214266308	0.753696	0.466858	-4.651971799
18	SSTotalX =	52.4				Math Aptitude	1.233870968	0.39070744	3.158043	0.009111	0.373929691
19						Tag 1	-5.987096774	1.768140033	-3.3861	0.006077	-9.878746747
20	btotal =	1.026717557				Tag 2	-2.433870968	1.783612627	-1.36457	0.199651	-6.359575892
21											
22	Means					Ancova					
23	*Group*	*Dependent Var*	*Covariate*	*Adjusted*		*Source of Variation*	*SS*	*df*	*MS*	*F*	*Significance F*
24	Human	6.8	8.4	6.553226		Adjusted Between	88.409	2	44.20442	5.838222	0.018706714
25	Computer	10.6	8.6	10.10645		Adjusted Within	83.287	11	7.571554		
26	Textbook	11.8	7.6	12.54032		Adjusted Total	171.696	13			

FIGURE B-2:
The Method 2 ANCOVA worksheet for the data in Table B-1.

The key is to somehow represent the group that each individual is a member of. Tag1 and Tag2 (in columns C and D) take care of that. If a child is in the Human Instructor group, Tag1 = 1 and Tag2 = 0. If a child is in the Computer group, Tag1 = 0 and Tag2 = 1. If a child is in the Textbook group, Tag1 = 0 and Tag2 = 0. In general, with *k* groups, *k*–1 columns can specify group membership in this way. Just to let you know, in the statistics world, columns B, C, and D are called *vectors*, but I won't go there.

WARNING

This categorization scheme works when you have the same number of individuals in each group. If you don't, things get a little dicey.

I drew lines to separate the three groups, but that's just to clarify.

What I've set up is a multiple regression with a dependent variable (Exam) and three independent variables (Math Aptitude, Tag1, and Tag2). What I'm saying is that Exam score depends on Math Aptitude, Tag 1, and Tag 2.

Below the data layout, cell B18 holds SS_{TotalX}. The formula for that cell is

```
=COUNT(B2:B16)*VAR.P(B2:B16)
```

meaning that I multiplied the number of scores in column B (15) by the variance in column B (treated as a population of 15 scores — hence, VAR.P) to give SS_{TotalX}, the numerator of a variance.

I also calculated b_{total} in cell B20:

```
=SLOPE(A2:A16,B2:B16)
```

What about b_{within}? Patience.

Below those values is a table of means and adjusted means, which I get to later.

You might not believe this, but the analysis is almost done.

All that remains is to run the Regression analysis tool and use its results to complete the ANCOVA table.

In Chapter 14, I show you how to use the Regression tool. The difference here (as with ANOVA in Method 1) is that I directed the output to this worksheet rather than to a separate worksheet. For this example, the Input Y range in the Regression tool dialog box is A1:A16. Because this is a multiple regression, the Input X range is B1:D16.

The ANCOVA table is below the Regression output. As earlier, I formatted the whole thing — labels, rows, columns, and all. Then I filled in the df.

I begin, as in Method 1, with the Adjusted SS_{Total}. Again, that's

$$Adjusted\ SS_{TotalY} = SS_{TotalY} - b_{Total}^2 SS_{TotalX}$$

$$Adjusted\ SS_{TotalY} = 226.93 - (1.03)^2 (52.4) = 171.70$$

So this time,

```
=H14-(B20^2*B18)
```

goes into cell G26.

What next? The values for the Adjusted Within row are in the ANOVA table for the Regression output. They're in the row labeled Residual. That's right — the Adjusted SS_{Within} is the $SS_{Residual}$ and Adjusted MS_{Within} is the $MS_{Residual}$.

That means

```
=H13
```

goes into cell G25 and

```
=I13
```

goes into cell I25.

The Adjusted $SS_{Between}$ is

```
=G26-G25
```

in cell G24.

I divided the Adjusted SSs by the df to produce the Adjusted MSs. Then I divided the Adjusted $MS_{Between}$ by the Adjusted MS_{Within} to compute F. The rightmost entry, Significance F, is based on FDIST as in Method 1.

Did I forget b_{within}? Nope. It's in the Regression output in cell G18 under Coefficients. It's the regression coefficient for Math_Aptitude. I used this value to calculate the Adjusted Means in the Means table. After using AVERAGE to compute the means for the dependent variable and the covariate, I put this formula into cell D24

```
=B24-$G$18*(C24-AVERAGE($B$2:$B$16))
```

and autofilled D25 and D26.

When you began reading this subsection, you might have wondered why I bothered to show you this method. Now that you've read it, you might wonder why I bothered to show you the first one!

After the ANCOVA

As I point out in Chapter 12, a significant F value indicates that an effect is somewhere within the data. It's still necessary to zoom in on where.

Post-analysis tests come in two varieties — the kind you plan in advance and the kind you don't. The first, *planned comparisons,* are motivated by your ideas about what to expect before you gather the data. The second, *post-hoc tests,* are motivated by what looks interesting in the data you gathered.

In an ANOVA, you perform those tests on group means. In an ANCOVA, you adjust the group means (of the dependent variable) just as you adjust the SSs and the MSs. You also adjust the error term (the denominator) of the tests.

I deal here with planned comparisons. After adjusting the means (which I did in each Method), the next step is to adjust the MS that goes into the denominator of the planned comparisons. I refer to the adjusted MS as MS'_{Error} and the way to calculate it is

$$MS'_{Error} = Adjusted\ MS_{Within}\left(1 + \frac{SS_{BetweenX}\left(k-1\right)}{SS_{WithinX}}\right)$$

in which k is the number of groups.

For the example, that's

$$MS'_{Error} = 7.57\left(1 + \frac{2.8\left(2\right)}{49.6}\right) = 8.43$$

In the Method 1 worksheet, I select a cell and enter

```
=D24*(1+(I24*2)/I25)
```

I can now proceed with planned comparisons, as I do in Chapter 12.

From all I show you here, it looks like Method 1 has the advantage over Method 2. Using the ANOVA analysis tool gives you the values you need for the planned comparisons, and it gives you the dependent-variable ANOVA to compare against the ANCOVA.

With the data arranged as in Method 2, you can't get all that information, can you?

Yes you can. And that sets the stage for looking at a particular statistical analysis (ANOVA) in a new way, as I mention at the beginning of Method 2.

Read on.

And One More Thing

In several chapters of this book, you see the interplay between ANOVA and Regression: After every regression analysis, ANOVA tests hypotheses about regression ideas.

In this section, I turn things around: I take an exercise normally treatable via ANOVA, turn it into a regression problem, and use regression to do an analysis of variance. This is called the MRC (multiple regression/correlation) approach. It's based on the work of psychologist /statistician Jacob Cohen, who in the late 1960s formulated the idea of multiple regression as a general system for data analysis.

Without going into all the details, Cohen's idea is that many kinds of data are expressible in the format that regression operates on. Performing a regression analysis is all that's necessary. In effect, various statistical techniques then become special cases of the general system.

The dependent variable data in Table B-1 provide an opportunity to illustrate this approach. With the groups identified under Tag1 and Tag2, and the Tags as independent variables, ANOVA is exactly the same as multiple regression.

You might already be a step ahead of me. Figure B-3 shows the data laid out as in Figure B-2 shown earlier, but with different analyses.

FIGURE B-3: The Method 2 ANCOVA worksheet with two different regression analyses.

	A	B	C	D	E	F	G	H	I	J	K
1	Exam	Math Aptitude	Tag 1	Tag 2		Dependent Variable					
2	6	10	1	0		ANOVA					
3	9	9	1	0			df	SS	MS	F	Significance F
4	7	8	1	0		Regression	2	68.13333	34.06667	2.574307	0.117412202
5	2	6	1	0		Residual	12	158.8	13.23333		
6	10	9	1	0		Total	14	226.9333			
7	9	7	0	1							
8	5	7	0	1		Covariate					
9	14	8	0	1		ANOVA					
10	10	11	0	1			df	SS	MS	F	Significance F
11	15	10	0	1		Regression	2	2.8	1.4	0.33871	0.719287208
12	9	7	0	0		Residual	12	49.6	4.133333		
13	12	9	0	0		Total	14	52.4			
14	9	4	0	0							
15	18	11	0	0							
16	11	7	0	0							
17											

I ran the Regression analysis tool twice and directed the output to this worksheet both times. I deleted everything except the ANOVA from each output.

The first time I ran the tool, the Input Y Range was A2:A16 (Exam) and the Input X Range was C2:D16 (Tag1 and Tag2). The result is the first ANOVA table, just below the heading Dependent Variable.

The second time, the Input Y Range was B2:B16 (Math Aptitude) and the Input X Range was C2:D16, resulting in the ANOVA table below the heading Covariate.

Do the numbers look familiar? They should. They're the same as the two ANOVAs I ran for Method 1. The only difference, of course, is the names in the Source of Variance column. Rather than Between and Within, these outputs display Regression and Residual, respectively.

To complete the post-analysis tests for Method 2 ANCOVA, you only need the ANOVA for the covariate. I show you both to illustrate the MRC approach.

You can extend the MRC approach to more complex hypothesis tests, like the ones I discuss in Chapter 13. When you do, it becomes a bit more complicated: You have to know more about multiple regression and how it applies to things like interaction. In any event, the MRC approach is definitely worth looking into.

Index

Symbols and Numerics

$ (dollar signs), 28

_ (underscores), 43–44

{ } (curly brackets), 43

| (given), 383

= (equal sign), 25, 35

∩ (intersection), 381–383

∪ (union), 381–382

α (alpha)

  confidence limits, 196

  defined, 200, 202

  hypothesis testing with more than two samples, 250–251

  two-sample hypothesis testing, 218

  using high, 215, 440

β (beta), 200, 202

ε (error in the relationship), 303–305

λ (lambda), 415

π (pi), 180, 396

Σ (AutoSum) button (Excel), 58–59

∑ (sum of), 102

σ (variance)

  averaging deviation versus squared deviation, 118–120

  population

    formula for, 121

    overview, 119–121

    `VAR.P` function, 121–122

    `VARPA` function, 121–123

  sample

    formula for, 123–124

    overview, 123–124

    `VARA` function, 124

    `VAR.S` function, 124

χ^2 (chi-square) distribution

  approximating multinomial distribution, 422–423

  formula for, 211

  independence testing, 452–454

  one-sample hypothesis testing

    `CHISQ.DIST` function, 213–214

    `CHISQ.DIST.RT` function, 214

    `CHISQ.INV` function, 214

    `CHISQ.INV.RT` function, 215

    overview, 211–212

    visualizing, 215–216

3D Map visualization

  creating, 97–99

  overview, 96–97

  rotating, 99

A

a posteriori tests (unplanned comparisons), 258–259, 498

a priori tests (planned comparisons), 256–258, 498–499

absolute deviation, 132–133

absolute referencing

  named arrays, 51

  overview, 27–28

  toggling between relative and, 28

Add-Ins dialog box (Excel), 54–56

alpha (α)

  confidence limits, 196

  defined, 200, 202

  hypothesis testing with more than two samples, 250–251

  two-sample hypothesis testing, 218

  using high, 215, 440

alternative hypotheses (H_1)

  defined, 15, 200

  two-sample hypothesis testing, 217–218

amount of numbers added up (N), 102

analysis of covariance (ANCOVA)

  covariance, 487–489

E

e (mathematical constant), 180, 456–459
elementary outcomes, 380
Enter button (Excel), 32–33
equal sign (=), 25, 35
Erlang distribution, 412
Error Bars menu (Excel), 447
error in the relationship (ε), 303–305
error term, 255
errors
  overview, 16–17
  Type I, 17, 200, 202, 218
  Type II, 17, 200
estimation
  Central Limit Theorem
    overview, 187
    simulation for, 189–193
  confidence limits
    CONFIDENCE.NORM function, 195–196
    finding for mean, 193–195
  general discussion, 185
  sampling distribution of the mean, 186–187
  t-distribution
    CONFIDENCE.T function, 198
    overview, 197–198
ETS (triple exponential smoothing), 358–359
events, 380
exam scores, 137–139
Excel. *See* Microsoft Excel
EXP function, 181, 459
expected value, 389–390
experimental control, 489
experiments, 388
EXPONDIST (old) function, 22
EXPON.DIST function, 22, 415–416
exponential distribution
  EXPON.DIST function, 415–416
  formula for, 415
  overview, 414–415
exponential smoothing
  damping factors, 356–357
  double, 358

single, 356–357
  triple, 358–359
Exponential Smoothing tool (Excel)
  overview, 356
  purpose of, 53
exponents, 454–456

F

FACT function, 387, 457
factorials, 457
Fahrenheit temperature scale, 13
FDIST (old) function, 22
F.DIST function, 240–241
F-distribution and *F*-testing
  ANOVA, 254–255
  regression, 306–307
  two-sample hypothesis testing
    F.DIST function, 240–241
    F.DIST.RT function, 242–243
    F.INV function, 243
    F.INV.RT function, 243–244
    F.TEST function, 240–241
    FTest tool, 244–246
    overview, 237–239
    using in conjunction with *t*-distribution, 239–240
    visualizing, 246–247
F.DIST.RT function
  for ANCOVA, 494
  general discussion, 22
  two-sample hypothesis testing, 242–243
fields, 471
fill handles (Excel), 25
Fill pop-up menu (Excel), 25–26
FINV (old) function, 22
F.INV function, 243
F.INV.RT function
  general discussion, 22
  two-sample hypothesis testing, 243–244
Fisher, Ronald, 238, 339
FISHER function, 348–349
FISHERINV function, 348

About the Author

Joseph Schmuller, PhD is a veteran of over 25 years in Information Technology. He is the author of several books on computing, including the three editions of *Teach Yourself UML in 24 Hours* (SAMS), and the three prior editions of *Statistical Analysis with Excel For Dummies*. He has created online coursework for Lynda.com, and he has written numerous articles on advanced technology. From 1991 through 1997, he was Editor-in-Chief of *PC AI* magazine.

He is a former member of the American Statistical Association, and he has taught statistics at the undergraduate and graduate levels. He holds a B.S. from Brooklyn College, an M.A. from the University of Missouri-Kansas City, and a PhD. from the University of Wisconsin, all in psychology. He and his family live in Jacksonville, Florida, where he is a Research Scholar at the University of North Florida.

Dedication

In loving memory of my wonderful mother, Sara Riba Schmuller, who first showed me how to work with numbers, and taught me the skills to write about them.

Author's Acknowledgments

As I said in the first three editions, writing a *For Dummies* book is an incredible amount of fun. You get to express yourself in a friendly, conversational way, and you get to throw in some humor, too. To write one more edition is a wonderful quadfecta (yes, that's a word!). I worked again with a terrific team at Wiley. Acquisitions Editor Katie Mohr initiated this effort. Project Editor Paul Levesque has been sensational throughout: His sharp eyes and keen sense of what's readable and what's not have made this the tightest of all four editions. Copy Editor Becky Whitney also contributed valuable insights that make the book you're holding easier to read. Professor Dennis Short of Purdue is unsurpassed as a Technical Editor. He has worked on three of these editions with me and they're all better because of his participation. His students at Purdue are lucky to have him, as am I. Any errors that remain are under the sole proprietorship of the author. My thanks to Margot Hutchison of Waterside Productions for representing me in this effort.

Again I thank mentors in college and graduate school who helped shape my statistical knowledge: Mitch Grossberg (Brooklyn College); Al Hillix, Jerry Sheridan, the late Mort Goldman, and the late Larry Simkins (University of Missouri-Kansas City); and Cliff Gillman and the late John Theios (University of Wisconsin-Madison). I hope this book is an appropriate testament to my mentors who have passed on. I thank Kathryn as always for so much more than I can say. Finally, once more a special note of thanks to my friend Brad, who suggested this whole thing in the first place!

Publisher's Acknowledgments

Acquisitions Editor: Katie Mohr
Senior Project Editor: Paul Levesque
Copy Editor: Becky Whitney
Technical Editor: Dennis Short
Editorial Assistant: Kayla Hoffman
Sr. Editorial Assistant: Cherie Case

Production Editor: Tamilmani Varadharaj
Cover Image: D3Damon/iStockphoto

pple & Mac

ad For Dummies,
h Edition
8-1-118-72306-7

hone For Dummies,
h Edition
8-1-118-69083-3

acs All-in-One
r Dummies, 4th Edition
8-1-118-82210-4

X Mavericks
r Dummies
8-1-118-69188-5

ogging & Social Media

cebook For Dummies,
h Edition
8-1-118-63312-0

cial Media Engagement
r Dummies
8-1-118-53019-1

ordPress For Dummies,
h Edition
8-1-118-79161-5

usiness

ock Investing
r Dummies, 4th Edition
8-1-118-37678-2

vesting For Dummies,
h Edition
8-0-470-90545-6

Personal Finance
For Dummies, 7th Edition
978-1-118-11785-9

QuickBooks 2014
For Dummies
978-1-118-72005-9

Small Business Marketing
Kit For Dummies,
3rd Edition
978-1-118-31183-7

Careers

Job Interviews
For Dummies, 4th Edition
978-1-118-11290-8

Job Searching with Social
Media For Dummies,
2nd Edition
978-1-118-67856-5

Personal Branding
For Dummies
978-1-118-11792-7

Resumes For Dummies,
6th Edition
978-0-470-87361-8

Starting an Etsy Business
For Dummies, 2nd Edition
978-1-118-59024-9

Diet & Nutrition

Belly Fat Diet For Dummies
978-1-118-34585-6

Mediterranean Diet
For Dummies
978-1-118-71525-3

Nutrition For Dummies,
5th Edition
978-0-470-93231-5

Digital Photography

Digital SLR Photography
All-in-One For Dummies,
2nd Edition
978-1-118-59082-9

Digital SLR Video &
Filmmaking For Dummies
978-1-118-36598-4

Photoshop Elements 12
For Dummies
978-1-118-72714-0

Gardening

Herb Gardening
For Dummies, 2nd Edition
978-0-470-61778-6

Gardening with Free-Range
Chickens For Dummies
978-1-118-54754-0

Health

Boosting Your Immunity
For Dummies
978-1-118-40200-9

Diabetes For Dummies,
4th Edition
978-1-118-29447-5

Living Paleo For Dummies
978-1-118-29405-5

Big Data

Big Data For Dummies
978-1-118-50422-2

Data Visualization
For Dummies
978-1-118-50289-1

Hadoop For Dummies
978-1-118-60755-8

Language &
Foreign Language

500 Spanish Verbs
For Dummies
978-1-118-02382-2

English Grammar
For Dummies, 2nd Edition
978-0-470-54664-2

French All-in-One
For Dummies
978-1-118-22815-9

German Essentials
For Dummies
978-1-118-18422-6

Italian For Dummies,
2nd Edition
978-1-118-00465-4

Available in print and e-book formats.

Available wherever books are sold. **For more information or to order direct visit www.dummies.com**

Math & Science

Algebra I For Dummies,
2nd Edition
978-0-470-55964-2

Anatomy and Physiology
For Dummies, 2nd Edition
978-0-470-92326-9

Astronomy For Dummies,
3rd Edition
978-1-118-37697-3

Biology For Dummies,
2nd Edition
978-0-470-59875-7

Chemistry For Dummies,
2nd Edition
978-1-118-00730-3

1001 Algebra II Practice
Problems For Dummies
978-1-118-44662-1

Microsoft Office

Excel 2013 For Dummies
978-1-118-51012-4

Office 2013 All-in-One
For Dummies
978-1-118-51636-2

PowerPoint 2013
For Dummies
978-1-118-50253-2

Word 2013 For Dummies
978-1-118-49123-2

Music

Blues Harmonica
For Dummies
978-1-118-25269-7

Guitar For Dummies,
3rd Edition
978-1-118-11554-1

iPod & iTunes
For Dummies, 10th Edition
978-1-118-50864-0

Programming

Beginning Programming
with C For Dummies
978-1-118-73763-7

Excel VBA Programming
For Dummies, 3rd Edition
978-1-118-49037-2

Java For Dummies,
6th Edition
978-1-118-40780-6

Religion & Inspiration

The Bible For Dummies
978-0-7645-5296-0

Buddhism For Dummies,
2nd Edition
978-1-118-02379-2

Catholicism For Dummies,
2nd Edition
978-1-118-07778-8

Self-Help & Relationships

Beating Sugar Addiction
For Dummies
978-1-118-54645-1

Meditation For Dummies,
3rd Edition
978-1-118-29144-3

Seniors

Laptops For Seniors
For Dummies, 3rd Edition
978-1-118-71105-7

Computers For Seniors
For Dummies, 3rd Edition
978-1-118-11553-4

iPad For Seniors
For Dummies, 6th Edition
978-1-118-72826-0

Social Security
For Dummies
978-1-118-20573-0

Smartphones & Tablets

Android Phones
For Dummies, 2nd Edition
978-1-118-72030-1

Nexus Tablets
For Dummies
978-1-118-77243-0

Samsung Galaxy S 4
For Dummies
978-1-118-64222-1

Samsung Galaxy Tabs
For Dummies
978-1-118-77294-2

Test Prep

ACT For Dummies,
5th Edition
978-1-118-01259-8

ASVAB For Dummies,
3rd Edition
978-0-470-63760-9

GRE For Dummies,
7th Edition
978-0-470-88921-3

Officer Candidate Tests
For Dummies
978-0-470-59876-4

Physician's Assistant Exam
For Dummies
978-1-118-11556-5

Series 7 Exam For Dummies
978-0-470-09932-2

Windows 8

Windows 8.1 All-in-One
For Dummies
978-1-118-82087-2

Windows 8.1 For Dummies
978-1-118-82121-3

Windows 8.1 For Dummies
Book + DVD Bundle
978-1-118-82107-7

 **Available in print and e-book formats.**

Available wherever books are sold. **For more information or to order direct visit www.dummies.com**

Take Dummies with you everywhere you go!

Whether you are excited about e-books, want more from the web, must have your mobile apps, or are swept up in social media, Dummies makes everything easier.

Visit Us
bit.ly/JE0O

Like Us
on.fb.me/1f1ThNu

Follow Us
bit.ly/ZDytkR

Watch Us
bit.ly/gbOQHn

Join Us
linkd.in/1gurkMm

Pin Us
bit.ly/16caOLd

Circle Us
bit.ly/1aQTuDQ

Shop Us
bit.ly/4dEp9

Leverage the Power

For Dummies is the global leader in the reference category and one of the most trusted and highly regarded brands in the world. No longer just focused on books, customers now have access to the For Dummies content they need in the format they want. Let us help you develop a solution that will fit your brand and help you connect with your customers.

Advertising & Sponsorships

Connect with an engaged audience on a powerful multimedia site, and position your message alongside expert how-to content.

Targeted ads • Video • Email marketing • Microsites • Sweepstakes sponsorship

For Dummies is a registered trademark of John Wiley & Sons, Inc.